CAMBRIDGE STUDIES IN GERMAN

CHRISTA WOLF'S UTOPIAN VISION

This is the first book-length chronological study in English of Christa Wolf's works. It traces the development and continuity of the writer's major themes and concerns against the backdrop of her constantly evolving relationship to Marxism, and documents the rise of her feminist consciousness. It does not, however, focus only on political and feminist issues, but addresses all facets of Wolf's identity (East – German – woman – writer) by showing how her works reflect her own self-understanding.

Forced by the clash between her vision of a humane socialism and the practice of socialism she observed in the German Democratic Republic to reassess her role as a writer and critic, Wolf broke through to her unique style in *The Quest for Christa T.*, a work initially repudiated in the GDR both for its unorthodox subject matter and for its unconventional form. Since then, Wolf has effectively challenged the restrictions placed on writers in the GDR by writing on topics such as the Nazi past (*Patterns of Childhood*), Romanticism (*No Place on Earth*), patriarchal attitudes in the GDR (*Cassandra*) and most recently the Chernobyl nuclear disaster (*Störfall*).

Anna K. Kuhn shows how Christa Wolf, by adhering to her self-imposed concept of writing as "subjective authenticity," has broadened the parameters of what is acceptable in her society.

CAMBRIDGE STUDIES IN GERMAN

General editors: H. B. NISBET *and* MARTIN SWALES

Also in the series

S. S. PRAWER
*Frankenstein's Island: England
and the English in the writings of Heinrich
Heine*

BENJAMIN BENNETT
*Hugo von Hofmannsthal:
The Theatres of Consciousness*

PHILIP PAYNE
*Robert Musil's 'The Man without Qualities':
A Critical Study*

Christa Wolf

Christa Wolf's Utopian Vision

From Marxism to Feminism

ANNA K. KUHN

University of California, Davis

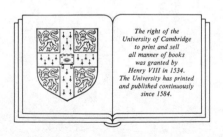

The right of the
University of Cambridge
to print and sell
all manner of books
was granted by
Henry VIII in 1534.
The University has printed
and published continuously
since 1584.

CAMBRIDGE UNIVERSITY PRESS

Cambridge

New York   New Rochelle   Melbourne   Sydney

Published by the Press Syndicate of the University of Cambridge
The Pitt Building, Trumpington Street, Cambridge CB2 1RP
32 East 57th Street, New York, NY 10022, USA
10 Stamford Road, Oakleigh, Melbourne 3166, Australia

First published 1988

Printed in Great Britain at the University Press, Cambridge

British Library cataloguing in publication data
Kuhn, Anna K.
Christa Wolf's Utopian vision: from Marxism to feminism.
– (Cambridge studies in German)
1. Wolf, Christa – Criticism and interpretation
I. Title
833'.914   PT2685.O36Z

Library of Congress cataloguing in publication data
Kuhn, Anna Katharina
Christa Wolf's utopian vision: from Marxism to feminism / Anna K. Kuhn
p.   cm. – (Cambridge studies in German)
Bibliography.
Includes index.
ISBN 0-521-32233-2
1. Wolf, Christa – Political and social views.
2. Utopias in literature.   3. Feminism in literature.
4. Socialism in literature.
I. Title   II. Series
PI2685.O36Z74   1988
838'.91409 – dc19   87-33768   CIP

ISBN 0 521 32233 2

CE

Creative practice is thus of many kinds. It is already, and actively, our practical consciousness. When it becomes struggle – the active struggle for new consciousness through new relationships that is the ineradicable emphasis of the Marxist sense of self-creation – it can take many forms. It can be the long and difficult remaking of an inherited (determined) practical consciousness: a process often described as development but in practice a struggle at the roots of the mind – not casting off an ideology, or learning phrases about it, but confronting a hegemony in the fibres of the self and in the hard practical substance of effective and continuing relationships. It can be more evident practice: the reproduction and illustration of hitherto excluded and subordinated models; the embodiment and performance of known but excluded and subordinated experiences and relationships; the articulation and formation of latent, momentary, and newly possible consciousness.

Raymond Williams
Marxism and Literature (1977)

CONTENTS

ACKNOWLEDGMENTS

This book was facilitated by generous financial support at various stages of its development. A University of Pennsylvania Women's Studies Summer Fellowship permitted me to devote the summer of 1984 to full-time research; a grant from the American Philosophical Society enabled me to travel to Germany; research grants from the University of Pennsylvania and the University of California, Davis, covered the costs of manuscript preparation.

I am indebted to many friends and colleagues for their support and help throughout this project. Without the unfailing encouragement of Walter Hinderer, this book might not have come into being. I am thankful for my years as a faculty resident at Van Pelt College House at the University of Pennsylvania, where students and colleagues, especially Ann Matter, provided me with distraction and a much-needed sense of community. Heartfelt gratitude goes to the SWAPOs, who lovingly and good-naturedly lived through the genesis and execution of this project. I am indebted to Patricia Herminghouse and Ruth-Ellen Joeres, and particularly to Helen Fehervary, for their thorough reading and helpful criticism of the original manuscript. I would also like to thank Andreas Huyssen and Magda Müller for reading and commenting on parts of the book. To Ruth Crowley, who meticulously prepared the manuscript and invariably helped me to sharpen my arguments, I owe a great debt of gratitude. Her intelligence, wit, generosity, unflinchingly honest criticism, encouragement, and superb editorial skills are greatly appreciated. I would also like to thank Luchterhand Verlag for generously making a copy of Christa Wolf's newest work, *Störfall*, available to me before it was published in West Germany.

But most of all I must thank Christa Wolf. When I started this project, I had no inkling of the adventure on which I was about to embark, an adventure in which I would learn more not only about this writer but about myself as well. The study of German language and literature (*Germanistik*) is a very male discipline. This may well account for the fact that during my years of study the only woman writer I encountered was Annette von Droste-Hülshoff, the one "accepted" female writer in the German academic canon. My work on Christa Wolf has forced me to reassess my life as a woman, a teacher and a scholar. I have learned to challenge the fundamental authoritarian bases of my profession and have questioned what, as a woman, my role at the university could and should be. I have had to confront the destructive structures of the academy and become painfully aware of the price of "success" in human terms in an institution predicated on competition, achievement and the belief that intellectual property is our most valuable commodity. I have become increasingly aware of how my profession causes human emotions to atrophy, preaching a religion of "objectivity," encouraging us to sever our emotions from our intellect.

While Wolf's writing has changed my view-scope in very fundamental ways, it has also made me painfully aware of how ingrained my own patterns of behavior are. So that while I have come to recognize that the assumptions at the very center of our discipline are wrong, are *verkehrt*, perverse in Wolf's sense of the word, that the concept of "objectivity" is itself an ideological construct, a subjective statement, I nonetheless still find myself a prisoner of those assumptions, having been trained by "experts" in that ideology. Like Wolf, I have found it difficult to say "I," at least in the context of the "objective" discourse of literary scholarship. It is very hard to unlearn years of training in which we were assiduously taught never, under any circumstances, to write in the first person. And in which the notion of relevance, relating our studies to our own realities, was considered bad form at best, pernicious at worst.

I am slowly learning to speak in my own voice, am beginning to articulate my needs as a woman engaged in the study and teaching of German literature and culture, am asking – more and more insistently – where all the women writers are whom we never read, am questioning not only the male valuation of female writers, but also the relevance of much male writing, with its one-sided perspective on the world. I've changed, or perhaps I should say, I'm changing. And by changing, I've challenged some very basic assumptions and called some cherished views into question.

Through Christa Wolf I have been introduced to the works of Karoline von Günderrode and Bettina von Arnim. *No Place on Earth* and Wolf's essays on the Romantics gave me access to the writers of this period, a period for which I had never had any use.

Acknowledgments

I've come to appreciate the subversive elements in their thinking, no longer consider them regressive and *weltfremd* (out of touch with reality). Wolf has led me to read Anna Seghers, Ingeborg Bachmann and, of course, Ernst Bloch. Perhaps I would have become familiar with these writers anyway. But they don't belong to the canon of *Germanistik* any more than she does, so I'm not certain. At any rate, it would have taken a lot longer and I wouldn't have seen them through her eyes. Christa Wolf's relentless honesty and self-scrutiny are inspiring and serve as a model for me, encouraging me to confront my own life. Ultimately her work has given me the courage to criticize, to review, to reassess, to rethink and to restart. I owe her an enormous debt.

This book is dedicated to SWAP.

ABBREVIATIONS

BE   Essay on Bettine von Arnim: "Nun ja! Das nächste Leben geht aber heute an." In *Fortgesetzter Versuch: Aufsätze, Gespräche, Essays*. Leipzig: Reclam, 1982.

BP   Büchner Prize Speech: "Von Büchner sprechen. Darmstädter Rede." Trans. Henry J. Schmidt, "Shall I Garnish a Metaphor with an Almond Blossom?" in *New German Critique* 23 (Spring/Summer 1981): 3–11.

C   *Cassandra* narrative. In *Cassandra: A Novel and Four Essays*. Trans. Jan van Heurck. New York: Farrar, Straus & Giroux, 1984.

CON   "Conditions of a Narrative." Wolf's Frankfurt Lectures on Poetics. In *Cassandra: A Novel and Four Essays*.

CP   "Change of Perspective" ("Blickwechsel"). Trans. A. Leslie Willson. In Elizabeth Rütschi Herrmann and Edna Huttenmaier Spitz, eds., *German Women Writers of the Twentieth Century*. New York: Pergamon, 1978.

CT   *The Quest for Christa T.* Trans. Christopher Middleton. New York: Farrar, Straus & Giroux, 1972.

DH   *Divided Heaven*. Trans. Joan Becker. New York: Adler's Foreign Books, 1981.

GE   Essay on Karoline von Günderrode: "Der Schatten eines Traumes." In *Fortgesetzter Versuch*.

MN   *Moskauer Novelle* (Moscow Novella). Halle: Mitteldeutscher Verlag, 1961.

NP   *No Place on Earth*. Trans. Jan van Heurck. New York: Farrar, Straus & Giroux, 1982.

PoC   *Patterns of Childhood*. Trans. Ursule Molinaro and Hedwig Rappolt. New York: Farrar, Straus & Giroux, 1984.

RW   *The Reader and the Writer: Essays, Sketches, Memories*. Trans. Joan Becker. New York: International Publishers, 1977.

S   *Störfall. Nachrichten eines Tages*. Darmstadt/Neuwied: Luchterhand 1987.

I

INTRODUCTION:
SETTING THE CONTEXT

In the twenty-six years since her emergence as a writer of imaginative literature, Christa Wolf has become one of the leading figures of German letters and the foremost female voice of the German-speaking world. Inherently political, her writing is both subtle and subversive. As she has matured, her themes have become more complex and the problems she addresses broader. The increasing universality of her writing, the immediacy and compelling relevance of her most recent works have helped earn her the international reputation she enjoys today. The East German writer of the early 1960s has evolved into a writer of world stature in the eighties. Abandoning the Socialist Realism that had influenced her early works, *Moscow Novella* (1961) and *The Divided Heaven* (1963), Christa Wolf established a distinctive style and set of concerns with *The Quest for Christa T.* (1968) and *Patterns of Childhood* (1976).

These novels were at first severely criticized in the German Democratic Republic (GDR) both for their complex experimental form and for their unorthodox subject matter. Christa T.'s claim to the right of individual self-fulfillment within the socialist collective and the narrator's need in *Patterns of Childhood* to come to terms with her Nazi past (from which the GDR totally dissociated itself) were considered taboo subjects. In the interim, the reception of *Christa T.* has changed radically – today the book is viewed as a classic, aimed at strengthening the socialist state through internal criticism.[1] It remains to be seen whether *Patterns of Childhood* will enjoy a similar rehabilitation.

In 1976 the dissident poet Wolf Biermann was expatriated, abruptly ending a period of liberalization that had begun in 1971, when Erich Honecker lifted all taboos for truly committed socialist writers at the Eighth Party Congress. Perhaps the precarious political situation in the GDR following Biermann's expatriation prompted Wolf to camouflage her social criticism in historical subject matter. Set in 1804, *No Place on Earth* (1979) portrays the fictitious encounter between the Romantic poets Heinrich von Kleist and Karoline von Günderrode, whose alienation and un- happiness obviously parallel the experiences of some citizens of the GDR – including Wolf, for whom Biermann's exile and its after- math precipitated a crisis. In her portrayal of these writers, both of whom committed suicide, Wolf treats the role of gender in their dilemmas and thus foreshadows concerns specifically addressed in *Cassandra* (1983).

Two trends are discernible in Wolf's work to date: a movement away from the present into the past in terms of subject matter, and an increasing concern with women's issues, particularly the role of the woman writer. These two trends converge in Wolf's feminist reinterpretation of the Cassandra story, in which Wolf moves into mythical times to continue her criticism of contemporary society.

The critical reception of Christa Wolf has been unique. No East German author has been as widely discussed by critics in both German states and in the United States. In the two Germanies, critics agree that Christa Wolf is a significant writer. With respect to particular works, however, the critical reception of Wolf in the Federal Republic has been almost the obverse of that in the German Democratic Republic. Molded by the Cold War politics of the fifties and early sixties, the ideological bias of most German criticism has led critics to praise or censure her works according to their opinion of the GDR and their perception of Christa Wolf's relationship to the socialist state. Critics in both countries, however, interpreted her first major work, *Divided Heaven*, in terms of the prevailing GDR aesthetic of Socialist Realism. This established a precedent that prevailed long after it ceased to be appropriate. The explicitly political theme of *Divided Heaven* predetermined the response to her later, less easily defined works. While noting the more personal tone of Wolf's second novel, *The Quest for Christa T.*, most German critics in both countries continued to interpret it and its successor, *Patterns of Childhood*, preeminently in the political context of GDR literature.

The reception of Christa Wolf's work in the context of GDR society and politics has tended to obscure the extent to which *Christa T.* marks a turning point in her writing. Political interpre- tation of her middle works in particular, by understating the utopian dimension of her more subjective writing, has caused Wolf's latest works to appear as greater anomalies than they are. While *No Place on Earth* disrupts the overtly autobiographical mode of Wolf's earlier works, the novel develops themes that have played an important role in Wolf's writing since *Christa T*. Indeed, even *Cassandra*, which uses myth to criticize patriarchal values and to reevaluate the literary canon, sustains a continuity with her earlier works through its criticism of both East and West and through its evocation of a utopian alternative.

Recent American feminist critics do not stress the GDR contextual aspect of Christa Wolf's writing, but instead see her in terms of feminist politics. The specifically female aspect of Wolf's writing, overlooked by (predominantly male) German critics, has been the focus of scholarship by women. Feminist scholarship has illuminated the problematic relationship of the woman writer to language in a patriarchal world, and has noted the interrelationship between the articulation of female subjectivity (the theme of the "difficulty of saying 'I'") and Wolf's narrative techniques. The chief virtue of this scholarship, in addition to making readers sensitive to gender issues in Wolf's writing, has been to point to the potential for a more formalistic, linguistically oriented approach to her works and to establish the methodological framework for such an investigation. However, to the extent that it focuses on the subjective experience of the female individual to the exclusion of the broader socio-historical and cultural context, this feminist scholarship is also reductionist.

Although Wolf is sometimes treated in the context of "New Subjectivity," her work differs from this West German literary movement of the seventies in that, despite the psychological depth of her characters, despite her emphasis on personal experience, she never presents subjective experience in a vacuum. Instead, the individual subject is always presented in a dialectical relationship with the larger social community. This relationship finds its linguistic expression in the shift between the individual ("I") and the collective ("we") voice in Wolf's texts. Just as Wolf speaks not merely for herself but also, and quite consciously, for her generation, her use of first-person narrative ensures at once specificity and typicality.

While the GDR context-related and the feminist avenues of inquiry have yielded the most fruitful insights into Wolf's work, each approach in itself is inadequate for a proper understanding of her complex and sophisticated writing. Christa Wolf is an *East German woman writer* and consideration must be given to each facet of her identity if one is to do justice to her work. Just as Wolf scholarship has often tended toward reductionism, it has also failed to clarify the interrelatedness of Christa Wolf's entire *œuvre*. As on a giant tapestry, strands from one work are interwoven into the next as new ones are being spun that connect with future works. This intermeshing is not limited to matters of content but includes formal aspects of Wolf's writing as well, making it virtually impossible to treat any of her works in isolation. Proceeding chronologically, I use a close textual analysis to examine Christa Wolf's fiction and essays as they interrelate. While I do not attempt to analyze each text exhaustively, I follow some of the strands of Wolf's literary tapestry, arguing that her work expresses the integration of the various aspects of her identity. (The following focus on each of the aspects of Christa Wolf's self-understanding is merely a heuristic device for placing her work in context and understanding the problems it presents. Indeed, the distinctions between aspects are artificial and cannot be sustained even in this introduction.)

East German woman writer: The highly politicized nature of literature in East-bloc countries means that any discussion of Christa Wolf must be framed in the context of the national and cultural politics of the GDR. A member of a society that experienced the imposition of socialism from above, Wolf enthusiastically embraced Marxism and has worked toward the realization of Marxist humanist ideals in GDR praxis. Augmenting her literary engagement with political commitment, she has been an active member of the Socialist Unity Party (SED = Sozialistische Einheitspartei Deutschlands) and for several years was a candidate for a position in the ruling Central Committee.[2]

Clearly Marxist theory, by providing her with the tools for an economic analysis of history, helped Wolf to understand what had happened in Germany between 1933 and 1945. More importantly, however, Marx's vision of an egalitarian, nonexploitative community filled her with hope. Like many of her compatriots, Wolf saw in socialism the means for achieving a qualitatively new and morally superior social order that would help prevent a repetition of recent German history by transforming human beings from objects into subjects of history.[3] Over the years, however, Wolf has become more and more critical of the form of socialism that has evolved in the GDR and increasingly more sceptical about her society's ability to implement the revolution in social relations necessary to create subjects of history.

Yet while Wolf's *œuvre* can be read as testimony to her increas-

ing disenchantment with her society, she is still a member of the
Party, chooses to live in the GDR, and remains committed to the
ideals of socialism as conceived by Marx. The theme of the
coming-into-being of human subjectivity (*das Subjektwerden des
Menschen*) so central to her work and her insistence on individual
self-actualization within the collective are compatible with Marx's
vision of free social individuality within a communal society. The
discrepancy between Marxist theory and the often repressive
reality of the GDR has not destroyed Wolf's faith in the possibility
of human community. In her recent works, in which she continues
to examine modes of human objectification and alienation, Wolf
has explored the feminist critique of Marxism. By analyzing patriarchal attitudes (still prevalent in the socialist East) and their
destructive effects on both sexes, she has created works that make a
universal appeal. In particular, her lament that reason has been
perverted to mere utilitarian pragmatism and her fear that the East,
by mimicking the West, by failing to repudiate instrumental rationality, has failed to present a viable alternative to this self-
destructive world view, has immediate global relevance. The
urgency of Wolf's argument, her belief that the lack of a viable
alternative may well lead to the annihilation of humankind, is
particularly compelling in light of recent world political events and
may explain the enormous popularity she has attained in the past
several years.

Despite their often bleak subject matter, Wolf's works never end
in despair. Indeed, one of the salient features of her writing is the
quiet optimism of even her most critical works. The element of
hope in Wolf's writing stems largely from her Marxist perspective.
Although Christa T., Karoline von Günderrode, Heinrich von
Kleist, and Cassandra succumb to the lack of livable alternatives,
Wolf holds fast to her belief in socialism's capacity to change
human consciousness and to create such alternatives. She shares
the socialist faith in literature's power to teach. But more than that,
she has a fundamental faith in human beings and their ability to
learn from the experiences of her characters. Literature for Wolf
allows both the writer and the reader to play through possible
(self-)destructive scenarios vicariously. Although many of Wolf's
figures die because they cannot exist in the societies into which they
are born, all remain uncompromising in their quest for self-
actualization. The implication that, given a different, more humane
social order, these figures could survive, is clearly meant as an
incentive to readers to attend to aspects of their society impeding

the development of human subjectivity. Thus Wolf's work keeps alive the hope of a humane socialism, even as it records the betrayal of contemporary socialism in the GDR.

One of Wolf's deepest commitments is to the emergence of nonalienated subjectivity as formulated by Marx. Perhaps the most serious obstacle to this is the GDR's self-deceptive attitude toward its National Socialist past. Marx believed that the basis of humane community was a revolution in social relations, which would allow people to see others as independent subjects and not merely in relation to themselves, that is, as objects. This community is predicated on the idea of reintegrative subjectivity. On the one hand, individuals must be able to recognize their objectification of and by others in order to overcome alienation and to attain mutual subjectivity, mutual regard for one another as human subjects. On the other hand, they must be able to empathize with one another's situation in order to experience a sense of their shared humanity. Yet clearly the ability to recognize another's subjectivity presupposes an individual's psychic integration. In the GDR, official Party policy has inhibited the process of psychological integration by effectively severing its citizens from their personal history. By calling the populace victims of National Socialism rather than its collaborators, it has prevented East Germans from becoming reconciled with their past and has fostered self-alienation, a phenomenon Wolf addresses most eloquently in *Patterns of Childhood*. Wolf's concern with achieving a heightened self-awareness as a prerequisite for overcoming alienation makes the question of *Vergangenheitsbewältigung* (a coming to terms with the Nazi past) an urgent one for her. Indeed, it informs her writing in *Patterns of Childhood*.

In order to understand the significance of *Vergangenheitsbewältigung* for the Germans, it will be helpful to recall their situation in 1945. At the end of World War II, a defeated, divided, and morally bankrupt Germany faced the task of rebuilding its cities, reconstructing its economy, and reassessing its history. The economic miracle (*Wirtschaftswunder*) of the Adenauer era and the Marshall Plan transformed the Federal Republic of Germany into the industrial and economic leader of Europe, and the German Democratic Republic emerged as the most prosperous Soviet-bloc country. Yet the accomplishment of overcoming seemingly insurmountable economic obstacles pales when compared with the task still facing the East and West German states and their people: the need to confront the National Socialist past.

Introduction

The occupation forces addressed the issue of moral culpability in the upper echelons of the Nazi party through the Nürnberg War Trials (1945–6), but such uniform, immediate, and direct action was not possible in the case of the populace at large. The Allies had agreed that a denazification program was needed. However, after the confrontation between the Western and Eastern powers (1947) and the escalation of the Cold War, methods for purging Nazi elements and for implementing reeducation programs varied in the four occupied zones. The French, British, and American sectors, operating with the concept of collective guilt, set up an elaborate bureaucracy for denazification that lagged behind the more rigorous and consistent measures of the Soviets.[4] In the Soviet sector the removal of former Nazi party members from public life (including the dismissal of more than 20,000 teachers in 1945), coupled with the institution of a "law for the democratization of the German school,"[5] that is, a centralized school system reform, ensured that education reinforced reeducation. Yet the Soviets, who had originally subscribed to the Allied concept of collective guilt, increasingly distanced themselves from this view as East and West moved toward an ideological division of Germany.

With the founding of the GDR on 7 October 1949 (in response to the creation of the Federal Republic on 21 September 1949) came an official severance of the East Germans from their Nazi past. Since its socialism was not the result of a revolution from below but had been imposed by Soviet occupation forces, the GDR felt obliged to legitimize itself by evoking the liberal legacy of 1848 and the social democratic heritage of the Weimar Republic (1918–33) and by creating the myth of wide-scale anti-Nazi resistance in the Third Reich. Viewing itself as the continuation of a progressive German tradition brutally crushed by the National Socialist state, the GDR accepted the Soviet definition of the Russian invasion as the liberation "of the German people from the yoke of fascism."[6] By casting its citizenry in the role of victims, the Party obviated the need to assess its immediate past and to assume responsibility for Hitler and the atrocities committed between 1933 and 1945. Rather than examining the events of the past, the GDR chose to develop the new socialist society, substituting the concept of the "scientific-technological revolution" for the revolution in social relations envisaged by Marx, that is, exchanging means for ends. Particularly in its early *Aufbau* phase, the period of socialist development and consolidation (*c.* 1949–61), it concentrated on changing the means of production. This reductionist view of socialism, prevalent long after the removal of the economic exigencies that had confronted the emerging socialist state, has been a frequent target of Christa Wolf's criticism.

Christa Wolf was sixteen years old in 1945. She belongs to the generation that experienced the transition from Nazism to socialism, an experience that not only shaped her but that also constitutes an important theme of her early and middle works. Her autobiographical novel, *Patterns of Childhood*, records the decisive experiences of her early years. Born in 1929 in Landsberg on the Warthe River, approximately 130 kilometers northeast of Berlin,[7] Wolf grew up in the Third Reich. *Patterns of Childhood* reconstructs her childhood under Nazism and records the traumatic break in her life caused by the invasion of the Red Army; her family's flight West; and her experiences under American, French, and Soviet occupation forces. By explicitly addressing the taboo issue of *Vergangenheitsbewältigung*, which had always implicitly informed her literary writing, Wolf was psychologically able to leave behind the inquiry into personal history that had characterized her writing. Delving ever further back in time, she was able to develop new narrative forms through which to examine broader historical contexts in their relationship to contemporary society.

Very much a product of her transitional generation, Wolf has treated, in literary and essayistic works as well as in interviews, the difficult and lengthy process of reassessment and reorientation that confronted her and her contemporaries after the war. Not until autumn 1948,[8] two years after graduating from the *Gymnasium* in Bad Frankenhausen near Schwerin, where her family had relocated, did Christa Wolf read her first Marxist work. Her encounter with Marxist thought and the subsequent rise of her socialist consciousness precipitated a fundamental reassessment of values.

Wolf's humanistic vision of socialism was intensified by her studies at the University of Leipzig (1949–53). In Leipzig, then the leading intellectual center of the GDR,[9] Wolf studied with the eminent Germanist Hans Mayer. Mayer was a Marxist thinker in the Hegelian dialectical tradition, a Third Reich émigré recently returned to the German socialist state. It is one of the tragic ironies of GDR history that thinkers like Hans Mayer and the philosopher Ernst Bloch (also lecturing in Leipzig at the time), people whose concern with the humanistic potential of Marxism might have helped implement a socialist order closer to the Marxian model, were among those attacked as revisionists.[10] With the erection of the Berlin Wall in August 1961, it became palpably clear to Mayer and Bloch that their vision of socialism could not soon be realized in the GDR, and they emigrated once again. Just as Mayer and Bloch were unable to endure the discrepancy between Marxist theory and GDR praxis, the tension between socialist ideal and reality was to become of increasing concern for Christa Wolf.

East *German* woman writer: Wolf's identity as a German is inextricably bound to the GDR's national self-understanding and its cultural politics with regard to the German tradition. Orienting itself politically in accordance with the Soviet model of communism, the GDR declared 1945 as a historical cesura and 1949 as the beginning of a qualitatively new social order. The official aesthetic governing literary production, Stalinist Socialist Realism, was deemed a necessity of cultural politics; its objective was to help develop and consolidate socialism in the GDR. Socialist Realism provides the mimetic theory of art with a socialist telos. That is, it holds that the purpose of art is to record social dynamics and conflicts from the perspective of the ultimate triumph of socialism. The doctrines of Socialist Realism, as articulated at the first congress of the Soviet writers' union in 1934, were appropriated in toto by the GDR. The four main precepts are: (1) the primacy of industrial production for society, hence a devaluation of portraying the private sphere in favor of the world of work in artistic production; (2) a mandate for the creation of positive heroes, portrayed as actively engaged in the socialist struggle, as the norm; (3) a call for socialist literature to appropriate critically its "classical heritage" (*klassisches Erbe*); (4) the positing of the inherently didactic function of literature which, by rendering a "truthful presentation of real life," is meant to effect an "ideological transformation and education of working people in the spirit of socialism."[11] Adherence to this restrictive aesthetic, with its insistence on *Parteilichkeit* (alignment with Marxist–Leninist Party policy) and on an ideologically conceived category of typicality (positive hero as norm, as an allegory of the State) severely inhibited or excluded nonmimetic experimental forms of literary production, bred homogeneity and sterility, and engendered fierce literary debates on the theory of realism.

This barren literary aesthetic was overturned by the Hungarian-born critic Georg Lukács. Until the Hungarian uprising in 1956, when he was deposed, Lukács enjoyed virtual intellectual hegemony in questions of literary realism in the GDR. He was responsible for broadening the parameters of the realist canon in the postwar period to include works by nonsocialist writers. His contribution to the realism debate must be assessed in the context of GDR cultural politics, which aimed at establishing the continuity of the German intellectual and literary tradition. To this end, literary historians evoked the humanistic heritage of the *Weimarer Klassik* (the classical period of Goethe and Schiller, *c.* 1786–1832) and engaged in lengthy debates as to which works of presocialist German literature were to be admitted into the new socialist canon (the *Erbediskussion*). Introducing the concept of "critical realism," which he opposed to Socialist Realism, Lukács entered the debate and reoriented the realist aesthetic toward the bourgeois novelists of the nineteenth century – Balzac, Dickens, and Tolstoy as well as Theodor Fontane and Thomas Mann. Lukács's concept of "totality," the basis of his theory of realism, enabled him to include writers who would otherwise have been condemned as late-capitalistic decadents. In Lukács's view, the great realists of previous eras were such masters at capturing the social dynamics of their particular society in its contradictory totality that unintentionally, by sheer virtue of their genius, they illuminate the irresolvable contradictions in their societies and thus point to the inevitable downfall of capitalism.

While Lukács's work greatly enhanced the realism debate in the GDR, it effectively stifled formal innovation through its anachronistic orientation and rejection of modernistic literary trends. Although the concept of totality allowed Lukács to reject certain mimetic art forms such as naturalism as the merely superficial reflection of external reality, his mandate for "objectivity" caused him to repudiate nonmimetic, subjective, "irrational," "solipsistic" movements such as Romanticism, Impressionism, and Expressionism. After Stalin's death (1953) Socialist Realist norms were ironically more – not less – rigorously enforced than before, and Lukács fell into disrepute as a revisionist. Only very recently has the GDR begun to reevaluate its position on writers excluded from Lukács's canon, the Romantics and modernist writers such as Kafka.[12] Thus it is obvious why Christa Wolf, who experimented with narrative perspective as early as *Divided Heaven* and has incorporated a number of modernist writing strategies, has thwarted her socialist critics. A further obstacle has been her insistence on active reader participation in the (re)constitution of the text, a phenomenon that is anathema to Socialist Realism's call for "objectivity." In place of Socialist Realism's emotional identification with typical characters, Wolf places intellectual demands on her readers, expecting them to fill in the lacunae of the text. While reader response theories of literature gained some currency in literary discussions in the late fifties and early sixties,[13] the concept of subjectivity remains problematic in the GDR to the present day. The rejection of individual (as opposed to class-based) subjectivity has been detrimental to the reception of Christa Wolf's works in East Germany, where her work has been criticized as "subjectivistic."

Wolf's study of German language and literature familiarized her with the socialist canon. Her career as a literary critic ensured that she was conversant with the nuances of GDR realism and the *Erbediskussion* debates.[14] Her contribution to the *Erbediskussion*, the reclaiming of the literary past, in *No Place on Earth* and her essays on the Romantics Karoline von Günderrode, Bettina von Arnim, and Heinrich von Kleist constitute important documents in the history of GDR literary reassessment and establish her as a writer in the German tradition. Subject matter for both *No Place on Earth* and the short stories written in the mid-seventies comes from Romanticism; more important, however, is the similarity between the formal and theoretical concerns of Romantic literature and those of Christa Wolf. Although Wolf's aims are somewhat different from those of the German Romantics, she, like them, writes about the act of writing; presents an open literary structure as an antiauthoritarian gesture; involves the reader in the creative act; and stresses that the lessons of creativity and self-determination learned from literature can be applied to life.

In essays and discussions, Wolf has stressed the importance of literature for her life, a fact to which her literary texts also bear witness. In addition to French and Soviet writers, her works reverberate with echoes from German writers as diverse as Goethe, Schiller, Thomas Mann, Robert Musil, Theodor Storm, Bertolt Brecht, Max Frisch, Novalis, Heinrich von Kleist, Sophie von La Roche, Bettina von Arnim, Karoline von Günderrode, Ingeborg Bachmann, and Anna Seghers. Clearly, Christa Wolf is acutely aware of her German heritage. In discussing Wolf in the context of the German literary and philosophical tradition so essential for her work, one must explore the ramifications of that tradition for the self-understanding of the GDR, just as one must consider Wolf's constantly evolving relationship to Marxism and to GDR praxis.

East German *woman* writer: With the exception of the sensitively drawn male figures of Manfred in *Divided Heaven* and Kleist in *No Place on Earth*, Christa Wolf's work deals almost exclusively with female experience. In *Moscow Novella* and *Divided Heaven*, Wolf does not explicitly differentiate between male and female experience, and her protagonists are developed in their relationships to men. Insofar as the dilemmas confronting her female characters were representative for both men and women under socialism, female experience seemed universally applicable. In *Christa T.* and *Patterns of Childhood*, male behavior is no longer viewed as the norm, and female consciousness is developed primarily in relationship to other women. Increasingly, Wolf has posed the question of self-actualization, fundamental to her work, in terms of women's possibilities in a patriarchal society. The initial generic treatment of her utopian theme has become ever more gender specific as she has delved further back in time for the roots of alienation. Wolf's feminism has evolved from her Marxist critique of scientific Marxism and can be viewed "not as an alternative to Marxism but as a qualitatively new and autonomous dimension that is a prerequisite for its renewal."[15]

In her short story "Self-Experiment: Appendix to a Report" ("Selbstversuch: Traktat zu einem Protokoll," 1973), Wolf first explicitly articulates a feminist perspective. By setting the action in the year 1992 she is able to express her criticism of socialist patriarchy indirectly. But the science fiction context is a thin veil: Wolf's criticism is clearly aimed at present-day GDR society, specifically at the crippling effects of a misguided concept of reason. The female protagonist, a scientist whose identity has been defined by her male-dominated profession, agrees to undergo a drug-induced sex transformation. Her qualitatively different perceptions of the world as a man convince her of the oppressive limitations of masculinity. She breaks off the experiment and demands to be changed back into a woman.

In her male incarnation the scientist recalls that "city" for her female self meant "an abundance of constantly disappointed hope constantly renewing itself. For him – that is, for me, Anders – it was a tight cluster of inexhaustible opportunities."[16] Yet rather than viewing the privileged male existence as liberating, s/he experiences it as restrictive. In contrast to the holistic,[17] mediating female way of appropriating the world that infuses external fact with subjective response, the male mode of existence is based on the dichotomous opposition of self and external reality. The lack of interaction between subject and object is seen to foster fragmentation, objectification, alienation, problems in communication, and ultimately the inability to love.[18]

Introduction

An anthology of interviews with women from the GDR, conducted by Maxie Wander, appeared in 1978.[19] Abandoning the typical question-and-answer format, Wander edited herself out of the interviews and allowed each woman to present herself directly. The result is a series of individual, highly personal monologues that, because they are directed at and incorporate the interviewer, take on a dialogic structure. *Guten Morgen, du Schöne* (Good Morning, You Beauty) constitutes an important document in GDR social history. Here women ranging in age from sixteen to seventy-four speak with remarkable candor about all aspects of their lives. They talk about their hopes and their fears, their pain and their joy, their successes and their failures, both in the workplace and in their intimate relationships. Lack of intimacy with their mates and stress resulting from the double burden of meeting domestic and professional expectations are recurrent themes of the book. What these interviews make abundantly clear is that the equality before the law that women in the GDR enjoy in no way ensures social or domestic equality. Instead, the women testify to the persistence of patriarchal patterns of thought and behavior in both the public and the private sphere, almost forty years after the founding of the socialist state. At the same time the book attests to the women's resistance to the current situation, a longing for a more egalitarian community in which all human needs can be met.

Christa Wolf wrote an introduction to *Guten Morgen* praising Maxie Wander's ability to encourage female self-expression and thanking her for giving a voice to these women, who would otherwise have remained silent. The essay "Touching"[20] enabled Wolf to continue her deliberations on gender-specific appropriation of the world. In it she identifies "sympathy, self-respect, trust, and friendliness" as "characteristics of sisterliness," a phenomenon she considers to be more prevalent than brotherliness, and she offers "unreserved subjectivity" as a possible means for social renewal, for overcoming alienation. The presence of supraindividualistic qualities – "longing, challenge, claim to life" – in these interpersonal texts by women strikes Wolf as heralding utopian community.[21] Through her concept of "touching" Wolf identifies a specifically female epistemological stance that, by regarding its object with understanding and sympathy, offers an alternative to positivistic objectivity.[22] "Touching" enables these women to transcend the limits of their own subjectivity by incorporating into it another's subjectivity. Through empathy they are able, however briefly, to transform the other into

13

a subject, hence to overcome their own alienation. Thus "touching" as transformative subjectivity adumbrates Marx's social individual.

In her literary (*No Place on Earth*) and essayistic[23] investigations of the German Romantics, Wolf further elucidates her feminist concern. Focusing on the utopian thought of the woman Romantics who longed for the possibility of a radically different, nonalienated human community, Wolf exemplifies her concept of "touching" and sisterliness. The ability to love is viewed as a female attribute, while the otherwise very different figures of Kleist, Savigny, and Friedrich Creuzer illustrate the severe emotional inadequacies common to men.

In *Cassandra*, male inability to love culminates in Achilles' necrophilia. *Cassandra*, Wolf's most feminist work, is literally radical. Not content to criticize contemporary self-destructive bellicosity in East and West, Wolf traces male aggression back to its source in patriarchy. Searching for the roots of dystopia, Wolf has been led further and further back in time as she has sought to uncover the origins of the petrified social structures that bring about alienation. Finally in *Cassandra* a utopian vision based on a matriarchal model replaces the earlier Marxist one as Wolf, through her reinterpretation of the Cassandra story, calls into question the foundations of male-dominated Western society, advocating the development of a (female) aesthetic of resistance to counteract the self-destructiveness of the patriarchy.

In addition to her feminist critique of patriarchy, Christa Wolf has helped recoup the writing of Karoline von Günderrode and sought to establish the existence of a female literary tradition in Germany. Recently, in the essayistic commentary to *Cassandra*, she has reflected on the existence of a female aesthetic and deliberated on the sociopolitical ramifications of such an aesthetic, especially on its potential for helping to create the alternatives needed for human survival.

East German woman *writer*: As a writer living in the GDR and writing primarily, though no longer exclusively, for the GDR public,[24] Wolf both enjoys certain privileges and faces the strictures encountered by all East-bloc writers. Officially the GDR does not exercise censorship; that is, there is no bureau of censorship. In fact, however, all literary production is under state control.[25] Fear of censorship and possible expatriation[26] are concerns for the GDR writer who seeks to express unorthodox views. All too often genuine material exigencies such as paper shortages serve as a pretense for outright silencing or for less obvious forms of censorship such as limited editions and delayed publication. The publication history of *Christa T.*,[27] as well as the excision from *Cassandra* of unconditionally pacifist passages and overt criticism directed against Warsaw Pact nations, indicate that Christa Wolf has had to contend with external censorship.

By her own admission she has also practiced a demoralizing self-censorship. Understood as a mechanism by which individuals living in totalitarian systems develop an exact sense of how far they can go without offending authority, self-censorship was inculcated into Wolf as a child growing up in the Third Reich. To the degree that she has become conscious of it, Christa Wolf's work can be read as an attempt to overcome this internal censorship.

Not merely a spokesperson for her society but also one of its most rigorous critics, Christa Wolf has become increasingly iconoclastic. The more she has violated the taboos of her society, the more she has had to discover means of articulating her criticism within the programmatic prescriptions for literary production placed on the GDR writer without compromising her integrity. This has led to indirect expression of criticism in historically distanced works such as *No Place on Earth* and *Cassandra* and at times to an opacity bordering on the obscure, such as in the story "Unter den Linden" (1974).

As compensation for some of the disadvantages described above, socialist writers, by virtue of their more integrated role, enjoy advantages of intellectual community virtually unknown to their counterparts in the West. Not only is there an intense interchange among members of the intelligentsia (writers, literary critics and scholars, editors and publishers are engaged in a continuous dialogue), but writers in the GDR play an important role for the populace at large. The dichotomy between "high" and popular literature characteristic of capitalist economies does not exist in East Germany, where the politics of publishing has led to the conflation of "high" and popular literature. Thus officially designated "classics" are often also runaway best-sellers.[28] Moreover, the voracious reading appetite of the populace[29] ensures that successful writers are a household word. For Wolf the integrated function of the socialist writer, the self-definition derived from work, the security that emanates from the sense of being needed[30] are weighty considerations. "Being needed" (*gebraucht werden*) is a theme that traverses Wolf's work and informs the creation of characters whose definition of self is derived from love and work.

In contrast to the outsider position to which German writers had traditionally been relegated – a "ghettolike internal realm of beautiful appearance"[31] – the GDR from the outset sought to liberate writers from their ivory tower existence and to make literature a public forum. The GDR's understanding of itself as a *Literaturgesellschaft*, a term coined by the country's first minister of culture, the poet Johannes R. Becher, points to a dialectic between literature and society and to the importance assigned to literature in cultural politics. Becher believed that literature was not only meant to advance the process of democratization and socialization in the newly established socialist state; it was also to serve as the agency for the self-understanding, the coming-to-consciousness of the populace. Ultimately it contributed to the perfectibility of a people, that is, of humankind within socialist society.[32] Literature in the GDR is conceived of as a nonelitist, democratic institution, based on an active communication among writers, readers, and producers of books. Its avowed goal is the inclusion of the working masses in the process of a literary production whose aim is the emancipation of all involved.

Again, there is a difference between theory and praxis. To counteract discrepancies between its ideal of a *Literaturgesellschaft* and the reality of a pervasive party organization and a hierarchy in social and communicative relations, in 1959 the Sozialistische Einheitspartei Deutschlands (SED) initiated the Bitterfeld Conference. Intended to unify the intelligentsia and workers and to break down the distinction between art and life, the so-called "Bitterfeld Way" sought to implement the motto of the Fifth Party Conference of the SED (July 1958): "sozialistisch arbeiten, lernen und leben" (socialistic work, learning, and life) and to advance the literary presentation of working conditions in factories. To assure authenticity, writers were encouraged to enter factories and work in brigades to obtain first-hand knowledge of working conditions. Alternatively, under the motto: "Kumpel, greif zur Feder, die sozialistische Nationalkultur braucht dich!" (comrade, take up the pen, the socialist national culture has need of you), manual laborers were called upon to document everyday conflicts, setbacks, and achievements in the sphere of economic production. Together the writer-worker and the worker *qua* writer were to help develop a socialist national culture and to break down hierarchical distinctions.

Introduction

The goals of the Bitterfeld Way were difficult to realize. Writers were reluctant to enter factories, and the cultural revolutionary impulses spurred by the program, such as workers' cultural clubs, the "circles of writing workers" (*Zirkel schreibender Arbeiter*), as well as the brief renaissance of the proletarian-revolutionary literature of the Weimar Republic, could not be sustained.

The years 1960–4 brought a revision in cultural politics that relegated workers to the sphere of material production and again measured literary production according to classical bourgeois norms. At the second Bitterfeld Conference (1964) it was clear that the GDR was more concerned with economic production and scientific-technological progress than with the development of a working-class culture. The possibilities for a broad-based mass cultural movement inherent in the Bitterfeld experiment were not realized; by the mid-sixties the professional writer was again firmly ensconced in an élite position. Nonetheless, its significance as an attempt to put socialist theory into practice should not be minimized.

GDR literary theory, which developed as an outgrowth of the Bitterfeld Conference and defined artistic creation not merely in terms of the writer's production but also in terms of the text's reception by the reader,[33] was to have far-reaching implications for Christa Wolf's work. In contrast to the autonomy concept that informs the aesthetic of *l'art pour l'art*, Socialist Realism, as didactic art, posits a dialectic between the author and the reader-recipient. Thus the relationship between the reader and the writer that constitutes the basis of Christa Wolf's reflections on literary theory, as articulated above all in her essay "The Reader and the Writer," has its roots in the socialist aesthetic that shaped her early works. Insofar as post-Bitterfeld theory conceived of mimesis not as a mere copy of reality but as a model through which essential social processes were made manifest in the hope of making the reader more receptive to the progressive forces of socialism,[34] it exerted a lasting influence on Christa Wolf. Much as she has distanced herself from Socialist Realism, all her works retain the modellike structure of this aesthetic.

Similarly, Wolf's innovative contribution to a socialist aesthetic, her focus on authorial subjectivity, can be seen as a response to the theoretical goals[35] of the Bitterfeld Way and the concrete situation of the writer in post-Bitterfeld society. Wolf rejects as impossible the notion of "objectivity" considered requisite for realist art. In her view, the basis of realist literature (to which she insists that all her work belongs)[36] is experiential, hence subjective. For her, literature is created through the appropriation of external reality by the author/subject and the transformation of that experienced reality into art. Wolf's focus on the individual in her works and her insistence on the primacy of subjective experience have been influential in changing the official Party stance toward subjectivity in literature.

Beginning with *Christa T.*, the work that established her own unique style, Wolf has accompanied her literary writings with essayistic and verbal commentary. She has introduced the concept of "subjective authenticity"[37] to describe her personal moral engagement as an author in her literary production. Subjective authenticity can manifest itself, as in *Christa T.* and *Patterns of Childhood*, through the introjection of authorial consciousness into the literary text or, as in *No Place on Earth* and *Cassandra*, as essayistic commentary that illuminates the text and clarifies the relevance of the material for its maker. As the concept of "subjective authenticity" makes clear, all of Christa Wolf's writing is ultimately autobiographical. In her early and middle works, the correlation between authorial biography and fictional narrative is more readily apparent than in her later narratives, where authorial subjectivity tends to be displaced into essays that elucidate the fictional texts. By creating an interdependence between personal, subjective essayistic commentary and the literary text, she undermines traditional generic categories and breaks down what she considers to be an artificial distinction between life and art.

The unique position Christa Wolf enjoys today, both in her own country and in the West, is largely due to the moral integrity she has displayed in her personal life and in her writing. Pursuing questions of personal conscience, she has criticized not only the policies of the West but increasingly those of the East as well. She has relentlessly scrutinized her own behavior and that of her compatriots and has refused to compromise her ethical standards, even when they have brought her into conflict with Party policy. As a consequence, she has come to be regarded as a voice of public conscience. Clearly Wolf's national and international reputation affords her special status within the GDR. Thus while the Party has the ultimate authority, Christa Wolf has become a force to be reckoned with. And that she *is* forcing a reckoning can be seen in her recent bout with the censors. Wolf insisted that the excised passages in the East German edition of *Cassandra* be marked by ellipses to signal censorship to her readers – and she prevailed, an unprecedented victory for a GDR writer.[38]

Ironically, Wolf's position in the GDR today is the outgrowth of another function that often falls to literature in socialist countries: in the absence of an open public sphere, political and social issues are often debated in the literary arena. The symbolic, multivalent nature of literary language, as opposed to more restrictive and ideologically charged political discourse, allows for greater freedom of discussion of volatile issues. Thus literature, which officially has a proselytizing function, can simultaneously serve as an impetus for implementing internal reform. The socialist writer's dual function as proselytizer/supporter and critic means that she walks a fine line between the accepted, the acceptable, and the taboo. A morally responsible writer such as Christa Wolf, who is acutely aware how precarious her situation is, has helped extend the boundaries of the accepted and the acceptable as she has ventured ever further into the realm of the taboo.

2

BEGINNINGS: EXPERIMENTATION WITH SOCIALIST REALIST PARADIGMS. *MOSCOW NOVELLA* AND *DIVIDED HEAVEN*

Moscow Novella

Christa Wolf's literary beginnings were not auspicious. The handful of politely encouraging reviews that greeted her first endeavor, *Moscow Novella* (1961) did not encourage wide translation of this work, so it is not available in English. Wolf herself agrees with the critical consensus that *Moscow Novella* is aesthetically inferior to her later works.[1] The naive, idealistic faith in socialism that determined the evaluative criteria of Wolf's literary reviews also stamped her first work of imaginative literature with an uncharacteristically evangelical tone.

By her own account,[2] Christa Wolf's initial encounter with Marxist thought was an epiphany: nineteen years old, horrified by the postwar revelations concerning the Nazi regime, she enthusiastically embraced Marx's humanistic social vision. Convinced that socialism offered the means of revolutionizing social relations, Wolf at first failed to distinguish between theory and praxis and accepted Party dogma uncritically. Her programmatic application of GDR cultural policy, reflected in her work as critic and editor for the publishing house "Neues Leben" and for the literary journal *Neue Deutsche Literatur*, carried over to her own creative writing.

Wolf's study of German literature had familiarized her with the prevailing Socialist Realist aesthetic. Her position as an editor of one of the leading GDR journals guaranteed that her (published) opinions and taste would not deviate greatly from official cultural policy. Wolf's years as an editor (1955–61) coincided with severe economic and political problems in the GDR – economic crisis; farmer resistance to collectivization; workers' demands for greater autonomy; general discontent and wide-scale emigration – all of which inhibited literary experimentation and flexibility still further. These factors undoubtedly contributed to the creation of Wolf's rather lackluster and contrived first work. Her adherence to

Socialist Realist criteria in *Moscow Novella* can be attributed also to a natural desire on the part of the fledgling writer to meet the expectations of her audience by working with established paradigms.

In both *Moscow Novella* and *Divided Heaven* (1963), Christa Wolf presents the dialectic between the individual and society as a conflict between duty and inclination, categories familiar from Schiller's debate with Kantian ethics. The duty versus inclination paradigm of an unviable love culminating in renunciation, a favorite constellation of the German *Klassik*, allowed Wolf to intertwine the personal and the political and to elucidate questions of personal fulfillment and social responsibility.

In *Moscow Novella* this conflict is presented in a straightforward and schematic fashion. As a member of a delegation sent to Moscow, East German pediatrician Vera Brauer is assigned to the Russian translator, Pavel Koschkin, whom she had met fifteen years earlier when the Red Army occupied her village. During her stay their love is rekindled. Both are married. When Pavel openly courts her, Vera must decide whether to pursue the temptation to explore their relationship.

Questions of moral responsibility, guilt, and atonement are raised not only in regard to their current situation but also concerning their past interaction. Their chance reencounter serves as a catalyst to review the past when Vera learns that an injury Pavel suffered had caused visual impairment, precluding his chosen career as a surgeon – an injury for which she had been indirectly responsible. Vera's recognition of her past culpability makes her more vulnerable to Pavel during their reunion in Moscow. While she fleetingly contemplates a life with her childhood love, Vera comes to realize that the needs of the larger whole must take precedence over their personal desires. Vera recognizes that "to love Pavel is to encourage him to fulfill his responsibility, that is, to stay with his wife and seek a new life with her on Russia's frontier."[3] She returns to her family and her work; the reader senses that her efforts to encourage the disheartened Pavel to take advantage of the teaching position offered him in the Far East will prove successful and that he will start a new, satisfying life. Thus, in the context of the novella, it is not respect for the institution of marriage but the need for both to be productive members of their respective societies that causes the lovers to separate. While Vera's renunciation is meant to reflect a socialist consciousness, the fact that the protagonists are both married allows the traditional bourgeois morality of the classical model to shine through.

Both thematically and formally, *Moscow Novella* conforms to Socialist Realist aesthetic norms. Its unambiguous presentation of moral choice, its black-and-white characterizations, and its judgment that self-fulfillment through interpersonal relationships must yield to commitment and responsibility to the collective offer the reader a clear-cut model of behavior. Thus it fulfills the mission of Socialist Realist literature to develop the moral consciousness of the reader toward socialist goals. The contrived, mechanistic plot and the linear narration with its obvious demarcations between past and present events made the text easily accessible, an essential formal criterion of Socialist Realism.

Twelve years after its publication, it was precisely this straightforwardness that Christa Wolf found most distressing about the work. In "Über Sinn und Unsinn von Naivität" (On the Sense and Nonsense of Naiveté, 1973), an essay for a volume in which well-known GDR authors commented on their first works, Wolf refused to address the questions put to her by the editor, maintaining that they were an invasion of privacy.[4] Instead of commenting on the genesis and development of *Moscow Novella*, she registered her reactions upon rereading the text: embarrassment and ambivalence. She attributed her own mixed emotions to the "almost total absence of mixed emotions in the text: . . . loyalty and faith, love and friendship, magnanimity and straightforwardness."[5]

Wolf did not disavow *Moscow Novella*. Instead, she stressed what she, from the vantage point of a later, more self-conscious stage in her development, perceived to be formal shortcomings of her first narrative prose work. In particular she was disturbed by "a tendency toward self-containment and perfection in the basic formal structure, in the merging of characters with the action of the plot, which is reminiscent of the ticking of a wound-up clock."[6] In her earlier essay "The Reader and the Writer," Wolf had rejected as anachronistic the mechanical, plot-oriented narrative structure dictated by Socialist Realism as belonging to a Newtonian world view. Similarly, in her criticism of *Moscow Novella*, she rejected its self-contained, predictable structure.

"On Sense and Nonsense" goes on to criticize the naive presentation of German–Russian interaction in her narrative, the failure to present adequately "the difficulties in the relationships between two peoples, one of which had fourteen years earlier tried to exterminate and enslave the other." Under such circumstances, Wolf claimed, it was not enough to depict a guilty conscience on the one hand and magnanimity on the other.[7] Faulting her narrative for its similarity to a political treatise, which she defined as "the dissemination of cherished beliefs,"[8] Wolf attributed her simplistic portrayal of complex events to her sincere belief in the transformative power of socialism. This belief allowed her to portray the main character of *Moscow Novella* as someone who had successfully and unproblematically put the Nazi past behind her and had wholeheartedly embraced the values of socialism.

Written at the time she was working on *Patterns of Childhood*, Wolf's criticism of *Moscow Novella* in "On Sense and Nonsense" was clearly influenced by the concerns addressed in the later book. Thus she (re)viewed *Moscow Novella* from the perspective of *Vergangenheitsbewältigung*. The shift in Wolf's perspective in the fifteen years between writing *Moscow Novella* and publishing *Patterns of Childhood* showed in the radically different conception of the main characters of these works. Vera Brauer conformed to the Party line of unproblematic transition from Nazism to socialism; Nelly Jordan is testimony to Wolf's recognition of the residual effects of Nazi indoctrination and ideology.

The autobiographical *Patterns of Childhood* also makes clear that Wolf had equipped her first fictional work with details from her own life. There are striking parallels between Vera Brauer and Nelly Jordan that coincide with the biography of the author. Both are the same age as Christa Wolf; they too are refugees from the Red Army and serve as secretarial assistants to the burgomaster in a small Mecklenburg village. The description of Vera's first encounter with Pavel, her fright and flight from the Soviet officer is duplicated in *Patterns of Childhood*.

Significantly, these autobiographical memories constitute the least contrived passages of *Moscow Novella*. Vera, recalling her meeting with Pavel, breaks through the distanced third-person narration that characterizes the rest of the work and, using the first-person pronoun, recalls:

Let it rain. The first time I met him it was raining too. To say we met is a good one . . . I panicked at the sight of his green-brown uniform and bolted out of the house, made a beeline across the meadows and fences and headed straight for the parsonage. And as I opened the door to the parish kitchen, muddy and out of breath, there he is sitting all by himself, in the middle of the room.[9]

Yet this authorial subjectivity remains anomalous in the text. The author immediately reasserts her "objective" stance, prompting speculation as to whether this was an "involuntary lapse" on Christa Wolf's part, "a brief glimpse of a narrative style that can tell a story without the self-censorship permeating the rest of the text."[10] We will have to wait until *The Quest for Christa T.* for the full development of that narrative style.

In contrast to *Patterns of Childhood*, however, Christa Wolf's experiences are merely superimposed onto the heroine of *Moscow Novella*, not placed in a dialectical relationship to the narrative and to the present. Only in the lengthy descriptions of Moscow does anything else approximating authorial subjectivity manifest itself in the text. Precisely these scenic descriptions, which were considered unintegrated, elicited objections from critics of *Moscow Novella*.[11] Yet these descriptions may well be an unsophisticated, if not unconscious, attempt at what will become a hallmark of Christa Wolf's prose: "subjective authenticity," the intrusion of authorial presence into the literary text. As such, they can be regarded as the presentation of Wolf's own Moscow experiences.

Despite its obvious shortcomings, *Moscow Novella* foreshadows some of Christa Wolf's major concerns and contains some quintessentially Wolfian features. Foremost among these are multitemporality and retrospectivity: past events are reviewed from a contemporary perspective, filtered through the consciousness of a remembering ego. In *Moscow Novella* Vera's reminiscences are activated by her fortuitous reunion with Pavel. Her initial failure to recognize Pavel indicates that without the stimulus of their meeting she would not have reexamined her personal history. Yet ultimately Vera's experience is not a productive process; the past is not successfully integrated into the present and hence cannot be made productive for the future.

Indeed, in highly un-Marxian fashion, the *Moscow Novella* at times appears to disavow the concept of a historical process that predicates understanding the present on the past and understanding the future on the present. In the key scene in which the German delegation, en route to Kiev with Pavel, collectively describes its vision of the man of the future, the future is seen as independent of the past and present. In response to Heinz's somber reflection that the momentous decision – permanent peace or self-annihilation – will probably be made during their lifetimes,[12] their younger colleague Gisela offers her naive utopia: "One day we'll wake up ... and the world will be socialistic. The atom bombs will be sunk in the ocean and the last capitalist will have voluntarily renounced his stock portfolio" (*MN* 51). Unlike the others, who ridicule Gisela for her illusions, Vera analyzes her situation empathetically and expresses the concept of generation-specific experience so important for Christa Wolf's later work.

The generation gap, a theme in *Moscow Novella*, *Divided Heaven*, *Christa T.*, and *Patterns of Childhood*, is measured not chronologically but experientially. Thus, although only six years separate them, Vera regards Gisela and her contemporaries as the new generation. For Vera, the difference between being ten and being sixteen in 1945 lies in a more conscious experience of war and Nazism; its consequences for the "older" generation were all too often disillusionment and cynicism. While the *Moscow Novella* explores this issue, Wolf does not present it as a problem until *Divided Heaven* when, in the figure of Manfred Herrfurth, she creates someone whose capacity for hope has effectively been destroyed by his conscious experience of the Third Reich.

Just as the mechanism for Vera's review of the past is contrived, the showcase discussion of the man of the future is also constructed to elucidate Wolf's humanistic ideals. In this respect Vera's and Pavel's contributions to the collective ethos are the most illuminating. Pavel's emphasis on technological mastery reflects the GDR policy of scientific technological revolution; this is offset by his humanistic vision that despite his technological achievements, the greatest achievement of the man of the future will be that "he will not become a robot, or a technologically perfected monster, but finally a human being. He'll walk upright on earth, will live long and intensely, will be happy and will know that this is his calling in life" (*MN* 52–3).

Asked to identify the most important characteristic of man in the year 2000, Pavel responds:

Brotherliness ... The ability to live with an open visor. Not to have to mistrust others. Not to envy them their successes, to help them endure their failures. Not to have to hide one's weaknesses. To be able to speak the truth. Guilelessness and naiveté, softness will no longer be insults. Fitness for life will no longer mean being able to dissemble.

Vera, on the other hand, considers "strength of character, the strength to overcome oneself" the most essential quality (*MN*, 53).

Together Pavel and Vera identify those attributes of moral strength and of egalitarian, caring human interrelationship that Christa Wolf presents as fundamental for human self-actualization in *The Quest for Christa T*. The fact that Wolf places the call for heightened vulnerability and brotherhood in Pavel's mouth is an anomaly: in her later works the desire for interrelationship is an almost exclusively female trait. Implicit in Pavel's utopian projection is a criticism of the present situation. The repeated use of negative formulations such as "no longer" indicates that Pavel's vision is an inversion or cessation of a current state of affairs. It is left to the reader, however, to draw conclusions about the implied contrast.

Jack Zipes identifies this conversation as the key to understanding all Wolf's works insofar as "their underlying purpose is to indicate ways in which humankind can actually become human, ways through which human beings can become the makers of their own history and not merely objects of history."[13] It is certainly true that all Wolf's works ultimately deal with the question of humanity's potential for self-actualization and that they explore the parameters of individual self-definition within the socialist collective. Yet as her relationship to Marxism evolves, Wolf's understanding of what constitutes self-actualization changes, as does the qualitative relationship of the individual to the collective. *Moscow Novella* and *Divided Heaven*, still heavily indebted to Party policy, stress the concept of self-mastery presented as renunciation and, in the tradition of the Enlightenment, affirm the role of reason in the development of moral consciousness.

Beginning with *The Quest for Christa T.*, her later works distinguish between reason and instrumental rationality and call for a broader, more integrative definition of self-actualization which emphasizes the development of the full range of human potential. To the extent that Wolf increasingly emphasizes the nonrational, the imaginative, the fantastic in her definition of what is human, her work can be seen as a movement away from the Enlightenment to Romanticism; away from orthodox Marxist–Leninism to Ernst Bloch.

Divided Heaven

Although it appeared only two years after *Moscow Novella*, Christa Wolf's second narrative, *Divided Heaven* (1963), represents a great step forward aesthetically. In contrast to the conventional structure of the novella, *Divided Heaven* is self-reflective and far more experimental; the more complex structure is also an essential carrier of meaning. Unlike Vera Brauer's reminiscences, Rita

Seidel's have bearing on the present and implications for the future. In *Divided Heaven*, which has been called "the socialist education of Rita Seidel,"[14] the heroine's reviewing of past events enables her to understand and reaffirm actions undertaken intuitively.

In addition to a short frame that establishes a sense of communality with the reader and places the story of Rita Seidel in the context of GDR society, *Divided Heaven* is framed by the present level of narration: Rita's gradual physical and psychic recovery from an ostensible accident in the railroad car factory where the teacher in training was working. This level of narration in turn serves as the impetus for bringing to consciousness significant past events that constitute the emotional level of the story. The sanatorium setting and Rita's condition are conducive to self-reflection and render the retrospective structure plausible. Although the story is told predominantly from Rita's perspective, Wolf restricts her use of interior monologue, accompanies Rita's reflections with the editorializing comments of an omniscient narrator, and augments Rita's perspective with that of Manfred. The inclusion of an omniscient narrator who shares his knowledge with the reader is in keeping with the didactic impulse of *Divided Heaven* and with the teleological orientation of Socialist Realism. However conventional *Divided Heaven* may appear to us today compared with Wolf's later works, by GDR standards of the time it was highly experimental. Its shifting narrative perspective and the ambiguities arising from the overlap of different temporal and narrative levels was challenging for a public unaccustomed to "formalist" narrative techniques.

By forcing readers to draw conclusions based on information implicit in the novel, Wolf engages us in the constitution of the text, a process that is given greater weight in *Christa T.* and subsequent narratives. Not until the end of the novel does a careful reading make clear to the reader that Rita's "accident" was actually a suicide attempt.[15] The subsequent revelation of the exact date of the "accident" adds the political dimension to Rita's personal story of renunciation on which most critics have focused. The thirteenth of August 1961 marks a momentous event in GDR history – the erection of the Berlin Wall. For Rita the Wall meant that her freely chosen decision not to follow her lover to the West had become irrevocable.

Divided Heaven answered the Socialist Unity Party's call at the Bitterfeld Conference of 1959 for artists and writers to enter factories to obtain practical work experience. The novel can be seen as Christa Wolf's contribution to the creation of a socialist national literature in the GDR; it is based on Wolf's experiences as a member of a brigade in the railroad car works in Halle, where she worked from 1959 to 1962. Thus *Divided Heaven* belongs to the "Literatur der Arbeitswelt" (literature of the world of labor) prescribed by the Bitterfeld Conference; that is, a literature reflecting the workaday experience of the GDR populace.

Yet despite its adherence to the precepts of Bitterfeld, the novel contains few details regarding the actual production process. Instead, as in *Moscow Novella*, Wolf focuses on relationships: Rita and Manfred, Rita and her mentors, Rita and the workers, the workers among themselves, Manfred and his parents. Thus the technical side of work is not of prime interest to Wolf, but rather the various possible human constellations within the world of labor.

"Dienstag, der 27. September" (Tuesday, 27 September), written for the Soviet newspaper *Isvestia*, makes the experiential basis of *Divided Heaven* clear. Written as a journal entry, the autobiographical sketch records the narrator/author's visit to the railroad works and outlines problems dealt with in greater detail in the novel. It also elucidates Wolf's frustration as she attempts to find a suitable beginning to what obviously will become *Divided Heaven*. She notes:

I look through the manuscript beginnings piled on top of each other on my desk. The tediousness of the process we call writing makes me bitter. A few faces have already emerged from the simple brigade story, people whom I know better than the rest and whom I have connected together to make a story – one which, as I can clearly see, is still much too simple. A girl from the country who for the first time comes to a larger city to study. Prior to that she does a practicum in a factory with a difficult brigade. Her lover is a chemist, he doesn't get her in the end. The third one is a young foreman who has been sent to the brigade on probation because he has made a mistake ... It is amazing that these banal events, "copied from life," intensify their banality to an intolerable degree on the pages of a manuscript. I know that my real work will begin once I find the overarching idea that renders the story tellable and worthy of being told.[16]

Wolf doubtless found her overarching idea, her decision to embed her love story in the context of the conflicting value systems of the divided Germany, in the wake of the construction of the Wall. Given the GDR's stagnant economy and its potentially explosive political situation, the decision to close off the border between East and West Berlin can be seen as a logical and necessary step. In the late fifties and early sixties the GDR had struggled in vain to catch up with the surging economy of the West. Crippled by excessively ambitious central planning, its economy could not begin to approximate the *Wirtschaftswunder* of the Federal Republic. The fact that East German émigrés were quickly absorbed into the West German economy resulted in a rise in emigration. Since those leaving were usually young skilled workers, the emigration seriously endangered the country's economic production. This situation was aggravated by the unprecedented number of farmers leaving in protest of agricultural collectivization. Confronted by a drastically reduced labor force that was in peril of dwindling still further, the GDR built the Wall, a measure that alleviated its most immediate economic problems and allowed the economy to stabilize.

Necessary though the Wall might have been for the economic survival of the socialist state, on the individual level it constituted a sorely felt loss of personal freedom. Although the Wall is never mentioned directly in *Divided Heaven*, the opaque reference to "the silent voices of imminent dangers, all fatal in that period" (*DH* 1) in the frame makes clear the psychological impact its erection had on the GDR's people.

While Rita Seidel's experiences in the railroad works, based on Christa Wolf's observations, reflect the problematic production conditions and other economic exigencies confronting the GDR in the early sixties, and while the portrayal of the Federal Republic is clearly informed by Cold War politics,[17] *Divided Heaven* focuses on the personal ramifications of the national division, registering the human costs of the Wall. Nowhere is Wolf's engagement clearer than in the poignant exchange between the lovers during Rita's brief visit to Manfred in West Berlin. Imploring her to stay with him, Manfred says:

Shut your eyes for a minute and think of the Schwarzwald, the Rhine, the Bodensee. Don't those names mean anything to you? Aren't they in Germany, too? Or are they only a legend, a page in the geography book? Isn't it unnatural not to want to see them? Not even to want to see them? Just to sweep aside the very thought? (*DH* 190)

And Rita, although repelled by the commercialism of West Berlin, is overcome by a "wave of longing for all those strange landscapes and faces, longing for a full life with Manfred" (*DH* 190). Bitterly she asks, "Who in the world has the right to make any human being – even if it is only a single one – make such a decision, which, no matter what he decides, demands a part of him."[18]

As "Tuesday, 27 September" makes clear, Wolf from the outset was concerned with the interaction of the lovers. The model established in *Divided Heaven*: an interpersonal story set against the background of great social conflict and change, is one that Wolf adheres to in all her works. As early as 1958 Wolf, expressing her faith in the ability of socialist ideas to change people, had nonetheless called upon socialist writers to construct plots rich in conflict, commensurate with the conflicts in the GDR's struggle to fulfill its socialist goals.[19]

More than any other of Christa Wolf's works, *Divided Heaven* reflects the sociopolitical structure of the GDR. In contrast to the distant, romantic setting of *Moscow Novella*, it deals with the world of production in Wolf's own country. Its uniqueness lies in the weight she assigns to the subjective component, her emphasis on interpersonal relationships.

As an outgrowth of Bitterfeld, *Divided Heaven* aroused expectations in Wolf's critics that the novel in many respects disappointed. Although it still conformed to Socialist Realist precepts, *Divided Heaven* resulted in a more critical, complex, and ambivalent presentation of socialism than had been the case in *Moscow Novella*. Precisely these characteristics precipitated widespread debate in the GDR. With the publication of *Divided Heaven*, Christa Wolf became a success in her country, earning the Academy of Arts Heinrich Mann Prize for Literature (1963). Indeed, the book created such a furore that in 1965 the Mitteldeutscher Verlag (the original publisher) released a volume of the collected East German reviews together with several West German reviews of the book followed by a critical assessment by the editor, Martin Reso.[20]

In the GDR, debate revolved around Rita Seidel's socialist models: were Schwarzenbach, Meternagel, and Wendland typical and exemplary? More dogmatic critics decried the fact that none of the socialist role models conformed to the paradigm of the antifascist resistance fighter and that their unorthodox tactics to improve production conditions seemed suspiciously individualistic, if not outright anarchistic. All had served in Hitler's army and their subsequent commitment to socialism appeared insufficiently motivated. The figure of Meternagel in particular came under attack as the character most directly connected with the world of labor and most revered by Rita. In addition, critics took issue with the portrayal of the foil characters, pointing out that while the role models remained relatively flat, the decadent bourgeois Herr and

Frau Herrfurth, but especially their son, Manfred, were drawn in far greater depth and were consequently more interesting.[21] In addition, Wolf's formal innovations in *Divided Heaven*, her break with strictly linear narration, her use of flashbacks, interior monologue, and the juxtaposition of subjective, lyrical passages with critical and reflective ones were still considered anathema by some critics in the early 1960s and also brought her into discredit.

More progressive voices in the GDR defended *Divided Heaven*, applauding its differentiated presentation of problems and contradictions in the country's developing social order. Chief among these was Martin Reso, whose essay assured that when the critical dust had settled, the vote was in favor of the more liberal reading of *Divided Heaven*.[22] The Reso book, an important document of GDR reception history, records the intricacies of one of the country's great literary debates and bears witness to the assertion of a more critical realism in the post-Wall period.

In the Federal Republic, reception of *Divided Heaven* proved to be as ideologically determined as in the GDR. Critics applauded what they saw as an honest presentation of production difficulties and problematic social relations in East Germany, while rejecting Rita's decision not to follow Manfred to the West as insufficiently motivated and hence unconvincing.

Despite Wolf's sympathetic portrayal of Manfred, there can be no doubt that Rita is the heroine of *Divided Heaven* and that the retrospective structure of the novel is designed to allow the reader to follow her development. She conforms to the Socialist Realist call for a positive hero, conceived on the Aristotelian model – that is, a figure with whom the reader can identify. The figure of Rita is thus consonant with GDR cultural policy, which is geared not only toward the development of a new consciousness about the production process but is also meant to develop the moral consciousness of the reader along socialist lines. At the second Bitterfeld Conference, Walter Ulbricht had maintained that works of Socialist Realist art

serve to foster the moral change of humanity in the spirit of socialism. They spur us on to great deeds for socialism, awaken in us the love of work, enrich the intellectual life of the people, develop the rational and emotional capacities of human beings in the socialist community, and educate us to take great joy in life.[23]

Divided Heaven clearly conforms to the spirit of Ulbricht's ideological aesthetic prescriptions. True, Wolf avoids the black-and-white characterizations typical of Socialist Realism that were present in *Moscow Novella*. She also experiments with new structures and styles and violates taboos by addressing issues such as *Republikflucht* (flight from the republic), nihilism (in the figure of Manfred), the Wall, and suicide.[24] Still, Wolf's socialist engagement and commitment to the Party's policy are unequivocally manifest in *Divided Heaven*.

In her portrayal of Rita Seidel's socialist education, Wolf for the first time refers back to the paradigm of the *Bildungsroman*, a genre favored by GDR writers of the fifties. The *Bildungsroman* (novel of personal growth) is a quintessentially German, teleologically conceived genre that depicts the moral and ethical development of the hero and culminates in his productive integration into society. It has a long history in German literature; its prototype, Goethe's *Wilhelm Meister*,[25] was informed by the German philosophical tradition since Leibniz and based on the concept of entelechy, the belief that every living being can develop to its full potential according to its own innate laws. In accordance with the *Humanitätsideal* (Humanism) of the German *Klassik*, the *Bildungsroman* portrayed the harmonious interplay between the individual and society, as the possibility of individual self-actualization without detriment to the collective. In the hands of the poetic realists Gottfried Keller and Adalbert Stifter, the *Bildungsroman* flourished in the nineteenth century. It has found its place in the twentieth century in modernist works such as Thomas Mann's *The Magic Mountain* and Hermann Hesse's *Steppenwolf*. In contrast to the inherently pessimistic undercurrent of Mann's and Hesse's critique of culture, the GDR's contribution to the *Bildungsroman* tradition reasserts the optimism of its classical model.[26] The classical vision of fully developed individuals who freely choose to work for the common weal is consonant with Marxist theory and had obvious appeal for Christa Wolf, for it embodied her ideal of socialism. Indeed, with the exception of *No Place on Earth*, all of Wolf's subsequent longer narratives will refer to paradigms of the *Bildungsroman*.

Obviously certain shifts in emphasis were necessary for a Marxist appropriation of an Idealist genre. Foremost among these was a movement away from a focus on the individual to a focus on society. Thus, in lieu of the Idealist entelechy concept, the socialist *Bildungsroman*, in keeping with the Marxist precept that social being determines consciousness, stresses the educative power of empirical models. Wolf retains the *Bildungsroman*'s optimistic belief in the educability of humankind but anchors her story firmly in the social matrix by fleshing out the role model figures. Rita Seidel's development from country innocent to a mature, committed member of her socialist society is unthinkable without Schwarzenbach, Meternagel, and Wendland. If we follow Hans Vaget in redefining the classical *Bildungsroman* as "the novel of socialization,"[27] then *Divided Heaven* represents the purest example of this genre created by Christa Wolf. In contrast to Christa T., Nelly Jordan, and Cassandra, who resist socialization, the more malleable Rita Seidel conforms to the expectations placed on her by her socialist society.

While still adhering in large measure to the Socialist Realist aesthetic, *Divided Heaven* broke with some of its programmatic prescriptions. In *Moscow Novella*, Wolf had cast old-time Party member Werner Kernten in the heroic mold; with *Divided Heaven* she abandoned this type as being outside her experience of everyday Nazism.[28] All Rita's role models share the belief in the socialist humanism articulated in *Moscow Novella*, coupled with an unfailing engagement to work to humanize social relations in GDR praxis. But their paths to socialism had been unheroic. The tension between ideal and realization is the root of Wolf's problematic characterization of these figures. Unlike *Moscow Novella*, *Divided Heaven* does not depict a utopian projection of a socialist society devoid of conflict, but instead focuses on the present, addressing the very real and immediate problems facing the GDR in the early sixties: shortages of material; bureaucratic red tape, inefficiency, and chicanery; residual bourgeois consciousness; lack of collective cooperation. It thus confronts issues that *Moscow Novella*'s flight of fantasy to the year 2000 had circumvented. Yet Christa Wolf's optimistic faith in socialism, operative in *Moscow Novella*, informed the creation of the educator figures in *Divided Heaven* as well.

Wolf clearly intended Meternagel's, Wendland's, and Schwarzenbach's paths to Marxism to appear as a rational choice, as evidence of the transformative power of the force of reason in the historical process. In a speech given in 1964, a year after the publication of *Divided Heaven*, Wolf reiterated her optimism regarding the ability of socialism as the force of reason to revolutionize social interaction:

In this part of Germany, which twenty years ago was still dominated by fascists and was inhabited by embittered, confused, and hate-filled people, the foundation has been laid for a reasonable human community. Reason –

we call it socialism – has penetrated into everyday life. It is the yardstick by which we measure here, the ideal in whose name we praise or censure here.[29]

Yet the educator figures' commitment to socialism emerges instead as a leap of faith. In keeping with the epihanic nature of their transformation, Wolf allows each character to speak in a confessional mode, to present the personal history of their transition from Nazism to socialism. Thus Meternagel matter-of-factly relates his experiences as a soldier to Rita, conveying his sense of helplessness at being a pawn of the existing powers. On the other hand, he credits his work experiences as a Soviet prisoner of war with teaching him the superiority of productive work to aggression and destruction. That work experience moved him to join the Socialist Unity Party immediately upon his return to Germany. Meternagel's development is meant to be exemplary, to show someone attempting to create himself through work, that is, struggling to become a subject of history. His account also conforms to the self-understanding of the GDR as the force of reason and peace opposing the capitalist militarism that led to fascism.

Wendland came to socialism through a similar prisoner-of-war experience. Sent to a work camp in Siberia for three years and to antifascist (denazification) school by the Soviets, Wendland was eager to join the Free German Youth upon his return home. Meternagel's and Wendland's experiences can be seen as examples of acquiescence to the moral force of socialism, as variations on the theme of making a virtue of necessity, as examples of self-mastery, or as reflective of Wolf's own idealistic belief in the moral superiority of socialism. Thankful for the circumstances that brought them to socialism, they embrace the new order with the fervor of converts.

Schwarzenbach's road to socialism was not through a positive prisoner-of-war experience nor as the result of a successful denazification program, but through Party benevolence. In his public self-revelation in the pedagogical institute, he admits that even though he is a worker's son, he had wanted to join the suicide squad, the "werewolves," at the end of the war in order to get himself killed:

We deserved hatred then and we expected people to hate us, but the Party was patient and tolerant with us, although it expected a great deal of us, too. You know, ever since then I've had a great respect for tolerance and patience. Those are real revolutionary qualities . . . (*DH* 132)

Wolf has justifiably been criticized both in the GDR and in the West for her optimistic and vague presentation of the ideological transformation of these figures. It is true that their perspectives change not because they come to understand Marxist–Leninist social analysis, but rather because of an idealistic humanism. Wolf's failure to provide specifics about the precise nature of Meternagel's insight and the curriculum at the antifascist school, for which she has been called to task,[30] may reflect a greater concern with ends than with means, which parallels her emphasis on relationship rather than production.

A more serious objection is the criticism of authoritarianism leveled against both the Party and Rita's mentors. Myra Love points out that much of Wolf's criticism of *Moscow Novella* in "On Sense and Nonsense" applies to *Divided Heaven* as well. Love maintains that Schwarzenbach's relationship to the Party is characterized by the same mixture of bad conscience and generosity as the earlier text. In her view, the acceptance of the "pat definition of the relationship of party and populace after the war legitimates the hegemony of the party on the basis of guilt" and explains its ability to hold "the population in a state of permanent dependency because of the Nazi past."[31]

Willkie Cirker, on the other hand, sees a dialectic between Wolf's idealistic humanism and what he terms her benevolent authoritarianism. "In her highly moralistic universe there is a constant danger that evil (the inhumane, the latently fascistic) will overcome good (the humane)."[32] While Cirker's reading of *Divided Heaven* as "an exhortation from above [the superstructure] to follow the socio-economic laws of the base as predicted by Marx"[33] is overstated, it is certainly true that Christa Wolf's faith in socialism leads her to place authority in the Party and to operate with antinomies of good and evil (precisely those categories she will reject in her essay "The Reader and the Writer"); moreover, her mentor figures, imbued with her own ideals about socialism, believe they have access to the truth and therefore come perilously close to imposing their views on others for their own good.

Unsatisfactory or nebulous as they may appear to the Western reader, such ideological transformations undoubtedly occurred during the war and postwar periods. Once we accept the genuineness of their conversion, Rita's mentors *do* offer concrete examples of how ordinary people can engage in productive work to realize their idealistic goals and give meaning to their existence. Wolf's characterizations embodied what she perceived to be the situation of many GDR citizens, for whom "the efforts for the ideas of socialism at the same time represented the first concrete possibilities in their lives to prove themselves as human beings and to realize their human potential."[34] Their examples encourage Rita and fortify her against the disillusionment that plagues Manfred and ultimately causes him to defect to the West. *Divided Heaven*, in the figures of Manfred and Rita, offers the reader models of two possible ways of being in the world, the one characterized by cynicism and indifference, the other by optimism and engagement,[35] models that recur often in her work. Rita's mentors play an extremely important role in her moral and social development toward the latter, clearly superior, stance.

The figures of Schwarzenbach, Meternagel, and Wendland must also be understood as foils to Manfred. Although they share with Manfred the burden of the Nazi past, their mechanisms for coping are quite different. It is important to note, however, that their commitment to socialism *is* a coping mechanism, for while all of Wolf's characters who have experienced Nazism suffer from it, not until *Patterns of Childhood* do any of them actively confront and come to terms with their past. In *Divided Heaven*, Wolf is obviously caught between her commitment to Party policy and to the authenticity of her personal experience. Unwilling to compromise her experience and create antifascist resistance fighters, yet wanting to portray members of the older generation as devoted socialists, Wolf conceives of the transformative power of prisoner-of-war experiences. For people of Meternagel and Wendland's generation, she can envisage the possibility of dramatic shifts in perspective only as the result of extraordinary events such as those they have experienced. The more usual case is that of Schwarzenbach's long period of relearning[36] or Manfred's utter disillusionment. A facile transition from Nazism to socialism such as Vera Brauer's in *Moscow Novella* is no longer a possibility for Wolf in *Divided Heaven*.

Wolf seeks the source of Rita's and Manfred's diametrically opposed world views in the generation gap. Rita, born in 1940, is ten years Manfred's junior. Manfred belongs to Christa Wolf's generation, young people whose biography was broken by the war and who consciously experienced the transition from Nazism to socialism. The generational differences between the lovers will prove a decisive factor in determining the outcome of their affair. Manfred exemplifies the situation of those described by Vera

Brauer in *Moscow Novella*: people psychically broken by the past, ruled by disillusionment, cynicism, and emotional frigidity.

In his cathartic monologue, Wolf has Manfred himself reflect on the generation gap separating him from Rita. More than the personal history of strained family relationships, Manfred's story is also the exposition of a youth under Nazism. It recalls the experiences of a sensitive child, an outsider who watches his parents embrace first Nazism and then socialism and who finds acceptance among his peers by attending Hitler Youth meetings, ultimately conforming to the prevailing brutish norms by joining a youth gang. In the midst of relating his story, Manfred interrupts himself to ponder:

> Why am I telling her all this? . . . Has she any idea of what things were like, then? Why, she wasn't even born! It's a queer thing, the new generation starts somewhere between us. She can't possibly understand that we were all injected early with this cynicism that's so hard to shake off.
>
> (*DH* 41–2)

Despite his recognition that the generation gap renders his experiences incomprehensible to Rita,[37] Manfred feels compelled to continue. He recalls his mother's black marketeering and her success in rehabilitating her husband. And finally he remembers his cynical response to the promise of a new and better social order:

> We idled about all through the summer and saw exactly what a mess the grown-ups had managed to make of everything, with all their cleverness and knowing better. We just laughed aloud at the posters which told us everything was going to be better and different. Who was going to make it different, we wondered. The same people who had got us into this mess? Our school opened again in the autumn. Our old Nazi song-books were still in our lockers. The new people had not even had time to get rid of all the old stuff.
>
> (*DH* 42)

Manfred's assessment of the postwar situation is a stinging indictment of his society. It represents Wolf's most graphic presentation of the problems resulting from the nonrevolutionary imposition of socialism. Manfred's use of the collective "we" is a linguistic feature Christa Wolf uses frequently to embed personal experience in a larger social context, thereby ensuring that it will be typical rather than idiosyncratic. Here the "we" stands in contrast to the "we" of the socialist collective of the frame and refers to Manfred and his cohorts.

Unlike subsequent fictional embodiments of Christa Wolf's generation such as Christa T. and the narrator of *The Quest for*

37

Christa T., these young men are unable to embrace socialist ideals and to give meaning to their lives by working toward their actualization. In Manfred's case this inability stems not only from his unreconciled Nazi past and from his disillusionment at the hypocrisy he perceives all around him, but also from personal betrayal after the war by the one friend of his youth. It is important to note that Wolf does not attribute Manfred's disillusionment to mere abstract intellectualism; his indifference is affectively motivated. At one time he had sought to effect change by publicly addressing what he perceived to be problems impeding social development in the GDR. His criticism of administrative errors in the university, of bureaucratic "ballast," and of hypocrisy as the most expedient policy for advancement earns him the condemnation of his peers, who consider his views "dangerous and corrupt" (*DH* 134). His journalist friend to whom he turns for support not only remains silent at the meeting but subsequently writes an article denouncing Manfred. His peers' reaction and his personal and intellectual betrayal by his friend prove the validity of Manfred's criticisms and he withdraws emotionally, retreating into coldness.

While his friend's self-serving betrayal has serious consequences for Manfred, the incident at the university conference has broader and more serious implications for his society. By failing to explore the criticisms raised the citizens of the GDR short-circuit the purpose of the public forum as a vehicle of social communication. By denying the contradictions in their society, they are unable to make them productive, that is, capable of transforming social relations. Thus the problem of (self-)delusional thinking and its relationship to (self-)destructiveness, so important for Wolf's later work, especially *Patterns of Childhood* and *Cassandra*, is prefigured in this early novel.

The destructive potential of doctrinaire fanaticism is one of the main foci of Wolf's criticism in *Divided Heaven*. It is at the heart of her portrayal of the pedagogue Mangold. A foil to Schwarzenbach, Mangold emerges as a cold, unimaginative functionary who uniformly enforces Party dogma, unwilling to take into account the particular circumstances of a given situation or the personalities involved. By adhering to the letter rather than to the spirit of socialism, Mangold comes under attack both from Rita and from Schwarzenbach.

Rita's immediate aversion to Mangold is prompted by his ready answer to every question. His unbending adherence to norms, his self-righteousness and complacency epitomize the dogmatism at the pedagogical institute that so disturbs her. Rita rejects Mangold as a pedagogical model because she recognizes that such a rigid personality cannot possibly foster the learning process, which presupposes openness and a willingness to explore. In Christa T., Wolf will create the positive counterpart of Mangold – a teacher concerned with the spiritual and intellectual development of each of her students.

The destructive effects of Mangold's intimidation tactics become apparent when the parents of one of the students flee to the West. Sigrid, afraid that her parents' actions will cost her her scholarship, does not report the flight as prescribed. By confiding in Rita, she implicates her as well. Mangold's response upon learning of the situation confirms Rita's worst suspicions about him:

So she had known about it. A fine conspiracy. A worker deserts our state, our republic. His daughter deceives this same state. And her friend, who also draws a stipend from this state, conspires with her. This will have serious consequences. His voice droned on and on.   (*DH* 123)

Rita's recollection of Mangold's response brings his cliché- and jargon-ridden language to the fore, while her use of the word "drone" reveals how ineffectual his speech is for her.

Schwarzenbach, interested not in abstract principles but in the human beings affected by them, intervenes, blaming not Sigrid but the pedagogical community for failing to inspire the trust that would have allowed her to seek advice. Mangold cannot admit a different perspective; his droning Party line response evokes Schwarzenbach's invidious comparison with "a Catholic talking about the immaculate conception" (*DH* 132). By confronting Mangold, Schwarzenbach radically changes the outcome of the meeting. Instead of a denunciation of Sigrid and Rita, it becomes an open discussion of fundamental issues concerning the relationship between the individual and the collective in the socialist state. It serves as a positive counterexample to the university conference scene described by Manfred. As proof of the importance of the individual in effecting constructive change, it takes its place next to the positive examples of Meternagel and Wendland, examples that Rita, in contrast to Manfred, has experienced first-hand.

Schwarzenbach's admonition that Mangold would do well to recognize that patience and tolerance are revolutionary qualities underscores Rita's perceptions. In what amounts to an either/or choice, Rita concludes that without people like Schwarzenbach, Meternagel, and Wendland, "people like the Herrfurths would gain the upper hand again" (*DH* 124). In a flash of insight Rita recognizes "how much alike Mangold and Frau Herrfurth were; was it possible for people to fight for quite opposite things in the same narrow-minded, selfish, nagging way?" (*DH* 125). Rita's analysis is remarkable: by categorically rejecting self-serving, fanatical behavior, regardless of its ideological context, she links doctrinaire communism with fascism.

Rita's equation of Mangold's and Frau Herrfurth's behavior is consonant with concerns later expressed by Christa Wolf in "On Sense and Nonsense." The tone of enthusiastic optimism that informed her speech of 1964, when she maintained that the foundation had been laid for the revolution in social relations, gave way to a more critical assessment in the essay of 1973. While acknowledging the importance of the changes that occurred in the GDR after the war, Wolf argues that these consisted primarily of a shift in ideological content rather than in fundamental structural changes in thought and behavior.

> For it is not enough to be deeply and lastingly horrified by the barbarism that had emanated from our country and that we had so long denied. Nor can one be content with a sobering up that concerns only past historical events. Even if mistakes in thinking had been recognized, regretted, and with considerable effort corrected; even if views and opinions, the entire image of the world [*Weltbild*] had been radically changed – the *way* of thinking could not be changed so quickly and even less could certain ways of reacting and behaving which, inculcated in childhood, continued to determine the structural relationship of a character to its environment: the habit of credulousness *vis-à-vis* higher institutions, the compulsion to deify people or at any rate to subordinate oneself to their authority, the tendency to a denial of reality and zealous intolerance.[38]

Wolf's aversion to *Weltbilder* and her criticism of the authoritarian personality can be attributed to her painful assessment of the deleterious effects of Nazi ideology and fanaticism on her own life (*Patterns of Childhood*). At the time she wrote *Divided Heaven* she had not yet consciously formulated her concern about the danger of substituting one ideology for another. Yet her portrayal of the Herrfurths, her criticism of hypocrisy and its counterpart, dogmatism, indicate that at some level she was aware that this was a potential problem for her society. Her aversion to political dogmatism undoubtedly shaped her conception of *Divided Heaven*, in which she sought to present Rita's choice of socialism as considered and reasoned and established on a realistic appraisal of existing conditions.

While Wolf is not always successful at avoiding stereotypes, she often uses situations or configurations that have become literary clichés and then plays new elements off against the reader's expectations. Thus Rita and Manfred's affair initially runs according to paradigms of bourgeois romances. Rita's emotions upon receiving Manfred's love letter testify to the romantic clichés that pervade her thoughts:

Rita, nineteen years old, had often been vaguely dissatisfied because she could not fall in love like other girls, but she had no trouble in understanding his letter. She suddenly felt that all her nineteen years, all her wishes, actions, thoughts and dreams, had had only one purpose – to prepare her for this letter. She felt that she suddenly knew things which she had never learnt. She was certain that nobody before her had ever felt or could ever feel what she now felt. (*DH* 7)

For a time Manfred becomes Rita's reason for living. Perhaps she would have defined her life entirely in terms of her lover, had not Schwarzenbach appeared in her village to recruit promising candidates for a teacher training program. Schwarzenbach, presented as a socialist *deus ex machina*, enables Rita to see "for the first time how a hand from above could influence the lives of ordinary people" (*DH* 15). Through benevolent state intervention, the course of her life is changed. Presented with an intellectual challenge, she is given the possibility of self-definition through productive work. Thus almost from the outset two means of self-actualization, love and work, exist in Rita's life.

At first it appears that Rita will be permitted to integrate the personal and the professional. Since the pedagogical institute is in Manfred's city, she moves in with her lover. Through his father she obtains the position in the railroad car factory that fulfills the requirement for students to engage in manual labor. Manfred's room, his only solace in the stifling environment of his hated, funereal parental home, becomes a haven for the lovers as well. In the privacy of their attic, Manfred, responding to Rita's openness and caring, lowers his defenses. In an apparent transformation of character, the cynic begins to hope again. This capacity for hope, which renders him human in the Blochian sense, is what he loses when his efforts to produce a spinning-jenny fail. The arbitrary rejection by Party functionaries of his friend Martin Jung's invention, in which Manfred also wholeheartedly believed, reinforces his scepticism and convinces him of the futility of individual action in the face of an inscrutable state machinery. Wolf, making us privy to Manfred's thoughts, relates how the shock of hearing that it [the spinning-jenny] had been rejected plunged him back into his old indifference; he mentally washed his hands of all responsibility for what was going on, and made up his mind not to let himself be drawn into anything again. A new feeling of cold detachment pervaded his thoughts. Real pain or happiness could only come from Rita now. (*DH* 111)

By attributing Manfred's ultimate retreat into cynicism to the contradictions he experiences in the new society, his disillusionment to the discrepancies between the ideal and the reality of socialism, and his decision to leave the GDR not to a misconception of the West but to his utter indifference, which enables him to live anywhere,[39] Wolf has created a new type in GDR literature.[40]

Manfred's situation reflects what Wolf then perceived as the most serious problem confronting young people in her society. In 1963, in a statement to the student newspaper *Forum*, she maintained:

The main problem of many young people is (and will remain) the tension between ideal and reality, between their expectations of happiness and the fulfillment of those expectations, the contradiction between the . . . possibilities which we already have and their often imperfect realization through all of us.[41]

Wolf's comment, based on the view of socialism as an ongoing process, also reflects her recognition of the discrepancy between socialist theory and praxis, a theme that is at the heart of her next work, *The Quest for Christa T.* Her motivation of Manfred's flight, together with her depiction of the difficulties encountered by Schwarzenbach, Meternagel, and Wendland must be read as a criticism of the failure of the existing East German socialist state to implement the changes necessary to realize socialist goals.

Although more sophisticated than *Moscow Novella*, *Divided Heaven* still operates with the antithetical structure so characteristic of Socialist Realist literature. Thus optimist/pessimist, East/West, old/young generations are juxtaposed. But these juxtapositions remain either/or oppositions. Not until *Christa T.* does Christa Wolf create a truly dialectical structure in which the reader must participate to create a synthesis.[42]

To motivate Rita's decision to remain in the GDR, to assure that she will not fall prey to Manfred's disillusionment, Wolf equips her with a series of encouraging experiences. Her education to socialism can be seen as an emancipation from Manfred and a movement away from a traditional female role. The evening at the professor's marks an important step in this process. In contrast to Rita's mentors, the professor and his group, like Manfred's family, are presented as steeped in bourgeois consciousness. Concerned with materialistic status symbols such as new automobiles, caught up in their personal success, their commitment to the socialist collective is presented as doubtful. The professor is shown as a vain, ambitious man; his inner circle as sycophants; their interaction as idolatrous.

The party culminates in a conversation that illuminates the differences not only between Rita and the professor and his entourage but between Rita and Manfred as well. Rita, appalled at Manfred's cynical collusion in baiting Rudi Schwabe, a Party liaison with the university administration, suddenly sees her lover in a new light. Commenting on this, the narrator remarks that such a moment of perception and evaluation, which supposedly coincides with the end of love, is "really only the end of enchantment, one of the things which real, enduring love must take in its stride" (*DH* 113). However, what is presented as a "moment of silent understanding" between the lovers is actually the expression of irreconcilable differences:

there was a moment of silent understanding between them when she saw in his eyes the decision not to build up hopes any more, and in her eyes he saw that she would never agree to this. She also realized that she could not comfort or encourage him and he, in a flash, understood that life could be a failure – that he had perhaps failed already. Many things which had seemed possible yesterday were quite unthinkable today, he was no longer very young and he could not believe in miracles. (*DH* 113)

If on that evening both Rita and Manfred had wished that time would stand still, Rita in retrospect recalls "the vague feeling of anxiety about the future which had come over her" (*DH* 117). Indeed, their mutual wish, ostensibly a desire to prolong indefinitely a commonality of experience and silent communication, can instead be interpreted as an intuition that this evening is a watershed in their relationship: from this moment on, it becomes increasingly strained, they become ever more isolated and unable to communicate with each other. This is also the first time that Rita openly asserts herself *vis-à-vis* Manfred. By defending Schwabe, she in effect offers her lover an example of the more humane behavior she had expected from him. At the same time, she challenges the behavior of the others.

Interpretations that read *Divided Heaven* as the story of star-crossed lovers driven apart by the politics of the Cold War overlook the fact that Rita and Manfred had become estranged before his flight and fail to take into account the degree to which Wolf prepares us for their separation. It is significant that Rita interprets her physical collapse as an unconscious attempt to flee the deadening repetition of everyday life. Her suicide attempt arises therefore not out of "desperate love, but rather out of despair that love is transitory like everything else."[43] Ultimately, their relationship fails because of Manfred's regression into indifference and stagnation. If Rita Seidel embodies the socialist ideal of caring, humane interaction, then Manfred represents the lost generation of the war – someone whose tainted consciousness and negative experiences render him incapable of socialist engagement. Rita has great capacity for change and growth, but Manfred is blocked. Their failure to articulate their differences indicates the erosion of their relationship and leads to increasing estrangement. So pronounced are the differences in their attitudes toward life that the physicality of their love can no longer hide the lack of shared interests and worldviews. In the face of adversity it becomes clear to the reader that their relationship was flimsily motivated, romantically overblown and sentimental.

In a radio interview, Wolf admitted that while she was working on the novel she considered an alternative ending, namely

that this couple separate, but without having either leave the GDR. Because in fact my main theme, my first theme for this book was not the division of Germany but rather the question: how does it happen that people have to go their separate ways?[44]

Wolf's statement underscores the ambiguity of the novel's title. It makes clear that it refers not merely to the political situation of Germany but also to the personal experience of the lovers. The overarching heaven is a symbol of unity. Divided, it represents both a nation alienated from itself and the shattered illusions, dreams, and hopes of individuals. Or as Rita, in response to Manfred's comment that they can't divide the sky, notes: "The sky? This whole arch of hope and longing, love and grief? . . . The sky divides first" (*DH* 198). Wolf's love story must be read as one in which internal differences estrange and separate the lovers as much as external politics. Rita and Manfred's relationship is jeopardized by her increasing involvement with Meternagel, Wendland, and her team, by her growing independence, and by his inability to resolve his past.

Not only is Manfred personally threatened by Wendland, he is also envious of Rita's emotional investment in her work. His grudging recognition that she will never belong solely to him testifies to the expectations he has of his future wife and expresses a stance that had theoretically become anachronistic with the advent of socialism in the GDR. Although his behavior can be explained historically and although Wolf does not pursue this avenue of inquiry in *Divided Heaven*, Manfred Herrfurth's attitude is an indication that woman's place in GDR praxis is not that of an equal, a view Wolf articulates both explicitly in the essay "Berührung" (Touching) and in the "Conditions of a Narrative," the essays accompanying *Cassandra*, and implicitly in *No Place on Earth* and the essays on the women Romantics, Karoline von Günderrode and Bettina von Armin, which augment the narrative text.[45]

In *Divided Heaven* Manfred's inability to take setbacks such as the rejection of the spinning-jenny is presented as more incriminating than his attitude toward Rita. The figure of Manfred can be understood properly only in comparison to Meternagel and Wendland. GDR criticism of Meternagel's individualism overlooks the fact that his tenacity in the face of adversity throws Manfred's resignation into sharper relief. His unswerving commitment to socialist production as the expression of his faith in the new order enables him to withstand injustice and to continue to work for the very men who had betrayed him. Meternagel's ability to put aside past injustices and devote himself selflessly to increasing the productivity of the brigade, fostering the communal spirit and sense of pride necessary for effective collective work, wins him not only Rita's admiration but the respect and ultimately the cooperation of his co-workers as well.

At the very end of the novel, Wolf qualifies her portrayal of Meternagel, thereby avoiding the black-and-white characterizations of *Moscow Novella*. She has Rita, just released from the sanatorium, visit the physically exhausted Meternagel at home. The insight she gains into his family life demands a reassessment of his way of life. From his wife Rita learns that Meternagel's compulsive self-sacrifice to the socialist cause was detrimental not only to his own health but also to the psychic well-being of his entire family, particularly his wife. Rita, aware of the seemingly insurmountable hurdles confronting Meternagel in his attempt to organize his brigade into an efficient team, had once likened him to "a hero in some old legend, set out upon a seemingly hopeless struggle" (*DH* 70); she now must question his self-sacrificing engagement, which has led to the sacrifice of another human being. Like the incident at the professor's house, Rita's visit to the Meternagels' represents a moment of disenchantment. Such disenchantment, necessary for a balanced assessment of reality, is seen as part of Rita's maturation.

It is possible to read *Divided Heaven* as a novel of lost illusions. There are similarities between Rita Seidel's education and that of Flaubert's Frédéric Moreau in *Sentimental Education*. In both cases the protagonist's preconceived romantic illusions are stripped away by experience. The fundamental difference between Flaubert's bitter conclusion and Wolf's quiet optimism is the faith Wolf places in socialism as the force of reason in society. Whereas in Flaubert's negative *Bildungsroman*, Frédéric Moreau's romanticism reverts to the opposite affective pole, cynicism, Rita Seidel's loss of romantic illusions is meant to give her critical distance with which to evaluate the world realistically and to affirm the socialist way of life.

Alexander Stephan has pointed out that Rita's socialization, in keeping with Christa Wolf's Marxist view of history, reflects the most essential stages of development from a precommunist to a socialist society. Her path leads

from unconscious, harmonious nature-connectedness over the intrusion of self-consciousness into this idyll, which rouses the intellectual bourgeoisie, to the threat posed to humankind by the introverted self-laceration of late capitalism on to the liberating arrival in the new, virtually intact, and constantly improving world of everyday socialism.[46]

It is certainly valid to read *Divided Heaven* as exemplifying Marxist historical consciousness. It is striking, however, that Rita, who throughout the novel had admired the male figures who dominated the work world,[47] should at the end empathize with Frau Meternagel. The issue of female bonding, an important component of all of Wolf's subsequent works, is not pursued in *Divided Heaven*. Indeed, it is questionable whether Wolf consciously confronted this issue until her incisive study of female interrelationship, *The Quest for Christa T.* Nonetheless, in Rita Seidel Wolf has created a figure who becomes increasingly self-defining. The previously male-identified Rita distances herself first from Manfred's influence,[48] then from that of her mentors, and develops the capacities for independent thought and action Wolf deems necessary for the future of the GDR.

These are the qualities Rita shares with Ernst Wendland, her other romantic interest. Of Rita's mentors Wendland emerges as the figure most to be emulated. Like Meternagel, Wendland has suffered both social injustice and personal betrayal, but he appears to lead a more balanced life. Indeed, the similarities between them serve to underscore their differences. Wendland serves as a point of contrast to both Meternagel and Manfred. He shares with the other exemplary figures in *Divided Heaven* a nonconforming pluckiness, a willingness to criticize his comrades and take issue with Party dogma – attributes that brought them under attack by more conservative GDR critics. For Wolf, however, Wendland's commitment to socialism coupled with his personal initiative and willingness to assume responsibility represent precisely those characteristics she considers necessary for the effective implementation and development of socialism in the GDR. By taking matters into his own hands and employing questionable means (including forging a telegram), Wendland is able to supply the railroad car works with the electrical fittings needed to fill their contract on time. Praised by the Party for accomplishing his tasks and censured for the means employed, Wendland admits the ambiguity of his situation: "They're right, but I'm right, too. Things like that do happen" (*DH* 104). In Wendland, a man who can tolerate ambiguity, Wolf has created a counterexample to the rigid Mangold and has moved toward the creation of more complex figures who can live with contradictions.

Wendland, in many respects Rita's male counterpart, is presented as her potential future mate. While his interest in Rita is made explicit, she does not consciously contemplate a future with him. Nonetheless, she considers this possibility subconsciously: during her stay in the sanatorium, she dreams that she is walking down a long road (the road of life?) not with Manfred but with Wendland. Rita's dream points to the possibility of their future union, as does the conclusion, which speaks of Rita's faith in getting her share of kindliness.

Wendland also has an important structural function in the novel. Rita is not a reflective character. Her decision to stay in the East is made intuitively, like all the important decisions in her life: entering the teacher training program, becoming involved with Manfred. She is unable to put her experiences into a rational framework as she is living them. In relating his experiences after the war, Ernst Wendland says: "Perhaps it's impossible to see the logic of things from above or below, but only later on, looking back" (*DH* 105). This remark provides the key to understanding

Rita's situation and the rationale for the novel's structure. Only by looking back can Rita perceive the logic of her experience. The two months spent convalescing and reflecting are meant to offer her, and with her the reader, insight into the events of the past two years and into the rationality of her choice. In Rita Seidel Wolf has created a figure who is educated from childlike spontaneity to rationality and socialist commitment.

The conclusion of *Divided Heaven* leaves Rita prepared to face the future and meets Socialist Realism's demand for a happy ending. Walking through the city streets, she

saw how inexhaustible supplies of kindliness, used up during the day, were renewed each evening. And she was not afraid that she would miss her share of kindliness. She knew that she would sometimes be tired, sometimes angry. But she was not afraid. And what made up for everything was the feeling that people could learn to sleep soundly again and live their lives to the full, as if there were an abundance of this strange substance – life – as if it could never be used up. (*DH* 212)

The future-directed conclusion also harks back to the last lines of the opening frame of *Divided Heaven*, in which the narrator, speaking of the sense of danger overcome, states:[49] "We learned to sleep soundly again and to live our lives to the full, as if there were an abundance of this strange substance life – as if it would never be used up" (*DH* 1).

The almost verbatim reiteration of the narrator's sentiments, the convergence of Rita's perspective with the communal "we" of the frame, indicates that Rita has been included in the socialist community, that she is to be viewed as a full-fledged member of the GDR. The conclusion of *Divided Heaven*, which advocates the ethos of fulfillment through work, presents us with the first of several female figures created by Wolf who are harbingers of the future. Rita Seidel is, however, the last of Wolf's Socialist Realist heroines, just as *Divided Heaven*, an example of GDR *Ankunfts-literatur* (literature based on the belief that the basis of socialism has been created), is the last of Wolf's works that can readily be categorized.

Wolf clearly conceived of Rita as a positive figure, whose renunciation of her lover and choice of the more difficult and demanding but more fulfilling life in the GDR was meant to inspire readers to persevere in the socialist struggle. Nonetheless, viewed from the perspective of Wolf's development, several aspects of Rita's education appear problematic. Foremost among these is her attitude toward her past. If her convalescence gave her the strength to face the future, then this capacity was won at the cost of severing herself from her immediate past. As the narrator tells us:

Without a doubt, she has been through a terrible experience. She is well again but, like many of us, she doesn't know how much spiritual courage she needed to look life squarely in the face day after day, without deceiving herself and without being deceived. Perhaps one day we will recognize that the fate of posterity depended on the spiritual courage of countless ordinary people – for a long, difficult, threatening, but hopeful moment in history.[50]

Looking back on those painful events of the recent past from her newly won "healthy" perspective, Rita feels "something approaching distaste at the thought of that sick state of mind. Time had done its work and let her regain the strength she needed to call things by their right names" (*DH* 202). By repressing rather than confronting trauma, by dissociating herself from her "sick state of mind," Rita is unable to mourn and become reconciled with her past. Thus, although she belongs to a different generation, she duplicates the behavior of Wolf's generation, who dissociated themselves from their (Nazi) past. Increasingly, Wolf calls such patterns of behavior into question as she reevaluates the ramifications of loss of spontaneity in the socialization process.

Rita's failure to reassess her past, her suppression of memory, is based on a coping mechanism similar to Meternagel's and Wendland's rationalizations of past injustices. Their interpretation of traumatic events as difficult moments to be overcome or endured in what is fundamentally a positive process is in keeping with the narrator's assessment of Rita's experiences in the larger context of GDR society: his hope that posterity will recognize this moment as a particularly trying period in the history of the socialist state.

Wolf subsequently rejected the view of history that informed *Divided Heaven*. She came to realize that a historical perspective that justified existing conditions on the basis of a future promise was an "apologia for the status quo."[51] Rejecting historical determinism, she no longer viewed individual experiences or events as moments in a predetermined totality but saw them as "loci of contradiction that can be made productive through a social praxis that does not exclude them from consciousness but makes them a focus of communication."[52] This change in perspective was accompanied by a change in Wolf's utopian vision. In *Christa T.*, the future-directed fantastic socialist utopia of *Moscow Novella* is replaced by a less overtly optimistic but more immediate concrete utopian view. In its emphasis on the present and in its more sober appraisal of the task confronting the GDR, *Divided Heaven* can be seen as a transition between these two perspectives.

3

CHRISTA T.: THE QUEST FOR SELF-ACTUALIZATION

This coming-to-oneself – what is it? Johannes R. Becher

Divided Heaven established Christa Wolf as a writer of note in the GDR; her second book, *Nachdenken über Christa T.* (*The Quest for Christa T.*, 1968) secured her position in the West. Of all Wolf's works, *Christa T.* has been the most heatedly debated, especially in the Federal Republic.[1] The limited first edition of the work[2] and its negative reception in the GDR[3] doubtless contributed to its success in the West, where critics read it as a statement of political dissent. In the symptomatic (if overstated) phrase of Marcel Reich-Ranicki, "Christa T. dies of leukemia, but her real sickness is the GDR."[4] While noting the more personal tone of *Christa T.*, most critics in both countries interpreted it and its successor, *Kindheitsmuster* (*Patterns of Childhood*, 1976) in the political context of GDR literature.

GDR critics, committed to thematic concerns and the mimetic theory of realism, responded negatively to Wolf's experimentation with perspective and narrative form. In the Federal Republic, the evaluation of *Christa T.* was almost the inverse of that of *Divided Heaven*. What critics in both East and West Germany *did* agree on was that *Christa T.* was an anomaly, in terms of both GDR literature and Christa Wolf's previous work. Both West German criticism, dwelling on the political relevance of *Christa T.*, and that of the GDR, bemoaning the abandonment of a political context in favor of a retreat into subjectivity, failed to see the broader implications of Wolf's work.

In Christa T., who is morally committed to the socialist state but is literally unable to live in it, Wolf has created her first casualty of irreconcilable contradictions. Like Karoline von Günderrode, Kleist, and Cassandra, Christa T. is an outsider. Whereas Rita Seidel was educated to conform with her society, Christa T., a diehard nonconformist, resists both Nazi and socialist attempts to

51

socialize her. Christa T.'s search for self-knowledge, her desire to explore and develop all aspects of her personality, is consonant with Marx's ideals of fully developed individuality. The failure of GDR critics to understand the political implications of Christa Wolf's personal story indicates the degree to which the humanistic goals of Marxism had been subordinated to economic and political exigencies. With *Christa T.* Wolf reasserted the rights of the human subject in the individual/collective dialectic.

Yet despite the social criticism it brings to bear, the truly revolutionary potential of *Christa T.*[5] lies in its form, a fact overlooked by political, theme-oriented critics. In *Christa T.*, Christa Wolf abandons the paradigmatic closed structures prescribed by Socialist Realism and breaks through to her own unique style. As the discussion of *Divided Heaven* has shown, Wolf was never comfortable with the normative strictures imposed by Socialist Realism. In *Christa T.*, she explodes the expectations of this aesthetic and creates a self-reflective, open-ended form, rich in ambiguity and contradiction. This self-reflexivity, the intermeshing of thematic concerns with formal structural questions, for example through the treatment of writing as a theme, is an underlying feature of both *Christa T.* and *Patterns of Childhood* and places Wolf squarely in the modernist literary tradition, a tradition repudiated in the GDR.[6] The new subjective component of Wolf's writing that found its sustained expression in *Christa T.*, the articulation of the emotional and intellectual engagement of the author, was the culmination of many years of reflection on reading, writing, and the function of literature, particularly in a socialist society.

Discussions, essays, letters, and prose writings from the mid-sixties reveal that Christa Wolf's reassessment of prevailing notions of literary realism had begun to merge with questions regarding the course of socialism in her country. In December 1964 Wolf participated in an international colloquium of socialist writers in Berlin.[7] Designed to foster self-evaluation and criticism, the colloquium, conducted as a public debate, was marked by extreme candor. Wolf's contribution to the discussion reaffirms her commitment to socialism and to the GDR as it specifically addresses aspects of her society that disturb her: "narrow-mindedness ... a leading by the nose, philistinism, false demands made on literature, false praise, false blame, lack of cosmopolitanism, failure to publish books whose publication" she considers "essential (that is, an inadequate publishing policy)."[8]

Contrasting her position with that of writers in the West, Wolf names despair and cynicism as common pitfalls of her West German colleagues and links their prevalence to the absence of a legal, truly socialist Left in the Federal Republic. As a socialist writer, she feels better equipped to resist the "maelstrom and the allure of the void"[9] confronting all of us in the twentieth century, in the shadow of possible self-extinction. For Wolf, belief in the perfectibility of humankind and the ability to think historically, to analyze social forces, and to confront disturbing contradictions in a productive way are part of socialism's legacy, a legacy she hopes will enable us to avoid the seemingly inevitable fate of the world.[10]

Wolf goes on to establish a reciprocity between literature and socialist society, a dialectic that reflects the utopian component of both. The function of literature, she believes, is to help society to self-awareness. Socialism in turn can regenerate literature. In contrast to Western novelists, whose stalemated bourgeois society offers no new conflicts to depict, socialist writers are not condemned to varying well-established themes. Instead, socialist society, by creating new, productive conflicts, has provided its writers with new literary subject matter. Wolf maintains that "literature in its essence is directly connected to socialist society insofar and inasmuch as this society approximates a greater perfection of the human, of the possibilities of human beings."[11]

Wolf's overriding concern with the humanistic goals of Marxism prompts her to interject a warning into the generally positive evaluation of her society. Noting the GDR's past and present industriousness, she poses a question she considers critical for the country at that particular historical moment: "What are we working for? Why are we creating this socialism, anyway? For it can happen that engrossed in the means – politics and economics – we lose sight of the ends: the human being."[12] In Wolf's view, the task of literature is to remind society of its proper goal. Thus she stresses that she is not interested primarily in future means of production but rather in the type of human being society is producing. "Will it be an apolitical technocrat? Will they be socialists?"[13] What distinguishes Wolf's colloquium contribution from her earlier comments on socialism is its emphasis on social contradiction and its explicit rejection of a mechanistic view of socialism, its refusal to equate socialism with a change in the mode of production.

Severing the economic and political means from the humanistic ends of socialism had significant ramifications for Wolf's future literary production. She has never since created a literary work in which the world of production featured prominently. Instead, her writing from the mid-sixties on has focused on socialism's goals: individual self-actualization and humane interrelationship. This shift in thematic emphasis was accompanied by the development of a new narrative style. Henceforth Christa Wolf conceived her own self-actualization as an ongoing process of self-exploration in which she as an author engaged in the act of writing itself and in which she sought to include the reader by means of the process of reading.

Her short story of 1965, "Juninachmittag" ("An Afternoon in June"),[14] in many ways prefigures narrative techniques and concerns consistently carried through in *Christa T.* and discussed in "The Reader and the Writer." The opening passage of the story marks the break with Wolf's previous narrative style: "A Story? Something solid, tangible like a pot with two handles, to be grasped and drunk from? A vision perhaps, if you know what I mean."[15] Here the first-person (clearly autobiographical)[16] narrator, reflecting on what constitutes a story, through the interrogative structure and her utilitarian analogy rejects traditional self-contained narration and attributes to literature transcendental qualities. Moreover, by explicitly addressing the reader (here in the formal "Sie" rather than the intimate "du" form)[17] she experiments with the dialogic structure that characterizes her writing from *Christa T.* on.

Thematically, the story is significant for Wolf's development in its appreciation of the human faculty of imagination. In the figure of the engineer, Wolf adumbrates the apolitical technocrat she describes in "Notwendiges Streitgespräch" and prefigures the "Hopp-hopp-Menschen" ("up-and-doing people") of *Christa T.*, whereas in the child she extols the spontaneity and openness to experience that she will so value in Christa T.

By the time she wrote "An Afternoon in June," Wolf was familiar with the work of Ingeborg Bachmann. Her essay of 1966, "Die zumutbare Wahrheit: Zur Prosa Ingeborg Bachmanns" (The Acceptable Truth: The Prose of Ingeborg Bachmann) pays tribute to the contemporary Austrian writer (1926–73) whose writing she greatly admired. Despite their political differences, Christa Wolf empathizes with the Western author, viewing her as someone who in her life and in her writing suffered from and struggled against the deadening effects of alienation. In the Bachmann essay Wolf attributes to her those characteristics that will become hallmarks of her own "subjective authenticity." Wolf warns Bachmann's readers not to expect plot-oriented stories with detailed descriptions of events or characters in the traditional sense. Instead, they will "hear a voice: bold and lamenting. A voice expressing itself truthfully, that is, according to its own experience, about things certain and uncertain."[18] Wolf's use of the term "truthful" (*wahrheitsgemäss*) recalls the mandate of Socialist Realism for the "truthful presentation of real life." Her equation of truth with experience adds a subjective dimension to the definition of realism. The Bachmann essay marks Christa Wolf's definitive break with the reflection theory of realism, a notion she will ridicule in her essay "The Reader and the Writer" (1968).

The reflection theory is based on the dichotomy between the authorial subject and the objects of external reality. It measures literary success in terms of accurate description, that is, mastery. Wolf posits instead the dialectical notion of the "appropriation of reality." First described in relation to Ingeborg Bachmann, the concept of the "appropriation of reality" has become a cornerstone of Christa Wolf's aesthetic. Wolf reads Bachmann's short story "Was ich in Rom sah und hörte" (What I Saw and Heard in Rome) as an attempt to "appropriate a city." In contrast to mimetic reflection, the appropriation of reality does not replicate external reality but, by incorporating the author's subjective and moral engagement in that reality, creates something qualitatively new. This new reality is, according to Wolf, "subordinated to an unexpected frame of reference, the production of an irrepressible and insatiable desire for the permeation of the natural and social environment with human standards."[19] Bachmann's infusion of external reality with subjective reflection and emotion is her attempt to overcome alienation both from other humans and from nature. It is precisely this epistemological stance that Wolf describes as specifically female in "Self-Experiment."

Wolf praises Bachmann for actively fighting against alienation, and her assessment is formulated in Marxist humanist terms. She sees in Bachmann's writing the articulation "of a human being's claim to self-realization, his right to individuality and the development of his personality, his longing for freedom."[20] Wolf's interpretation of Bachmann's prose as a moral institution and as a utopian construct[21] clearly reflects her own understanding of the function of literature. Similarly, her reading of Bachmann as a writer whose work explicitly relies on the active participation of her readers manifests her concerns with reader involvement.[22] Because "Juninachmittag" and the Bachmann essay document the new emphasis of Wolf's subsequent writing, they have been called "prolegomena to *Christa T.*"[23]

Both *Christa T* and *Patterns of Childhood* are personal history. They reflect Christa Wolf's conscious effort to take a productive attitude toward herself. Viewed together, they encompass the period 1927–63, a period that saw the rise of Nazism, World War II, the defeat, occupation, and division of Germany, and the foundation and development of the socialist state. Both are intensely personal accounts of experiences of this period. *Christa T.* emphasizes the postwar period and the development of socialism, whereas *Patterns of Childhood* concludes with the year 1947, two years before the German Democratic Republic was founded. Yet the reverse chronological order of these works is hardly accidental; it is doubtful whether Christa Wolf would have written *Patterns of Childhood* had she not first written *Christa T.* The narrator's work of mourning in the earlier work, her reconstruction of Christa T.'s past, seems to have served as a catalyst enabling the author to attend to her own past and to work through her own experiences.

It has been suggested that hostile prepublication response to *Christa T.* in the GDR prompted Wolf to justify herself by writing her essay "The Reader and the Writer."[24] In an interview with Hans Kaufmann (1973), Christa Wolf explained the circumstances that gave rise to this essay. *Christa T.* had been completed for a year and while it had not yet appeared, there had been sufficient preliminary response for her to predict its reception. According to Wolf, the essay examines her experience of writing *Christa T.* to determine what was specific to that particular work and what could prove fruitful for her future writing.[25] Clearly Wolf was distressed by the lack of understanding that greeted her book. Yet the tone of the essay and of the two interviews that hark back to and expand upon it (the Kaufmann interview and an interview with Joachim Walther, 1972)[26] is hardly apologetic and makes clear that "The Reader and the Writer" was written as much for Wolf herself as for the arbiters of GDR cultural politics. Both the essay "Interview with Myself" (1966)[27] and the more theoretical "The Reader and the Writer" represent Wolf's attempt to articulate the significance of the process of writing that informs the text of *Christa T.* Thus literary praxis precedes theory. This essayistic reflection on her own literary undertakings established a pattern for Christa Wolf that continues to the present: for Wolf, essay and fiction are not distinct but rather mutually illuminating genres.[28] The fluidity between biography and literature is further underscored by the lack of generic subtitles in both *Christa T.* and *Patterns of Childhood*. While much of her work is designated as narrative (*Erzählung*), Wolf consciously refrained from relegating these works with their essayistic self-reflective components to the realm of fiction.[29]

The most salient characteristic of Wolf's writing from *Christa T.* on is the presence of authorial subjectivity in the literary text, a narrative technique she attributes to Georg Büchner. In "The Reader and the Writer," Wolf, speaking of Büchner's novella "Lenz," praises his discovery "that the scope of narrative has four dimensions: the three fictive co-ordinates of the invented characters and the fourth, 'real' dimension of the narrator. This is the co-ordinate of depth, of contemporaneousness, of inevitable involvement that determines not only the choice of material but also its coloring."[30]

In the same essay she defines "depth" in terms of subjective time: as the ability of human consciousness, by virtue of its manifold and multilayered possibilities of experience, to stretch (with the aid of memory and prescience) almost to infinity a finite (objective) stretch of time.

Depth: if depth is not a property of the material world, it must be a result of experience, an ability gained through human beings living together over long periods of time that has not only survived but also developed, because it was useful. So it is tied to us, subjects living in objective conditions. It is the result of unsatisfied needs, the resulting tensions, inconsistencies and tremendous efforts people make to grow beyond themselves or, perhaps, to reach up to themselves. This may be the meaning and task of depth in our consciousness; so we must not abandon it in favor of superficialities. (*RW* 180–1)

Wolf's concept of "depth," at once subjective and utopian, informs all her writing from *Christa T.* on. Encompassing the past, present, and future, the individual and the community, it serves as a constant reminder of human potentiality. It is for Wolf inextricably bound up with the function of authorial subjectivity and with the task of writing.

In her middle works, authorial subjectivity, a phenomenon she later terms "subjective authenticity,"[31] takes the form of the author's presence, as narrator, in the literary text. It wreaks havoc with traditional modes of literary interpretation that insist on the strict separation of author and narrator.[32] Trained as a Germanist, Wolf is surely aware that her approach begs the critic to commit the biographical fallacy by conflating author and narrator. Wolf plays with this distinction. On the one hand, she warns against identifying the narrator with the author. At the same time she experiments with autobiographical and essayist forms seemingly predicated on precisely such an identification.

The following statements from "Interview with Myself" reflect Wolf's ambivalence:

Q. Can you say something about the subject matter of this story? [*Christa T.*]

A. This is difficult ... I must confess to a purely subjective urge. Someone very close to me died, too young. I don't accept this death. I am looking for some means to defend myself effectively against it. Searching, I write. The result is that I have to pin down this searching, as honestly, as exactly as possible ...

Q. So you are writing a kind of posthumous biography ...

A. That is what I thought at first. Later on, I noticed that the object of my story was not at all, or did not remain so clearly herself, Christa T. I suddenly faced myself. I had not foreseen this. The relations between "us" – Christa T. and the narrator "I" – shifted of themselves into the center; the differences in character and the points at which they touched, the tensions between "us" and the way they dissolved or failed to dissolve. If I were a mathematician I should probably speak of a "function" – nothing tangible, visible, material, but extraordinarily effective.

Q. At all events, you have now admitted that there are two authentic figures in it – Christa T. and an "I."

A. Have I admitted that? You would be right if, in the final analysis, both characters were not invented ... (*RW* 76–7)

Wolf's remarks point to the essential differences between *Divided Heaven* and *Christa T.* Where the earlier work focused on the outcome of the story, the socialization of Rita Seidel, in *Christa T.* the process (of writing) is the outcome. Where *Divided Heaven* offered models of behavior, *Christa T.* calls into question so-called exemplary modes of behavior. From the point of view of both the writer/narrator and the reader, moreover, *Christa T.* can be seen as an anti-*Bildungsroman*. The narrator, in reviewing Christa T.'s life, deconstructs her own socialization and calls upon her readers to follow suit.

In speaking of a shift in emphasis away from the figure of Christa T. to the "relations between 'us' – Christa T. and the narrator 'I,'" to the "differences in character and the points at which they dissolved or failed to dissolve," Wolf is ironically positing an author/narrator identity she retracts a few lines later by her statement that in the final analysis, both characters are invented. The disclaimer that precedes the novel offers similar problems of interpretation. There the statement that Christa T. is a fictional character stands in contrast to the next sentence, in which we are told that some of the quotations from diaries, sketches, and letters are authentic. The English version reads: "Christa T. is a fictional character. Several of the quotations from diaries, sketches and letters come from real-life sources." It is misleading in that it masks the implied contradiction between the sentences by easing the ambiguity regarding the source of the documentary material. The inverted word order in the original conveys the impression that the documentary material stems from Christa T., who has just been declared a fictional character.[33]

To compound the issue still further, Christa Wolf, in a radio interview with Karl Corino, called for a straightforward naive reading of the disclaimer. The proclivity of critics to view her prefatory remarks as a "trick," she maintained, has prevented them from being taken seriously and has led to misinterpretations.

There was this Christa T., there was her life, whose facts and individual stations I knew or learned of after her death . . . and there were also these documents, some of which I quote in part. Then however . . . I was also confronted with the problem that these were not sufficient and that some of what was very important for me in the interpretation of this life of course had to be invented.[34]

The ambiguity, if not outright contradiction, of Wolf's statements has precipitated much critical debate as to the precise relationship between author, narrator, and Christa T. What has been overlooked in this discussion is that Wolf's playing with literary convention is an estrangement technique in the Brechtian tradition that, by defamiliarizing accepted "truths," encourages us to reassess them. Thus Wolf's new way of writing, which is intrinsically connected with her "new [socialist] way of living in the world" (*RW* 177), is intended to overcome distinctions informing traditional realist literary production. In "The Reader and the Writer" Wolf describes a dialectical process whereby people, events, and things one has encountered leave their imprint on the writer and enable her to *see* everything differently and thus become the impetus for her new creative perception (*RW* 177–9). A corollary of this transformation of external reality, which she later, echoing the Bachmann essay, calls "the appropriation of reality" and which she considers more suited to literary realism than mere mimetic reflection of external reality,[35] is a breakdown of subject/object boundaries and a sense of interrelationship and interconnectedness.

Elaborating on the process of transforming external reality, Wolf maintains:

One sees a different reality from before. Suddenly everything hangs together and is in flux, objects perceived as unchangeable "givens" become soluble and disclose social relationships objectified in them (we are no longer dealing with that hierarchically ordered social cosmos, in which human particles move according to sociologically or ideologically preconceived paths or diverge from this expected movement); it becomes much more difficult to say "I" and at the same time often essential to do so.[36]

Wolf rejects the distanced, controlling relationship between writer and subject that informs the Socialist Realist aesthetic and asserts instead a reciprocity between author and subject matter in which the two touch and affect each other. Subject matter is thus for Wolf not inanimate but living material, constantly evolving and being evolved in its relationship with the author, changing and causing the writer to change as well. Wolf's relationship to her material conforms entirely with her view of the task of writing as a means of "bringing forth new structures of human relationships in our time."[37]

The discrepancies within the disclaimer and "Interview with Myself" and between these and Wolf's position in the interview with Karl Corino are too self-consciously contradictory to be unintentional. Wolf is obviously playing with reader expectations, calling into question assumptions about narration, narrative technique, and literature in general. Her remarks imply that the distinction between art and life is artificial, and advocate a more integrative approach to writing. This technique is in keeping with her call for a more differentiated socialist literature. In "Interview with Myself" Wolf, addressing the issue of *Christa T.* as a "retreat into inwardness," views the work in the context of the GDR's historical development. Repudiating the old Socialist Realist norms, she maintains:

No one will any longer bring up the absurd idea that socialist literature cannot deal with the fine nuances of the life of the spirit, with differences in individual character, or that it depends on creating types that move along prescribed sociological paths. The years in which we were building the socialist conditions of production, in which the individual could find himself lie behind us. Our society is becoming more and more differentiated. And the questions people ask are also more differentiated, in the form of art as well. People's willingness to accept divergent answers has also developed. The subject is increasingly sovereign in our society, which it feels to be its work, not only thinks and knows, but feels this. (*RW* 79)

While defining her own work in the tradition of literary realism and rejecting its categorization as "new subjectivity,"[38] Wolf rejects the traditional realist claim to objectivity. Objectivity is for her a misleading category, a false construct impossible to attain. She replaces this pseudo-objectivity with the concept of "subjective authenticity" and views literature as a vehicle through which the author can address issues of personal concern. By her own admission, Wolf can only write about things that disturb her.[39] Her use of the term *Betroffenheit* ("being struck"; it implies an affective impact) makes clear that these concerns are not merely intellectual but emotional as well.

Writing as "subjective authenticity" can have a therapeutic function.[40] By transforming potentially destructive emotions into the imaginative realm, Wolf believes the writer is sometimes able to work through these emotions vicariously. Thus, in Georg Büchner's "Lenz" – for her the prototype of modern prose writing – Büchner's situation parallels that of the Storm and Stress writer Johann Michael Reinhold Lenz, whose flight into insanity is recorded in Büchner's novella. According to Wolf, Büchner:

has included himself, his own insoluble conflict, the danger he himself faces and of which he is fully aware. A conflict which sharply reflects the thousandfold threats to human beings hungry for progress and longing for truth in restorative times: the writer faced with the choice of adjusting himself to unbearable conditions and destroying his talent, or perishing physically.

The variant madness – Lenz – cannot have been entirely foreign to the later-born Büchner. He may have played it through in order to escape it.[41]

(*RW* 198)

Thus, while the literary construct can mitigate the emotional immediacy of the issues addressed, the underlying authorial engagement is at all times perceptible in the work. It is this engagement that creates the sense of contemporaneousness of which Wolf speaks. According to her, the "author has to take a stand. He cannot hide himself from the reader behind his invention; the reader should be able to see him along with it."[42]

In both *Christa T.* and *Patterns of Childhood*, Wolf's subjective authenticity takes the form of the introjection of a self-reflective consciousness into the literary text. It shows the author in the *process* of artistic creation, not as a sovereign over a closed world, and seeks to engage the reader in the same process. This technique conforms to her reason for writing: self-exploration, self-actualization. The narrator, as a projection of Wolf, is learning as much about herself in the process of writing as she is about Christa T. Nor is the self-exploratory force of literature limited to the writer; it extends to the reader as well. In "The Reader and the Writer," Wolf rejects the traditional concept of plot as antiquated and calls for a shift of emphasis away from a plot-oriented, closed form of narrative, as reflecting a mechanistic attitude toward the world, in favor of an open-ended form, as the expression of a dialectical stance. She calls for a new kind of prose, "epic prose," that like Brecht's epic theater would use models in order to encourage people to think dialectically (*RW* 201). Like Brecht's epic theater, Wolf's epic prose would deflect attention from *what* is being said to *how* it is said. In her interview with Joachim Walther, Wolf elucidates this Brechtian component of her writing. She maintains that her purpose is "always to work up the past, those processes whose external course is known, where the tension lies not in what happens, but rather in how it happens and why people act in a certain way."[43] The author Wolf knows from the outset what will happen to her "hero" and is ultimately concerned with her relationship to her figure and its power to change her, rather than with plot line. Analogously, she does not try to manipulate her readers' emotions by creating tension,[44] but instead allows their rational and imaginative faculties to come into play in the co-creation of the text.

In *Christa T.* the outcome of the narrative is anticipated from the outset. Christa T.'s death and the narrator's response to it, her fear that her own omissions prevented her from seeing her friend as she actually was, serves as the impetus for the text we, as readers, have before us. Thus the opening of the story points to its conclusion, the death of Christa T., bringing it full circle with the beginning. *Christa T.* shares this circularity of narrative structure with *Divided Heaven*. Just as the convalescing, reminiscing Rita Seidel reflects on past events in order to gain insight into the reasons for her crisis, the remembering, reflecting narrative consciousness in *Christa T.* reconstructs the past in order to come to terms with both her grief and her sense of remorse about things left undone. Here, however, the similarities end. While Rita Seidel gains sovereign access to her past via memory, the narrator's task in *Christa T.* is far more complex. Indeed, given the circumstances, the narrative stance of *Christa T.*, its interweaving of first-person and third-person perspective with the subjective "I" voice given precedence, initially seems incongruent. Since Rita Seidel is concerned with her own past, narration in the first person seems more appropriate to her than it does to the narrator of *Christa T.*, who is ostensibly concerned with someone else's past. Since her memories of her friend are not only limited, but, as her reading of Christa T.'s letters, diaries, and literary sketches has convinced her, probably deceptive, the narrator can at best hope to give an elliptical account of Christa T.'s life.

The interspersed excerpts from Christa T.'s own writings serve not only to augment but also to test the narrator's memories. Thus the text *Christa T.* has the dual function of viewing and (re-)viewing. Through it the narrator hopes to let us "see" Christa T. and thereby save her from oblivion. Moreover, since the narrator, after reading Christa T.'s literary remains, believes she knows her friend as she actually was, the text also serves as a means of testing her memories against her new-found understanding. This (self-)evaluative function of the text justifies the narrator's use of first-person narration. Moreover, since both the tenuous nature of the figure of Christa T. and the narrator's respect for her as an autonomous subject militate against the consistent use of third-person narration, Christa T. is also allowed to present herself directly in those incorporated documents (letters, diary entries, and literary sketches) written in the first person.

Christa T. does not appear clearly delineated, but the narrator remains an even more imprecisely drawn character. This very fluidity constitutes the genius of the narrative voice in *Christa T.* The lack of clear boundaries reproduces the connectedness that Wolf experienced while writing and is the expression of her new, uncensored writing style. In her discussion with Hans Kaufmann, Wolf recalled the emancipatory power of the new spontaneity she experienced while writing *Christa T.*, a spontaneity she had believed irrevocably lost. She linked this spontaneity to a new attitude toward her subject matter, with a need to question the assumption that had informed her previous writing – Anna Seghers's belief that "what can be narrated is something one has overcome." For Wolf had experienced the contrary, namely the need to narrate *in order to* overcome, the need to abandon "the strict temporal sequencing of life, 'overcoming,' and writing and, for the sake of the inner authenticity" toward which she was striving, "to incorporate directly into the process of writing the process of thinking and living informing the work."[45] Thus, the intentional ambiguity of the text is designed to sustain uncertainty, to use the act of reading to engage the reader in the same process in which the narrator is engaged.

The lack of definition of the narrator, together with biographical similarities between the author and her figure (including the shared first name) have led several critics to conclude that Christa Wolf is synonymous with Christa T. Others posit the identity of the narrator and Christa T., and see Christa T. as the narrator's alter ego. The fact that Christa T. in her autobiographical writings tended toward third-person narration lends weight to this reading. Her reluctance to use the first person, identified in the text as "the difficulty of saying 'I,'" allows us to read *Christa T.* as Christa Wolf reads Büchner's "Lenz": as the literary working through of potentially (self-)destructive emotions.[46] Such a reading, however, overlooks the dialogic structure so essential to the work. Moreover, it fails to take into account that some similarities between Christa Wolf, the narrator, and Christa T. can be attributed to the common experience of their generation. Despite Christa Wolf's emphasis on subjectivity, she never loses sight of the specific historical context and often serves as a spokesperson of her generation.[47] Though their responses are different, both Christa T.'s and the narrator's experiences are representative of Christa Wolf's generation.

Clearly, the speculations as to the precise relationship among Christa Wolf, narrator, and Christa T.[48] reflect the bewilderment of the critics when confronted with Christa Wolf's new and challenging narrative technique, which encompasses author, narrator, and reader. Neither identification (Christa Wolf/Christa T.; narrator/Christa T.) seems adequately justified by the text. Since there is no textual evidence of narrative unreliability, it is reasonable to assume that the narrator and Christa T. are two discrete individuals. Nor are the narrator and Christa Wolf identical, although there are striking similarities between their situations. Ultimately the narrator is an invention of the author. The premise on which I will proceed is that the text of *Christa T.* consists of a multiple refraction: in order to come to terms with her grief at the loss of her friend, Christa Wolf creates a narrator who, in order to come to terms with *her* grief, "creates" Christa T. anew and also creates *Christa T.*, the literary work, and who seeks to engage the reader in her creation.

Wolf elucidates her undertaking in the prologue and the closing paragraph that frame the text. In contrast to *Divided Heaven*, the frame of *Christa T.* does not seek to subsume the individual into the collective. Instead the prologue (opening prong of the frame), told from the narrator's perspective, underscores her relationship to Christa T., while the frame's closing prong, by calling upon others to create her for themselves, points to the intersubjectivity of the text. Both the narrator's and the potential reader's creation of Christa T., governed by the desire to know her, by "the compulsion to make her stand and be recognized," is seen as essential, not for Christa T., but for us: "Useless to pretend it's for her sake. Once and for all, she doesn't need us. So we should be certain of one thing: that it's for our sake. Because it seems that we need her."[49] The function of Christa T. lies not in what she as a model can teach us, but in what we as readers can learn about ourselves and about our society in the process of creating her.

In *Christa T.*, Christa Wolf emphatically rejected the Socialist Realist category of exemplary typicality. As her narrator maintains:

It would never have occurred to me, I swear, to think of her as an exemplary person. For she isn't an exemplary case at all . . . Just for once, for this once, I want to discover how it is and to tell it like it is: the unexemplary life, a life that can't be used as a model.   (*CT* 45)

If Rita Seidel's story, although banal, was exemplary, Christa T.'s story, although unexemplary, serves as a reminder of what still remains to be done, as an incentive to the narrator/reader to attend to their own lives.

This complex construct and the twofold purpose of narration, viewing and reviewing, account for the text's multitemporal, multivalent complexity. Its articulation is tentative because its narrator is groping and searching and because its object is vague. In addition to the narrator's reminiscences and excerpts from Christa T.'s documents, the text incorporates the narrator's reflections on these writings, her reflections on her own memories and on experiences shared with Christa T., and memories of experiences shared with others that excluded Christa T. The resulting twofold referent for both the individual "I" (narrator and Christa T.) and the collective "we" (narrator and Christa T., narrator and others), coupled with the sometimes almost imperceptible transition from one referent to another, is unsettling to the reader. Furthermore, the narrative proceeds by an associative linking of events rather than in a straight chronology. A chronology of Christa T.'s life can be deduced from the text, but it remains the reader's responsibility to establish the linear sequence of events.

As Dieter Sevin's extrapolation of the time structure of *Christa*

T. makes clear, the Stalin period of the early fifties is given the most space in the text.[50] The text consists of twenty chapters of approximately the same length; the first three describe the first meeting between the narrator and Christa T. and use flashbacks to construct the first twenty-four years of Christa T.'s life, concluding with the reunion with the narrator in Leipzig in 1951. Christa T.'s four-year study of German (1951–55) is the focus of the next eight chapters, whereas the following three chapters cover her year (1955–56) as a teacher in Berlin. While Christa T.'s six-year marriage (1957–63) to the veterinarian, Justus, are condensed into the next three chapters, the final three chapters deal with events from New Year 1961/62 until her death in February 1963.[51]

This skeletal biography of Christa T. serves as the point of departure for the narrator's (re)creation of her friend. Since factual (Christa T.'s documents) and cognitive (the narrator's interpreted memories) material do not suffice to evoke the figure of Christa T., the narrator calls upon the power of imagination: she invents. Her imaginative interpolations primarily show Christa T. interacting with other people: the young schoolteacher's courtship of Christa T. (summer love); her conversations with the school principal; her decision to marry Justus; her visit to the psychic, the General. These encounters thus crystalize the existential issues of love, work, and death and are fundamental to an understanding of Christa T.'s character. By inventing precisely the most essential episodes in her life, the narrator fulfills her mediating role. But she also relativizes her presentation of Christa T., for she leaves open the possibility of other scenarios. In fact, she at times revises her own invention, just as she constantly reevaluates her perceptions of Christa T. The net effect of this continual relativizing is to foster a tentativeness that has frustrated many critics who fail to see that Wolf's intentionally nonreductionist narrative technique is meant to sustain complexity. In "The Reader and the Writer" Wolf had after all attributed to prose the ability break up "deadly simplifications by displaying the possibilities of living in a human way" (*RW* 212).

Critics who fault Wolf for formalism and excessive experimentation with narrative perspective fail to see that her shift in address and her nonlinear narration are meant to challenge the reader. By forcing us to attend fully to detail, by compelling us to fill in the lacunae in the text, Wolf actively engages us in the constitution of the text. By necessitating constant reevaluation of assumptions about the text, she forces the reader to duplicate the process that it is unfolding. By shifting the focus of her narrative away from content-based categories toward the function of relationships, by blurring the distinctions between herself and the narrator and between herself and Christa T., Wolf actualizes her aesthetic of intersubjectivity. In describing the first-person narrator and Christa T. as both authentic and ultimately invented figures, Wolf is only partially playing with literary conventions; she is also alluding to the transformative power of imagination which, through the process of inventing and the act of writing, at once allows her to cope with her emotions and to confront herself. Writing for Christa Wolf thus serves as a form of therapy in its self-exploratory function and as a utopian model in its transformative function. These models she in turn makes available to the reader.

The English translation of the title *Nachdenken über Christa T.*, *The Quest for Christa T.*, is not entirely felicitous. It relays the idea of a search but fails to make clear that this search takes place only in acts of remembering and imagining. The opening lines of *Christa T.* bear witness to a linguistic scrutiny that Wolf employs both in this work and in *Patterns of Childhood* and in *Cassandra*. The noun *Nachdenken*, derived from the verb "to think about," is commonly used with the preposition "über" to signify "to think about something." Wolf had already personalized the noun in the title; in the opening lines she takes the verb literally and, contrary to usage, transforms it into a dative verb: "Nachdenken, ihr nach-denken."[52] This neologism has the literal sense of thinking after her, that is, it connotes following her in thought and following her thoughts. It can, however, also refer to the act of recreating her in thought. Consciously used in lieu of the more usual verb, *sich erinnern*, "to remember," it places the narration in relation to Christa T. "Reflection about Christa T. is thus the integration of Christa T. into the conscious history of the narrator and the transformation of the narrator into one who is receptive to Christa T.'s way of thinking and being."[53]

Wolf introduces this distinction in order to differentiate between her undertaking, seen as an active, creative, empathetic and sympathetic process, and the act of remembering, which is dependent solely on memory. Between the writing of *Divided Heaven* and *Christa T.* memory became suspect for Christa Wolf. "Memory puts a deceptive color on things," says the narrator in the prologue to *Christa T.* (*CT* 3). In "Interview with Myself" Wolf had spoken of "deceptive memory" (*RW* 76). She elaborates on this concept in "The Reader and the Writer":

We seem to need the help and approval of the imagination in our lives; it means playing with the possibilities open to us. But something else goes on inside us at the same time, daily, hourly, a furtive process hard to avoid, a hardening, petrifying, habituating, that attacks the memory in particular.

We all carry with us a collection of miniatures with captions, some quaint, some gruesome. These we occasionally bring out and show round, because we need confirmation of our own reassuringly clear feelings: beautiful or ugly, good or evil. These miniatures are for the memory what the calcified cavities are for people with tuberculosis, what prejudices are for morals: patches of once active life now shut off. At one time one was afraid to touch them, afraid of burning one's fingers on them; now they are cool and smooth, some of them artistically polished, some especially valuable bits have cost years of work, for one must forget a great deal and re-think and re-interpret a great deal before one can see oneself in the best light everywhere and at all times. That is what we need them for, the miniatures. You will know what I mean.

But we are in the habit of calling it "remembering" when we show people these prettily made pieces of arts and crafts and call them genuine, so that they can show their market value and measure up with the other pieces on show; and the more like these others they are the more genuine they are said to be.   (*RW* 190–1)

In speaking of one of her own miniatures, Wolf uses the image of film, an image she had first introduced in *Christa T*. In the prologue the narrator, unsettled by her ability to conjure up her image of her friend at will, says:

I can still see her. Worse, I do what I like with her. I can summon her up quite easily with a quotation, more than I could do for most living people. She moves, if I want her to. Effortlessly she walks before me, yes, that's her long stride, her shambling walk . . . But all the time I know that it's a film of shadows being run off the reel, a film that was once projected in the real light of cities, landscapes, living rooms. Suspicions, suspicions: what is this fear doing to me?   (*CT* 4)

It is against her own reified image of Christa T., her objectification of a human subject, that the narrator undertakes the reconstruction of her friend's life. She recognizes that by allowing her filmlike miniatures of Christa T. to stand, she makes herself culpable of a moral death. Prompted by Christa T.'s letters, diary entries, and literary endeavors to question her perception of her friend, the narrator undertakes the task of reanimating her calcified miniatures. Recognizing with a start that "for a whole year, her image in my mind hasn't changed; and there's no hope of her changing," she realizes that "this is what departure means" (*CT* 4).

So the narrator vows to think Christa T. further (*sie weiterzudenken*), "to let her live and grow older as other people do." By resolving to "work on her" with the purpose of making "her stand and be recognized" (*CT* 5), the narrator sets into motion what "The Reader and the Writer" juxtaposes with reified memory: imagination, "the playing with the possibilities open to us" (*RW* 190).

Wolf links the act of remembering with the faculty of the imagination and distinguishes it from memory. For the narrator oblivion is the same as memory ("we try to find consolation in the oblivion which people call memory," *CT* 4). Memory reifies the living past into lifeless, frozen images, simplifies the past, makes it smooth. Memory is a kind of forgetting. But the act of remembering is "swimming against the current, like writing – against the apparently natural current of forgetting" (*RW* 192). In *Christa T.*, her friend's writings help the narrator in her swim against the "current of forgetting": they serve as a corrective to the narrator's memories. Indeed, these documents make clear to her that she must abandon her memory of Christa T. (*CT* 5). But seeking to reconstruct the life of her friend authentically and not merely as a reified image has implications for the narrator as well. Memory brackets out traumatic or painful psychic experience, so the reactivation of ossified memory (miniatures) means the reexperience of the narrator's own past pain. Presumably this is what Christa Wolf was describing when she said that "the object of my story was not at all, or did not remain so clearly herself, Christa T.; I suddenly faced myself." Thus Christa T. serves as a catalyst for the narrator. Just as she grants Christa T. the potential for growth and change, she also grants herself that potential. By reliving and reassessing her past she comes to understand the negative aspects of her own socialization. In retrospect, she comes to recognize the deadening effects of conformity and points up the rigidifying effects of society.

Among Christa T.'s documents there is a letter written after her romance with Kostia had ended, in which she contemplated suicide. Since the letter was never sent and no one knew of its existence, the narrator considers suppressing it. Questioning her motives, she wonders whether it is "because people won't want to read it? I'd understand that. Certainly, too, one can be silent from strength. But there are scars which only give pain when one has to go on growing. Should one keep quiet because one's afraid of the pain?" (*CT* 71). This statement makes clear that suppressing the letter would be an injustice not only to Christa T. but to the narrator and the potential readers of *Christa T.* as well. In contrast to Rita Seidel, who survives by not touching the "wound" caused by her separation from Manfred, the narrator in *Christa T.* consciously probes those wounds. In her interview with Joachim Walther, Christa Wolf addresses this issue. Responding to Walther's remark that she "always probes where it hurts, even when it is she herself who feels the pain," Wolf says:

With me it is always the case that I am concerned with the sore spot that is the sore spot for me at the moment. And if it happens that others also feel the same way – that is the best case. At that point, of course, the debate begins as to whether one should leave the sore spots alone so that they can heal better or whether they should hurt in order to mobilize forces in society that can help in the healing process.[54]

Christa Wolf's uncompromising position in this debate in favor of the pain that accompanies growth underscores the social and communal implications of her writing. Her criticism is levelled by an individual with the intention of mobilizing a collective response to effect change.

This social nexus of her writing is made explicit in "The Reader and the Writer." In our technological world, which has the potential to annihilate itself, epic prose, the mode of writing appropriate to the scientific age,[55] is for Wolf inextricably bound up with "trends of thought that give man a future," and she posits a "close correlation between this way of writing [epic prose] and socialist society" (*RW* 201).

Epic prose is similar to socialism in that it seeks to stimulate individual and collective growth through the full personal and moral development of the individual reader. In Wolf's view we as individuals must develop a personal interest in ourselves if we are to survive as a species. Epic prose is meant to promulgate the development of the individual's self-interest, to enable us to live in a technological world without the self-denial that is implied in a drastic adaptation to the norm. For Wolf, epic prose has a utopian dimension. Conceived of "as an instrument, sharp, accurate, attacking, changing, to be used as a means, not as an end in itself," it is seen as "a means to shift the future into the present."

Intensely personal, it is viewed as an antidote to the dehumanizing effects of mass society. It is

a genre which undertakes to penetrate along paths not yet traveled into the innermost parts of this individual, the reader of prose. Into the very inmost part, where the nucleus of the personality develops and consolidates . . .

Christa T.

The voice of another person, in prose, can reach this region, it can be touched and opened up by language, not in order to gain control of it, but to set free spiritual forces that can be compared in power with the energies bound up in the atom.   (*RW* 201)

Wolf's faith in the emancipatory power of prose, its ability to touch[56] the core of another person, merges with her cautious optimism about humanity's ability to employ reason to ensure its survival. At a time in which our self-confidence is so severely diminished that "many people in highly technologized countries take refuge in suicide or in the dead end of neurosis" (*RW* 211), Wolf rejects as "romantic nonsense" the Rousseauist back-to-nature solution propagated by some and as pernicious desensitization modern psychiatric methods aimed at producing mass conformity (*RW* 211). She concludes: "So the only way left is the narrow path of reason, of growing up, of a maturing of the human consciousness, the deliberate step out of prehistory into history. The decision to grow up remains to be taken" (*RW* 212). Wolf believes that prose, as a genre evolving late in human development, can be instrumental in furthering humankind's coming-of-age.[57] According to her, "it helps mankind to become conscious subjects. It is revolutionary and realistic; it entices and encourages people to achieve the impossible" (*RW* 212).

The point of departure for the narrator's recreation of her friend is her own experience of and with Christa T. From the outset, she is presented as a nonconformist. The fact that the independent newcomer had not sought the approval of either her classmates or her teachers, that she had, on her first day in class, circumvented the authority of the teacher and turned the statutory interrogation into a conversation by declining "to name a favorite school topic because her favorite activity was walking in the woods" (*CT* 7), that she had appeared offended by the teacher's liberty in using the condescendingly familiar form of address, had relegated her to the position of an outsider. It is significant that the narrator locates the inception of their relationship at that moment when she first became aware of Christa T.'s uniqueness, although this occurs months after their first meeting. Christa T.'s sudden and spontaneous gesture: "she put a rolled newspaper to her mouth and let go with her shout: HOOOHAAHOOO" (*CT* 9), causes the narrator suddenly to "see" Christa T. for the first time.[58]

The image of the trumpet-blowing Christa T. functions as a leitmotif in the novel. As a symbol of spontaneous self-expression, it characterizes not only Christa T.'s nonconformity, but also her effect on the narrator. While she reacts with the same ridicule as the others, the narrator is uncomfortable about acquiescing to peer pressure. The remembering narrator recalls her response: "Never, never again did I want to stand outside the town park, outside the fenced-in-deer meadow, on a day without any sunshine – and it was another person who'd let go with that shout which erased everything and for a fraction of a second lifted the sky up higher. I could feel it falling back again on my shoulders" (*CT* 10). Thus for the narrator Christa T.'s shout calls the established order of things into question.

Intrigued by her spontaneity, the narrator actively cultivates Christa T.'s friendship. She is the supplicant throughout, while Christa T. remains elusive. Nonetheless, this new relationship allows her to see things in a different light, to (re)view things. Thus the feared and admired authoritarian teacher is regarded by Christa T. as "calculating." Seen through Christa T.'s eyes the teacher's walk "wasn't a stride anymore but a self-righteous strut, and her stockings, darned all the way up the calf, were ugly and clumsily darned stockings, not the proud sacrifice of a German woman in the war's fifth year amid a textile shortage" (*CT* 12). For the narrator, then, the relationship between the two is from the outset a dialectical one, one that engages her in self-examination, self-reflection, one in which Christa T.'s more unique, more developed sense of self causes the narrator to reevaluate her own self-awareness.

The invasion of the Red Army brings an abrupt end to the incipient friendship between the two girls. As both their families join the ranks of the refugees fleeing west, the girls lose contact with each other and do not see each other again for seven years. Since the Soviet invasion occurred in 1945, and the two friends separated for Christmas break in December 1944, the reader can fix their reunion at the university in 1951, when the fledgling socialist state was in its period of consolidation.

While she is pleased to see Christa T. again, the goal-directed narrator's perception of and relationship with her friend is now different. Caught up in her studies, she tends to be impatient of Christa T.'s nonconformity. Her autonomy, previously seen as her most positive attribute, is no longer regarded with the same enthusiasm. Whereas the narrator had severed herself from her peers during her school days and cultivated the friendship of the outsider Christa T., now her identification with her fellow students at the university is stronger, her spirit of community more highly developed. Thus when Christa T. drops out of sight in order to read Dostoyevsky instead of preparing for her examinations, thereby jeopardizing the collective class grade, her classmates are uncomprehending and somewhat exasperated. The collective voice, in the figure of Günther, tries to impress upon her her responsibility to the group and the state that has allowed her to study. While the narrator does not explicitly join in the implication of irresponsibility, she does not distance herself from it either. This incident effectively illustrates the contradictions between the individual and the collective that constitute an important focus of the book.

During her university days Christa T. seems closest to Gertrud Born, with whom she spends hours pondering whether Dostoyevsky's proposition that extreme softness vanquishes extreme hardness is true in all circumstances, or deliberating "how one could make a whole life out of the bits one was presented with," and whether such wholeness is really the aim and "if not, then what is?" (*CT* 36). While the rest of the students are memorizing dates and rhyme schemes and amassing factual information they will regurgitate in their exams,[59] Christa T. is posing existential questions. In retrospect the narrator realizes that Christa T.'s role in Gertrud Born's life was to make it questionable for her (*CT* 48), just as she is posthumously causing the narrator to question her own life and society.

The narrator also realizes in retrospect one source of the tension between herself and Christa T. Identifying herself with the collective "we," she asserts:

The truth is: we had other things to do. We were fully occupied with making ourselves unassailable ... Not only to admit into our minds nothing extraneous – and all sorts of things we considered extraneous ... also to let nothing extraneous well up from inside ourselves, and if it did so – a doubt, a suspicion, observations, questions – then not to let it show. Less from fear, although many people were frightened, than from insecurity. A feeling of insecurity that is more difficult to shed than anything else I know. (*CT* 50–1)

The narrator's description of the collective "we" of the Stalin period calls to mind the idealogue Mangold from *Divided Heaven*. By linking dogmatism with insecurity, she concedes that Christa T., despite (because of) her vulnerability, was morally superior to them.

Unassailability is of course the antithesis of Christa T.'s scepticism, her perpetual questioning of everything and everyone, especially herself. The point of intersection between the collective "we" and Christa T. is the faith they shared in the "new world," the socialist state that was being built. If the "we" were building up the new world by doing what they deemed necessary: making not only themselves but it unassailable with a singleness of purpose, then Christa T. was contributing in her own way. Where they were concerned with the means, her emphasis was on the ends. Yet this becomes apparent to the narrator only in hindsight. When the narrator claims responsibility for that new world, pointing out "whatever happened or will happen to that new world remains our affair," and credits Christa T. with having had "precisely the kind of imagination one needs for an understanding of it," she defines socialism as a process. Comparing Christa T. with the "new world of people without imagination" to the detriment of the "factual people, up-and-doing people [*Hopp-hopp Menschen*] as she [Christa T.] called them," she again aligns herself with her friend against the collective voice of her society. In doing so, she implies that the development of socialism has occurred at the cost of a pervasive conformity and a concomitant atrophy of essential human faculties. For it is precisely the imagination, by stretching the parameters of human thought, possibility, and potentiality, that can perpetuate the socialist utopian vision. Its transcendent, future-directed gesture extends the limits of the attainable and guards against stasis, complacency, and conformity with the status quo. Christa T., by envisioning the possibility of humane community, keeps alive the memory of a future.

The narrator's evaluation of Christa T.'s role implies a criticism of GDR society based on a belated recognition of its shift from perceiving socialism as an ongoing dialectical process to a narrow focus on and acceptance of existing conditions. This conformity with the status quo, presumably a result of faith in the inevitability of socialism, characterizes vulgar Marxism as distinct from fundamentalist Marxism. By bracketing out individual responsibility, this reductionist view relegates human beings to the status of objects of the historical process instead of dignifying them by making them agents of social change, as Marx had done. By fostering uniformity, conformity inhibits the productive contradiction necessary for the dialectical process.

While Christa T. never explicitly articulated these insights during her lifetime, she did register the shift of emphasis in her society as it manifested itself in language: "She felt how words begin to change when they aren't being tossed out any more by belief and ineptitude and excessive zeal but by calculation, craftiness, by the urge to adapt and conform." Thus during the Stalin period, a time in which people retreated "behind the gigantic cardboard placards they carried around" (*CT* 56), Christa T. watches the rise, not of the new human being, but of the one-dimensional human being. In retrospect, the narrator is able to discern the process by which the collective "we" internalized the slogans and values of these one-dimensional people until

> there emerged around us, or in us too, it is the same thing, a hermetic space which had its own internal laws, with its stars and suns, revolving with apparent effortlessness around a center which was subject to no laws, to no change, and least of all to doubt. The machinery which made it all move – or did it move? – the cogs, chains, and rods, were submerged in darkness; one rejoiced in the absolute perfection and purposiveness of the apparatus, and to keep it going smoothly seemed worthy of any sacrifice, even the sacrifice achieved by self-extinction.[60]   (*CT* 56)

The images of stasis that permeate this passage: "hermetic space," "internal laws," "center . . . subject to no laws, to no change"; the questioning of the motion of the machinery *per se*; but most significantly the dehumanizing, self-destructive effect of a system which "seems worthy of any sacrifice . . . even . . . self-extinction" – these are severe indictments of a mechanistic system at variance with the dialectical process in the service of humankind postulated by Marx.

In sensing the discrepancy between the goals of her society and its praxis, in suffering from its pressure for homogeneity, in deploring the fact that the individual is subjugated to the system, that human beings exist to serve the "apparatus" of the state and not vice versa, Christa T. was ahead of her time. For the collective "we" of the narrator, this awareness comes only later: "Only today do we feel any proper surprise: feelings have a long way to travel" (*CT* 56).

As an "untimely phenomenon" (*unzeitmäßige Erscheinung*), Christa T. is the first in a line of Wolf's characters (Karoline von Günderrode, Heinrich von Kleist, Cassandra) who live in a period of transition and who, unable to reconcile the contradictions confronting them, cannot find a viable form of existence. Inextricably connected with this theme is the question of human productivity, our need to contribute actively to our society. Rita Seidel's contribution to the process of socialist development is immediately discernible. Christa T.'s less tangible one can be understood only in retrospect, upon closer scrutiny. Always out of step with her society, yet believing in its goals, Christa T., as the narrator tells us, could not doubt her world, so she had no recourse but to doubt herself (*CT* 71). Ultimately this self-doubt, fostered by a society intent on conformity, destroys her.

Alternating with this self-doubt are feelings of superiority and a hopeful desire to be needed by her society. In her desperate suicide letter she states her belief that her contribution can best be made through writing. Writing for Christa T. is a bulwark against the alienation she experiences. The narrator attributes Christa T.'s autobiographical sketches to her student period when, unable to find affinity with those around her, she looked inward. Already as a child, the antidote to fear and pain for Christa T. had been writing. Thus, on the cover of her precious journal that she had brought safely through the war and the flight west stands written in a ten-year-old's scrawl: "*I would like to write poems [dichten] and I like stories too*" (*CT* 16).[61]

Going back to the etymology of *dichten*: "*condensare*, make dense, tighten," the narrator, in a formulation reminiscent of Rainer Maria Rilke, sees this activity as characteristic of Christa T. Like Rilke's Malte Laurids Brigge, Christa T. hates imprecision and formlessness. Writing affords her a means of giving form to experience. The consolation the child gains in thinking about writing foreshadows the therapeutic function that writing will assume in her adult life, when it will provide her only means of coping with reality.

Writing for Christa T. is a means of increasing self-awareness. Her sketch "Child in the Evening," for instance, captures an important moment in the human individuation process: the recognition that one is different. Having been sent to watch the expulsion of a group of gypsies from her village,[62] Christa T. fears the contempt of the little gypsy boy who earlier that day, in the ultimate gesture of antiauthoritarian defiance, had "pulled his pants down in the street and left a heap right in front of the burgomaster's office." Her lack of identification with the voyeuristic villagers prompts her much later to write about the child's differentiation: "'I,' the child thinks, 'I' am different." In a conscious play on Thomas Mann's "Tonio Kröger," this act of self-identification is marked by "longing, a little fear, misery and something like a birth" (*CT* 22).[63]

When Christa T. writes down this experience of ego-formation thirty years later, she is, the narrator implies, reiterating her sense of self-discovery. Yet in so doing, she again sets herself off from the collective. Just as she could find no community under National Socialism that would allow her to develop as an individual, she is also unable to find one under socialism. Moreover, since her sense of self is achieved against the definition of the norm, she knows only what she is *not*. She will spend her entire life learning what she *is*, what she could be.

Christa T.'s generic answer to the question what she would like to become: "a human being" (*CT* 35), harks back to the Johannes R. Becher quotation which Christa Wolf places as the motto to *Christa T.* In her "Interview with Myself" Wolf puts Becher's question: "This coming-to-oneself – what is it?" back into its broader context: "'For this profound unrest of the human soul is nothing but the premonition and the ability to sense that man has not yet come to himself. This coming-to-oneself – what is it?'" (*RW* 77). In so doing she makes clear its ramifications for the interpretation of the work. Clearly, coming-to-oneself is what Christa T. grapples with throughout her life. She herself articulates this concept when she speaks of *"the attempt to be completely oneself"* (*CT* 3), or of becoming *"oneself with all one's strength"* (*CT* 149), or when she calls writing this *"long and never-ending journey toward oneself"* (*CT* 174).

Yet Becher had provided an answer to the question as to what constitutes the coming-to-oneself. "It is," he maintained, "the fulfillment of all those possibilities which are given to mankind."[64] The Becher quotation in its entirety offers valuable insight into Christa T.'s position *vis-à-vis* GDR society. The "profound unrest of the human soul" of which Becher speaks and which manifests itself in Christa T. as a sense of longing is, as Heinrich Mohr[65] was the first to point out, a productive force that points to what must still be accomplished. The open-ended "not yet" in Becher's remark allows for the possibility of self-realization in the future; indeed it implies that this will be achieved.

The Becher quotation is crucial to the interpretation of *Christa T.* It contains the element of hope that links it with the philosophy of Ernst Bloch. In his *Philosophy of the Future*, Bloch states: "I am. But without possessing myself. So we first come to be."[66] In its emphasis on wonderment and doubt as requisite attributes for humankind's coming-to-itself, Bloch's philosophy has strong similarities with the figure of Christa T. Bloch's observation that "doubting is imbued with openness of endeavor – a readiness to be tested. Hardly fortuitous, then, as a scientific mistrust of convention it demanded a break with the taboo of hitherto received opinions,"[67] captures Christa T.'s restlessness, her probing of convention. Similarly, Bloch recognizes the importance of the reciprocity between the inner and outer worlds, sees empathy as a means of bridging the subject–object dichotomy, and believes that a fully open subject–object relationship can effect a utopian "external self-encounter";[68] these views directly parallel Christa Wolf's new way of writing. In his *magnum opus, The Principle of Hope*, Bloch defined the human being as forever hopeful, maintaining, "expectation, hope, intention towards possibility that has still not become; this is ... a basic feature of human consciousness."[69] Thus for Bloch, humankind is by nature future-directed, striving to become something it is not yet, "the stress being on the two words 'Not Yet' with their potential for the future. To be human means being on the way to something."[70]

The development of utopian thought in a socialist context posed problems for Bloch when he returned to Germany in 1949 from his Nazi-imposed exile and chose to settle in the GDR. Since he considered the future to be the most important subject of philosophy, and since utopian thinking had been a proscribed topic for socialist theoreticians since 1883, when Friedrich Engels published his treatise *Socialism: Utopian and Scientific (Entwicklung des Sozialismus von der Utopie zur Wissenschaft)*, Bloch sought to rehabilitate the term "utopia" in Marxist philosophy through the dialectical concept of "concrete utopia." Bloch's "concrete utopia," as distinct from purely speculative utopian thought, recovers traces of humane social interaction in the past and present and using these as bases, foresees the possibility of the concrete realization of a future utopia. In an uncannily similar formulation to Bloch's dialectical concept of "the memory of a future," Wolf, speaking of the potential of prose, maintains that it "can keep awake in us the memory of the future that we must not abandon on pain of destruction" (*RW* 212). For Bloch, as for Wolf, Marxism is seen as the sole concrete or realistic possibility of attaining these goals.

Ehrhard Bahr has pointed out the aesthetic ramifications of the principle of hope, noting that it creates a new time structure for art and philosophy. This principle, he maintains, is antithetical to the prescribed Socialist Realist perspective of the GDR. "It is a dialectical concept that tries to take into account the differentiations and contradictions of social reality as well as the frustrations of human progress without being excessively optimistic or persistently stoic."[71] Bahr sees Christa T. as the embodiment of the Blochian concept of "Not Yet" as well as of the potential utopia as delineated by the struggles of her unexemplary life. Furthermore,

Christa T. represents a utopian element in Bloch's terms insofar as she passes her legacy on to the narrator who, by reiterating Christa T.'s impatient leitmotival question: "When, if not now?" (*CT* 69, 70, 101) at the end of the work (*CT* 185), calls for the actualization of her friend's "concrete utopia." *Christa T.* ends with that question which seems to echo Bloch's language and philosophy. The manifestations of utopian thought in *Christa T.* will not allow us to read the text as one that ends in pessimism, resignation, or suicide.

Viewed in its historical and political context, *Christa T.* can also be read as a call for internal reform. In the GDR, the early sixties, the period of destalinization, were marked by a more liberal cultural and political policy. The success of the country's new economic policy aroused hope that more fundamental issues of individual civil rights would now be addressed. Revelations about the Stalin regime and the public rehabilitation of some "revisionists," among them Ernst Bloch, as well as the development of a reform communism in neighboring socialist countries, intensified this hope. For many in East Germany, the success of Alexander Dubček's reform efforts in Czechoslovakia seemed particularly propitious. By the time *Christa T.* was finally released in the GDR, the "Prague spring" had come to an abrupt end. Nonetheless, the text of *Christa T.* can be viewed as a reminder of its legacy.[72]

The discrepancy between ideal and reality, between Christa T.'s vision of herself and her society, also shares an affinity with German Romanticism in its use of the theme of *Sehnsucht* (longing). The Romantics use longing to express dissatisfaction with the banality of everyday existence and a yearning for the exotic, extraordinary, fantastic. The avatar of this Romantic longing is the eponymous hero of Novalis's *Heinrich von Ofterdingen*,[73] who spends his entire life in pursuit of the blue flower that has become symbolic of Romantic longing in German literature.[74] Christa T. shares with the Romantics dissatisfaction with her life as it is, but the object of her longing is different. While the Romantics long to transcend empirical reality, Christa T. longs to be able to engage in it more fully. She desires not to be anywhere, anywhere out of this world, but to be needed by it, to play a more active role in it. Her inability to find a means of active involvement calls forth her longing for death, which she articulates in her suicide letter.

At first glance the letter, addressed to her sister and found among her effects by the narrator, seems prompted by her unrequited love for Kostia. Closer analysis reveals a more pervasive malaise. Given the lack of historical specificity in *Christa T.*, especially with respect to events in the postwar period, it is striking that this letter, unlike the rest of Christa T.'s documents, is dated: early summer 1953,[75] and that the narrator underscores this date. Asking herself why she hadn't noticed that Christa T. had vanished before the beginning of the summer vacation, the narrator wonders: "What can have been on our minds that summer of 1953?" (*CT* 71). The seemingly innocuous question, unanswered in the text, would immediately strike a chord in a GDR reader, for the summer of 1953 marked a momentous event in GDR history: the 17 June populist uprising and its suppression by the Soviets. Yet in retrospect the narrator seems to regret having been so involved in political events that she failed to notice her friend's crisis.

Of all Christa T.'s documents, the letter to her sister is the most self-reflective and self-revealing. The epistolary form by definition necessitates saying "I," something which had always been problematic for her, yet the "I" here is not self-affirming. Instead, Christa T. reproaches herself for her "fruitless ponderings," her softness, her lack of determination. Faulting herself with "remaining everlastingly out of it, unfit for life," she recalls "how simple and natural everything seemed when I first read about it in the books." Confronted with the discrepancy between the promise of socialism and its imperfect realization, unable to find a niche for herself: "The whole world like a wall facing me. I fumble over the stones: no gaps. Why should I go on deluding myself: there's no gap for me to live in" (*CT* 70), she contemplates suicide. It is important to note that her feelings of despair are elicited by her inability to contribute productively to her society: "I don't know what I'm living for" (*CT* 70). She rejects emphatically a position as outsider: "I wouldn't want to live among a lot of other stranded people; that's the one thing I do know with any certainty" (*CT* 71). Recognizing her need for both privacy and community and given her desire for productivity: "I want to work. You know – with others, for others," she contemplates writing, in its public and private aspects, as a possible solution: "As far as I can see my only possible kind of activity is in writing; it's not direct. I have to be able to grapple with things quietly, contemplating them," only to drop it again: "All of which makes no difference; the contradiction can't be resolved – none of this makes any difference to my deep sense of concurring with these times of ours and of belonging in them" (*CT* 71).

Interpreting the letter, the narrator concludes that Christa T. "wasn't able to doubt the world, so all that was left was to doubt herself. Fear: she couldn't live in a world of fear. The inevitability of things in the world as it is: that frightened her" (*CT* 71–2). Thus the narrator attributes Christa T.'s situation to her inability to effect change, her fear to a discord between the prevailing determinism of her society and her utopian vision of the world. Her frustration arises out of her concurrence with and sense of belonging to her times and her inability to find a way of contributing to her society without compromising her integrity. Her inability to make the contradiction productive through writing precipitates her crisis of self-doubt. Thus the dialectic between the individual and society operates at all times in *Christa T.*

Although she finds professional self-definition restrictive and is reluctant to delimit in any way her aspiration to become a human being, Christa T. does try to make a place for herself in the public sphere through her work as a teacher. To this role she brings humanistic ideals and an antiauthoritarian attitude – she is an "equal among equals" (*CT* 102). Her pedagogical approach contrasts sharply with the manipulative and doctrinaire teaching techniques under which she had suffered as a child. Challenging her students, she spurs them on to excellence and tries to inculcate in them moral values. Encountering the blasé pragmatism of her students, Christa T. is once again forced to recognize how different she is. Three episodes during her teaching days: the Goethe poem; the class essay and the ensuing conversation with the school principal; and the Toad Story, serve to convince Christa T. of her marginality.

Christa T. takes seriously Goethe's humanistic values and attempts to instill them in her students. "Edel sei der Mensch" (Let the human being be noble) (*CT* 102) is the opening line of Goethe's poem "Das Göttliche" (The Divine). The verses of the first stanza read: "Let the human being be noble, helpful and good; for this alone distinguishes us from all other beings that we know." The closing stanza again returns to the concept of nobility: "Let the noble human being be helpful and good! Untiringly let him create what is useful and just, let him be an example to us of those intuited [divine] beings."[76] Christa T. believes in Goethe's message: these are the values by which she conducts her life. Her students' incredulous reaction to her, to the poem, and to her attitude toward the poem's ideas emphasizes the gap that exists between them – a gap she perceives to be generational. Believing along with Gorky in "the half-real, half-imaginary existence of human beings" (*CT* 111), Christa T. is intent on doing justice to both components, whereas for her students, human nature has been reduced to the real. Learning for them does not represent a means of growth and exploration but rather a chore. Thus they are content to learn the poem by heart rather than to take its message to heart.

In contrast to *Divided Heaven*, the failure to adapt to socialism is not attributed to bourgeois consciousness. Like Rita Seidel, Christa T.'s pupils have grown up under the socialist order; unlike her, they are uncommitted and apathetic. Christa T., on the other hand, belongs to Manfred Herrfurth's and Christa Wolf's transitional generation and is receptive to socialist humanist goals. Wolf thus inverts the concept of the generation gap as presented in *Moscow Novella* and *Divided Heaven*.

The differences between Christa T. and her students become even more apparent in the class's self-serving essays on the regulation topic: "Am I too young to contribute to the development of the Socialist society?" (*CT* 102). The essays precipitate a crisis of conscience for Christa T., again underscoring the dialectic between the individual and the collective. While she feels morally obliged to give all her students a D, to do so would jeopardize the standing of the school. Confronting her students, especially Hammurabi, who had described in glowing colors what a member of the Youth Association can do for society but was not himself a member, Christa T. is taught "about certain rules of the game in practical life" by her students. A blasé girl informs her naive teacher that no one could "actually force her to be so stupid as to mess up the grades, and a D, if the teacher really wanted to risk that, well, she for one wasn't going to put up with it" (*CT* 103). For Christa T., the most painful aspect of this lesson in opportunism is the fact that "the class made it quite clear that they understood the teacher's anger but saw it as the anger of inexperience, the sort of feeling they'd got over long ago" (*CT* 103).

In Christa T.'s pupils, Christa Wolf has given literary expression to a phenomenon of grave concern to her: the political apathy of her country's youth. It was this attitude of apathy, the result of disillusionment, that she described as symptomatic of her own generation after the war[77] and that informed the conception of Manfred Herrfurth. In "Zu einem Datum," Wolf also described how her introduction to Marxist thought had enabled her to overcome her apathy. In both the *Forum* article and her correspondence with Gerti Tetzner,[78] Wolf articulated the problem slightly differently: how to engage young people who had grown up under socialism and who were less tolerant of the discrepancies between the ideal and reality than those who had lived under Nazism. In their total lack of political or moral engagement, Christa T.'s pupils are spiritual cousins of the youth of the immediate postwar period in *Divided Heaven*. It is precisely this lack of caring and of interest in themselves that Wolf finds so dangerous to humankind and that she believes literature must rekindle to counterbalance the development of technocracy.

Christa T.'s distress at her students' cynical conformity is initially compounded by her visit to the principal. Her experiences with her students convince her of the differences between her generation (for at this point, Christa T. is still seen as a representative of her generation)[79] and the next; her encounter with the principal elucidates the differences between her generation and the previous one. The principal, a die-hard socialist survivor of the Nazi period, has learned to accommodate itself to the exigencies of the particular historical period. The invented "conversation" between the two actually consists of the alternating presentation of their unvoiced thoughts and impressions. Wolf's narrative technique in this scene functions much like an interior monologue:[80] it grants the reader greater insight into the characters' consciousness than they themselves have. At the same time, it makes clear the extent of nonverbal communication between them. This communication is based on recognition that each is projecting their image on the other, and on acceptance of the fact that they can never really understand each other. What emerges from their encounter is, if not a meeting of minds, then a recognition of mutual respect. The principal recognizes in the idealistic girl ("for he can only see her as a girl," *CT* 103) before him the enthusiasm of his own youth. A vague nostalgia for that period of his life echoes through when, in one of his few articulated thoughts, he says: "You want to have everything at once: power and goodness and I don't know what else besides" (*CT* 105). At this Christa T. suddenly understands that the principal has

trained himself to want only as much as he can reach by using all his powers. Otherwise he wouldn't be alive today, or he wouldn't be sitting here ... But the easy sayings – like One's actions should match one's thoughts, or The Integrated Life, or No Compromise, The Truth, and Nothing But The Truth – he'd put them all behind him.   (*CT* 105–6)

This insight enables her to break through the image she had had of the principal and to reaffirm her own aspirations. For the first time, she realizes that "she has wishes which go beyond herself" (*CT*

106) and beyond the time that she will see in her life, and a feeling of gratitude overcomes her for the man who helped make these wishes possible. In other words, she recognizes the historical context of his perspective, its relationship to her own perspective and that of her perspective to future generations.

If the outcome of the essay incident was ultimately self-affirming, the Toad Story proved demoralizing for Christa T. In contrast to the meeting with the principal, which the narrator, for want of documentary material, must invent, the Toad Story had been recorded by Christa T. in a twelve-page manuscript which, according to the narrator, serves as the basis for the story as it appears in *Christa T.* (*CT* 107–10). The Toad Story, which Christa T. makes light of in a drafted letter to her teacher-training professor: "What does a young lady teacher do, dear Herr Professor, when in her presence an almost grown-up student is overcome by the desire to bite off the head of a common country toad?" (*CT* 107), in fact calls into question both her profession and the capacity of the new social order to create the new, more humane person.[81] When Hammurabi decapitates the toad on a bet, Christa T.'s response, sorrow and tears rather than disgust, indicate her emotional involvement and sense of failure.

To cope with her defeat, she invents an alternative ending to the story, a projection of her own hopes and wishes, in which Hammurabi runs into the house, vigorously brushes his teeth and rinses out his mouth, and then "cries his eyes out," "howling and weeping like a little child" (*CT* 110). Christa T.'s alternative conclusion to the Toad Story, which invents a repentant, remorseful Hammurabi in order to sustain her view of a moral world and which reflects her inability to "accommodate herself to the true naked reality" (*CT* 110), is not upheld by the narrator. Instead, she invents a more probable conclusion in which the principal, pursuing a complaint by Hammurabi's parents, reprimands Christa T. for not intervening. The Toad Story clearly illustrates the schism that exists between Christa T.'s future-directed vision of an ideal society and present-day reality in the GDR.

Although there is a great discrepancy between the present and the future ideal, Christa T. does not perceive such great differences between the present and the past. Defining Hammurabi as hard-working and brutish, Christa T. notes that it's "only his good luck that he's living here. Anywhere else he'd be . . . I don't know what. There's still a demand for people like him. Only don't let's be deceived about that kind of ability. For – what could it lead to?"

(*CT* 110). The implied continuity between the brutal behavior of Hammurabi and his Nazi predecessors is made explicit in a passage interspersed in the scene of Hammurabi biting the toad:

> Then the black tomcat smashes against the stable wall, the magpie's eggs splinter against the rock, and again the snow is brushed away from the small rigid face. The teeth bite once more. It doesn't stop.   (*CT* 109)

Christa T.'s other salient characteristic, besides imagination, is conscience. Her sense of shared humanity causes her to be deeply affected by the acts of others. Thus the memory of the senseless killing of the family tomcat she had witnessed as a child haunts her. The sound of the animal's bones cracking as it was flung against the stable door will accompany her throughout her life, as will the knowledge that her father had passively watched the inebriated farmer kill the animal. Helplessness meshes with stunned incomprehension when one of her pupils purposely smashes a magpie's eggs and culminates in her pain at Hammurabi's brutal killing of the toad. These events in turn mesh with her survivor's guilt, engendered by the sight of the child that had frozen to death outside the stalled truck in which she had fallen asleep on the flight west. Tomcat, magpie, toad, and child serve as leitmotifs in the novel. Pointing to the dark side of life, to mankind's cruelty and indifference to the pain of other creatures, their recurrence indicates that the founding of the socialist state has not yet brought about the promised new age.

The ethical shortcomings of Christa T.'s society not only manifest continuity between the past and the present but jeopardize the future as well. At the New Year's party the year of her death, Christa T., asked what is indispensable for the survival of humankind, responds: imagination and conscience (*CT* 172). The importance of imagination for the sustenance of a utopian vision is thus coupled with the call for ethical behavior in the here and now.

Christa T., in the words of the narrator, has precisely the kind of imagination needed for the actualization of socialism; her moral consciousness is highly developed as well. Respect for the individual and an affirmation of community are two essential and mutually reinforcing aspects of her character. By regarding everyone she encounters as an equal, by treating people not as means to an end but as ends in themselves, Christa T. complies with Kantian moral principles as put forth in both *The Groundwork of the Metaphysics of Morals* and *The Critique of Practical Reason*. It is clear that Christa Wolf considers compliance with Kant's moral imperative essential for humane interaction.[82]

In her concern for the interrelatedness of human community, Christa T. broadens the parameters of Kant's moral code, which is justice-oriented and based on the primacy of duty, to include a moral consciousness based on responsibility and care. Christa T.'s sense of morality coincides with the vision of maturity articulated by Harvard psychologist Carol Gilligan in her work, *In a Different Voice*. Working with the six-stage theory of moral development put forth by Lawrence Kohlberg, a theory formulated without specific consideration of female subjects, Gilligan found that women, when placed in situations of moral conflict and choice, addressed issues involving the relationship between self and others in ways distinct from their male counterparts. Young male adults tended to base their decisions on a morality of rights expressing a sense of equity while young women tended to manifest a morality of responsibility based on connection and need.[83]

Gilligan attributes the differences in response to gender-specific ego formation. Male identity is founded on separation from the mother (who, in most Western cultures, remains the chief source of nurture) and involves the empowerment of the self in its awareness as other and in the renunciation of everything perceived as feminine, e.g., attachment and emotionality. Female identity is based instead on attachment to and sustained connection with the mother. For the men in Gilligan's study, involvement represented a qualification and limitation of self; for the women, identity was defined through relationships of intimacy and care. Overall, women's sense of self as separate tended to be less highly developed than men's, whereas men's sense of relationship tended to be less highly developed. These developmental differences elicited different moral responses also. Male consciousness tended to stress justice on the basis of separate but equal rights; female ethics revolved around relationship and sought the inclusion of diversity. While male ethics generated transcontextual absolutes, female ethics showed a commitment to context.

Gilligan is careful to note that these male and female voices are not mutually exclusive, nor do they remain totally divergent. In the mature individual they converge to create a morality that embraces both an ethic of fairness and one of care. Her criticism of Kohlberg centers on the limitations of his theory: its male bias through its exclusion of women's experience and its definition of morality in terms of a principle that subordinates the relational and privileges individualism.

While Gilligan's work has been criticized for overpsychologizing morality and for failing to take sociological factors adequately into account, it is revolutionary in broadening the definition of morality to include relationship. It is this aspect of her work that bears on Christa Wolf's. In language strikingly similar to Wolf's, Gilligan points to the perilousness of the current world situation and to the need for ethical judgment informed by a recognition of the interrelatedness of the human community to ensure the survival of humankind.[84]

Wolf and Gilligan approach the dialectic of individual and society from opposite ends of the spectrum. Gilligan, writing in the context of a highly capitalist society, perceives the need for a greater sense of collective, whereas Wolf, speaking from a socialist perspective, addresses the need to reaffirm individualism within the collective. According to both Wolf's and Gilligan's criteria, Christa T.'s sense of morality is more highly developed and differentiated than that of her compatriots.[85] She does not conceive of individualism and communality as dichotomous oppositions but as mutually reinforcing modes in which the individual voice sustains the community and in which the collective allows and sustains the individual voice. Similarly, while her definition of self is initially formulated in terms of her uniqueness, it never loses sight of interrelationship.

It is her feeling of interrelationship that precipitates Christa T.'s frustration, her "bitterness as the fruit of passion" (*CT* 132) when confronted with the battered street-car conductress who refuses to improve her situation. Similarly, Christa T.'s decision to marry and bear children need not necessarily be interpreted as a retreat into a petit-bourgeois idyll, but can be seen as an attempt at self-actualization through relationship. Perceiving herself to have failed in the public sphere, Christa T. resorts to the private sphere, traditionally viewed as the domain of women.

Critics have noted the primacy of moral issues in Wolf's work since *Christa T.*[86] She views literature as a moral institution[87] and her role as author as that of a moralist. In keeping with a Marxist perspective, Wolf believes in the primacy of the social infrastructure, that is, that being determines consciousness and not vice versa. At the same time she denies that the existing structure leads to the development of a moral society. She cites fellow GDR writer Johannes Bobrowski's question: "How must the world be constituted for a moral being?"[88] as germane to her own concerns, and stresses: "Bobrowski's question is and remains stimulating because it helps to adjust the world to a morality worthy of human beings, and not to adjust the morality of human beings to a world that is still not worthy of human beings . . ."[89]

Wolf's acknowledgment of her moral perspective echoes sentiments found in Christa T. She admits that she does not

> share with some Marxists the contempt for the (little) word "morality" . . . I cannot and will not admit to a narrow historical determinism which sees individuals, social strata, classes, and peoples simply as the objects of a historical inevitability corresponding to a totalistic philosophy of history. Nor can I admit to a barren pragmatism, which sees in the morality of classes and individuals, nothing other than a means to an end, able to be manipulated at will, able to be ignored at will, at times a useful, at times a useless vehicle.[90]

Morality for Wolf

> has nothing to do with Christian antinomies of good and bad, with the rigid juxtaposition of thinking and action, nothing to do with abstract, barren, and in the final analysis paralyzing demands for integrity. Indeed, even our mistakes can be moral, if they continually bring us anew to the productive side of our contradictions. Immoral on the other hand is everything that prevents us, prevents the masses from being the subject rather than the object of history. And using that as a starting point – why shouldn't the socialist author also conceive of himself as a "moralist"?[91]

Wolf's emphasis on morality has been criticized for its failure to assign proper significance to the material basis of historical development, for in fact trying to obscure or deny that basis.[92] Yet Myra Love's reading of Wolf's statement as "an attempt to formulate the principle of revolution in moral terms: as the necessity for a praxis that can change the world to make it fit for a humanized humanity" and as an indirect challenge to the "self-understanding of GDR socialism as a system that is as humanized as possible because organized in a manner aimed at maximal technological rationalization,"[93] seems more accurate.

Love's distinction between *praxis* and *techné*[94] is an important one. Wolf has become increasingly concerned about the GDR's reduction of reason to technological rationalism. Her society has abolished private ownership without revolutionizing social relations, and its prime focus since the 1960s has been "the revolution in science and technology." Wolf's emphasis on the development of moral consciousness to effect a fundamentalist Marxist revolution in social intercourse, her interpretation of the crucial role of literature in helping effect the changes necessary, thus marks a radical deviation from the norm, as does her plea for a socialism whose main focus is the human being.

Christa T.'s view of writing converges markedly with that of Christa Wolf; the personal and moral implications for both are strikingly similar. The principle of subjective authenticity that informs Wolf's writing is adumbrated in Christa T.'s writing and emerges most distinctly in her thesis on Theodor Storm. Just as Wolf's authorial presence is perceptible in her texts, just as in *No Place on Earth* and *Cassandra* she will use historical subject matter to articulate contemporary issues of relevance to her, so Christa T. is present as subject in her study of the nineteenth-century realist writer.

The narrator interprets Christa T.'s interest in German poetic realist writers Wilhelm Raabe, Gottfried Keller, and Theodor Storm as a perhaps unconscious attempt to combat her attraction to "complicatedness, multisignificance, subtlety, the-end-of-an-epoch feelings" (*CT* 94), symbolized above all by her love for Thomas Mann. She sees the circumscription, sobriety, and simplicity of these writings, their focus on the "world of small things" (*CT* 93), as a refuge for Christa T. against her own complexity and against the onslaught of a world in which she cannot find a proper place. The fact that of the three realists mentioned, she chooses to work on Storm, the least critical of his society and the most private writer, is revealing.

In 1954, when Christa T. wrote her thesis, Georg Lukács was still dictating the GDR literary canon: his assessment of Storm as a poet of resignation, whose retreat into inwardness and idyll rendered him unworthy of consideration by socialist society, assured that Storm was a *persona non grata*.[95] While Christa T. does not overestimate Storm's works, she does appreciate the fact that he was able to write at all, in light of his "'predominantly lyrical'" nature and his historical age, which was a "period of cultural inertia and derivativeness" (*CT* 95). The parallels between Storm's time and Christa T.'s are obvious, and she can identify with Storm's dilemma: "*The conflict between willing something and the inability to do it thrust him into a corner of life*" (*CT* 97); the dissimilarities between them, the fact that unlike him, she is unable to write, are therefore all the more poignant.

The narrator reading the thesis anticipated "the haughty tone and ready-made, clattering sentences with which in those days we attacked rather than grasped our topics. I didn't anticipate compliant understanding, the confessions, even less the self-questioning and almost undisguised self-portrayal, the eruption of personal problems into the dispassionate inquiry." By establishing a relation between Storm and another person unspecified but present in the text, by structuring her study around a question of great import to her: "how, if at all, and under what circumstances, can one realize oneself in a work of art?" (*CT* 95), by injecting her own voice and experience into the so-called objective study,[96] and through her empathy with Storm's situation, Christa T.'s thesis attains the dimension of depth described in "The Reader and the Writer" and serves as a model for Christa Wolf's new way of writing.

In the final part of her thesis, Christa T. actually succeeds in overcoming what she had thematized in her journal as "the difficulty of saying 'I.'" Comparing her own childhood with Storm's, she recalls similar experiences in her life evoked by his descriptions. Her assessment of Storm as a "*writer who made a landscape of longing, of Sehnsucht*" (*CT* 97) is applicable to herself as well. Her failure as a writer does not invalidate the example of her life: it too can be described as a "landscape of longing."

Writing for Christa T. represents a means of combating the dark sides of life, the brutality and immorality (nowhere is this more apparent than in her alternative ending to the Toad Story). Yet insofar as all her writing represents an attempt at self-understanding and self-actualization, it must be seen as a moral endeavor in Christa Wolf's terms: it helps facilitate the development of Christa T. as a conscious subject ("das Subjektwerden des Menschen"). Besides being a survival tactic, a means of coping with reality, and an instrument of growth for Christa T., her writing has posthumous implications for the narrator who, in grappling with Christa T.'s life, comes to confront herself as well. Thus the narrative shows not only Christa T. but also the narrator in the process of becoming an autonomous conscious subject – a process which the reader is meant to replicate as well. Precisely herein lies the revolutionary potential of the text.

Christa T.'s and Christa Wolf's writing has a ripple effect. The open-ended style of both must be contrasted with Christa T.'s antipode, the successful opportunistic writer Blasing, whose clearly defined stories with their preconceived structures are seen as lethal:

He's put us all into tins long prepared and even labeled to receive us, tins in existence perhaps even before we were born. All Blasing had to do was clap the lids on, and now we'd been dealt with, we knew all about ourselves and nobody had the slightest reason to stir a finger or make a single move. Nobody had any reason to go on living, and Frau Blasing ... told her husband bluntly she'd always suspected he wanted to kill her. (*CT* 166–7)

Blasing's objectifying writing serves as a foil to Christa T.'s and Christa Wolf's respect for the subjects of their writing. His commodity-oriented, consumer attitude toward art focuses on the work of art as an end product rather than on writing as a creative, self-reflective and liberating process capable of effecting change. He manifests precisely that positivistic stance which Wolf had criticized in her discussion with Hans Kaufmann. He is a writer who

in order to present his art must concoct a plot, a kind of lasso with which he then ropes in and tries to interpret his pitiable material. He, the writer, can be on foot or on horse-back, he can be a boorish cowboy or a master of his craft, indolent or industrious – he still remains who he was, when at the end he exhibits his booty. Of his readers, however, he dares to hope that by reading his book they might be fundamentally "changed"![97]

Clearly the description of Blasing's mechanistic writing, devoid of any subjective dimension, his use of preconceived types who move along preordained paths, is meant as a criticism of Socialist Realism. His anachronistic orientation and his commercial success as an author who panders to his audience's literary taste, coupled with Christa T.'s "failure" as a writer who engages in self-exploration (which doubtless contributes to her death), can be seen as an indictment of GDR society.

As Dieter Sevin has pointed out, the theme of writing in *Christa T.* consciously points to the difficulties confronting the narrator in the construction of the text and thereby makes the reader aware of the enormous difficulties confronting the GDR writer who seeks to write in a new, subjective mode.[98] In addition to the restrictive Socialist Realist prescriptions regarding the positive hero against which the narrator rebelled in order to create her unexemplary model, Christa T., the writer is inhibited from free self-expression ("the difficulty-of-saying-'I'" motif) by the prevailing suspicion of subjectivity on the part of GDR cultural arbiters.[99] Sevin's reading lends too negative a cast to the presentation of this theme in *Christa T.* It fails to make clear the far-reaching implications the text has for the reader and for GDR society at large, an undertaking that informs Myra Love's study "Das Spiel mit offenen Möglichkeiten: Subjectivity and the Thematization of Writing in the Works of Christa Wolf." Love has argued persuasively that

Christa Wolf's writing is intended to create a basis for open communication that is missing in the public sphere of the GDR.

Part of Christa T.'s problem is the scepticism she feels toward language, an attitude she shares with Christa Wolf. Jeanette Clausen, examining this scepticism from a gender-specific perspective, points out that feminist writers have widely acknowledged the difficulty of saying "I," a theme in both Christa T.'s and Christa Wolf's writing, as a basic experience of women under patriarchy. Clausen maintains that the conscious self-assertion necessary for saying "I" is possible only when the grammatical subject has an "authentic relationship to his/her self and the world."[100] For women the situation is compounded by the need to use a male-oriented, male-dominated discourse to articulate the self. Clausen draws upon French feminist Monique Wittig's observations regarding the implications of the use of the pronoun "I" for women: the fact that by masking the sexual identity of the speaker/writer it may make her feel deceptively at home in a male-dominated language; that the use of this pronoun may allow her to forget that the pronoun "she" is obliterated in the false generic "he"; the fact "'that the female saying "I" is alien at every moment to her own speaking and writing. She is broken by the fact that she must enter this language in order to speak or write.'"[101] She then argues that Christa Wolf's theme of self-reference can be seen as a response to what radical feminist theologian Mary Daly has called "grammatical silencing devices."[102] These observations are illuminating in that they point to the compounded difficulties confronting the GDR woman writer. Not only does she share with her male counterpart the exigencies of literary production in a repressive system, she is also, by virtue of her sex, alienated from the language that men have created and to which they have privileged access. In *No Place on Earth* Wolf will address the double burden facing the woman writer explicitly.

In a similar vein Love, in her essay "Christa Wolf and Feminism: Breaking the Patriarchal Connection,"[103] called for a reading of *Christa T.* as a process of deconstructing the system of dichotomous oppositions that informs the patriarchal model of perception and discourse. The implicit point of departure of Love's argument is the concept of logocentricity, derived from the work of deconstructionist theoretians Jacques Derrida and Jacques Lacan and elaborated by French feminists Hélène Cixous, Luce Irigaray, and Monique Wittig. These women argue that male domination is established and sustained through logocentric and phallocentric structures of thought and discourse. Logocentric, paradigmatic positing of a central term of logos and its opposite or negation, based on a conceptualization of the world as a system of polarities (e.g., subject/object; speech/silence; presence/absence), in conjunction with patriarchal phallocentricity, relegates woman to the position of other.[104]

In *Christa T.*, Love argues, the patriarchal experimental model is subverted and transcended through the overcoming of two oppositions: presence/absence and speech/writing. Christa Wolf's purpose in *Christa T.* is to make her absent (dead) friend present in the text through reflection. The presence of Wolf in "the text which constitutes itself in relation [not in opposition] to the absence which is *Christa T.*" signifies a "process of self-constitution in intersubjective relationship" and represents the "coming-into-being of subjectivity free of domination."[105] Another essential function of the text is the subversion of the opposition of literature and communication, of speech and writing. Citing Roland Barthes's juxtaposition of written and spoken language and his assertion that the "closed" structure of written language militates against communication: "'writing is an anticommunication, it is intimidating,'"[106] Love argues that *Christa T.*, in contrast, through its use of a nonlinear, self-interrupting mode of discourse, through its use of the familiar you (*du*) and the inclusive "we," creates the aura of conversation between narrator and reader and in so doing overcomes the polarity between writing and speech. Attributing women's silence not only to "the lack of a voice capable of speaking female experience beyond the limits set upon it by patriarchy" but also to "the lack of practice in occupying the position of authority which has traditionally characterized authorship,"[107] Love credits Christa Wolf with bridging the gap between experience and culture and with demystifying "authorship by removing it from its traditional position of depersonalized authority and returning it to its function as a means of social communication."[108]

In her recent dissertation (1983) Love embeds her interpretation of Wolf's concept of literature as a form of social communication in the context of GDR sociopolitical history and praxis. She believes Wolf's emphasis on the communicative function of literature arises from the lack of a public sphere of communication. Love connects the feminist utopian concept of intersubjectivity, of subjectivity free of domination, with the socialist utopian vision of the coming-into-being of conscious subjects. By augmenting her feminist perspective with an analysis of the political and critical theoretical context of Wolf's writing (she draws on the philosophy of Jürgen Habermas and to a lesser degree on Max Horkheimer and Theodor Adorno), Love averts the danger of ahistoricism sometimes attendant upon feminist interpretation.[109]

Just as one cannot ignore the fact that Christa Wolf is a GDR writer who upholds the fundamental precepts of socialism, one cannot overlook the fact that Christa Wolf is a woman writing about women and women's experiences, and that these experiences differ fundamentally from men's. While it can be assumed that Christa Wolf at the time of the writing of *Christa T.* was not consciously criticizing patriarchy, it is also clear that the alternative model of human interrelationship that she creates stems from women's experience.

For this reason Alexander Stephan's consistent refusal to address the gender specificity of Wolf's writing[110] constitutes a definite omission in his otherwise useful analysis of Wolf's work. Indeed, the most glaring example of Stephan's shortcoming can be found in the essay in which he undertakes to discuss Wolf as a woman writer. His assessment of her writing in general and of *Christa T.* in particular must be repudiated. He argues that "Christa Wolf's books do not deal with problems of women, with a specifically female appropriation of reality or a specifically feminine aesthetic (insofar as this already exists) nor are they especially written for women" and rejects the gender specificity of the text of *Christa T.* His statement that apart from minor insignificant details, Christa T. is interchangeable with Christian T.,[111] cannot be substantiated by the text. It is true that Christa Wolf by her own admission does not write for a specifically female audience.[112] Nonetheless, her books have found the greatest resonance among women,[113] not only in socialist countries but in capitalist countries as well. Given Wolf's increasingly sharp criticism of patriarchy, which culminates in *Cassandra*, the feminist perspective which enriches our understanding of her texts and elucidates an additional depth of meaning of her work, is of particular interest.

Yet if her model for overcoming alienation in *Christa T.* is based on female experience and a female mode of being in the world, in no sense can one interpret Christa Wolf as a separatist. As both her discussion with Hans Kaufmann and her essay "Berührung" make clear, Wolf is striving for the humanization and emancipation of all, men and women alike. In 1968 when she wrote "The Reader and the Writer," Wolf placed her hope for the realization of her utopian goals in socialism. By 1977 when she wrote "Berührung,"

94

"brotherliness" (*qua* socialism) had been replaced by the concept of "sisterliness" as a means toward realizing her end. Yet precisely those attributes of sisterliness described in the later essay, attributes that point to a community whose laws are "sympathy, self-respect, trust and friendliness," are operative in the text of *Christa T.* It is clear that the narrator's treatment of her "subject matter," Christa T., is informed by what Wolf later calls "touching," the "spirit of the actually existing utopia."[114]

4

PATTERNS OF CHILDHOOD: THE CONFRONTATION WITH THE SELF

How did we get to be the way we are?

Patterns of Childhood is part of the second wave of GDR literature dealing with the war and the Nazi past that appeared in the mid-seventies. In contrast to the earlier literature of the *Aufbau* period, which propagated the tradition of resistance to Nazism, these works document the traces of fascist mentality and behavior still manifest in everyday life in the GDR – authoritarianism, moral cowardice, conformity – as well as widespread self-deception in the refusal to admit to earlier political convictions. The timing of the literary reassessment of the German past is due in part to the convergence of political and psychological factors. The more liberal cultural politics of the early seventies following Erich Honecker's call to lift taboos (1971) and the simple passage of time finally allowed writers such as Christa Wolf, Hermann Kant, Volker Braun, Erich Loest, and Heiner Müller to break their silence about their personal experiences in Nazi Germany.[1]

In *Patterns of Childhood*, Christa Wolf places the theme of the continuity between the past and the present, touched on in the Hammurabi incident in *Christa T.*, at the forefront of her investigation. While the treatment of this question remains abstract in *Christa T.*, it is made concrete in the figure of the narrator in *Patterns of Childhood*, who embodies both the Nazi past and the GDR present. The relationship of Christa Wolf to the narrator of *Patterns of Childhood* is like the author/narrator relationship in *Christa T.*; the two are strikingly similar without being identical.

As discussions with Christa Wolf make clear, *Patterns of Childhood* is autobiographical;[2] yet it is not written as a first-person narrative. Wolf says that she spent over a year experimenting with alternative beginnings to the book. Most of these alternatives were in the first person, and in each instance the subjective narrative form inhibited her writing. Only later did Wolf realize that her

resistance to first-person narration arose out of a sense of estrangement from her own biography during the period of her life lived
under National Socialism.[3] Wolf's situation is reflected in the poem
by Pablo Neruda that she places as a preface to the book:

> Where is the child I used to be,
> still within, or far away?
>
> Does he know I never loved him,
> or that he never loved me?
>
> Why when we grew up together
> did we later grow apart?
>
> Why when my childhood years were dead
> didn't each of us die too?
>
> And if my soul fell from my body,
> why does my skeleton remain?
>
> *
>
> When does the butterfly in flight
> read what's written on its wings?
>
> Pablo Neruda, *Book of Questions*[4]

Wolf's sense of self-alienation was so profound, the schism
between childhood and adult self so pronounced, that she was
unable to cast her autobiographical narrative in the first-person
form. The difficulty of saying "I" for the narrator of *Patterns of
Childhood* is directly attributable to the Nazi past: "Because it is
unbearable to think the tiny word 'I' in connection with the word
'Auschwitz.' 'I' in the past conditional: I would have. I might have.
I could have. Done it. Obeyed orders" (*PoC* 230). Instead, her
narrator must objectify her childhood self into a third person in
order to be able to write at all. Confronted with the dilemma: "to
remain speechless, or else to live in the third person. The first is
impossible, the second uncanny" (*PoC* 3),[5] the narrator chooses
the latter alternative. Consequently, the childhood self is named
"Nelly," while the reactivating consciousness of the trip to Poland
and the reflective, creative consciousness of the writing self are cast
in the second-person familiar form, "du."

Wolf raises questions about self-reference throughout the book.
In a passage from the opening page of the original, unfortunately
deleted from the English translation, the narrator states:

In cross-examination with yourself the true reason for the linguistic
breakdown becomes apparent: Between the monologue and the address a
perplexing sound shifting occurs, a fatal change in grammatical relation-

ships. I, you (*du*), she, merging together in thoughts, are supposed to be estranged from each other in the articulated sentence. The chest tone toward which language seems to be striving withers under the acquired technique of the vocal cords. Linguistic disgust. Opposed to that the almost indomitable tendency to platitudinous chatter in the same person.

To give interim information, to avoid assertions, to give perceptions in lieu of oaths; a procedure intended to give the rupture which goes through time the respect it deserves.[6]

The intimate "du" is not only the most appropriate form of self-address; it can also mean the reader and creates a sense of community between the writer and the reader. Thus it is in keeping with the generational implications of Wolf's inquiry, which in turn are underscored by the narrator's use of the communal "we."

In 1975, a year before *Patterns of Childhood* appeared, Christa Wolf discussed her work in progress. Asked how the book would end, she maintained that the third person of Nelly and the "du" person would converge into an "I" about whom she would have to write in a very different way.[7] Yet Wolf's predicted coalescence of third and second person into the first person was to prove more difficult than anticipated. At the end of the book the narrator contemplates the success of her undertaking:

The child who was hidden in me – has she come forth? Or has she been scared into looking for a deeper, more inaccessible hiding place? Has memory done its duty? Or has it proven – by the act of misleading – that it's impossible to escape the mortal sin of our time: the desire not to come to grips with oneself? And the past, which can still split the first person into the second and the third – has its hegemony been broken? Will the voices be still?

I don't know. (*PoC* 406)

Some critics have called Wolf's failure fully to achieve this avowed goal of her narrative a shortcoming. Such criticism, based on the notion of the narrator's sovereignty over the subject matter, forgets that Wolf's "subject matter" is the relationship of the self to its past and diminishes the importance of the *process* of self-examination and of writing for her. In a highly conscious and far more systematic fashion, *Patterns of Childhood* continues the confrontation with the self inadvertently triggered by the writing of *Christa T.* As with her previous work, *Patterns of Childhood* was based not on experience overcome but on experience to be overcome. Clearly, Wolf had hoped that by addressing her National Socialist past she would be able to exorcise it. Her "failure" to synthesize her two selves should be seen not as an aesthetic shortcoming[8] but rather as a courageous confession that her self-alienation had not yet been completely overcome. Moreover, by leaving the process of *Vergangenheitsbewältigung* open, Wolf calls upon readers to participate actively in that process, by confronting their own childhoods.

The difficulty of saying "I" and the tenuousness of the first-person narrator's statement ("I don't know," *PoC* 406), with its confession of doubt and self-doubt, are evidence of the power of the past and the complexity of Wolf's undertaking. Judging the book according to Wolf's own criteria and bearing in mind Wolf's understanding of the moral function of art and of the writer as a mediator of experience, this ending should be read not as a failure but as an expression of subjective authenticity. It is the reflection of a never-ending process that is ultimately the end in itself.

In her short story of 1970, "Blickwechsel" ("Change of Perspective"), Christa Wolf had still envisaged the possibility of writing her autobiography in the first person. She had the "I" narrator, who is clearly a synthesis of Nelly and the narrator "du" of *Patterns of Childhood*, relate the final stages of her family's flight west and their liberation by American troops. In many ways the short story can be read as a prelude to the later work. It includes characters who reappear and incidents that are only slightly varied in *Patterns of Childhood*.[9] It also documents Nazi anti-Soviet propaganda, which manifests itself in the terror tactics of the SS officer who seeks to persuade the narrator's grandmother of the need to continue fleeing from the invading Soviet armies[10] and the narrator's astonishment at hearing one of the concentration camp inmates utter "the unheard-of word *Communist* as though it were a permissible everyday word like *hate* and *war* and *destruction*" (CP 100). More significantly, however, "Change of Perspective," in recording the emotions of the narrator – dismay at learning of the Führer's death and at the soldier's indifference and lack of deference in relaying it; reluctance to be liberated; desperate fear of the Soviet armies – effectively undercuts accepted notions of the German citizenry as victims of Nazism longing for liberation. Moreover, it not only implicates the citizenry in the Hitler regime but attributes to them knowledge of the Holocaust.

Thus the narrator is granted an insight that is denied to child Nelly and attributed only to the adult "du" narrator of *Patterns of Childhood*: the fact that the Germans knew about the concentration camps.

Then we saw the concentration camp inmates. Like a ghost the rumor had been weighing on our minds that the inmates of Oranienburg were being herded along behind us. I never suspected, at the time, that we were also fleeing from them. . . . We involuntarily retreated before them. But this retreat also betrayed to us – it indicated, in spite of everything – what we affirmed to one another and to ourselves: We did know what had gone on. All of us – we knew . . . I knew for the fraction of a second that we were to blame. I forgot again.   (CP 99)

The fact that the sixteen-year-old narrator of the earlier short story "forgot" this important insight helps explain the complex structure of *Patterns of Childhood*, with its emphasis on the function of memory. The narrator of the later work must unearth that insight from beneath years of "forgetting," that is, repression. Although a far more traditional narrative, "Change of Perspective" contains glimpses of the reflexive structure characteristic of *Patterns of Childhood*. Thus the narrator is able to document the precise moment when she became aware of her self-alienation.

I wasn't a changeling, but I was no longer myself either. I never forgot when this stranger entered me, who had meanwhile grabbed me and did with me as she would. It was that cold morning in January, when I left my town on a van for Küstrin in great haste, and when I was really very surprised how gray this town was, in which I had always found all the light and color I needed. Then someone in me said slowly and distinctly: You'll never see it again.

My fright can't be described. There was no appeal to this judgment. All I could do was keep to myself truly and honestly what I knew . . . go on doing everything that I owed others, say what they wanted to hear from me. But the stranger in me gnawed about and grew, and possibly she would refuse to obey in my place.   (CP 96)

This experience, which anticipates Cassandra's introspection on self-alienation and refers back to Wolf's reflections on narrative stance in "The Reader and the Writer," is carried over into *Patterns of Childhood*. Similarly, the narrator's statement that "you can't see yourself when you're in yourself. But I saw all of us, as I see us today, as though someone had lifted me out of my skin and set me aside with the command: Look there!" (CP 95) anticipates the dual focus of narration of Wolf's autobiographical work and its narrator's sophisticated ruminations on the uses and abuses of memory and the power of self-deception. Wolf's decision to expand the reflexive component of her later narrative obviously also prompted her to abandon the more straightforward, linear narration of

"Change of Perspective" in favor of a form that would reflect the process of self-examination she was undertaking.

As in *Christa T.*, the process of reviewing the past through the prism of the present determines the narrative structure of *Patterns of Childhood*. There are three levels of narration at work in the text, each of which constitutes a distinct temporal frame of reference. The first is that of the reflecting and creating consciousness writing the book. The temporal parameters of this level are clearly delineated: from 2 November 1972 to 2 May 1975. The second level is that of the consciousness reliving and describing memories and emotions reactivated by a forty-six hour visit to the narrator's home town in what is now Poland on 11–12 July 1971. Finally, there is the level of reconstructed childhood experiences, comprising the years 1931–47, from the child's first awareness of herself as an independent ego until two years after the end of the war. Wolf carefully establishes a temporal frame for her narrative, which moves from the present ever deeper into the past and at the end reverses the temporal movement. However, as Sandra Frieden has pointed out, the three time levels can be separated from each other only heuristically, "since the remembered, the remembering and the reflective levels of consciousness are interwoven from the outset."[11] Wolf points to the danger of simplification as she reaffirms the interrelationship of biography and literature and elucidates the difficulties of transmitting experience through writing:

Ideally, the structure of the experience coincides with the structure of the narrative. This should be the goal: fantastic accuracy. But there is no technique that permits translating an incredibly tangled mesh, whose threads are interlaced according to the strictest laws, into linear narrative without doing it serious damage. (*PoC* 272)

The reflective level provides the conceptual framework for Wolf's narrative. It introduces the elements of contemporaneity and unavoidable engagement which for Wolf constitute subjective authenticity and which are essential for her task: the coming to terms with the past in the present. At this level the narrator reflects on memory, writing, and childhood and introduces and comments on documentary material on events of the Nazi past and the GDR present as well as psychological and scientific findings on the act of remembering. As in *Christa T.*, the narrator at this metafictional level, concerned with making the reader aware of the process of writing, reflects "upon the self in its own introspection."[12] Wolf comments on world political events that occurred during the writing of the book – the American bombings of Vietnam, the military junta in Chile, the Pentagon Papers, Watergate – which for her represent the continuity of fascist and fascistic attitudes into the present. Other events not so immediately relevant to her topic, such as the precarious situation in the Middle East and the launching of the spaceship Apollo, are woven together with everyday life in the GDR and with events of particular personal concern to her, such as the death of Ingeborg Bachmann and the suicide of her daughter's teacher. By recording and commenting on these contemporary events, the narrating consciousness personalizes them and embeds them into her subjective historical inquiry. The narrator thereby encourages the reader also to relate the past to the present.

In her essay on the "Diary, Aid to Work and Memory" (1964), Wolf had maintained that personal entries, diaries, and sketches function as vehicles for experimentation, often serving as a dry run for the fictional narrative.[13] Since Nelly's mother burned her daughter's incriminating journals at the end of the war, the narrator must rely completely on her memory to reconstruct her subjective past. Wolf's attitude toward memory was critical in *Christa T.*; it is even more so in *Patterns of Childhood*. Memory is deceptive not only in falsifying images but in erasing them as well. Gaps in memory become apparent around sensitive or volatile issues. Indeed, one of the reasons for writing *Patterns of Childhood* was to discover whether the narrator's memories were elusive because they were so far in the past or because she could not bear to recall them.

The narrator feels a need to reactivate her memory, to facilitate the deconstruction of miniatures, those falsified images of the past that have superceded authentic experiences by their predictable familiarity. She wants to probe past the superficial levels from which miniatures are fashioned to the recesses that house the complexities, ambivalences, ambiguities, the "mixed feelings of adulthood that, more than anything else, mean being grown up" (*RW* 192). This desire prompts her, twenty-six years later, to visit her home town G. (= Gorzów/Wielkopolski), formerly L. (= Landsberg/Warthe), along with her husband, H., her brother, Lutz, and her teenage daughter, Lenka. Her companions serve as foils or prods to the remembering adult. They prompt her to pursue avenues of inquiry she might not otherwise have explored and thereby buttress the associative structure of this level.

The trip to Poland serves as a catalyst to reactivate memory, leading the narrator to consult documentary material – notably local newspapers from the period, including the Nazi *Landsberger General Anzeiger*, as well as speeches by Hitler, Himmler, and Goebbels – to augment those aspects of the past about which she has little or no recall. This material also proves to her that events about which Germans claim to have had no knowledge were matters of public record: the burning of Communist flags, the beating of Communists, the founding of Dachau. The narrator's own "forgetting" mirrors that of her society.

The narrator's intermingling of documentary research and individual memory is one aspect of her attempt not to be a sovereign narrator. She lets documents speak in their own voice. In the same way, she tries to resurrect the child, her former self, and let her act autonomously and interact with her adult self. The dialectic between the two selves is that between the remembered child who is "presented in the immediacy of its experience [and] the remembering adult [who] provides a conjuncture for the flood of memories and the awareness of implications, a filter of hindsight through which former deeds and values must now pass."[14]

In "The Reader and the Writer," Wolf had attempted to determine the locus of the narrator in an episode that was to become part of *Patterns of Childhood*.

And the narrator? She lies in the potato furrow, sees the potato plants to the right and left and the broad segment of sky, is startled by the lizard and holds her breath; but at the same time she is grown up and looks down at the fourteen-year-old. Thinks it worthwhile after twenty-five years to remember that at that time she was happy and should not have been. Tries to be honest in writing and finds that the twenty-five years have not only worked on her, but also on that early scene. Must admit that she has not described it "objectively" – that is not possible. This does not discourage her. She decides to tell, that is invent, truthfully on the foundation of her own experience. (*RW* 193)

And in fact, by again swimming "against the apparently natural current of forgetting" (*RW* 192), Wolf's narrator does recall the child lying in the furrow in the potato field with a lizard sunning itself on her stomach, violently suppressing the habit of obedience in not answering calls from the house, who will appear as Nelly in *Patterns of Childhood*. In presenting the child's happiness and her guilt at being happy during the war, Wolf abandons the simplified memories characteristic of miniatures and thereby deconstructs the original miniature. It is this task, the breaking down of reified memory, that Christa Wolf undertakes in *Patterns of Childhood*.

Patterns of Childhood begins with a descrption of its own difficult beginnings. The narrator tells of numerous alternative beginnings, most of which centered around the child's first memory: her consciousness of herself as independent subject:

> Yes, most of the time you started with the description of this seldom-remembered moment, which you were able to summon up after some thought. Yours is an authentic memory, even if it's slightly worn at the edges, because it is more than improbable that an outsider had watched the child and had later told her how she had sat on the door step of her father's store, trying the new word out in her mind: I . . . I . . . I . . . I . . . I . . . each time with a thrilled shock which had to be kept a secret, that much she knew right away. (*PoC* 5)

Elaborating on this image of her childhood self, the narrator, in language reminiscent of the way in which the narrator of *Christa T.* initially conjured up her friend, relays her manipulative attitude toward her former self:

> You've got it, then. She moves, walks, lies down, sits, eats, sleeps, drinks. She can laugh and cry, dig sand pits, listen to fairy tales, play with dolls, be frightened, happy, say mama and papa, love and hate and say her prayers. And all with deceptive authenticity. Until she strikes a false note, a precocious remark – less than that: a thought, a gesture – exposing the limitation for which you had almost settled. (*PoC* 7)

Somewhat reluctantly the narrator gives up her control over her childhood self and decides to try to get to know her. That is, she credits this child with being an autonomous subject and seeks to place her present self in relationship to her former self. In so doing, she implicitly admits to a schism in the self that she seeks to overcome through the creation of connectedness.

Throughout the book the narrator will experience and discuss the danger of objectification inherent in writing. Her inability to write in the first person exacerbates this problem: by writing about her childhood self in the third person, she is by definition objectifying her. The narrator's awareness of the fundamental paradox of her undertaking and her moral compulsion to proceed nonetheless contribute to the psychological and moral imperatives of the text. In order to become a subject, she must first objectify a part of herself. Although her goal is similar to that of the narrator in *Christa T.*, knowledge of another and self-knowledge are even more closely intertwined in *Patterns of*

Childhood: knowledge of the other is identical with knowledge of self:

It hurts to admit that the child – aged three, helpless, alone – is inaccessible to you. You're not only separated from her by forty years; you are hampered by your unreliable memory. You abandoned the child, after all. After others abandoned it. All right, but she was also abandoned by the adult who slipped out of her, and who managed to do to her all the things adults usually do to children. The adult left the child behind, pushed her aside, forgot her, suppressed her, denied her, remade, falsified, spoiled and neglected her, was ashamed and proud of her, loved her with the wrong kind of love, and hated her with the wrong kind of hate. Now, in spite of all impossibility, the adult wishes to make the child's acquaintance. (*PoC* 7)

This passage evokes the Neruda poem that prefaces the book. The interrogative structure of Neruda's poem is consonant with Christa Wolf's undertaking in *Patterns of Childhood*. The final stanza of the poem: "When does the butterfly in flight read what's written on its wings?" adumbrates Wolf's concern with blind spots in the individual and in society that plays a crucial role in *Cassandra* but that actually became a cornerstone of her writing with *Christa T.* In a discussion at Ohio State University on 1 June 1983, Wolf maintained:

Every human being experiences – if he experiences himself at all – that he has, at every stage of his life, a blind spot. Something that he does not see. This is connected with his powers of perception, with his history. Similarly, a society or a civilization has a blind spot. It is precisely this spot which brings about self-destruction. To not only describe, but rather to penetrate into this blind spot, to so to speak enter the center of the hurricane: that is, in my opinion, the task of literature.[15]

Christa Wolf, in breaking the silence and in dealing with the Hitler period from a personal point of view, has ventured into the center of the hurricane in the hope of preempting the (self-) destructive potential of the unconfronted past, on both a personal and a social level. The highly personal nature of her investigation transcends the more circumscribed, class-defined concept of subjectivity that prevailed until recently in the GDR. However, what distinguishes Wolf's narrative from the West German confessional literature of the 1970s, generally subsumed under the heading of "New Inwardness" (*Neue Innerlichkeit*) or "New Subjectivity" (*Neue Subjektivität*), is its highly developed dialectic between the individual and society.

As Wolfgang Iser points out, the novel as a genre, although it deals with social and historical norms, does not merely reproduce contemporary values. Instead it transposes them from the realm of empirical reality, where they function as social regulations, to the realm of literature, where they become a subject of discussion. The novel thus often ends up calling these norms into question.[16] Precisely that is Wolf's intention: in *Patterns of Childhood* she seeks to uncover the socialization processes in the Third Reich that led to widespread conformity with the values of Nazism. In many ways, *Patterns of Childhood* can be read as a response to the lesson Christa T.'s former student seeks to teach her, that "the essence of health is adaptation or conformity" (*CT* 111). In the later work conformity, far from leading to health, is seen as the root of neurosis and self-alienation. In her attempt to discover how the members of her generation got to be the way they are, Christa Wolf has written an anti-Nazi anti-*Bildungsroman* in which both narrator and reader are meant not to (re)affirm but to reject the process of socialization to which she and some of her readers were subjected.

By speaking not merely for herself but for her entire generation, Wolf violates one of the basic assumptions of the genre of auto-biography: its emphasis on the uniqueness of the individual. Similarly, by showing self-reference to be a problem, Wolf again flies in the face of generic expectations, based on the identity between writing self and author as articulated through the pronoun "I" and representative of a continuity between past and present writing self. The complex narrative structure also disappoints the expectation of linear chronology of past events and the clear demarcation of temporal levels.[17] Thus Wolf's work throughout exhibits a tension between expectation and actuality.

Patterns of Childhood, like *Christa T.*, is preceded by an ironic disclaimer:

All characters in this book are the invention of the narrator. None is identical with any person living or dead. Neither do any of the described episodes coincide with actual events.

Anyone believing that he detects a similarity between a character in the narrative and either himself or anyone else should consider the strange lack of individuality in the behavior of many contemporaries. Generally recognizable behavior patterns should be blamed on circumstances.

C.W.

Wolf's preface, at once a parody of conventional novelistic dis-claimers and a criticism of conformity,[18] is paradoxical for auto-biography, which claims to portray verifiable truth. It may, moreover, be a conscious allusion to the 1968 novel *Klassentreffen*

(Class Reunion) by GDR writer Wolfgang Joho,[19] a complacent and politically accepted treatment of the Nazi past that relegates the legacy of the Third Reich to the Federal Republic. To compound the problem of classifying the work by genre, Wolf added the subtitle "novel" to the West German edition. As in *Christa T.*, Wolf's play with generic conventions in *Patterns of Childhood* challenges reader expectations. It thus underscores the challenge to the implied readers of the text (among whom we must count above all Wolf's contemporaries, who would most clearly feel themselves addressed by the "du" of the text) to compare the social reality of the Third Reich reconstructed by the text with their own recollections of this period.

German critical response to *Patterns of Childhood* was largely based on a reading of the book as autobiography and was determined by the political ideology of the critics. By focusing almost exclusively on political content, GDR criticism again underestimated the significance of structure for the transmission of meaning. Indeed, many critics faulted the book's complex narrative structure as being excessively experimental or self-consciously formalistic.[20] The most ferocious criticism was levelled by the writer Annemarie Auer. She attacked the book ostensibly on personal, but ultimately on ideological grounds, for its failure to articulate the experience of those who, like herself, perceived the defeat of Nazi Germany as a liberation and who had actively helped to implement social revolution in the GDR.[21] Like his GDR counterparts, Marxist critic Hans Mayer focused on the self-reflective third level of narration, accusing Wolf of dishonesty in failing to include Communist aggressions in her discussion of the continuity of fascist tendencies into the present.[22] In the FRG, leading critics such as Fritz Raddatz and Marcel Reich-Ranicki totally missed the point of Wolf's narrative. Raddatz, applying outdated normative aesthetic criteria, found the reflective level of Wolf's narrative too intrusive to constitute "great art." *Patterns of Childhood*, in his estimation, could at best be classed as a "noble essay."[23] Reich-Ranicki dismissed the book as "dilettantish," containing merely the "raw material for a novel," and deemed it a "failure."[24] So wide of the mark was most of the criticism that it prompted Norbert Schachtsiek-Freitag to speak of "The Failure of Criticism" with respect to *Patterns of Childhood*.[25]

Perhaps understandably, the most sensitive, least defensive readings of the book have come from non-German critics. On the whole, Anglo-American criticism has succeeded in presenting a politically neutral assessment of *Patterns of Childhood*.[26] Thus Jackson and Saunders, situating *Patterns of Childhood* in the context of Wolf's fictional and theoretical work, consider it "the most daring challenge of her career as an autobiographical writer and literary innovator."[27] They argue that the presence of a reflective, self-questioning narrator who juxtaposes issues that seem mutually exclusive but that are actually interdependent – such as the author's concern with the possible consequences of probing an officially "resolved" past and Nelly's first awareness of self – makes us aware of her "broad self-questioning stance." They also argue that the narrator's sceptical scrutiny of language "encourages the reader to question every word and every cliché."[28] Like *Christa T.*, *Patterns of Childhood* poses questions; the interrogative structure in this work is even more pronounced than in the previous one. By not offering ready answers, by leaving readers to draw connections between the past and the present, Wolf again actively engages us in the process of investigation. Her belief that both individuals and societies who are unwilling to learn from their past experiences are doomed to repeat them, prompts her to explore the origins of (self-)destructive behavior and to challenge the reader to do the same. By making these patterns of behavior conscious, she hopes to help in overcoming them.

The original English translation of the title, *Kindheitsmuster*, as *A Model Childhood* is grievously misleading. Nothing could be further from Christa Wolf's intention than to imply that her childhood experiences in Nazi Germany can in any way be regarded as exemplary. Reflecting on the title, the narrator notes that "'pattern' is derived from the Latin 'monstrum' which originally meant 'sample' [*Probestück*] . . .[29] But monsters in today's sense of the word will also appear."[30] Wolf, in probing "the terribly intimate experience"[31] of her childhood, in seeking to uncover the means by which patterns of behavior become ingrained and values become inculcated in a child, and in examining their residual effect, is addressing superindividual phenomena. By speaking for herself, Christa Wolf is also speaking for her generation.

Born in the late 1920s, Wolf's generation was too young to be directly responsible for the rise of Hitler, yet old enough to become aware in retrospect of how fascism translated itself into everyday life under National Socialism. Given the enormous burden of guilt involved, it is perhaps understandable why the older generation, those immediately culpable, should envelope themselves in silence.

It is a testimony to her level of involvement (*Betroffenheit*) that it took Christa Wolf, a member of the middle generation, more than twenty-five years to be able to break the silence and to write about her experiences during this period.[32]

The significance of Wolf's work lies in the ruthlessly honest and unapologetic way in which it breaks the silence – both self- and externally imposed. It defines the concept of *Bewältigung* psychologically rather than sociopolitically. Wolf calls for

a confrontation of the individual with his uniquely personal past, with that which he has personally done and thought and which he cannot delegate to someone else; with that for which he cannot excuse himself by pointing to the masses of people who have done the same or worse. Sociology and statistics fail in this instance. It's a question of personal and societal morality and the conditions which abrogate both.[33]

Patterns of Childhood is generally classed with the literature of *Vergangenheitsbewältigung*. Yet Wolf herself rejects the concept of *Bewältigung* in its traditional sense, maintaining that one cannot really "come to terms" with the murder of six million Jews and the death of twenty million Soviet people.[34] Wolf's method for examining the National Socialist past was moreover still anathema to official cultural and political policy of that time. By exploring the commonality between the past and the present, *Patterns of Childhood* challenges the GDR's claim of discontinuity between Hitler's Germany and the postwar socialist state. From the opening lines of the book: "What is past is not dead; it is not even past. We cut ourselves off from it: we pretend to be strangers" (*PoC* 3), Wolf challenges her country's self-understanding.

Lamenting the absence of the phenomenon of "moral memory" (*PoC* 36), Wolf uses personal history as a springboard to examine the patterns of behavior that gave rise to fascist attitudes such as the fear of authority and the unquestioning obedience still discernible in people of her generation. According to Wolf, the impetus to treat this subject came from a profound sense that the easy transition from fascist to socialist values recorded in the extant literature was not in keeping with her own experience. "My experience was different. In my experience it took a very long time until at first tiny insights, later deepseated changes were possible."[35]

Addressing a fundamental socialist issue, the possibility of changing one's character (*sich verändern*), Wolf maintains:

The answer to that essentially boils down to getting the severely damaged apparati for perception and for the proper reaction to reality back into order; that one succeeds in living in reality, with reality, and in a way that does justice to reality [*realitätsgerecht*] – that is, to act so that reality will be influenced by one's actions. All of that was not even present as a possibility. There was an entire generation, and not only one, which was deeply impaired in the basis of its psychic existence. And that is not that easy to repair. That isn't over and done with if two years later one says: By Jove, Marx is right.[36]

Christa Wolf considers herself fortunate to have found people after the war who helped repair her damaged psyche (in *Patterns of Childhood* the teacher Maria Krangold is one of these). By telling her what was not found in history books, they rectified her distorted perception of reality. Nonetheless, this was a slow and painful process, one that essentially caused her to dissociate herself from her childhood self. Not until she was writing *Patterns of Childhood* did she realize that "between the period of childhood up to age sixteen and the emergence of a new period based ... on a new world view a kind of no man's land had formed which separated the two periods from each other."[37]

Christa Wolf's appropriation of the term "no man's land" from the political sphere (it is used in Germany today to designate the treacherous strip of mined territory along the border separating the GDR and the FRG) is particularly poignant in this context. When the temporal dimension (of memory) is added to this geographical metaphor, it assumes geological dimensions. The past is seen as strata of sedimental deposits in which the two periods of Wolf's life, her childhood to age sixteen and her adult self, informed and transformed by Marxian consciousness, are separated by a molten and imprecisely defined stratum that impedes access to the earlier strata. Wolf's narrator consciously plays with the geological metaphor. Quoting a friend who had maintained that the Nazi period was for her "tertiary," she describes the tertiary as a geological era basically similar to the present era, "except that man is still absent," and ponders:

Why, then, stir up settled, stabilized rock formations in order to hit on a possible encapsulated organism, a fossil. The delicately veined wings of a fly in a piece of amber. The fleeting track of a bird in once spongy sediments, hardened and immortalized by propitious stratification. To become a paleontologist. To learn to deal with petrified remains, to read from calcified imprints about the existence of early living forms which one can no longer observe. (*PoC* 151)

Her musings reflect her misgivings about her endeavor and are but one example of the self-doubt that accompanies and at times overpowers the narrator throughout her writing. At the same time, read in conjunction with Wolf's thesis articulated in the opening lines of *Patterns of Childhood*, her reflections call into question her friend's analogy. The geological metaphor on the other hand seems more appropriate when one recalls that Freud likened the work of the analyst to that of the archaeologist.[38] The task of Wolf's narrative is precisely the reanimating of her fossilized childhood past.

Wolf felt compelled by the "laws of morality of her profession" (*Gesetze der Berufsmoral*)[39] to confront her past in order to be able to move on to other subjects. At the same time, she felt obliged to document both for her generation and for succeeding ones what it was like to live and grow up in this period. *Patterns of Childhood* is for Wolf as much about the present as it is about the past because "as long as people who had this childhood, who experienced these years as children or young people, are alive, it is all in them. Our contemporaries live with it."[40] Her investigation is not guided by the question that prompts most queries into the National Socialist past: "How could it have happened?" but rather by: "How did we get to be the way we are?" Her intensely personal confrontation with her childhood self is aimed not at a merely rational working through of the past, but rather at an emotional reclaiming of it in the hopes of thereby attaining the psychic integration necessary to actively participate *realitätsgetreu* in the world. Thus the writing of *Patterns of Childhood* serves a threefold function: it is personal, generational, and political/public. It is in keeping with Wolf's belief in the ability of literature to touch people at their innermost core that she assigns to it the difficult task of breaking the silence surrounding the Hitler period. Wolf maintains:

My access to literature, the compulsion to write arises out of the fact that I am very strongly, very personally affected [*betroffen*] by history, by the history of our people, our state and by all the events that I have experienced consciously since my childhood. It seems to me that it is necessary, that it could be useful – apart from the fact that it is useful for me – if one tried to bring movement into the strata, the sediments which events have left behind in all of us . . . It is, I believe, really the task of literature to bring some movement into the inner strata, with whose immobility one likes to comfort oneself by confusing numbness with true peace, which can only emerge out of an inner freedom.[41]

Just as the writing of *Patterns of Childhood* is meant to help bring about this inner freedom in the author, the constitution of the text through the reader and the reactivation of the reader's experiences is meant to perform a similar emancipatory function for members of Wolf's generation.

The psychological ramifications of Christa Wolf's undertaking are made explicit in the work of West German psychologists Alexander and Margarethe Mitscherlich. In their pioneering study of the collective social conduct of postwar Germany, *The Inability to Mourn: Principles of Collective Behavior* (1967)[42], the Mitscherlichs analyze why the vast majority of Germans who survived the war are unable to come to terms with their Nazi past. In their view, the inability of these survivors to mourn their loss – the loss of their Führer – can be seen as a psychological defense mechanism. Mourning would mean recognizing the intensity of their love for Hitler and accepting their own responsibility for the atrocities committed during the war. In light of the enormity of the guilt, shame, and anxiety such mourning would release, it is perhaps understandable why the Germans fail to mourn. They deny individual and/or collective responsibility, projecting sole responsibility on the Führer and his accomplices. In order to avoid the intolerable insights and emotions mourning would discharge, they sever "all affective bridges linking them to the immediate past."[43] In emotionally repudiating the past, they rob it of its substance; "it fades like a dream."[44] This has grave consequences, for in the Mitscherlichs' view, "no matter how much in the forefront of one's conscious mind there may be a sense of breach with and estrangement from the past – a sense of starting over from scratch – if what came *after* is to be understood, it must be considered in conjunction with what happened *before*."[45]

According to the Mitscherlichs,

working through the losses is a prerequisite to experiencing guilt and remorse. No such working-through occurred. Instead, the recollection of a whole segment of national history soon faded; and naturally on the individual level that meant losing segments of one's own life from memory – how one had thought, acted, and hoped in them. Blanks developed in the autobiography of the individual.[46]

Christa Wolf's debt to the Mitscherlichs is strikingly apparent from this passage. In her autobiographical work, she explicitly raises the issue of collective and individual memory gaps, introducing the concept of the "black box" (*PoC* 281) or memory blank and the "black hole," a term borrowed from modern astrophysics, as a metaphor to describe Nelly's psychic state at the end of the war: "collapsed horizon of events" (*PoC* 295).[47]

The inability of post-Hitler Germany to mourn the loss of its leader, and its failure to reexperience its past and thereby to release the psychic energy necessary for a vital existence in and a coming to terms with the present, is inextricably linked with the German way of loving, in the Mitscherlichs' opinion. The German people's incredible obedience to the Führer arose, they believe, out of the German predilection for narcissistic, idealizing love relationships. Thus Hitler is viewed as the embodiment of the *collective ego-ideal* of the German people, able to instill feelings of omnipotence in his followers. Consequently the exposure of Hitler as a criminal dealt a crushing blow to the very core of the Germans' self-esteem. His "death, and his devaluation by the victors . . . implied the loss of a narcissistic object and, accordingly, an ego- or self-impoverishment and devaluation."[48] Using the distinction drawn by Freud between *mourning*, in which "the individual feels impoverished, but . . . suffers no diminution of his own sense of worth," and *melancholia*, in which there is "'an extraordinary diminution of his self-regard, an impoverishment of his ego on a grand scale,'"[49] the Mitscherlichs maintain that any grieving for the Führer in post-war Germany would have resulted in mass melancholia. The primary reason for the general emotional repudiation of the past after the war was avoidance of the trauma caused by the loss of an ego-ideal. The avoidance of mourning for the victims of the Hitler regime was a secondary psychological process that occurred only later.[50] In order to avoid the work of mourning, Germans, according to the Mitscherlichs, focused their psychic energy on reconstruction and the economic development of their new state.

The Mitscherlichs' study was written primarily, although not exclusively, for a West German audience. It clearly reflects the situation of the Federal Republic in the mid-sixties. The Auschwitz trials held in Frankfurt from December 1963 to August 1965 and the public debate about the statute of limitations on war crimes had brought the Holocaust back into public consciousness. Documentary plays like Rolf Hochhuth's *Der Stellvertreter* (*The Deputy*, 1963), indicting the Catholic Church and especially Pope Pius XII for refusing to speak out against the mass extermination of the Jews, and Peter Weiss's *Die Ermittlung* (*The Investigation*, 1965), based directly on the Auschwitz trials and revealing a continuity between Nazi and post-war attitudes, fueled public discussion of the Nazi past. Both the war trials and the statute of limitations debate made painfully clear the degree to which Germans had repressed their Nazi past. The formation of the Great Coalition (1966), which included the Socialist Party, signaled the end of the conservative Adenauer era with its emphasis on economic recovery and Cold War politics. The severe economic crisis of 1966 intensified speculation, voiced since the fifties,[51] that the German commitment to democracy was merely a commitment to the affluence that democracy had promised the Germans in the post-war period.

It is against this backdrop that the Mitscherlichs' study must be understood. Like many of the liberal intellegentsia, the Mitscherlichs had hoped that the citizens of the Federal Republic would develop truly democratic attitudes. Instead, their case histories convinced them of the ominous continuities of patterns of behavior between pre- and post-war German society. The Mitscherlichs were prompted to undertake their analysis of psychosocial behavior patterns by the volatile situation of the sixties, together with what they identified as a German inability to address social problems in a socially progressive way. They argue that the German way of loving caused Germans merely to substitute a symbiotic unity with the Führer for unity with the occupation forces, without internalizing the principles on which these new forms of government were based. The Cold War in turn furnished each of the German states with ready-made enemies onto which responsibility for the past could be projected in order to avoid the work of mourning. According to them,

the German people's basic attitude – the attitude they were able to reconcile with National Socialism – they now bring unchanged to the conduct of the affairs of their present governments. Here, too, the idealization of Germany's political guardians, both in West and East Germany, is far more intense than would be called for by the objective situation. Both West and East Germans prop up their badly damaged self-confidence through such identifications.[52]

Mindful that the generation that had experienced Nazism firsthand was dying out, they urged the German people to mourn their past in order to break this disastrous pattern of behavior and to release the psychic energy so necessary to confront productively problems in the present.

Although they deal primarily with West Germany, many of the Mitscherlichs' insights are clearly applicable to the GDR as well. For both Germanies it is surely true that "when, as had been the case in the past, social problems were dealt with in the manner of the 'final solution,' no effortless transition to civilized 'normality' could ensue without entailing a dangerous split in consciousness."[53] Indeed, it can be argued that the GDR, by insisting on calling the Soviet invasion of Germany "liberation" and by dissociating itself from the Third Reich, only intensified this schism in consciousness.

It is precisely this split in consciousness that Christa Wolf describes as "no man's land" in *Patterns of Childhood*. Wolf, who was impressed by the Mitscherlichs' work,[54] sets about in her monumental narrative to do the work of mourning[55] they call for. Her interest in patterns of behavior and patterns of experience are testimony to the similarity of concerns between the writer and the psychologist. Christa Wolf's contention that writing can be a form of therapy is substantiated by *Patterns of Childhood*.

In addition to the individual psychological work of mourning, Wolf's work is an investigation of the phenomenon of widespread memory loss. For both the individual and society, the narrator's following contention holds true:

In the age of universal loss of memory . . . we must realize that complete presence of mind can be achieved only when based on a clear past. The deeper our memory, the freer the space for the goal of all our hopes: the future. (*PoC* 153)

On the personal and generational level, *Patterns of Childhood* is intended to help Christa Wolf and her contemporaries confront the fear and guilt engendered during their formative years. Wolf argues that the empathy which this generation was forced to deny or repress during their childhood surfaces later as fear and an inability to identify with other people. The consequence of this fear is forgetting. To overcome or at least reduce this fear by making it conscious is one of the goals of *Patterns of Childhood*.[56] Not merely an intellectual undertaking but an emotional one as well, *Patterns of Childhood* is intended to work against collective amnesia.

The theme of fear, which is an undercurrent in the narrative, surfaces in chapter seventeen, entitled "A chapter of fear – the arch" in the German edition,[57] and becomes the focus of reflection. After relating Nelly's visceral fear at seeing a Russian soldier, a fear instilled by Nazi anti-Soviet propaganda, the narrator goes on to describe the fear she experiences in March 1975 while writing the book. As in Wolf's other works, her holistic approach causes her to consider body and mind a unity in *Patterns of Childhood*. The trauma of war and occupation send the sixteen-year-old Nelly into the hospital with tuberculosis. Resistance to boring into the wounds sends the narrator to the hospital with palpitations of the heart, insomnia, and anxiety. In a passage deleted from the English translation, the narrator reflects that "the attempt to touch the untouched, to speak the unspoken makes fear 'free.' This freed-up fear in turn makes him who is seized by it unfree." In attempting to analyze her anxiety, she asks:

Is it a question of the banal fear of the consequences of violating a taboo, a question of cowardice, which could be overcome through a moral act? . . . Or is it the fundamental fear of discovering too much and of being forced into a zone of nonagreement, whose climate you haven't learned to tolerate? A fear that reaches far back into time and has been inculcated since childhood, a fear of self-betrayal and guilt. Unhappy legacy.[58]

On the political level, *Patterns of Childhood* confronts the accepted paradigm of socialist resistance to Hitler that had been used to create a continuity between the presocialist and the socialist state. The fact that the names of Sophie and Hans Scholl, members of the Catholic student resistance group "The White Rose," were unknown to Nelly and that there was "no mention ever of the uprising of the Jews in the Warsaw ghetto" (*PoC* 257) indicates that resistance activity had not impressed itself onto the consciousness of Nelly's family. On the other hand, the family's horrified reaction to the news of the assassination attempt on Hitler on 20 June 1944 and the depiction of Nelly's undying loyalty to the Führer deconstructs the paradigm of widespread antifascist resistance. As Judith Ryan has pointed out, "in eliminating any but such brief references to the resistance movement, Wolf shows sovereign disregard for the idea of an East German resistance heritage (and certainly she makes no mention of the Communist resistance, which is what is meant by this term)."[59]

In a discussion, Wolf made her iconoclastic position explicit:

Our past was the antifascist tradition. Our point of departure was the fact that many leading positions were held by anti-fascists. But the common people [*Volk*] were of course the same as in the Federal Republic. *Patterns of Childhood* attempted to describe everyday life at that time and everyday life of today to show: those are the same people who were living then and who are still living today.[60]

Wolf's portrayal of the people living then is limited almost exclusively to the petite bourgeoisie. By focusing on the shop-keepers Bruno and Charlotte Jordan and their extended family, she is able to present a colorful and fairly representative cross-section of the common people in the Third Reich. By using the child's memories as her starting point, she ensures that the political will be meshed with the private. One of Wolf's achievements in *Patterns of Childhood* is the rendering of everyday speech. Her skill at capturing not only the simple language of the child but also the aphoristically laden language of her elders, especially Charlotte Jordan's, authentically (re)creates the petit-bourgeois milieu.

The fact that the remembering narrator is female necessarily shapes the experiences remembered. In addition to biological events like the onset of menstruation and psychological factors like the strong, unbroken identification with her mother, the narrator also recounts historical events specific to women's experience. The war, from the perspective of an adolescent female civilian, signified the absence and possible death of Nelly's father; his infrequent home leaves; her mother's struggle to maintain the shop; bombings and air raid shelters; and most significantly, the trek west. *Patterns of Childhood* differs from most German war narratives in describing the flight from the Red Army in terms of experiences specific to old people, children, and (particularly) women. For Nelly the flight meant watching her mother become suddenly transformed into an old woman; seeing her father return from a Soviet gulag, changed beyond recognition; and watching her grandparents die from different ailments all emanating from the same cause: their superfluity.

Wolf's narrator demonstrates the presence of fascism in everyday life by weaving Hitler and Goebbels speeches, political rallies, and Nazi indoctrination into family conflict, petty jealousies, and gossip. Events whose ramifications are unclear to the child, such as Charlotte Jordan's indignation at being denounced as part Jewish, and the mysterious death of the mentally ill Aunt Dotty (killed under the euthanasia program), are presented along with other family events from which the children are shielded, like Uncle Emil Dunst's affair and Aunt Liesbeth's looming divorce. Nelly's parents are presented not as active Hitler supporters but as passive fellow travelers. Content to profit from the barracks built in their neighborhood, they are delighted that Hitler's war economy elevates them to the status of independent shopkeepers and homeowners.

The class-conscious, materialistic, apolitical stance of the Jordan family, typical of the German petite bourgeoisie of this period, accounts for their friendship with a Nazi book dealer, and their fear of alienating people in the Party. Bruno Jordan, whose contribution to the socialist organization *Rote Hilfe* (Red Help) was to make him vulnerable to SA leader Rudi Arendt's blackmail attempt, does not actively seek membership in the National Socialist party. Instead, he becomes a member when his rowing team, along with the rest of the town's sports clubs, is taken over by the Nazi party. Bruno Jordan's opportunistic acquiescence in the National Socialist program contrasts with his wife's more sceptical stance. Charlotte's doomsday prophesizing, which earns her the name Cassandra, also makes her less enthusiastic about National Socialist policies. She curses Hitler when her husband is called up; she prophesies in 1944 that Germany has lost the war, precipitating a visit by the Gestapo; after the war, in an echo from "Change of Perspective," she calls Hitler " 'that goddamned lousy criminal' " (*PoC* 167). Granted, her rancor against the Führer arises from self-interest; still she is the only one with the courage to articulate a dangerous minority viewpoint. Her assessment of the war situation is an example of clairvoyance as Wolf will define it in *Cassandra*: the ability to predict the future based on an undeluded appraisal of the present. Yet only in retrospect can the narrator see her mother's lack of sympathy with the National Socialist cause.

On the whole, Nelly's parents are presented as hard-working, decent people. Her father's horror at the news that his troop had "executed" Polish hostages while he was on leave and her mother's clandestine help to a pregnant Ukranian worker exonerate them from direct complicity with the Hitler regime. Nelly's uncle, Emil Dunst, on the other hand, makes himself morally culpable by using Nazi racist politics for economic gain: in 1937 he acquires a candy factory far below fair market price from a Jew forced to emigrate. Yet Emil Dunst, a prime example of German memory loss, maintained after the war that the Jew was

just an old man, on his way out, who was glad to be able to get away. He was grateful to me, if you want to know the truth, really grateful ... Some things may have happened, they may have, that weren't quite on the level, but not with me, with me, never. Folks like us didn't know what was going on, and if anyone has a clear conscience, that's me, I'm the one, yes, sir.

(*PoC* 150)

This ability to clear his conscience makes Emil Dunst the only character the narrator names who would have been capable of carrying out the "final solution." Reading the notes of Auschwitz Commandant Rudolf Hoess, the narrator concludes that Emil Dunst could have played a role in this book ... He would have qualified. You remember how he used to pronounce certain words. Dirty Polacks! Jew bastards! Russian swine! He fitted every aspect of the extermination machine which Hoess was describing. (*PoC* 242)

After the war Charlotte Jordan is asked by a released concentration camp inmate: "Where on earth have you all been living?" when she expresses disbelief that he could have been imprisoned merely for being a communist. And a year and a half later, an emaciated Bruno Jordan, just released from a Soviet prisoner of war camp, asks: "What have they done to us?" (*PoC* 39). Wolf's portrayal of the Jordan family begs the reader to pose the question of individual moral responsibility: "How could you *allow* them to do this to you?" Despite Wolf's careful differentiation of the private personae of her characters, there is an overriding conformity in their public personae. They are unwilling to know what is going on in the political arena and they want to obliterate the immediate human ramifications of state policy: the persecution of the Jews, concentration camps, the meaning of the "final solution." What one refuses to know, one cannot forget.

The question as to how the wartime generation learned to refuse to know is one of Wolf's chief concerns in examining her own past. She sheds light on the socialization processes that induced conformity and compliance in the child Nelly. From the outset it is explicit that Nelly "has been accustomed to obedience" (*PoC* 6) and that "somewhere along the road she has learned that obeying and being loved amount to one and the same thing" (*PoC* 14–15). In reexamining her past the narrator discovers that she must relinquish her false memory of a happy childhood.

Swiss psychologist Alice Miller's studies on childrearing closely parallel Wolf's literary examination of childhood. According to Miller, "there is one taboo that has withstood all the recent efforts at demystification: the idealization of mother love."[61] Wolf consciously violates this taboo in *Patterns of Childhood*. Relating her initial difficulties in writing, the narrator describes a scene she has imagined: on a table she saw a manuscript with the single word "mother" on the first page. She fears that her dead mother will be hurt by what she will write. The narrator is aware of the psychological ramifications of treating this taboo subject; she consciously expresses this when she says that parental love, like conjugal love, is sacrosanct. Her brother Lutz also articulates this taboo when he cautions her to respect the limits in regard to her parents, that is, warns her against speaking the unspeakable. Presumably this is the reason the narrator did not write the book during her mother's lifetime. It is no accident that she starts to write when she herself is the same age her mother was at the end of the war (forty-five) and her daughter is approximately the same age the narrator was when the Hitler regime collapsed and brought about the devaluation of self that triggered a psychological crisis in Nelly.[62]

In portraying the specificity of women's experience in *Patterns of Childhood*, the narrator focuses on the mother–daughter relationship. She depicts three generations of mother–daughter interaction, although the relationship between Whiskers Grandma and Charlotte is sketchy. As Margarete Mitscherlich has pointed out, in the consciousness of all the bourgeois families described in *Patterns of Childhood*, "the patriarchal social order and the apotheosis of the man were totally accepted. Unconsciously, however, the man in the family tends to be experienced as weak, even ludicrous."[63] It is certainly true, as Mitscherlich indicates, that Nelly's father is less mature than her mother; the same holds true for Nelly's maternal grandparents, Whiskers Grandpa and Whiskers Grandma.[64] The women are portrayed as stronger than the men. It is also true that of all the characters, the narrator's mother alone possesses the prerequisites for what is commonly called conscience. She alone has the capacity to identify emotionally with people completely different from herself. Her high opinion of her mother makes the narrator's criticism of her even more traumatic.

The narrator's fear of hurting her mother is well founded, for one of the things Nelly will have to reproach Charlotte with is her failure "to find out about her daughter's inner self" (*PoC* 23). By failing to accept Nelly in her own right, by projecting her own needs onto her daughter, Charlotte Jordan fails to treat Nelly as a subject. Thus *Patterns of Childhood*, like *Christa T.*, treats the theme of knowing (*kennen*) and being known (*gekannt werden*), a theme that will sound again in *No Place on Earth*. Indeed, it seems that an important reason for writing *Patterns of Childhood* is to ensure that the narrator does not repeat the fate of her grandfather. At his deathbed Nelly had wept not "for Hermann Menzel's death, but for the fact that he hadn't found the chance to know himself and to be known by others" (*PoC* 386).

By failing to accept Nelly for herself, Charlotte Jordan crushes her daughter's spontaneity. She effectively silences her. When Nelly's jealousy of her brother translates itself into overt action and she dislocates his arm, Nelly's mother warns her it will be her fault if his arm remains stiff. Later, when the injury turns out to be a trifle, "not a word is said about the culprit who caused the dislocation. Nelly is alone with her parents' good graces. Her anguish is being rewarded with cocoa and hot buns, while Lutz, the absent victim, has to stay in the hospital for observation. She quickly learns the lesson: to rejoice in undue praise. She catches on" (*PoC* 19).

Not only does Nelly receive undue praise, she also receives unwarranted punishment. After having been betrayed by her best friend Helmut Waldin, Nelly, instead of being consoled, is thrashed with a carpet beater by her mother. Charlotte, who had witnessed Nelly's unsuccessful attempts to seek recourse with Helmut's father, Police Chief Waldin, beats her daughter without giving her a chance to explain. Her actions arise out of her own fears: it is dangerous to be on bad terms with the police chief. In the face of such injustice, Nelly remains mute. Thus both undue praise and undue censure act as silencing devices.

One element of Nelly's silence concerns her feelings. She has been taught that she must keep her negative emotions from her parents.

Nelly had the disconsolate feeling that even the good Lord insisted on the brave, truthful, intelligent, obedient, and most of all happy, child she pretended to be during the day. Words like "sad" or "lonely" have no place in the vocabulary of the child of a happy family; as a result the child starts early to assume the difficult task of sparing his parents. To spare them misfortune and shame. (*PoC* 23)

To ensure that they are spared, the child does not speak about anything important, about anything that affects her. Instead of real communication, platitudinous chatter prevails. The dissembling child hides herself.

Having rattled the skeletons in her childhood closet, the narrator, overcome by fear of what she has unearthed, feels the ground moving underfoot. Yet she also recognizes that the child she left behind on 29 January 1945, when her family started their flight west, may well "have been more deeply hidden under the thinner layers of years than she is today, as she begins to stir, independent of certain promptings" (*PoC* 24). This unprompted stirring is testimony to the fact that the narrator's probings are reactivating areas formerly closed to memory.

Reflecting on the psychological impediments to violating taboos, the narrator asks:

Who wouldn't wish to have had a happy childhood? Anyone who stirs up his childhood, can't expect to make rapid progress . . . He can be assured of the guilt feelings inherent in actions that are contrary to nature: it is natural for children to thank their parents all their lives for the happy childhood they have given them, and not to touch it. Thanking? Language behaves as expected, and derives "thinking," "bethinking," "thanking" from the same root. So that investigative bethinking, and the emotion inevitably prompted by it, can, in case of need, also be taken for the "expression of a thankful state of mind" – though a better term might exist.   (*PoC* 25)

The narrator's desire for a happy childhood parallels her mother's desire for a happy marriage and family life. Yet whereas Charlotte Jordan sustains the myth of a happy marriage in the face of serious marital problems, the narrator at last calls her happy childhood into question. Her idealized mother love is severely tested by Charlotte Jordan's actions in 1945, when, confronted by the imminent invasion of the Red Army, she at the last moment decides to abandon her children rather than her possessions. Sending Nelly and Lutz on in the truck with the rest of her family, Charlotte returns to her house instead of bringing her children to safety. While she can find mitigating circumstances for Charlotte's actions, a nagging question still remains: "You have to ask yourself whether such extreme situations do indeed reveal a person's greatest values, irrefutably, conclusively" (*PoC* 26). The undeniable fact remains that Nelly's mother abandoned her children – a fact that is stated by the narrator: "The way Nelly's mother acted in January 1945, during the 'flight,' when, at the last minute, she did not abandon her house but rather her children, has of course given you much food for thought" (*PoC* 25–6).

The acumen of Wolf's presentation of childhood is substantiated by Alice Miller's psychological studies of childrearing. In her first two books, *The Drama of the Gifted Child: How Narcissistic Parents Form and Deform the Emotional Lives of Their Talented Children* (1979) and in *For Your Own Good: Hidden Cruelty in Child-Rearing and the Roots of Violence* (1980),[65] Miller discusses the consequences of the type of parental behavior manifested by Charlotte Jordan. The original English title of her first book, *Prisoners of Childhood*, is a graphic description of her theory and points to the concerns Wolf and Miller share.

Miller posits a neutral, value-free definition of the term "narcissistic." "Healthy narcissism" characterizes someone who is able to experience his true feelings, culminating in "the ideal case of a person who is genuinely alive, with free access to the true self and his authentic feelings."[66] Miller argues that parents who project their needs onto a child are narcissistically wounded adults who themselves were not accepted for themselves in their childhood. These parents, prisoners of their childhood, perpetuate narcissistic dysfunctioning by training their child to accommodate to parental needs. Thus the child is not taken seriously as a subject in its own right, but is objectified as the projection of its parents' needs. Those individuals who are not taken seriously in childhood learn to hide their true emotions as adults. This dissociation from one's emotions leads to self-alienation, which manifests itself in psychological dysfunctioning. If one is loved not for what one is but for qualities one possesses, then it follows that depression will ensue when these qualities, such as intelligence, beauty, youth, are on the wane or are in some way jeopardized.

Two aspects of Miller's argument are of particular relevance to Christa Wolf's concerns. The first is that the child's fear of losing love brings about a readiness to conform that results in a loss of spontaneity and individuality. A serious consequence of early emotional adaptation, according to Miller, "is the impossibility of consciously experiencing certain feelings of his own (such as jealousy, envy, anger, loneliness, impotence, anxiety) either in childhood or later in adulthood."[67] A "false," "as-if" self, geared to anticipating and meeting parental needs,[68] emerges from the repression. The "loss" of the authentic self, as described by Miller, is directly applicable to Nelly's situation in *Patterns of Childhood*.

This split into a false and a true self would also help explain the "hexing" game Nelly played with Lieselotte Barnow in which they changed themselves into repulsive creatures:

into a frog, a snake, a toad, a bug, a witch, a pig, a newt, a slug. Never a higher being, always vermin, living in filth and mud, fighting each other tooth and nail. Scratched up and filthy, they'd come home in the evenings, let themselves be scolded and told to stop. The parents of the Frog Prince had also sat by and watched their beautiful golden-haired son turn into a slimy disgusting frog under their very eyes – which the son must certainly have wished to do, deep down. (*PoC* 24)

The hexing game allows Nelly to rebel against the image of the dutiful daughter imposed upon her by her mother. This rebellion in the realm of fantasy corresponds to one of the turning points in the therapy of the narcissistically disturbed patient: the recognition that the love he had obtained as a child was an illusion, that he had not been loved for who he was, but for what he was, for his beauty and achievements.

In analysis, the small and lonely child that is hidden behind his achievements wakes up and asks: "What would have happened if I had appeared before you, bad, ugly, angry, jealous, lazy, dirty, smelly? Where would your love have been then? And I was all these things as well. Does this mean that it was not really me whom you loved, but only what I pretended to be? The well-behaved, reliable, empathic, understanding, and convenient child, who in fact was never a child at all? What became of my childhood? Have I not been cheated out of it? I can never return to it. I can never make up for it. From the beginning I have been a little adult. My abilities – were they simply misused?"[69]

Nelly's acting out of attributes excluded by her parentally imposed self-image serves as a hedge against conformity. As for Christa T., so too for Nelly Jordan: imagination, the playing with the possibilities open to us, has a liberating function. It also facilitates the narrator's work of mourning for her false childhood self as an adult and the (re)creation of an authentic self.

A second striking parallel between Miller's and Wolf's work lies in Miller's assertion that the person not taken seriously as a child is incapable of loving others, because he cannot love himself as he really is. "And how," she asks, "could a person do that, if, from the very beginning, he has had no chance to experience his true feelings and to learn to know himself."[70] The connection Miller makes between self-knowledge, self-acceptance, and the ability to love is one that Wolf implies in *Patterns of Childhood* and explicitly states in *No Place on Earth*, "Self-Experiment," and *Cassandra.*

While both Wolf and Miller seek to accomplish similar tasks – the confrontation with and mourning for the childhood self, the striving for psychic integration – each chooses means of dealing with the past consonant with her chosen métier. Wolf, the writer, invents a narrator who writes about her experiences; Miller, whose first book is primarily addressed to the psychoanalytic community (which she considers particularly prone to the narcissistic disturbance she describes), advocates therapy as a vehicle for becoming whole, authentic, and vital. In both cases an essential component of their treatment and recovery is making the private public. By writing (Wolf) and by speaking (Miller), these women break the silence; they find a voice.

The similarities between Wolf and Miller are all the more startling in that their works are quite independent of each other. *Patterns of Childhood* appeared three years before Miller's first book. Yet despite the strong similarities between the two, significant differences do exist. Miller's focus is on the individual;

Wolf's criticism is more broadly based. Wolf portrays the petite bourgeoisie as a whole as conformist, subservient to an ideal of respectability, and dependent on the opinion of their social group. Exaggerated fear about what the neighbors will think often motivates behavior. This desire to conform manifests itself linguistically in a predilection for proverbial sayings. Charlotte Jordan embodies the German propensity for sententious adages. Use of such prefabricated and generalizing language robs an individual situation and the emotions associated with it of their uniqueness.

These conformist tendencies are perhaps most clearly manifested in Bruno Jordan. When Bruno is made a Party member through his sports club, the narrator attributes to both parents the following sentiments: happiness "composed of the following elements: relief (the unavoidable step has been taken without having had to be taken on one's own); a clear conscience (the membership in this comparatively harmless organization – the Navy storm troops – could not have been refused without consequences. What consequences? That's too precise a question); the bliss of conformity." It is specifically about her father, however, that the narrator says: "it isn't everybody's thing to be an outsider, and when Bruno Jordan had to choose between a vague discomfort in the stomach and the multi-thousand-voice roar coming over the radio, he opted, as a social being, for the thousands and against himself" (*PoC* 42–3). Thus conformity is seen in increasingly negative terms in Christa Wolf's work, while the role of the outsider assumes ever more positive attributes. In *No Place on Earth* and *Cassandra*, the status of the outsider will once again be redefined.

Bruno Jordan's acquiescence in Nazism conveyed itself clearly to Nelly. In a description that reveals an astute understanding of mass psychology, told from the perspective of the five-year-old child, the narrator relates the electrifying excitement created by the expected visit of the Führer and captures the emotional impact of such an event for Nelly. In retrospect, however, the narrator must ask herself how the five-year-old not only knew,

but felt what the Führer was. The Führer was a sweet pressure in the stomach area and a sweet lump in the throat, which she had to clear to call out for him, the Führer, in a loud voice in unison with all the others, according to the urgings of a patrolling sound truck ... Nelly could neither understand nor remember what was being talked about, but she took in the melody of the mighty chorus, whose many single shouts were building up toward the gigantic roar into which they were meant to break, finally, in a display of powerful unity. Although it frightened her a little, she was at the same time longing to hear the roar, to be part of it. She longed to know how it felt to be at one with all, to see the Führer.   (*PoC* 45)

Nelly Jordan's experiences differ sharply from Christa T.'s. The counterpart to this scene in *Christa T.* is the expulsion of the gypsies. Whereas Christa T. had psychologically distanced herself from the townspeople, Nelly seeks to merge with them. The gypsy incident had initiated Christa T.'s awareness of self in opposition to others; in the Hitler scene Nelly seeks to obliterate her individuality in the crowd. Thus Wolf establishes Nelly as far more ego-identified with the Hitler regime than was Christa T. This would also account for their very different reactions at the collapse of the National Socialist state. While Christa T., hearing the fanatical voice demanding "loyalty, loyalty to the Führer, even unto death" on the flight west, suddenly understands that "that is what it was all about, and this is how it must end" (*CT* 19) and refuses to salute or sing the German anthem any more, Nelly Jordan *is* willing to swear undying loyalty to the Führer.

Family pressure on Nelly to conform is compounded by the tendency of her society under Hitler to hide, forget, or otherwise distort everyday reality. A conspiracy of silence is formed around forbidden topics. Just as Bruno Jordan does not pursue the possible consequences of refusing membership in the Navy storm troops, people "forgot" or "didn't know about" the concentration camps – even though Nelly recalls euphemisms for them such as "concert hall" and even though the founding of Dachau was reported in the local Nazi paper, as was news of the beatings of Jews, the burning of Communist flags, and the boycott of Jewish shopkeepers and professions. In some cases the use of "glitter words" signal to Nelly that a taboo subject is being mentioned. In her perception such words cause the eyes of the adult using them to glitter. Nelly, taught to anticipate the needs of her parents, is so adept at spotting these words, and at interpreting the message being communicated, that she refrains from asking about them. Among the glitter words the narrator mentions are: "not normal," "oversexed," "consumption," "alien blood," "sterilization," "venereal disease," "hereditary illness" (*PoC* 57–60), all words in some way connected either with sexuality or with the Nazi eugenics program (also reported in the *General-Anzeiger*). Sex is taboo in the Jordan household (Nelly must seek enlightenment from the more open Aunt Lucie); so too is Nazi policy, of which one did not necessarily approve but which one also did not contest. By including the psychiatrist's assessment of Adolf Eichmann as one of the most "normal" people he had ever met, the narrator forces the reader to review the term "not normal."

If some topics are mentioned obliquely, there are others about which strictest silence prevails. One of these is the burning of the Communist flag at the Hindenburgplatz, to which normally garrulous and open Aunt Lucie never alludes, even though as a resident of that neighborhood she must have witnessed the flag-burning rally. Another is the help extended to the pregnant *Ostarbeiterin* (woman "laborer from beyond the Eastern border," *PoC* 66) by Nelly's mother and grandmother. When Charlotte is asked to help the woman, Aunt Emmy brusquely sends Nelly away. Not until long after the war does Nelly learn that the women had sent pieces of linen and rags as swaddling. So strong is the conspiracy of silence that no one, not even Charlotte Jordan, ever asks about the infant, which probably died in the barracks, nor does the Ukranian woman ever mention it.

The fact that twelve-year-old Nelly, by nature inquisitive, does not insist on pursuing the truth, leads the narrator to ponder how a child's natural curiosity can be suppressed – whether curiosity diminishes when left unsatisfied for a long time; whether it is possible to numb a child's curiosity totally; finally, whether the implied ability to do so might not be an answer to the question about "what enables human beings to live under dictatorships: that they learn to restrict their curiosity to realms that are not dangerous to them [since] all learning is based on memory" (*PoC* 67). Clearly the mechanism the narrator describes here is one of (self-)censorship, a form of repression Wolf practiced. The narrator had been pursuing this line of thought in order to determine why Nelly told no one about the maid's admission that her family were Communists and that she had wept when the Communist leaders had been forced to burn their own flags. She decides that Nelly might have been reluctant to pass on the information because she knew that adults were avoiding the word "Communist." Wolf here presents a remarkably accurate account of inhibition conditioning.

This is most succinctly presented in the narrator's recollection of the shocked look on her mother's face in response to the statement that the Russians in the men's foreign laborers' barracks were "dying like flies."

(The expression was used. Nelly must have heard it: "like flies.") The only reply to this sentence was a dark shocked look from her mother. Not a word. Nelly knows what is expected of her. She plays deaf and dumb. And

that's what she became. Only the memory of her mother's look, a look
without a context. (*PoC* 68)

The context is furnished on her visit to Poland. Her unsuccessful
search for the site of the former labor camp brings the narrator a
sudden, unexpected answer to a fundamental question of her
investigation: how much people knew: "Suddenly you know that
everyone knew. Suddenly a wall to one of the well-sealed vaults of
memory breaks down. Snatches of words, murmured sentences, a
look – all kept from re-creating an incident which one would have
had to have understood. Dying like flies" (*PoC* 69).

When she reaches school age, Nelly readily transfers her desire
to please from her parents to her authoritarian teachers. She
particularly loves her anti-Semitic religion teacher, Herr Warsinski, whose internalization of Nazi propaganda manifests itself in
the interspersion of Hitler slogans ("'Within a hundred years the
swastika will become the life blood of the German nation'"; "'The
athletically disciplined person of either sex is a citizen of the
future'"; *PoC* 99, 100) into everyday speech. He inculcates guilt in
his students by pointing to the discrepancy between the noble
self-sacrifice of the Führer, who works without pause for Reich and
Volk, and their own slovenly behavior. He also makes blas-
phemous statements such as "Jesus Christ would be a follower of
our Führer were he once again to walk this earth" (*PoC* 102) and
articulates such decidedly non-Christian teachings as "[a] German
girl must be able to hate, Herr Warsinksi said: Jews and Communists and other enemies of the people. Jesus Christ, Herr Warsinski
said, would today be a follower of the Führer and would hate the
Jews" (*PoC* 128). Nelly readily obeys when Herr Warsinski orders
her to exercise her weak arm muscles in order to sustain the Hitler
salute for the hundred seconds it takes to sing the "Deutschland"
and "Horst Wessel" songs. She is desolate when he fails to notice.
Nelly is certain that "all her accomplishments mean absolutely
nothing to Herr Warsinski, whereas he disapprovingly notices
every one of her shortcomings" and "perhaps not consciously,
increases her efforts to guess Herr Warsinski's expectations of her"
(*PoC* 99–100).

The narrator portrays Nelly's first school year as a process of
increasing conformity with a concurrent movement toward deception. Well versed in the German way of loving, Nelly had idealized
her teacher as completely truthful, and her faith is called into

question by the orthography lesson. She cannot understand why Herr Warsinski should insist that the Führer be spelled with a capital "F" since according to him the rules for capitalization dictate that everything in the German language that can be seen or touched be capitalized, "and in Nelly's experience neither quality pertains to the Führer." Rather than admit the pedagogical short-comings of his explanation, Herr Warsinski ridicules his student, encouraging the entire class to laugh at her. Her parents, instead of challenging the teacher, concur in his assessment of Nelly as a "dum-dum." The geranium pots are her last act of defiance; she throws five of them from the nursery window in rebellion against Herr Warsinski. But Nelly soon learns to conform to his inconsistent teaching, capitalizing "the noun 'rage' even though rage can neither be seen nor touched nor heard nor smelled nor tasted." Her compliance, perceived as "finally listening to reason" (*PoC* 92), causes the narrator to speculate about "what has happened to reason throughout the decades, reason as grounds for approval. Reason as the damper. A regulating mechanism which, once installed, stubbornly insists on flashing the 'happiness' signal only under certain reasonable conditions ... A reasonable child gets kissed good night" (*PoC* 91).

What honesty had not brought her – recognition and acceptance – lying does. Nelly is conditioned to believe that "all the things that had gone wrong up to then righted themselves if one just held one's own for once and lied. The good Lord had no objection. He meted out no punishments; if anything, he rewarded you. He did, however, insist that one repeat the feat. That one did it again and again, and always for the same reason: out of pride" (*PoC* 116). Thus Nelly's familial experiences are repeated at school. Conditioned to conform, Nelly deceives, putting forth a false self and hiding her true self more and more. The socialization process described in *Patterns of Childhood*, its education to mendacity, its perversion of reason and of the liberating functions of spontaneity and imagination, is a biting indictment of Nelly's society and its authoritarian childrearing practices.

Perhaps the most poignant example of Nelly's repression of her true emotions is her reaction to the fire in the synagogue during *Kristallnacht*. Nelly, for once allowing her innate curiosity to surface, had visited the synagogue. The tension between her spontaneous human reactions and the caution to which she has been conditioned are brought forth in the following passages:

Nelly couldn't help it: the charred building made her sad. But she didn't know she was feeling sad, because she wasn't supposed to feel sad. She had long ago begun to cheat herself out of her true feelings. It is a bad habit, harder than any other to reverse. It stays with you and can only be caught, and be forced to retreat, step by step. Gone, forever gone, is the beautiful free association between emotions and events ... It wouldn't have taken much for Nelly to have succumbed to an improper emotion: compassion. But healthy German common sense built a barrier against it: fear.

(*PoC* 160–1)

Compassion was not a new emotion for Nelly. It was something she had experienced while watching a member of her Hitler Youth group be reprimanded. In both cases the repression of spontaneous empathy results in its distortion into hate, guilt, and fear, emotions inextricably bound to her childhood. The narrator deliberates on the negative effects of this:

You realize that the emotions which you have suppressed will take revenge, and you understand their strategy to the last detail: they apparently withdraw, taking related emotions with them. Now it's no longer just the sadness, the pain that are nonexistent but regret and, above all, memory, as well. Memory of homesickness, sadness, regret ... Emotions are not yet fused with words: in the future emotions will not be governed by spontaneity but – no use avoiding the word – by calculation. (*PoC* 275)

Whereas Nelly loved Herr Warsinski, she admired and sought to emulate her history and German teacher, Dr Juliane Strauch. ("Among the women she knew, not one led a life Nelly would have wished or might have imagined for herself: except Julia" *PoC* 221.) Presumably Nelly chooses Julia Strauch as a role model because she is the only female intellectual she encounters. She is in many ways a walking contradiction: decidedly non-Aryan in appearance (short, dark-haired with pronounced Slavic features), she espouses Aryan ideology and seeks to reconcile appearance and essence by calling attention to a "consequence of European history," namely that "as the result of an unfortunate godforsaken mixture of the noblest blood with the vilest ... pure Germanic thinking and feeling could often be found in persons whose exterior appearance didn't permit such an assumption: in short, that a Germanic soul was hidden inside such persons" (*PoC* 220). Unmarried, she violates the Nazi ideal of woman as mother and, as Nelly perceives, despises her own sex – a perhaps understandable sentiment, given the severe limitations placed on women during this period.

There are numerous indications that Dr Juliane Strauch is based on the same model as the class teacher in *Christa T.* In a conversation with Julia, Nelly mentions Christa T., "the new girl from the Friedeberg area, who didn't show off and had no need for Julia, and from whom Nelly had just extorted the halfhearted promise that she would write to her during the Christmas vacation" (*PoC* 227). The narrator has already fixed the narrated time as the winter of 1944–5, which coincides with the meeting between Christa T. and the narrator in the earlier work. In speaking of Julia, the narrator of *Patterns of Childhood* uses images and vocabulary taken from Christa T. The image of Julia strictly supervising the class during break in the schoolyard coincides with that of the class teacher in *Christa T.*, while her long strides and "her stockings darned way up her calves" (*PoC* 223) and Nelly's "sneaking suspicion that Julia might be calculating" (*PoC* 228) are direct quotations from *Christa T.*[71]

Another indication that the narrator of *Patterns of Childhood* is identical with the narrator of *Christa T.*[72] is their common response to Nazi fanatic Horst Binder, who has a crush on Nelly. Binder, whose murder of his parents and subsequent suicide is alluded to in *Christa T.*, is fleshed out in *Patterns of Childhood*. Indeed, the narrator invents in detail the description of the double murder and suicide. Binder's pathological emulation of Hitler, described in some detail, has comic overtones and induces Nelly to toy with her smitten admirer. Repulsed by him, Nelly is also attracted to him. Her ambivalence toward Binder is a not uncommon response for Nelly during the Third Reich.

By the time she meets Julia Strauch, Nelly has become adept at currying favor. In order to impress, she distinguishes herself both politically, by taking on a leadership position in the Hitler Youth, and academically, through her German compositions. While writing, she is at all times aware of her audience. The dutiful daughter has become the model student. "A touch of deceit permeated every line; she had described her family as just a trifle too idyllic and herself as just a trifle too virtuous: exactly the way she thought Julia wished to see her" (*PoC* 224). Nelly, who in this regard bears a striking resemblance to Christa T.'s students, has become a shrewd strategist. She knows that "in order to win Julia over – or to deceive her, which seemed to amount to the same thing – she had to refrain from blunt maneuvers and ensnare the demanding teacher, who was not easily flattered, in a web of the subtlest weave: looks, gestures, words, lines that lay within a hair's breadth of her true emotions' without ever fully blending with them" (*PoC* 225). Nelly's machinations prove successful: Julia selects her as a confidante, seeks her advice on class matters, encourages her to reflect about her own friendships, gives her private lessons, invites her over to her house, and finally, by admitting to the special status of their relationship ("Well, you and I know what we mean to each other, don't we?" *PoC* 228), acknowledges that Nelly has succeeded in her courtship.

Yet Nelly's first experience of requited love is an ambivalent one, experienced at once as a deep affinity and as a sense of captivity, a sentiment doubtless arising from the fact that she is not loved for herself, but for her teacher's image of her, to which she must conform. In her interaction with Julia, her deceit and her consciousness of it allows her to sustain a sense of authenticity in spite of her intense devotion. Reflecting on this issue, the narrator ponders whether "the deceit, and the fact that she remained conscious of it, as much as her longing for truthfulness, was this perhaps some form of salvation? A vestige of independence, which she was able to resume later?" (*PoC* 224).

Nelly's self-consciousness ultimately leads to a split in self, which causes one part of her to watch and judge the other part incessantly. Presumably it is this alienation that in turn prevents total self-abnegation and unquestioning acceptance of Nazi policy. Nelly is, after all, able to reject the *Lebensborn* (Well of Life) eugenics program and to condemn the actions of Christine Torstenson, a fictional character who during the Thirty Years' War intentionally contracts the plague in order to transmit the disease sexually to the enemy camp. In both instances Nelly is caught between conflicting ideologies: on the one hand the bourgeois ethos of respectability (embodied in her mother) mandates against sexual licentiousness in women, on the other hand the political ethos of total subservience to the state or a cause calls for sexual surrender. Speaking of Nelly's conflicting emotions when confronted with *Lebensborn*, the narrator notes that "it was one of those rare, precious, and inexplicable instances when Nelly found herself in conscious opposition to the required convictions she would have liked to share." Feeling guilty for not being able to conform, Nelly at the time could not "have known that bearing guilt was, under the prevailing conditions, a necessary requirement for inner freedom" (*PoC* 223). This becomes apparent to the narrator only in retrospect, as she explores the parameters of self-expression under totalitarianism.

Through the figure of her daughter, Lenka, the narrator is able to examine whether childhood experience is universal or historical, that is generational. While some patterns of behavior, such as reluctance on the part of children to hear secret or painful experiences from their parents' past and a fondness for political songs, seem to perpetuate themselves from one generation to another, heartening changes in the mother–daughter interaction are discernible in the narrator's relationship to Lenka compared with the Charlotte–Nelly relationship. The narrator had contended that in order to understand Rudolf Hoess, one first had to understand his father; the same applies to Lenka and to herself. The narrator's experiences have made her very different from her mother. Both she and Lenka reject Charlotte's notion that the child should be transparent to the mother. The narrator allows and respects her daughter's privacy. In contrast to Charlotte she is nonjudgmental and aware of the dangers of imposing her morality upon her child. She does not attempt to make Lenka conform to her values but rather appears to encourage her daughter's individualism. It remains unclear to what degree the differences in Lenka's responses are due to different childrearing practices or to the socialization process of the new socialist regime. For her, however, the vocabulary of nationalism has been devalued. Thus the word *Heimat*, a term whose closest English equivalent, "homeland," does not capture the sentimental overtones of the original, has no meaning for her. She substitutes the word *Zuhause* (home), which for her connotes a few people: "Where those few people are, that's home" (*PoC* 120) for the term *Heimat* with its connotations of blood and soil. Thus the concept of being-at-home is not defined geographically but in terms of relationships.

Lenka's respect for the individual is apparent in her rejection of songs that extinguish the "I" in favor of an exalted "we." Clearly more self-sufficient and independent than her mother was at her age, she is unafraid of being out of step with the majority. The idea of currying favor with a teacher is "idiotic." Her perception of moral issues is also markedly different from her mother's, as witnessed by her reaction to the picture of the American GI holding a gun to the temple of an old Vietnamese woman. Accustomed to seeing the atrocities of war, Lenka is not interested in what motivates a murderer, but how the photographer can witness this scene without intervening and still carry out his professional duties. Her demand for "unconditional involvement" is an indirect indictment of the failure of the German people to intervene during the Third Reich.

In Lenka, Wolf creates a figure who is at once a critic of her society and a product of it. Unlike Nelly at her age, Lenka is politically astute and more independent in her thinking. In her insistence on the integrity of the individual in the community, in her absolutist moral stance, she calls to mind Christa T. Like Christa T., Lenka embodies the principle of hope; like her, she serves as a reminder of the discrepancy between socialist theory and praxis. Her questioning of authority, her rejection of the "pseudo" people (a variation on Christa T.'s "up-and-doing people"), her indignation at the inhuman working conditions at the factory make clear that socialism has not succeeded fully in ameliorating the conditions of the workers and that the danger of inauthenticity continues to be a serious threat to GDR society in the seventies.

These two tenets of Wolf's criticism converge in the story of the double suicide of Lenka's German teacher M. and his girlfriend. The narrator attributes his death to the fact that, like Christa T., he had failed to find a suitable part to play in his society. Similarly, his girlfriend, despite brilliant entrance exams, had inexplicably failed to gain entrance to medical school. Thus the irrationality of her situation parellels that of Manfred Herrfurth in *Divided Heaven*. The lines in Robert Musil's *Man Without Qualities* underlined by M. before returning the book to the narrator: " 'There's only one choice: either to play the game of these vicious times (to travel with the pack), or to become a neurotic. Ulrich chose the latter' " (*PoC* 107) indicate that the need to fight against the pervasive and debilitating conformity was still a relevant issue for the GDR in the seventies.

However positively Lenka is portrayed as an individual, like her mother she is also a member of her generation, a generation that grew up entirely in the post-war period. As such she feels totally dissociated from the German past that is causing the narrator such anguish. It is on the generational level that the narrator presents her criticism of Lenka. She reflects what the consequences will be for a society whose youth cannot fathom the ordinariness of Adolf Eichmann and for whom a map showing the sites of World War II concentration camps has no more resonance than any other historical document. This attitude leads to the offensive behavior of the tourists at Buchenwald who eat their lunches and listen to blaring music while viewing the site of mass murder.

Wolf's social criticism is sharper and more direct in *Patterns of Childhood* than it is in *Christa T.* Her indictment of the GDR not only for its failure to reckon with its Nazi past but also to address the question of Stalinism is a feature that is downplayed by Western critics who accuse her of distorting the truth in favor of the East.[73] Wolf had already obliquely alluded to Stalinism in *Christa T.*, but the allusions to this period are far more numerous and overt in *Patterns of Childhood*. By equating the thirties with the fifties, she explicitly draws a parallel between fascist and Stalinist repression. "What does it mean: to change? To learn to get along without delusions. Not having to evade children's looks that are directed at our generation when – rarely enough – the talk turns to 'back when': back in the thirties, back in the fifties" (*PoC* 147–8). She embeds a seemingly parenthetical reminder that Krezentia Mühsam, wife of the persecuted socialist writer Ernst Mühsam, was interned in a Soviet concentration camp in a discussion of the repressive Pinochet regime in Chile (*PoC* 276–7). She explicitly and repeatedly refers to the 1937 Moscow trials when discussing the communist air attack in retaliation for Guernica (*PoC* 145–7). The result of such juxtapositions is to blur distinctions between fascist(ic) and communist repression. The clearest indication of the force of the social taboo surrounding the Stalin regime is the fact that it, like the Nazi past, has psychosomatic implications for the narrator: a bizarre dream of Stalin's funeral repeatedly interrupts her sleep. "When," the narrator asks herself, "will we start speaking about that, too? To get rid of the feeling that, until we do, everything we say is temporary, that only then would we really begin to speak" (*PoC* 245).

Yet the focus of the entire book, Wolf's exploration of the continuity of fascist behavior in the East German populace (presented most directly in Lenka's story of the anti-Polish song from the Third Reich, sung by her countrymen in Czechoslovakia), is a more subtle, but more pervasive form of criticism, one that calls into question the basis of the GDR's self-legitimization. Moreover, by considering the possibility that all patterns of behavior and perception are irrevocably established during a child's formative years, the narrator also questions a fundamental socialist precept; the individual's ability to change. This challenge is intensified by the fact that we are not made privy to the *process* of the narrator's change of consciousness between 1947 and 1971 (when she returned home) but are instead presented with two conflicting moral systems, embodied in the child Nelly and the adult narrator. Thus in a sense Wolf's autobiographical work again presents us with *Weltbilder*.

Judith Ryan has faulted *Patterns of Childhood* for being excessively ambitious, with framing its questions "in such a way as to make them virtually unanswerable, such as whether one's perceptual patterns are set in the first years of life or are capable of further change."[74] She argues that the dialectic between Nelly Jordan and the narrator essentially fails. "In contrast to the mutual interplay between the perspectives and value systems of Christa T. and her narrator, the relationship between Nelly Jordan and her narrator is simply one where the earlier viewpoint is put into its proper context and corrected by the later one."[75] Ryan's argument that the narrator's judgment of Nelly is too thoroughly consonant with the judgment of current readers to be provocative begs the question about precisely who these "current readers" are. If they are assumed to be Western readers, then Ryan's point is valid. If, however, they are assumed to be GDR readers, or indeed FRG readers of Wolf's generation, then Ryan's reading is problematic. It also overlooks the nonjudgmental tone of the book. The desire of Wolf's narrator to know, that is, to understand and accept the child Nelly, is the personal (and symbolic) expression of a desire to gain a reconciliation with the past. Moreover, *Patterns of Childhood*, like all Wolf's work, is more concerned with posing questions than with offering answers. If the questions are indeed unanswerable, that too is in keeping with the spirit of her writing.

If, as we have seen, this reconciliation remains problematic in the novel, it does not detract from the significance of Wolf's undertaking, which lies not in the outcome but in the process. As Annemarie Auer's reaction shows, the questioning of Wolf's narrator proved provocative for the audience to whom the book was primarily addressed: Wolf's own generation. Aware that the appeal of *Patterns of Childhood* was, by its very nature, more circumscribed than that of other works, Wolf underestimated its appeal for the children of her contemporaries, who gained insights not only into life under Nazism but also into the attitudes of their parents.[76]

Wolf does not conclude with the narrator's equivocation regarding the hegemony of the past. Instead the new first-person narrator abandons her hesitant articulation and projects a future-directed dream vision:

At night I shall see – whether waking, whether dreaming – the outline of a human being who will change, through whom other persons, adults, children, will pass without hindrance. I will hardly be surprised if this outline may also be that of an animal, a tree, even a house, in which anyone who wishes may go in and out at will. Half-conscious, I shall experience the beautiful waking image drifting ever deeper into the dream, into ever new shapes no longer accessible to words, shapes which I believe I recognize. Sure of finding myself once again in the world of solid bodies upon awakening, I shall abandon myself to the experience of dreaming. I shall not revolt against the limits of the expressible.   (*PoC* 407)

Through the dream the narrator is able to articulate potential for change not yet considered possible in empirical reality. The fluid transitions of the human being seen by the narrator (it is unclear whether it is intended as the projection of the narrator herself), the vision's half-real, half-fantastical nature call to mind Gorky's definition of human kind which is so important for Christa T. The dream state allows the transcendence of all the limitations confronting us in the waking state: freedom from patterns, from the boundaries of the self, and from the limits of language.[77] By allowing the same play with open possibilities afforded us by imagination, the open-ended conclusion of *Patterns of Childhood* becomes an expression of hope. It leaves us the possibility that the discontinuous nature of the narrator's biography, appropriately expressed in a discontinuous prose, may sometime in the future be overcome.

5

NO PLACE ON EARTH: REVISION OF THE ROMANTIC HERITAGE

In 1976 Wolf Biermann, the dissident poet and songwriter whose satiric verses had long been a thorn in the side of Party officials and who had been banned from performing in East Germany since 1965, was refused reentry into the GDR after a West German tour. On the following day, 17 November 1976, a group of concerned intellectuals including the writers Stephan Hermlin, Christa Wolf, her husband Gerhard Wolf, and Sarah Kirsch sent an open letter of protest to *Neues Deutschland*, the official Party newspaper, and to the French news agency AFD. Implicitly referring to Honecker's lifting of taboos, they argued that the GDR, having passed out of the initial developmental stages of socialism, was sufficiently established to sustain internal criticism and urged the government to reconsider its sanctions against Biermann. The Biermann petition, the first public group protest in the GDR, met with reprisals ranging in severity from expulsion from the SED (for Gerhard Wolf) to censure by the Party (for Christa Wolf and Hermlin). Two months later, on 20 December, Christa Wolf and other prominent writers including Jurek Becker, Günter de Bruyn, Sarah Kirsch, Ulrich Plenzdorf, and Volker Braun were expelled from the board of directors of the Berlin branch of the writers' union.

Inconsistent as the measures taken against the petitioners were, the message was unequivocal: the Party would not tolerate what it perceived as a public challenge to its authority. *Neues Deutschland* immediately responded to the petition by launching a campaign against Biermann and the critics of his expatriation. Later Klaus Hopcke, the acting minister of culture, underscored the official Party stance by denouncing those who had signed the petition as "enemies of socialism."[1]

For Christa Wolf, Biermann's expatriation and its aftermath was a watershed. The official reaction manifested exactly the dogmatism to which she so vociferously objected. It abruptly curtailed prospects for democratizing the public sphere, which she con-

sidered vital for the development of socialism. The most demoralizing consequence of the Biermann affair for Wolf, however, was
that the Party's reprisals against these dedicated socialists fundamentally challenged the accepted role of the socialist writer-as-
critic. Thus Christa Wolf, who had stressed the socially integrated
role of the socialist writer and who in "The Reader and the Writer"
had emphasized that "the author is an important person,"[2] suddenly found herself relegated to the position of outsider. The
dialectical relationship between literature and socialist society on
which her "epic prose" is based had been definitively negated.
Earlier, Wolf's Nazi childhood had threatened to silence her; the
existential crisis she faced in 1976, the feeling of no longer being
needed by her society, posed a similar threat.

By writing her autobiography in the third person, Wolf had
succeeded in breaking the silence surrounding her National Socialist past. At first glance it appears that her aesthetic response to the
volatile political situation of 1976 was to abandon her concern with
personal history and in *No Place on Earth* (1979) to treat the lives of
two historically distant figures – Heinrich von Kleist and Karoline
von Günderrode. Yet it soon became clear that Wolf focused on
these Romantic writers – outsiders *par excellence* – because she
perceived their situation as analogous to her own at that time. By
historicizing the exigencies of her own situation, by writing a
Künstlerroman about these Romantic poets, she was able to work
through her own crisis.

GDR readers were attuned to the political ramifications of *No
Place on Earth*.[3] In an interview with Frauke Mayer-Gosau for
alternative, a West German Leftist journal, Wolf made the contemporary relevance of her historical narrative explicit for Western
audiences as well. She admitted that her impulse for writing *No
Place on Earth* had been autobiographical and elucidated the
contemporaneity of her text at length:

I wrote *No Place on Earth* in 1977. That was a time when I found myself
obliged to examine the preconditions for failure, the connection between
social desperation and failure in literature. At the time, I was living with
the intense feeling of standing with my back to the wall, unable to take a
proper step. I had to get beyond a certain time when there seemed to be
absolutely no possibility left for effective action.

1976 was a caesura in cultural policy development in our country,
outwardly indicated by Wolf Biermann's expatriation. It led to a polarization of culturally active people in various fields, especially in literature: a
group of authors became aware that their direct collaboration, the kind

that they themselves could answer for and thought was right, was no longer needed. We are socialists after all; we lived as socialists in the GDR because that's where we wanted to be involved, to collaborate. To be utterly cast back on literature brought about a crisis for the individual, an existential crisis. It was the origin, for me among others, of working with the material of such lives as Günderrode's and Kleist's. It wouldn't even have been possible for me to work on the problem with contemporary material. It would have become naturalistic, banal and flat.

I took these two figures in order to rehearse their problems for myself ... That was the compelling impulse. It was self-communication; it was also a kind of self-preservation when the solid ground was pulled out from under my feet ... it was a question of existence altogether.[4]

Thus just as in "The Reader and the Writer" Christa Wolf suggested that Georg Büchner played out the variant of madness in his novella *Lenz* in order to escape it himself, so in *No Place on Earth* she played out the despair and depression that arose from a sense of being superfluous. As with *Patterns of Childhood*, the writing of *No Place on Earth* was therapeutic for Christa Wolf: playing out the variant of suicide allowed Wolf to continue living and writing. Moreover, it apparently enabled her to remain in the East, in contrast to many writers who left the GDR in the wake of Biermann's expatriation.

Clearly, the historical setting of *No Place on Earth* afforded Wolf both the political and the personal distance needed to address volatile issues. Nonetheless, the narrative, like *Christa T.* and *Patterns of Childhood*, is also conceived as a model.[5] The reconstruction of this parabolic text by the reader serves a didactic function: to encourage us to draw connections between the situation of 1804 and contemporary society. Thus the hidden references to Biermann both in the essays and in *No Place on Earth*[6] had particular significance for GDR readers. Yet the issues raised in the narrative are not specific to socialist society. In exploring why some individuals are unable to find a viable mode of existence, Christa Wolf probes the sources of human alienation and destructiveness – issues relevant to all of us.

Of all of Christa Wolf's works, *Kein Ort. Nirgends* (*No Place on Earth*)[7] is the least accessible to readers not thoroughly familiar with the German political and literary tradition. Set in 1804, the narrative reflects the crisis of the progressive German intelligentsia in the face of the Napoleonic wars. The collapse of the French Republic and the disillusionment engendered by the Republic's failure to institute a new social order built on the democratic ideals of *liberté, égalité, fraternité* (ideals that anticipate the goals of the socialist state) precipitated a spiritual crisis in those who had hoped for a more egalitarian society. Coupled with this disillusionment was the sense of alienation brought about in part by the propagation of Enlightenment values of rationality and progress and the exclusion of newer, more subjective, emotional values. In probing for the deep-seated roots of their feeling of homelessness, the Romantics, the literary generation of 1800, isolated as a primary cause the one-sidedness of their culture. Rebelling against the utilitarian ethos of their time, they sought to revitalize their emotionally atrophied society, to reestablish a harmony between intellect and emotion, and to infuse society with their vision through the integrative power of the poetic imagination.

Against this intellectual historical backdrop, Christa Wolf unfolds her *erwünschte Legende* (wished-for legend),[8] the fictitious encounter between the Romantic poets Heinrich von Kleist and Karoline von Günderrode.[9] Wolf's characterization of both Kleist and Günderrode rests on a carefully researched and sensitive understanding of their individual psychology and empathy with their historical and personal situations.[10] A close textual analysis has revealed the authenticity of many of the quotations that constitute the text's dialogues.[11] The majority of these quotations are from the historical Kleist and Günderrode, but are not identified as such in the text.[12] Instead Wolf, by appropriating the exact language of the historical figures for her fictional characters, again blurs generic boundaries (are we to read *No Place on Earth* as historical fiction or as biography?[13]) and the boundaries between art and life.

Wolf's sympathetic portrayal of her protagonists in *No Place on Earth* ran counter to the attitude then prevalent toward Kleist in the GDR. It thus tackled a controversial issue of literary reception of presocialist German literature. Until recently reception of German Romanticism[14] in general and of Heinrich von Kleist in particular was dictated by George Lukács's aesthetic of realism. Goethe, lauded by Lukács for his harmonious representational art, was accepted into the presocialist literary canon, but Kleist was seen as his antipode. Kleist's subjectivism was deemed solipsism; he was written off by Lukács as reactionary and decadent.[15] Using Goethe and Kleist as representative types, Lukács, in keeping with Goethe's dictum "The Classical is healthy, the Romantic is sick,"[16] rejected Romanticism *per se* as pernicious. The repudiation of Romanticism by the grand old man of Marxist criticism, coupled with the corruption of certain tenets of Romantic thought in National Socialist *völkisch* ideology, assured that this movement would be rejected out of hand by literary critics of the emerging German socialist state.

As early as 1937 Anna Seghers had taken issue with Lukács's theory of realism and with his assessment of Kleist. She had contested the narrow, mimetically defined basis of his realist aesthetic and called for a more broadly defined concept that would allow the inclusion of subjective factors. Placing the Romantics in their specific historical context, she attributed their immediacy of expression to the "shock effect" that their reality had upon them. She deemed this form of expression the only possible and appropriate response to their situation. Thus for Seghers the subjectivity of the Romantics' *œuvre* was not a solipsistic end in itself; rather, it reflected and expressed their experience of the crisis evoked by the rise of a new epoch. Pointing to the high incidence of insanity and suicide in this literary generation, Seghers implicated their society in the etiology of their illness and death.[17] Among the suicides she mentions are Kleist and Günderrode. It is a clearly established fact that Anna Seghers's broader, experientially based concept of realism inspired Christa Wolf's own aesthetic.[18] It is also obvious that Seghers's assessment of the Romantics in general and of Kleist in particular influenced Wolf's conception of *No Place on Earth*. Anna Seghers, moreover, first introduced Christa Wolf to the works of Günderrode.[19]

Despite the extensive correspondence between Seghers and Lukács that contributed substantially to the long-standing *Realismusdebatte* (debate on literary realism) in the GDR, Seghers's voice went largely unheard. Lukács's assessment of the Romantics prevailed in the GDR until the mid-seventies, when it was challenged by writers, notably Christa Wolf. Thus, *No Place on Earth* can be seen as part of an attempt by members of the socialist literary avant-garde to rehabilitate the Romantics.[20]

The fact that Wolf does not restrict herself to the well-known figure of Kleist, but also includes the perspective of a figure outside the generally known tradition, reveals her intention: not merely to rehabilitate a well-known male figure of the German literary canon but also to recuperate a female writer lost to that tradition. In addition to placing Karoline von Günderrode next to Kleist at the nexus of the narrative of *No Place on Earth*, Christa Wolf was instrumental in having Günderrode's poetic *œuvre* reissued.[21] *Der Schatten eines Traumes* (The Shadow of a Dream, 1979), edited by

Wolf, consists not only of a selection of Günderrode's poems chosen to support her reading of this poet's life, but also of Günderrode's correspondence with friends and the testimony of contemporaries. The introduction Wolf wrote for this volume, "Der Schatten eines Traumes," together with her letter-essay "Nun ja! Das nächste Leben geht aber heute an!" (Yes indeed! But the next life starts today!),[22] written for the recently reissued auto/biography of Günderrode by her friend Bettine von Arnim,[23] testify to Christa Wolf's endeavor to reclaim women writers.

Wolf's interest in the women Romantics reflects her increasing concern with issues of gender and her criticism of patriarchal structures. In "Self-Experiment" (1979) Wolf had first presented the problem of gender relationships and had repudiated dominant male values, leaving to the female protagonist the possibility of creating an alternative way of being in the world, one based not on the male model of acquisition of a monolithic truth but on interpersonal relationship and intimacy. In her essay "Touching" of 1976, her reflections on women's potential for developing viable alternatives were rooted in her belief in the inherent destructiveness of patriarchy caused by instrumental thinking and by the atrophy of human emotions, particularly by male inability to love. This belief also informs her analysis of the Romantics, whom she regards as the precursors of us moderns. Wolf's discussion of the friendship between Karoline von Günderrode and Bettine von Arnim highlights the egalitarian, nonobjectifying interaction of these two very different women, documented above all in Bettine's epistolary novel, *Die Günderode*, and valorizes their caring, reciprocal relationship. Wolf views the unreserved (inter)subjectivity of this friendship as an antidote to the alienation arising from the incipient capitalism and division of labor of the early Romantic period and as a positive model of humane community.

Wolf's essays on Karoline von Günderrode and Bettine von Arnim offer invaluable insights into the text of *No Place on Earth*. Functioning essentially as a commentary on the narrative, they make the opaque text more transparent. In the three works dealing with female German Romantics – *No Place on Earth*, the Günderrode essay, and the Bettine essay – the intertextuality between essays and narrative achieves an unprecedented density. The essays refer not merely to the fictional world of *No Place on Earth* but to the autobiographical and fictional works of Günderrode and Bettine as well and make explicit Wolf's *modus operandi* in the literary text: the incorporation of authentic unidentified citations.

This writing strategy is similar to a technique favored by the Romantics – their montage of unidentified literary citations. For example, Clemens Brentano commonly borrowed from the works of contemporary and earlier writers, and E. T. A. Hoffmann massively appropriated material from other authors in his *Kater Murr*. By following their lead, Wolf is able to replicate romantic writing itself in *No Place on Earth*. Much of the dialogue of *No Place on Earth* is drawn from quotations from Brentano, Savigny, Kleist, and Günderrode. The title of the Günderrode essay, "Shadow of a Dream," is paradigmatic for Wolf's technique. It is, as we are told in the essay, a quotation from a letter of Günderrode's to a woman friend shortly after meeting the lawyer Savigny, enjoining the friend to tell her everything about "S" (Savigny), adding " 'it is after all the only thing I can have from him: the shadow of a dream' " (GE 340). Günderrode's letter to her friend, from which this quotation is taken, is included in Wolf's *Schatten eines Traumes*.[24] The quotation then reappears in *No Place on Earth*. Recalling a dream about Savigny, Günderrode upon waking thinks: "That is all I can have of him: the shadow of a dream" (*NP* 7).

While the incorporation of citations serves to make the text more authentic, it has another function as well: to activate reader participation in the (re)construction of the text. Christa Wolf, by making Günderrode's *œuvre* readily accessible to the reading public (as Kleist's work had always been), not only invites comparisons with her sources, but challenges the initiated reader to decode a hermetic text.[25]

In her essays on Karoline von Günderrode and Bettine von Arnim, Wolf highlights written quotations by Günderrode that are germane to the two most important aspects of her life, on which she focuses in her narrative: her interpersonal relationships and her poetry. Discussing the negative review of Günderrode's poetry in Kotzebue's conservative journal, *Der Freimüthige*, Wolf quotes Günderrode's response to Brentano's query about why she had published her poems: "the pure and alive longing exists in me to articulate my life in an eternal form" (GE 347) – a quotation from her letter of 10 June 1804 to the poet[26] that also appears in Günderrode's important discussion about poetry with Brentano in *No Place on Earth*. Similarly, drawing upon the Bettine–Günderrode correspondence, which is also incorporated into Bettine's *Die Günderode*, Wolf extracts Günderrode's statement that not only through her circumstances, but also through her nature, narrower limits are drawn on her actions than on her friend's (GE 352). This sentiment is articulated by Günderrode in the climactic finale of the narrative, her conversation with Kleist. Here too is found that line from her love poem "Die Einzige" (The One and Only):[27] "to bear that which slays me" (GE 358), which for Christa Wolf so succinctly captures Günderrode's inescapable predicament.

The Günderrode essay also elucidates Günderrode's relationship with Carl Savigny, elaborates upon the significance of the incident in which Günderrode jams Savigny's hand in the carriage door, and quotes in full the poem "The Kiss in the Dream" which Günderrode sent Savigny, along with a rather unambiguous postscripted declaration of love, two weeks before his wedding (GE 346–7) to Gunda Brentano. It makes more explicit than the narrative her untenable situation *vis-à-vis* Savigny and Gunda; quotes Gunda's criticism that it offends Günderrode's feelings to be dependent on anything in the world, not to be "the first and only one in every relationship"; and interprets Savigny's reproach to Günderrode, that she harbors "republican inclinations" (GE 339), as a covert response to Günderrode's attempt to extricate herself from the triangular relationship. Both quotations as well as the one from Savigny's letter to Günderrode in which he asks himself "whether he should believe the rumor which would have her coquettish or proud of a strong masculine spirit" (GE 341) find their way into the text of Wolf's narrative.

The Bettine essay, which deals primarily with the intense relationship between the two women and with Bettine's development, brings a clearer understanding of the significance of Bettine (who plays a secondary role in *No Place on Earth*) for Günderrode. It specifically refers to Günderrode as Bettine's "disciple in inconsequentiality" (BE 402) – a term taken from Bettine's novel *Die Günderode* that appears again in Wolf's narrative – and elaborates upon the importance of such training for someone whose life work aims at being significant.

Wolf's fictional Günderrode, reflecting on Clemens Brentano's reproach that she is arrogant, notes:

Arrogance. In her heart of hearts, where she is ruthless in self-judgment, Günderrode knows that this reproach is not so far off the mark, even if, like most reproaches, it does not get down to the core of the matter. Arrogant, that she is. Just a little while ago, when she was sitting with Bettine in the window alcove and Bettine was speaking to her in her animated way about the genius of the inconsequential, it dawned on Günderrode how necessary this genius was to her, and how necessary

Bettine was to her, in enabling her to dissolve, over and over, that secret feeling of superiority which has always cut her off from other people. The inconsequential! Bettine does not suspect how this word has preyed on her ever since, for the first time, it appeared in one of her letters. (*NP* 72–3)

Thus the essays, which represent the fruits of Christa Wolf's reading of Günderrode's and Bettine's works, especially *Die Günderode*, open up a text that initially seems hermetic.

No Place on Earth has been faulted for being both esoteric and static. While it is true that there is a minimal plot line, the essence of the narrative lies not in what occurs on the level of external action but rather in its exploration of the inner landscape of the two protagonists. The external plot can be summarized as follows. The Prussian writer Heinrich von Kleist, who has suffered a breakdown after burning his most ambitious, uncompleted manuscript, "Robert Guiscard," has found refuge with the physician Wedekind in Mainz in the Rhineland. Wedekind takes him to an afternoon tea at the home of a merchant, Merten, in Winkel on the Rhine. There Kleist meets and interacts with the circle surrounding the poet Clemens Brentano, a member of the early Romantic group centered in Jena. His attention is caught in particular by a young woman peripherally connected to the Brentano circle, Karoline von Günderrode. Günderrode, driven by the desire to see Savigny, to whom she is emotionally attached, has left her convent to attend the tea party. Neither Kleist nor Günderrode wants to attend the gathering; both consider themselves outsiders in the circle of businessmen, politicians, and successful writers. During the course of the afternoon they are drawn together by an intuition of their elective affinity. For one brief moment they transcend the painful isolation of their alienation as they reveal their inner essence to each other.

The complex, constantly shifting narrative perspective moves from Kleist's and Günderrode's interior monologues, the most subjective of figural perspectives, in which characters spontaneously and freely express their most personal thoughts without mediation of a narrator, to "narrated monologue" (*erlebte Rede*),[28] in which the characters' own mental language is again reproduced verbatim but in which the first person is replaced by third-person reference. These monologue forms often merge into dialogue, the unmediated, neutral mode of characterization. And finally, there is an authorial perspective at work which, through its use of the pronoun "we," posits a communality at times with the reader and at times with the two protagonists. This method of converging authorial and figural perspectives underscores the intimate relationship between the two perspectives evoked through the technique of the narrated monologue and points to the interrelatedness of past (figural) and present (authorial) perspectives. The extensive use of interior and narrated monologue juxtaposed with dialogue makes the reader privy to both the private and public personae of Kleist and Günderrode. By differentiating between the two, by determining what is censored in the public sphere, we gain insight not only into the psychology of the characters, but into their society as well.[29]

In the Günderrode essay Wolf explicitly draws parallels between the bourgeois Romantic society of 1804 and GDR society of her own time: both are societies in a state of transition. The former is moving from a feudalistic to a bourgeois structure, the latter from a bourgeois–fascist to a socialist order; the former is dominated by "sterile rationalism," the latter by "vulgar materialism" (GE 330). Thus neither Kleist and Günderrode's society, which constitutes a perversion of Enlightenment ideals, nor Wolf's society, which constitutes a perversion of Marxist ideals, affords the creative artist the possibility of integrating life and work.

Calling them "precursors," Christa Wolf immediately establishes the contemporaneity of the text of *No Place on Earth* by creating a connection between Kleist and Günderrode and us. The opening sentence of the narrative: "The wicked spoor left in time's wake as it flees us" (*NP* 3), establishes the link between the past and the present, a link which in the following sentence: "You precursors, feet bleeding,"[30] is seen as a painful, bloody one. The evocation of Kleist and Günderrode, their resurrection out of separate graves, leads into the actual story and, together with the open-ended conclusion "we know what is coming" (*NP* 119), frames the narrative. It also points to "centuries-old laughter" (*NP* 3) which, emitted in the Kleist–Günderrode dialogue, still reverberates.

Wolf's use of stretch-of-time phrases such as "still" ("still greedy for the ashen taste of words") and "not yet" ("Not yet mute as is suitable," *NP* 3) in her juxtaposition of the "we" and "you" establishes a continuity between past and present, between the "you" and the "we." On the other hand her inversion of conventional images and metaphors ("descended heavenward") and the repeated use of estranging negatives ("Gazes without eyes, words that stem from no mouth. Shapes without bodies") convey the perversity of their situation.[31] Relegated solely to the realm of literature, language for both Kleist and Günderrode and for writers such as Christa Wolf becomes problematic; words take on an "ashen taste." Wolf consciously draws attention to her fluidly shifting, multidimensional narrative perspective by interjecting the question "Who is speaking?" several times throughout the text (*NP* 4, 113). By challenging readers to differentiate between the various perspectives, she also forces them to draw connections between then and now, between the figures and the author/narrator.

The narrator's evocation of predecessors with whom she feels a spiritual affinity is consonant with the Romantic philosophy Bettine attributes to Günderrode in her epistolary novel. Speaking about the possibility of a union through affinity between totally distant and disparate people, Bettine's Günderrode had maintained that "similar thoughts of different people, even if they never knew about each other, constitute a union in a spiritual sense," and that a union with the deceased can occur, provided they continue to be in harmony with us.[32] Perhaps the most striking parallel between the Romantic ideas of Günderrode as mediated by Bettine and Wolf's interpretation of her is the notion of subjective reception. According to Günderrode, "a great person does not attain permanence in me in *his* fashion but rather in mine. How I receive him, how and if I want to remember him."[33] Wolf's meticulously researched portrayal of Karoline von Günderrode and Heinrich von Kleist in *No Place on Earth* as well as of Cassandra in her more recent work is ultimately a subjective reception of these figures. These recreations enable her to address issues of personal relevance to her and are the expression of the way the figures continue to live in her. They are in short a manifestation of her concept of subjective authenticity.

Wolf prefaces her text with two identified quotations, by the historical Kleist and Günderrode respectively, which are eloquent testimony to their alienation, their psychic dissociation, their homelessness. Kleist's statement: "I carry around a heart the way a Northern land carries within it the germ of a semitropical fruit from the South. It sprouts and sends forth shoots, but it cannot grow ripe," is based on the juxtaposition of North and South that has played such an important role in German letters since Goethe's Italian journey (1784–6). Ironically, Kleist, either unconsciously or by design, used the vocabulary of his archrival Goethe to articulate his own alienation. His imagery is furthermore reminiscent of the concept of entelechy so important to Goethe, the belief that living things evolve and develop toward the fulfillment of their innate essence. Günderrode's imagery, on the other hand, is more concrete and static: "But for this reason I fancy that I am seeing myself lying in the coffin, and my two selves stare at each other in wonderment."[34]

The differences in the imagery employed by Kleist and Günderrode reflect different expectations that can be attributed to their genders. Kleist's broad spatial imagery contrasts sharply with Günderrode's, which is the most restrictive imaginable: the coffin. Kleist's comparison of his heart to the seed of a semitropical fruit that constantly puts out shoots indicates that he expects to actualize himself. Such an expectation is absent in Günderrode's statement. Her imagery is not one of development but of ultimate regression. As the Günderrode essay makes clear, Christa Wolf considered Günderrode's mutually exclusive aspirations as woman and as poet to be a cause of her failure, and included her physical and psychic ailments as symptoms of self-alienation (GE 336). Thus the schizophrenic image of Günderrode's two selves can be interpreted as a feminine and an artistic ego.

The inherent differences in world view reflected in these quotations shapes Christa Wolf's portrayal of Kleist and Günderrode. In the figure of Kleist, Wolf for the first time grants a man equal stature in her literary work. Intended to be representative casualties of their time, they are, as Wolf states in the Günderrode essay, victims of their transitional historical situation. She describes the situation of the young Romantic writers as follows:

They experience the Revolution as foreign rule. They, sons and daughters of the first generation of the educated German bourgeoisie [*Bildungsbürger*] and of impoverished noble families that have become bourgeois, have a choice between the crippling repressive practices of petty German princes and subjugation by Napoleon; between the anachronistic feudalism of petty German principalities and the introduction by force of long-overdue administrative and economic reforms by the usurper who, of course, strictly suppresses the spirit of the Revolution. If this can be called a choice, then it is one that destroys action at its root, in the very thought. They are the first to experience to the depth of their beings that they are not needed. (GE 329)

Wolf's description calls to mind Ernst Bloch's concept of *Ungleichzeitigkeit* (nonsynchronicity), which may have helped shape her conception both of Kleist and Günderrode and also of Cassandra. First introduced in *Erbschaft dieser Zeit*[35] (Heritage of This Time, 1935), Bloch's attempt to analyze the reasons for the National Socialist Party's victory in 1933, the term *Ungleichzeitig-*

keit was intended to explain "the contradictory coexistence of developed capitalistic and remnants of precapitalist means of production [objective nonsynchronicity] and ideologies [subjective nonsynchronicity],"[36] contradictions successfully exploited by the Nazis. *Gleichzeitigkeit* (synchronicity) refers to the agreement between the means of production of a given society and the existing working conditions and consciousness of individuals in that society. In its subjective manifestation *Ungleichzeitigkeit*, which became a key concept of Bloch's philosophy, helps explain the historical lag between material conditions and consciousness in any period of transition. Thus Wolf's description of the overlap between feudalistic and capitalistic material conditions constitutes an example of objective *Ungleichzeitigkeit*. Her following description of the generation of 1800, on the other hand, illustrates subjective *Ungleichzeitigkeit*:

A small group of intellectuals – avant-garde without a hinterland, as so often the case in German history since the peasant wars – equipped with a worthless ideal, differentiated sensibility, an uncontrollable desire to apply their newly developed consciousness encounters the narrowmindedness of an underdeveloped class without self-esteem but full of blissful subservience, which has appropriated for itself from the bourgeois catechism only the commandment: Enrich yourself ... They become strangers in their own country, precursors whom no one follows, enthusiasts without reverberance, callers without an echo. And those among them who are not able to make the compromises demanded by their time: victims.

(GE 327–8)

Bloch's concept of *Ungleichzeitigkeit* is helpful not only for understanding the generation of 1800 but also for explaining the coexistence of a socialist means of production and presocialist (i.e., bourgeois capitalist) consciousness in today's GDR. It thus provides the basis of a philosophic-theoretical reading of Wolf's narrative(s). Within the text of *No Place on Earth*, *Ungleichzeitigkeit* is attributed both to the present time of narration by the narrator and to the narrated past by the narrative voice of Günderrode. The novel's opening passage clearly refers to contemporary readers of the text who can see the traces of the past ("wicked spoor") in the present.[37] Günderrode expresses the concept of *Ungleichzeitigkeit* more opaquely when she reflects that "between one time and another ... is a twilit region in which it is easy to go astray and to get lost in some mysterious way" (*NP* 118). Wolf's metaphors for describing *Ungleichzeitigkeit* at the beginning of the nineteenth century are most graphic in her Günderrode essay.

There she speaks of the dissonance of Günderrode's soul as the "Unstimmigkeit" (inconsistency, discrepancy) of her time (GE 375) and maintains that the "rupture of her times" runs through her, causing her to split herself into several persons (GE 375). Bloch broadened his discussion of nonsynchronicity by adding the concept of *Übergleichzeitigkeit* (hypersynchronicity),[38] by which he meant a consciousness that was in advance of existing material conditions, specifically a socialist consciousness. To the extent that the holistic ideal of harmony between the emotional and the rational and the ethos of intersubjectivity (articulated above all by the women Romantics and practiced in the salons) foreshadows the goals of socialist society, the Romantics can be considered hypersynchronistic.

Clearly Kleist and Günderrode belong to those untimely (hypersynchronistic) individuals described by Wolf in the Günderrode essay who, incapable of compromising, unable to reconcile the discrepancy between their ideals and the crass materialism of their age (as manifested most directly in the figure of Merten), are doomed to be its victims. In examining the reasons for their destruction, Wolf distinguishes between external and internal causes, between the function of a repressive social order and the peculiar psychological make-up of the individuals involved. She also enunciates the gender specificity of their situation.

The sociological similarities between Kleist and Günderrode are striking: as members of the impoverished nobility both are inhibited from freely pursuing their literary vocations. Kleist, an officer in the Prussian army who will later be forced to earn his living as a civil servant, is resentful of the time his service takes away from his writing. Günderrode, having spent years caring for her ailing mother, is forced for financial reasons to enter the Kronstetten–Hunspergische Evangelical Sisterhood in Frankfurt am Main at the age of nineteen. While subjected to a more circumscribed, confining existence than Kleist, Günderrode has more leisure time for her writing. Unlike Kleist, however, she is excluded from the public sphere by virtue of her sex. Since as a woman Günderrode lacks a public voice in her society, it is understandable that when she publishes her poetry, she does so under the male pseudonym Tian.

Apart from the similarities in the external exigencies of their situation, Kleist and Günderrode share an inability to compromise; however, their failure to conform takes its psychological toll. To both Kleist and Günderrode Wolf attributes "a pity, a compassion for the repressed language of their bodies, a mourning for the all too precocious taming of their limbs by the military uniform and the religious habit, for the morality in the name of regulations, for the secret excesses they commit in the name of breaking the regulations" (*NP* 97–8). Yet despite these similarities, significant differences, due in part to gender and in part to personal psychology, exist between them. The gender distinction is underscored from the outset. Used to introduce the main characters, it is sustained throughout the narrative.

A man, Kleist, afflicted with this overly acute sense of hearing, flees on the pretext of excuses he does not dare to see for what they are. Aimlessly, it seems, he sketches with his eccentric footprints the lacerated map of Europe. Happiness is the place where I am not.

The woman, Günderrode, banned by a spell to the confines of a narrow circle, reflective, clairvoyant, unassailed by the transitory, determined to live for immortality, to offer up the visible to the invisible. (*NP* 4)

In these portraits it is revealing that Kleist is cast as the Romantic wanderer, in a state of perpetual, frenetic motion, while Günderrode is introduced through a sentence fragment conspicuously lacking a verb. The absence of an action word immediately identifies her with the passivity that is her lot.

Although Kleist fails to find a niche for himself anywhere, he, unlike Günderrode, is free to travel and to gather life experience. In a later passage Günderrode's restrictive life situation and the discrepancy between reality and her potential are elucidated. She is portrayed as being

poised between the two contradictory poles of a spirit which was by nature soaring, and living conditions of the most restrictive kind. Those first nights in the convent, at the age of nineteen, on the hard narrow bed in the small room with the open windows, through which, when the last of the night birds had gone mute, there shouldered its way a silence which grew ever more dense, more threatening, and more final, and before morning seemed to fill up and to suffocate the entire universe. (*NP* 15)

For both of these marginal figures, writing compensates for the lack of a livable life. Kleist, driven by a compulsive ambition to succeed, writes to make his mark on the world, whereas Günderrode's desire to express her life in an enduring form reflects her desire to communicate. For her "poems are a balm laid upon everything in life that is unappeasable" (*NP* 64).

For both there is much that is unappeasable. In *No Place on Earth*, her most pessimistic work to date, Wolf seems to abandon the Blochian notion of a concrete utopia and to return instead to the original Greek meaning of *u-topos*, "no place." For both

Heinrich von Kleist and Karoline von Günderrode, the explicit utopian reference of the title appears to have meaning only in terms of its opposite – a dystopia. By appending the word "Nirgends" (Nowhere) to her title, Wolf underscores the impossibility of Kleist and Günderrode finding a home on earth. However, Wolf's repeated use of the term "home" already evokes a Blochian mood, for it is clearly to be understood in Bloch's sense of *Heimat*, that is, as a philosophical concept, denoting a spiritual being-at-home in the world as opposed to alienation. For both Kleist and Günderrode, the solution to their irremediable homelessness will be suicide. According to Wolf, the Romantics "were probably one of the first generations to feel torn inside by their inability to realize in action the possibilities which they sensed were there, inside them, very much alive and alert; which they rehearsed in debates and literary experiments."[39] Drawing the connection between the situation of the Romantics in general and of Kleist and Günderrode in particular to our own time, Wolf maintains:

It's been my experience that the alternatives we live in are collapsing one after the other, and that fewer and fewer real alternatives are left ... It now seems there are fewer and fewer productive contradictions and that the number of unlivable alternatives is increasing. That's precisely the source of so many people's tension, that they feel they've gotten into a corner.[40]

The average German reader, encountering the figure of Kleist in Christa Wolf's narrative, is apt to be aware that the historical figure took his own life. Since Günderrode does not belong to the literary canon, the reader is unlikely to know that she also died by her own hand. Yet the narrative leaves little doubt as to this outcome. The themes of homelessness, alienation, and death, first sounded in the mottos of Kleist and Günderrode, are used leitmotivally in the narrative. These themes, repeated and varied throughout, lend a musical quality to the work. This theme-and-variation structure is apparent in the dialogue between Kleist and Günderrode. In the nonverbalized thoughts that constitute part of Kleist's narrated monologue in the dialogue between the two, he gives expression to his sense of hopelessness:

Kleist reckons up the number of countries he knows. It has become a compulsion for him to do so. He has learned that conditions in these countries run counter to his needs. With the best will in the world and a timid trust he has tried them out, and rejected them only against his will. The sense of relief when he abandoned his hope for an earthly existence in any way corresponding to his needs. Unlivable life.

No place on earth. (*NP* 107–8)

This dystopian view refers back to the opening image of Kleist as the wanderer who had discovered: "Happiness is the place where I am not" (*NP* 4), and varies it to read that happiness for Kleist exists no place, nowhere. As the Günderrode essay points out, Kleist's sentiment is shared by Günderrode. Her lament: "'Earth did not become a home for me'" (GE 374), echoes Kleist's view almost verbatim. Together these two quotations form the basis of the English translation of the title.

While the theme of homelessness is varied as the motif of the outsider, the death motif, first introduced in Günderrode's motto, is repeated and varied as suicide. This motif is taken up again in Günderrode's dream, in which she, in lieu of the doe hunted by Savigny, is wounded in the neck and in which she foresees bleeding to death as the most natural thing in the world (*NP* 7). If the dream state allows a fairy-tale-like happy end (in the dream, a magical brew allows Savigny to cure her wound), the waking, conscious Günderrode takes precautions to learn how best to die.

She knows the place beneath her breast where she must drive home the dagger, a surgeon whom she jestingly asked about it showed her the spot, pressing it with his finger. Since then, whenever she concentrates, she feels the pressure and is instantly at peace. It will be easy and certain, she need only take care that she always have the weapon with her. If one thinks about anything long and often enough, it loses all its terror. Thoughts get worn out like coins which are passed from hand to hand, or like images that one calls to mind over and over. She is able, without flinching, to see her corpse lying anywhere she looks, even down there by the river, on the tongue of land beneath the willows on which her gaze rests.[41]   (*NP* 7)

As the dramatic encounter between Günderrode and the other guests over Günderrode's dagger makes clear, the dagger has symbolic value for her: it represents the only freedom she has, the freedom to die. Bettine takes the weapon from her friend's bag; it is snatched away and passed around among the guests. When Wedekind confiscates it as a dangerous object, Günderrode emphatically retrieves her property. This episode interjects an ominous note into the tea party setting. While everyone knew about Günderrode's dagger, no one realized that she carried it around with her at all times. The sight of the dagger and Günderrode's insistence on retaining it are sobering to the guests. For the reader, too, the dagger scene makes concrete the idea of suicide, articulated as an abstraction in the earlier passage, and thus clarifies the depth of her commitment to a *Freitod* (a freely chosen death). The knowledge that she can at any time choose to end her life is a great source of comfort to her after the devastating review of her poems. "She will not allow herself to be humiliated. She has the remedy to prevent this, and she will not hesitate to use it. What consolation lies in the knowledge that one does not have to live" (*NP* 23).

For Günderrode a prime source of unhappiness lies in her inability to find love. The motifs of homelessness, death, and love converge in her reflection on lack of belonging: "My friend, my friends! I understand their glances only too well, I am not at home among them. There, where my home is, love exists only at the price of death" (*NP* 35). Thus for Günderrode, as for Lenka in *Patterns of Childhood*, *Heimat* is defined in terms of relationship.

Yet her thwarted longing for intimacy and relationship is merely one aspect of Günderrode's predicament. Wolf, deriving her dilemma from her particular historical situation, sees Günderrode as one of the first female intellectuals. Like other women Romantics, such as Karoline Schlegel-Schelling, Dorothea Schlegel, Rahel Varnhagen, and Bettine von Arnim, Günderrode was educated as previously only men had been. (In contrast to her more privileged female compatriots, however, Günderrode was an autodidact.) As men's intellectual peers, these women could no longer abide by traditional role expectations. Born into a time of upheaval and transition, they had no models of behavior to fall back on. Called upon to create new ones themselves, they at times revert to outdated models while simultaneously establishing new, unprecedented goals for themselves. This is clearly the case with Günderrode, who attempts to reconcile the irreconcilable, the public and the private spheres. "Günderrode wants to unite what cannot be united. To be loved by a man and to bring forth a work of art that asks to be judged by absolute criteria. To be a wife and a poet: to have and care for a family and to step into the public sphere with her own bold literary products: unlivable wishes" (GE 340).

The uncompromising Günderrode wants to devote herself absolutely to two contradictory modes of existence. As a poet who adheres to canonical literary norms, she is subservient to critical taste; as a woman seeking fulfillment through marriage and motherhood, she is subservient to traditional female role expectations. Her desire to develop all aspects of her personality is not tolerated by her society and can lead only to frustration, schizophrenia, the self-alienation manifested in the motto, and ultimately to death. It was impossible for the women Romantics to unite their private and public selves. What was possible, as the case of Bettine von Arnim demonstrates, was to devote oneself first to one and then to the other. As a counterpoint to Günderrode's story, Christa Wolf's Bettine essay documents what amounts to the three lives of Bettine von Arnim: the young Bettine, a precocious free spirit (this self-image, which Bettine retroactively recreated in *Die Günderode*, is essentially also the Bettine of *No Place on Earth*); Bettine, the wife of Achim von Arnim and mother of seven children, a woman who conforms to the expectations placed on her by her society; and Bettine the widow who, reasserting her nonconformity, becomes a well-known writer and an influential and critical member of her society. Günderrode's aspirations could conceivably be realised in sequence, but not simultaneously. Her awareness that her situation is hopeless is reiterated in the line from her poetry that so horrifies Kleist: "To give birth to what slays me" (*NP* 97), which Christa Wolf in the Günderrode essay interprets as her commitment to her writing, a commitment that will negate the possibility of a conventional life as wife and mother.

Kleist too suffers from mutually exclusive wishes, wishes remarkably similar to Günderrode's. When asked by Bettine what he would wish for if he had three wishes and could wish for anything he liked, he chooses: "Freedom. A poem. A home" (*NP* 86), readily conceding that these wishes are an attempt to reconcile the irreconcilable. For both Kleist and Günderrode, their ambivalence is crippling. Kleist himself gives the most poignant expression to the debilitating effects of ambivalence in the anecdote about his experiment with Wedekind's dog. Called simultaneously by Frau Wedekind and Kleist, Bello was overwhelmed by being "trapped between two contradictory commands, each of which necessarily appeared to him absolutely binding" (*NP* 61). When both parties refused to release him from their commands, the animal, overpowered by its insoluble dilemma, succumbed to an irresistible urge to sleep. This retreat from consciousness in the face of a situation it cannot resolve parallels the retreat into unconsciousness of many of Kleist's protagonists when confronted with an empirical reality diametrically opposed to the subjective reality driving them, a reality expressed by Wolf's Kleist: "I bear an inner precept inscribed in my heart, compared to which all external maxims, were they sanctioned by a king himself, are of no value whatever" (*NP* 67).[42]

Bello's dilemma becomes an emblem for Kleist's existential situation. His identification with the dog is implicit in his wish to be able to sleep his whole life away. It is made explicit by Wedekind and is in turn elucidated by Kleist; in presenting the group with an example of an insoluble human dilemma similar to that of the dog, he is obviously describing his own life situation:

> Whether rightly or wrongly, someone feels in himself the compulsion to follow a certain vocation. His circumstances do not permit him to live abroad, where he would be free to pursue his plans, nor do they permit him to go on living in his native land without taking a civil-service post. But this post, which he would be forced to degrade himself beyond endurance to obtain, would in every way run counter to his vocation. (*NP* 63)

While Kleist cannot sleep his life away, he can choose to enter the realm of eternal sleep. Suicide is an option he has actively pursued; he had attempted without success to persuade his friend Pfuel to enter into a suicide pact with him.[43] Whereas with Günderrode the death motif is linked to her inability to find love, with Kleist it is connected to his inability to realize his ambition. Thus Kleist interprets his recurring dream, in which he shoots and kills a beautiful boar after unsuccessfuly trying to tame it,[44] as symbolic of his lack of viable alternative. Confronted with the choice – "either to systematically annihilate in himself that consuming dissatisfaction which is the best thing in him, or to give free reign to it and be destroyed by his temporal misery. To create time and space in accordance with the necessity of his own being, or simply to vegetate in a run-of-the-mill existence" (*NP* 29) – Kleist is determined to rise to the challenge. "No one other than himself will execute judgment upon him. The hand which was fated to commit the crime will carry out the sentence" (*NP* 30).

In contrast to Günderrode with his desire for relationship, Kleist is totally self-absorbed. It is significant, for example, that he defines himself in negatives, in terms of the discrepancy between the reality of his existence and the expectations he places on himself. "Who am I. A lieutenant without a sword knot. A student without learning. A civil servant without a post. An author without a book" (*NP* 42). Kleist's insoluble dilemmas are not restricted to the public sphere. They extend into his personal life as well, as his eloquent description of Wedekind makes clear: "The calamity, Privy Councilor, of being dependent on ties which suffocate me if I put up with them, which tear me apart if I break free" (*NP* 39).

The ties he alludes to are those of his sister Ulrike. Kleist's intense relationship with his sister, as well as his inability to relate to women sexually, is an issue raised by Christa Wolf both in the narrative and in her essay on Kleist's *Penthesilea*. In a passage that can be attributed to both Kleist and the narrator, the narrative voice reflects on the love between siblings of the opposite sex:

> But what does that mean, that love between a brother and a sister which human beings cover up that they may not see. Which they tolerate by failing to perceive what their blood is urging deep down in its abysmal muteness. The benefaction of blood kinship, a thought that is never thought through to the end. A kinship which mitigates one's incomprehension of that alien sex to which one cannot surrender oneself. (*NP* 94–5)

Wolf also attributes to Ulrike an ambiguous sexual identity and interprets the latently incestuous love between the siblings as a buffer for the man and the woman, both of whom fear the opposite sex.

In her *Penthesilea* essay, written after her Cassandra project, Wolf is far more critical of Kleist in general and of his relationship with Ulrike in particular:

> Kleist, oblivious to his sister, proposes in 1808 from Chalons-sur-Marne to set up a small household after all, so that he can board with her. "You could read all of Rousseau again, and Helvetius, or you could look for places and cities on maps; and I could write." This is followed by one of those sentences whose innocent candor only increases their impudence: "Maybe you'll learn again in a peaceful hour what your real purpose in life is. We'd be happy! The feeling of living together must be a need for you, as it is for me. For I feel that you are my friend, the only one on earth!" This is presented as a firm commitment in the same letter whose postscript nonchalantly overturns the entire plan, because the way to Dresden has been opened to him, which was his real goal.[45]

In Wolf's later assessment, Kleist becomes one of the first of a series of poets whose "genius carelessly makes use of the less talented woman for the fulfillment of his needs and ends."[46]

Just as Wolf views Kleist's treatment of his sister as manipulative and objectifying, this reification characterizes all of Günderrode's romantic relationships with men. In the Günderrode essay Christa Wolf notes that "three men played a role in her life: Savigny, Clemens Brentano, Friedrich Creuzer – three variations on the same experience: what she desires is impossible. Three times she experiences that which is most intolerable: she is made into an object" (*GE* 340).

At the time of the tea party Günderrode has not yet met the professor of comparative mythology, Friedrich Creuzer, on whose account, allegedly, she will commit suicide in 1806.[47] Yet her future involvement with an unidentified "someone" is alluded to several times in the text. At one point the omniscient narrator,[48] clearly alluding to Creuzer, projects Günderrode's fate: "One day she would encounter a man of whom she knows nothing. Of whom she can experience nothing, but through whom she will experience herself to the very depths, to her ultimate limits and beyond. And then beyond that there is nothing any more" (*NP* 106).

Günderrode's interaction with both Clemens Brentano and Savigny testifies to their objectification of her. Neither Brentano, whose romance with Günderrode lies three years in the past, nor Savigny, with whom she is currently involved, is able to relate to her as an independent subject. Both project an image of her and attempt to mold her into that image. While the precise nature of Günderrode's relationship with Clemens Brentano remains unclear, it is clear that she has rejected him and that he is resentful. His wounded pride avenges itself through his proprietary attitude toward her and his patronizing attitude toward her art. Jealous of Savigny, he contrives ways of separating them. In his attempt to comfort her about the condescending review of her poetry, Clemens is too egocentric to see past himself and to divorce himself from the issue. Irritated that she had not consulted him before publishing her verses, he initially undermines the credibility of the critic, attributing his caustic review to the envy of the poet manqué when confronting genuine poetic talent.[49] He then, however, goes on to claim to hear reflections of his own sentiments in her poems. It escapes him that in doing so, he reiterates the most hurtful remark of the review: "Many people mistake for original ideas what are merely reminiscences" (*NP* 22).

It does not, however, escape Günderrode, who points out that Brentano would not have made that remark to a man. Nor is that the only occasion during the course of the afternoon on which Günderrode takes Brentano to task. When he insists on reading aloud one of her poems as proof of her inconsistency, everyone recognizes that the choice of these intimate verses is a violation of their friendship. The unidentified verses quoted by Brentano are from Günderrode's poem "Wandel und Treue" (Change and Constancy). The poem is printed in its entirety in both Bettine's *Die Günderode* (pp. 35–7) and Wolf's *Schatten eines Traumes* (pp. 68–71). The stanza included in *No Place on Earth* redefines the notion of constancy. Narcissus calls those inconstant who maintain a calculating consciousness even in love. This must have appealed to Wolf, who has consistently criticized calculating behavior (*Divided Heaven*, *Christa T.*, *Patterns of Childhood*). Günderrode's response to Brentano's betrayal is direct: "Clemens . . . there is no way I can fight the obtuse reviewers. But how then am I to fight a friend who deliberately sets out to hurt me?" (*NP* 75). Günderrode is aware of and distressed by Clemens's manipulative behavior. She recognizes for instance that in order to separate her from Savigny, he has hauled her off to the window as if she were his property, to laud the beauty of the landscape (*NP* 14). She is offended by his indiscretion, his inability to recognize things about which he should keep silent. She is particularly offended by the sexual obtrusiveness of his glances:

> She feels the skin of her face grow taut so that it may become impermeable to his glances, which palpate her mouth, forehead, cheeks. She finds it intolerable that a man can take such liberties with a woman simply as a matter of course, and that she cannot defend herself against his importunity without, in the end, appearing prim, prudish, and unwomanly.
>
> (*NP* 21)

Although Günderrode is able to recognize similar breaches of friendship in Savigny's behavior, her love for him makes her vulnerable to his manipulation. Whereas the tension between Günderrode and Clemens is resolved, for that day at any rate, by his conciliatory dedication of his most recent song to the beautiful poet Tian,[50] her relationship to Savigny ends on a less reconciled note. Günderrode's complicated relationship to Savigny, the fact that his marriage to Clemens Brentano's sister Gunda created a triangle in which she is the outsider, renders the situation emotionally unviable for her. Savigny's marriage of convenience to the banal Gunda frees him to pursue his fascination with the more interesting and challenging Günderrode, safe from the danger of commitment. After his marriage, Savigny continues his relationship with Günderrode via an intense personal correspondence. The cipher language they develop ensures that Günderrode will for a time remain emotionally entangled in a hopeless situation, a relationship without prospects. In the Günderrode essay, Christa Wolf calls Savigny to task:

> How easy for Savigny. Since he knows he is in safe hands, he allows himself the luxury of starting a humorous, ironic, undangerous correspondence with the woman who after all fascinates him, a correspondence conducted in a nonobligatory manner, which only hurts the woman who loves . . . One could call him a bit cruel, if he had given it much thought. (GE 341)

Savigny's lack of awareness and concern are readily apparent in the narrative. The intimacy he and Günderrode share is based on a mutual understanding of his emotional supremacy. Engaged in a power play of sexual politics, Savigny, by virtue of his domestic situation, has the upper hand. Nor is Günderrode unaware that Savigny excels in putting her off. Highly attuned to the secret gestures that exist between them, Günderrode notes:

> As Clemens was dragging me away, Savigny signaled to me with his finger. He has come. He knows that I am waiting and counts on my being able to conceal it. He understands that when I love I am constant and selfless, and takes advantage of the fact, and I in turn must love him all the more. This, too, he has taken into account. And so it goes, on and on. (*NP* 14)

In *No Place on Earth* Wolf allows Günderrode to engage Savigny in a "dream conversation" (*NP* 48). Their two-part conversation, separated by a section devoted to Kleist, prepares the reader for the narrative's climax, Günderrode and Kleist's dialogue, in that it also documents Günderrode's attempt to communicate authentically. Almost the entire Günderrode–Savigny interchange is taken verbatim from their correspondence from 1803–4[51] and deals with Günderrode's relationship to both Savigny and Gunda. By splicing the most critical passages from the historical Günderrode's letters into her dialogue with Savigny,[52] Wolf creates a character with a well-defined sense of self. In contrast to her historical model, who was more inconsistent in her attitude toward Savigny, Wolf's Günderrode has the strength to extricate herself unequivocally from her unhappy affair. Her desire to speak with Savigny is prompted by the sense that "something of decisive importance still remains to be said." Probing further for her motives, the narrator and/or Günderrode wonders: "Does she feel a need for some kind of reparation? Is she making one last attempt to obtain from someone else an absolute understanding of her nature?" (*NP* 57), and thereby identifies the precise function of this dialogue.

Günderrode's mocking air and ironic stance serve as a shield behind which she can mask the depth of her emotional involvement. They allow her to touch on intimate topics with impunity. Embedded in this bantering exchange are numerous reproaches to Savigny: for prohibiting her from using the familiar *du* form of address; for not having kept silent about the love poem "Kiss in the Dream" and the confessional note she wrote him two weeks before his marriage. But her most poignant lament is for having been invisible to him, not having been understood or known. In the Günderrode essay, Christa Wolf names the desire to be known as the "urgent wish of women who do not want to live through men, but rather through themselves" (*GE* 342). Since the prerequisite for knowing another person is the ability to regard the other as an autonomous subject, and since Günderrode is repeatedly objectified by the men with whom she is involved, she will never experience what she so ardently desires.

In the Günderrode–Savigny dialogue, Günderrode essentially curtails their relationship. Expressing Wolf's view of their relationship, she tells Savigny that she now knows that they were compelled to miss each other because he knew nothing of her and that her heart has turned away from him. She declares her dedication to the study of history and philosophy and to her art – "I am," she asserts, "writing a drama, and my whole being is wrapped up in it. I project myself so vividly into the drama, I become so much at home within it, that my own life is becoming alien to me" (*NP* 60). By devoting herself to her work, Wolf's Günderrode is able to extricate herself from her unhappy love.

The Günderrode who confronts Savigny in *No Place on Earth* is clearly refracted through the prism of Christa Wolf's twentieth-century consciousness. The historical Karoline von Günderrode was more ambivalent toward her work and more unsure about her poetic calling than is the Günderrode Wolf invents. Her letters reveal a more conciliatory attitude toward Savigny and less self-awareness as an artist and as a woman. While the historical Günderrode was aware of Savigny's manipulation and suffered from her untenable position in the friendship *à trois*, with him and Gunda, nowhere do we find anything approximating the reproachful assessment that Wolf's fictional character gives:

How well I know him. Do not be too tender and too melancholy and too yearning – be lucid and stable and yet full of *joie de vivre*. Ah, Savigny. What does all that really mean? It means that Günderrode-my-pet is not supposed to molest you further. She is not only supposed to understand what is appointed to her: to stand in the background and wait, to play second fiddle, but she is also supposed to keep quiet about it. And – this of course was the most agreeable, the most convenient thing of all – she was supposed to be cheerful about it, that horrid little Günderrode-my-pet, you dear little duck. She is not supposed to make anyone feel the least twinge of guilty conscience. – And of course he is right.   (*NP* 45)

Christa Wolf has thus augmented her authentic material with a utopian projection. Like her meeting with Kleist, Günderrode's conversation with Savigny is a wished-for encounter, one in which the author allows her character to settle accounts with Savigny as the historical Günderrode never did. This conversation is indeed Günderrode's reparation. As an examination of Wolf's sources reveals, Günderrode's behavior in *No Place on Earth* is not implausible; that is, it is not a fantastic utopian construct. Instead, by distilling the historical Günderrode's most self-affirming impulses, it represents the realization of her human potential; it constitutes the praxis of utopia.

Moreover, Wolf attributes to Günderrode a prescience that points forward to *Cassandra*. During her conversation with Kleist, Günderrode realizes that she can pinpoint the exact moment when she began to distance herself from Savigny. Drawing on an authentic biographical event in which Günderrode had injured Savigny's hand by jamming it in a carriage door, Wolf reinterprets the literal departure as a symbolic leave-taking. In a moment of clairvoyance,[53] Günderrode had foreseen her future, a future that did not include Savigny. Rather than rekindle the flame, Günderrode gave in to this vision. The fact that Savigny's marriage to Gunda Brentano appears to her as a *déjà vu* indicates that Günderrode believes in the self-actualization of her inner reality. Her prophecy fulfills itself in her private conversation with Savigny at Merten's party.

As the Günderrode essay makes clear, Savigny continued to play an important role in the historical Günderrode's life after 1804; he even played a part in her last, tragic affair. Savigny, having helped finance Friedrich Creuzer's studies, became his confidant during his thwarted relationship with the poetess. Günderrode's affair with the married Creuzer was from the outset doomed to failure. Creuzer was unwilling or unable to leave his wife. His relationship with Günderrode was characterized by clandestine trysts, letters written in code, subterfuge, ambivalence, and indecision. The guilt-ridden Creuzer eventually called upon Günderrode to renounce her erotic love and begin a platonic relationship with him instead. Finally unable to endure his situation any longer, Creuzer, unaware of the intensity of Günderrode's longing for death, terminated their relationship. His farewell letter was her "death sentence" (GE 368); upon reading it, she stabbed herself. Her body was found on the meadowy spit of land by the river.

As an epilogue to the tragedy[54] of Günderrode's life, Christa Wolf recounts the tragedy of her art. After her death, Creuzer succumbed to his friends' urgings and turned her letters over to a friend who burned them. A greater loss, however, was the disappearance of the manuscript of *Melete*, a heterogeneous collection of poems, drama, and letters that Günderrode had sent Creuzer and which he was to help her publish. Creuzer's enthusiastic if somewhat threatened response to Günderrode's poetry contrasts sharply with his subsequent actions: he withdrew the manuscript, it disappeared from sight, and but for a minor miracle[55] it would be lost to us. The background information furnished by the Günderrode essay, the knowledge of what Günderrode's future holds in store, lends an ominous note to the conclusion of the narrative: "We know what is coming" (*NP* 119).

The narrative leaves little doubt about the tragic outcome of Kleist's and Günderrode's lives. Clearly, Wolf felt bound to abide by the historical reality of their deaths. However, by bringing them together she introduces an element of hope into their bleak existences. As a counterpoint to the theme of alienation and homelessness, as a possibility for transcending their isolation, the theme of *kennen* forms another link between Günderrode and Kleist. Both Günderrode and Kleist suffer from being *verkannt* (misapprehended, misunderstood). Both articulate their pain at not being known. Yet there is a fundamental difference between their situations. Günderrode's failure to be known is inextricably bound to her sex, to the reification she is forced to endure. While for Günderrode, being *verkannt* is a personal loss, for Kleist it takes on public ramifications; it bears overtones of the theme of the *verkanntes Genie* (misunderstood genius). Kleist both desires intimacy and is terrified of it. More than for personal intimacy, Kleist longs for public acclaim. The driving force of his existence is ambition, an emotion the woman does not share.

And yet there is sufficient affinity between them to enable these two, between whom, as is made clear, there is no sexual attraction, to share a moment of true emotional and intellectual intimacy. The subliminal eroticism that constitutes the subtext of Günderrode's encounters with both Brentano and Savigny gives way in the Kleist–Günderrode dialogue to an intellectual and emotional intimacy that is sensuous. The integrative power of their exchange is made explicit in Kleist's response to Günderrode: "This exchange with her, which does not arouse him as a man, closely resembles a sensual intoxication" (*NP* 118). Through it, the dualism between the sensuous and the intellectual is overcome. It thus approximates that Romantic synthesis of thinking and feeling which Christa Wolf calls for in the Bettine essay, an overcoming of the false dichotomy between rational and nonrational.

The dialogue between Kleist and Günderrode, the climax of *No Place on Earth*, distinguishes itself from the conversations at Merten's, which both view as empty chatter, in that it is an exchange of intellectual equals who are able to perceive each other as autonomous subjects. For Kleist and Günderrode, the conversations with other members of the tea party were frustrating and unfulfilling because the others either were not their intellectual or emotional peers and essentially philistines (Merten and to an extent Wedekind) or were fundamentally egotistical (Brentano, Savigny).

Merten, Wedekind, and Savigny had been unsympathetic to Kleist's need for unity between art and life. All three had maintained the need to uphold the boundaries between the two realms. They had valorized science and progress and had valued reason to the detriment of other human faculties, notably the imagination. There can be no meeting of minds between Kleist's view that "the path of science has separated from that of art . . . Our modern-day civilization is steadily expanding the sphere of the intellect, steadily restricting that of imagination. We have almost reached the point at which we can predict the end of the arts" and that of the scientist Nees von Esenbeck: "I would give everything I have in exchange for the chance to live again on this earth two or three centuries from now, and to share in the paradisiac conditions which – thanks to the advance of the sciences! – mankind will then enjoy." "There is," as the narrative voice tells us (who is speaking?) "a flaw underlying this thinking, but it is still too early to give it a name" (*NP* 79). It remains the task of the reader, as one historically located in the time projected by von Esenbeck, a member of the atomic age, to judge the beneficence of the sciences.

The tea party discussion on poetry enabled Wolf to crystallize many important themes and to elucidate their contemporary relevance. Thus Kleist's "vision of an age founded on empty talk rather than actions" reflects Wolf's pessimistic perspective of 1977, and the ambiguous narrative perspective makes the following statement applicable to her situation as well: "And there we are, still sitting there, and acting on the basis of the catch phrases of the century before, splitting hairs and struggling against our weariness, which keeps gaining ground on us, and all the time knowing: this is not anything we could live or die for. Our blood will be shed and no one will tell us why" (*NP* 78–9).

Moreover, the parallels she has established between Kleist's time and her own lend contemporary resonance to the poet's sceptical analysis of the state's limitations. In response to Merten's question, "how could a single individual who is not cut to the measure of the crowd urge his extraordinary aims upon a state, urge those high-flown demands he makes of life on a commonwealth, which, after all, has to satisfy the needs of all – the farmer, the merchant, the courtier – as well as the poet?" (*NP* 67), Kleist says vehemently:

Good! . . . If the state rejects the demands I place upon it, let it reject me as well. If only it could convince me that it does in fact satisfy the needs of the farmer and the merchant: that it does not compel all of us to subjugate our higher aims to its interests. The crowd, it's called. Am I fraudulently to transform my aims and views to accord with theirs? And above all the question remains: What would really benefit this crowd in the first place? But no one poses this question. Not in Prussia.   (*NP* 67)

Günter Kunert picked up the gauntlet thrown down by Christa Wolf when he drew the connection between Kleist's and Wolf's Prussia and maintained that in the GDR Kleist's question is still not being posed.[56]

The distinction Kleist draws between truth and pragmatism poses a similar challenge to the GDR (and to the West):

Is the state concerned with truth? The state? A state recognizes no other value than that which can be reckoned in terms of percentages. It desires to know truth only to the extent that it can make use of it. What for? For arts and trades. But arts are not something that one can extort from people, like the manifestation of military skills. If the arts and sciences do not help themselves, no king will come to their aid.   (*NP* 69)

Like Goethe's tormented artist figure Torquato Tasso, with whom he is identified, Kleist rejects the dualistic world view in which practical men of action like Savigny (the counterpart of Tasso's foil Antonio) believe. Günderrode, describing Savigny's antinomic thinking, defines it in terms of gender: "Savigny . . . Savigny sees everything in terms of Either-Or. You must know, Kleist, he has a masculine brain. He knows only one kind of curiosity: curiosity concerning that which is incontrovertible, logically consistent, and soluble" (*NP* 80). The narrator, commenting on Günderrode's assessment, ascribes to her an uncanny prescience, which echoes Wolf's own views on the inherent destructiveness of antinomic thinking and anticipates the dilemma presented in *Cassandra*: "This woman. As if she had some special intimation of the hidden contradiction on which the ruination of mankind is predicated" (*NP* 80).

It is no accident that the dialogue between Günderrode and Kleist takes place not indoors but outside, on a stroll which she has instigated. For Günderrode, a follower of Schelling's nature philosophy, the natural setting constitutes the proper backdrop for an exchange that qualitatively surpasses any that preceded it in its interpersonal intensity. In this dialogue, it is Günderrode who takes the initiative. She pulls Kleist aside; she sets the tone of their conversation by articulating her reflections on the etiology of human destructiveness.

> Günderrode says to herself, but as if she were replying to him: Yes, it has been her most painful experience to learn that only that within us which wishes to be destroyed is destructible; that only that can be seduced which meets seduction halfway; that only that can be free which is capable of freedom; that this realization conceals itself, in the most monstrous fashion, from the person to whom it is of greatest moment; and that the battles we exhaust ourselves in fighting are often no more than shadowboxing that takes place in our minds.   (*NP* 87–8)

An elaboration of Christa Wolf's concept of the blind spot, Günderrode's belief that only what is vulnerable in us can succumb to external forces, makes clear that for her destructiveness consists of a dialectic between objective and subjective factors. As such it anticipates a topic Günderrode and Kleist will discuss in the course of their solitary walk: fate versus free will. Equipped with a seismographic intuition and an acute, emphatic sensibility (she is, we are told, able to read Kleist's thoughts), Günderrode, by articulating an intensely personal experience as though in response to Kleist, indicates that she recognizes that this question is essential for him and that an unspoken affinity exists between them.

Like Kleist, Günderrode is not only alienated from other people; she is also alienated from her own sexuality. Sexual identity plays an important role in *No Place on Earth*. Günderrode, who suffers from the restrictions placed on women, aspires to be a man. Kleist, groping for a description of her, comes up against the inadequacies of commonplace language to define this unusual woman. "The way she stands there, not imposing herself, not expressly withdrawing. Highborn lady. Girl. Female. Woman. All designations glide away from her again. Virgin: absurd, even insulting; later I'll think why. Youth-maiden. Curious notion; enough of that" (*NP* 19). Repeatedly we are told that Günderrode's countenance, her way of speaking, do not conform to Kleist's expectations about women. "Should a woman have such a look about her?" (*NP* 8); "Ought a woman to speak in this manner?" (*NP* 93), he asks himself, and admits that he prefers more passive, more predictable women – in short, women who conform more closely to stereotypical gender expectations. One by one Kleist rejects the usual labels affixed to young women of his society, ultimately coining the term *Jünglingin* for her. *Jünglingin*, the feminization (by means of the "-in" ending) of an obviously masculine noun meaning "young man, youth," makes clear Günderrode's androgynous nature. Her androgyny is further underscored in the use of the masculine "der Freund" (rather than the feminine "die Freundin") which she and Savigny use to refer to her, and by the use of the diminutive neuter form "Günderrödchen" (the translation into the English, "Günderrode-my-pet," captures the endearing quality of the nickname, but not its gender neutrality). The fact that Kleist labels the terms he has invented "curious" and that he seeks to repress it ("enough of that") indicates that the term has struck a disturbing resonance in him. The probable source of his discomfort is revealed later. Reflecting on his relationship with his sister Ulrike, he admits that there is an "insoluble residue which does not fit into the overall diagram. This is the thing concerning which they cannot and must not ever, with a single word, with even so much as a single glance, show each other that they understand their own and one another's feelings. He not wholly a man, she not wholly a woman" (*NP* 94).

Christa Wolf has attributed the resistance many men have shown to *No Place on Earth* in part to Kleist's androgynous character-istics, to a "diffuse discomfort with everything androgynous, with the fluid transitions, with the fact that it isn't only one way or the other, friend-foe, male–female. A fear of learning how to live with not against each other. Not in rigid antinomies, but in fluid transitions, in productive alternatives that wouldn't have to be fatal. We haven't learned this, weren't brought up for it. Having to weigh its consequences creates fear."[57] The sexual ambivalence[58] Kleist and Günderrode share, together with the similarities in their situation, constitutes a bond that does not exist between any other characters in the work. Casting about for suitable topics to talk about, Günderrode invariably touches on those, be they personal or metaphysical, that render Kleist most vulnerable, those that are areas of deeply concealed self-doubt: "the appointed role of her sex and his" (*NP* 93), his sister Ulrike, blind fate versus free will, his love-hate relationship to Goethe, his ambition, his own literary work. Thus Günderrode, by intuitively touching on Kleist's taboos, induces him to speak the unspeakable. Her attitude is consonant with Christa Wolf's belief that it is essential for individual and societal well-being that problems be confronted and aired.

In the Günderrode–Kleist conversation, the main themes of the narrative converge in a resounding coda. Kleist's problems of sexual identity, alluded to in connection with his engagement to

Wilhelmine von Zenge and with his sister, are elaborated on and converge with Günderrode's sisterly interest in Ulrike. The theme of sisterliness, solidarity between women, expands the theme of friendship between women that plays such an important role in the Bettine essay and points forward to *Cassandra*. When queried by the suspicious Kleist about her interest in his sister, Günderrode responds that

from what she has observed, the lives of women require more courage than those of men. When she hears about a woman who has managed to summon up this necessary courage, she very much wants to know her. For things have reached such a pass that women – even women who are far removed from each other in many respects – must lend each other support, since men were no longer capable of doing so. (*NP* 93)

Lack of male support Günderrode in turn attributes to the particular exigencies of the historical situation. "It's because the men for whom we might care are themselves entangled in inextricable dilemmas. The constant round of responsibilities you men must deal with cut you into pieces which scarcely bear any relation to each other. We women are looking for a whole human being, and we cannot find him" (*NP* 93). Günderrode's statements closely approximate Christa Wolf's own views on gender relationships both in the specific historical context she is portraying (the beginning of the modern period) and in her own time. She attributes the intense female friendships of the women Romantics to their need for caring community and regards these friendships as a prelude to the salons. The dialogic nature of salons in turn with their aura of mutual confession and exchange, their free expression of subjectivity, makes them "a perhaps unconscious attempt to integrate feminine elements into a patriarchically structured culture" (GE 350). In Wolf's interpretation, the alienation brought about by the onset of industrialization and division of labor in Germany was experienced more acutely by men, because they were in the public sphere. Women, excluded from the public domain, were less likely to be coopted by the establishment of which the men sought to be a part. Hence women were – and are – often in a better position to see the deficiencies of their society. As the objects of men, who are themselves objects, women are paradoxically in a privileged position to see society's blind spots. There is a direct line between *No Place on Earth* and *Cassandra* in terms of making this function of women explicit.

While Kleist fails to understand Günderrode's interest in his sister, the discussion of a topic which has for so long been taboo frees him to speak about another topic of passionate concern to him: Goethe. For the tormented young dramatist, the fifty-five-year-old Goethe represented all that was unattainable. An impoverished orphan, Kleist is consumed with envy for the man of means who has found his place not only as the most influential German writer of his time but also as a statesman and natural scientist. Kleist's image of Goethe is informed by Schiller's distinction between the naive and the sentimental poet in his treatise *Naive and Sentimental Poetry* (1795–6). For Schiller, the naive poet is at one with nature; naive poetry is "imitation of nature," that is, mimetic and impersonal. The sentimental poet, on the other hand, is alienated from nature and divided within himself; sentimental poetry is reflective, self-conscious, and subjective.[59] Goethe represented the modern "naive" poet whose naturalness, spontaneity, and objectivity the "sentimental" Schiller admired and envied. For Kleist as well, the quintessentially sentimental artist, Goethe is the object of intense love and hatred. Yet his ambition propels him to confront the poet who is temperamentally his antipode. Kleist's self-proclaimed goal is to "tear the laurel from his brow" (*NP* 100).

Finally, prompted by Günderrode, Kleist is able to talk about his unfinished play "Robert Guiscard," which he had destroyed. Relating its content to Günderrode, he touches upon metaphysical questions that affect not only his art but also his life, and it becomes clear that Kleist's tragic world view and his innate self-destructiveness inform his aesthetic as well. He draws in the sand an "absurd geometrical construction, a mechanical device gone awry," which he calls his blueprint for a tragic drama. "He would like to know what she thinks of this impossible object, the presupposition of which is that, once it is set into motion it is condemned to destroy itself" (*NP* 84).

Kleist's fatalism also underlies the conception of "Robert Guiscard."[60] Günderrode immediately understands the insoluble dilemma in which the dramatist finds himself. Giving expression to Bloch's concept of *Ungleichzeitigkeit*, she assesses Guiscard's situation: a man caught between two value systems, someone as much bound by the laws of the ancients as by those of his own day, governed as much by his belief in fate as in the power of man to shape his own destiny. By recognizing that Kleist has worn himself out trying to capture inexpressible content in form, she absolves him of artistic incompetence. He has set himself an impossible task. Through her, Kleist is momentarily able to recognize and accept this as well. Once he understands that it is no disgrace to have failed at this task, he is free to make peace with himself. Thus the Kleist–Günderrode dialogue contributes to Kleist's self-knowledge. Significantly, during their encounter both Kleist and Günderrode are free of the physical ailments that so often plague them, an indication that their symptoms are psychosomatic and may well arise from a withdrawal of love.[61]

The high point of the dialogue between Kleist and Günderrode, indeed of the narrative as a whole, is the *Wesensschau* (eidetic intuition) of their spiritual touching.

They examine each other candidly, without reserve. Naked gazes. Self-abandonment, a tentative experiment. Smiles, first hers, then his, ironical. Let's pretend it's a game even if it's deadly earnest. You know it, I know it too. Don't come too close. Don't stay too far away. Conceal yourself. Reveal yourself. Forget what you know. Remember it. Masks fall away, superincrustations, scabs, varnish. The bare skin. Undisguised features. So that's my face. This is yours. Different down to the ground, alike from the ground up. Woman. Man. Untenable words. We two, each imprisoned in his sex. That touching we desire so infinitely does not exist. It was killed along with us. We should have to invent it. It offers itself to us in dreams, disfigured, horrible, grotesque. The fear in the pale morning light, after one wakes up so early. We remain unknowable to each other, unapproachable, craving disguises. The names of strangers in which we wrap ourselves. The cry of lament forced back into the throat. Grieving is forbidden, for what losses have we suffered?

I am not I. You are not you. Who is "we"?

We are very alone.   (*NP* 108–9)

In moving from the "I" to the "we" (the text continues at some length in the first-person plural), Kleist and Günderrode are briefly united; their existential loneliness is assuaged by mutual recognition. They are aware that the touching they long for is not possible for them; they cannot be known. At the same time this recognition is a form of knowing each other. In experiencing the seemingly impossible, they share a utopian moment. Thus the hope of which Günderrode speaks finds concrete expression, however fleetingly. Just as the unreserved subjectivity of Maxie Wander's interviews with women from the GDR and the "touch-fest" in *Cassandra* are for Wolf characterized by the spirit of a really existing utopia, Kleist and Günderrode's touching also offers a glimpse of truly humane social interaction. While this utopian moment is not sustained and cannot avert the tragic outcome of their lives, it serves to keep alive the memory of a future both for the characters and for the reader. Although for Kleist and Günderrode there is no place on earth, by bringing them together and granting them this interchange, Wolf inscribes their meeting as a concrete utopia.[62] We as readers are meant not only to draw the parallels between their situation and ours but also to recognize, affirm, and work toward creating viable alternatives. As a passage that clearly echoes Bloch's philosophy of hope warns: "If we cease to hope, then that which we fear will surely come" (*NP* 117).

For one brief moment as the masks fall away, alienation is overcome. After that, Günderrode and Kleist return to their isolated lives. In an omniscient projection, the narrator informs us that Kleist's fleeting regret at not knowing her poetry will subside, that he will not follow through on his resolve to read her works, that news of her death will evoke merely a twinge in him. It also projects Kleist's bleak future, indicating that he will in fact attempt to accommodate himself to the expectations of his society, will take a civil service position that will aggravate his precarious emotional situation. He will suffer another breakdown.[63]

It is hardly accidental that Christa Wolf chose the Romantic period as a setting for her narration. Her interest in Romanticism was obvious as early as 1969/70, when she published the stories "Unter den Linden" and "Neue Lebensansichten eines Katers."[64] "Neue Lebensansichten" (New Memoirs of a Tomcat) takes its title and its literary device from the fragmentary novel *Lebensansichten des Katers Murr* (Memoirs of Tomcat Murr, 1820/2) by the late-Romantic author E. T. A. Hoffmann (1776–1822). Like its predecessor, it presents the scribblings of a gifted tomcat who observes the human world and affirms its dominant values. The story of Hoffmann's tomcat was interspersed with the journal of a sensitive musician whose genius makes him less able to survive in philistine society than his pet. Wolf's story does not give excerpts from the human journal in which the tomcat writes, that of his master's teenage daughter, but the counterpoint is the same; her tomcat is an advocate of his master's science project aimed at generating total human happiness by eliminating all instances of the non-rational, including creativity. Both Hoffmann's novel and Wolf's much less ambitious story use irony to make a point about what is irreducible and valuable about human beings: imagination, the nonrational. Hoffmann's tomcat represents the philistine position and Wolf's that of the technocrats, but in both cases it is those spheres of human activity repudiated by the tomcats that are seen to have the most value.

"Unter den Linden" again uses Romantic motifs and techniques to portray the narrator's confrontation and reconciliation with her earlier self, first introduced as "das Mädchen" (the girl). Wolf's most obvious borrowing from Romanticism is her use of the popular motif of the *Doppelgänger* (here, older and younger selves). More important for the development of the narrative, however, is its use of dreams. As in Romantic works, dreams in "Unter den Linden" (as in many of Wolf's other works) function to reveal aspects of reality hidden from normal waking consciousness. They uncover connections among seemingly discrete phenomena and make clear that the force that unifies them is individual consciousness, guided by the faculty of imagination. As the vehicle of the nonrational, dreams for both the Romantics and Wolf allow the play of imagination and grant access to more significant truth than the truths of rationality. Schiller's privileging of the imagination, his assessment that the human being "is only fully a human being when he plays"[65] holds for both Wolf and the Romantics and illuminates one of the fundamental affinities between them. Play is liberating; the play of the imagination frees the mind to create connections and significances that overcome alienation and make the world a home for humans. It is the act of creative play, the process and not the result, that is liberating in a general sense; for the reader the significance of a work of literature lies less in the content, that is, in the specific plot or situation described, than in the experience of participating in the creation of a world. Moreover, the sense of subjective power and responsibility granted us *vis-à-vis* the world of the work of art can be extended to empirical reality as well and can help us realize our human potential, both individually and communally.

In analyzing Wolf's work I have mentioned features of her style that draw the reader into the creative process. Her narrators tend to be noncoercive and nonauthoritarian, to allow the reader to see the "open possibilities" of situations or characters rather than presenting them as finished and closed structures. She (along with many other modern authors) shares this trait with the Romantics, who experimented with ways of breaking open the traditional paradigm of the self-enclosed world presented by literature. Romantic works are replete with examples of self-aware experimentation with literary form aimed at creating alternatives to the omniscient narrator. The ideological point of these experiments is to give the reader first-hand experience of creative freedom. The fragmentary nature of Romantic works such as Novalis's *Heinrich von Ofterdingen*, for instance, can be seen as a rejection of closed structures. Similarly, the radical shift in perspective that occurs when the narrator of Brentano's *Godwi* dies of boredom in mid-narration and one of the characters is drafted to take over his function undermines the idea of an authoritarian narrator. Or the narrator is sometimes made superfluous when a character's unmediated voice speaks for itself in a Romantic text, as in Bonaventura's *Nachtwachen* (Night Watches) – and in Wolf's *No Place on Earth*. All these techniques are highly conscious attempts at a nonauthoritarian narrative stance consonant with Romantic theory, which regards literature as a means to liberation.

Wolf's formal experimentation indicates more than an attenuated reception of Romantic ideas that have become common currency. Rather, it can be seen as the manifestation of an elective affinity with Romanticism. Wolf shares in good part the Romantics' belief in the function of literature. Her choice of the Romantics as a theme for *No Place on Earth* makes her affinity with Romantic thought explicit.

A focus of the indoor conversation at Merten's is literature, art, poetry. The social setting of the work and the fluid narrative perspective, which often allows the characters' voices to occupy the foreground in dialogue, call to mind the literary salon so popular among the Romantics. Wolf was acutely aware of the salon's importance as a forum. Indeed, a quotation by Rahel Varnhagen, who led one of the most prominent Berlin salons, serves as a motto for "Unter den Linden." The Romantic emphasis on conversation, on co-philosophizing (*symphilosophieren*), which is in keeping with their emphasis on process and their belief that poetry should become an ever more inclusive undertaking, made the salon an obvious arena for literary exchange.

The salon, comprised of a closed circle of men and women, met weekly to engage in continuing literary discussion. In its emphasis on friendship and sociability, the salon represented the personal and private sphere while at the same time serving as a forum for public discourse. Precisely this merging of the private and public spheres constitutes its uniqueness. As Hannah Arendt pointed out in her study of Rahel Varnhagen, "the salons were the meeting places of those who had learned to represent themselves through conversation. The actor can always be the 'seeming' of himself."[66] Thus the salon can be seen as a new form of "theater" in which "there was no need for an audience, for this theater was not the representation of life but its verbal enactment."[67] For Helen Fehervary the fact that "the form of the salon demanded subjectivity – as intersubjectivity – on everyone's part" renders it a "literary utopia whose participants might have transformed the genres of the novel and the drama, had it not been for the ensuing Restoration and its cultural conservatism."[68]

Merten's tea party cannot be considered a salon, even though the gathering includes the circle around Brentano and even though writing is a topic of discussion. Nor can Merten be considered a genuine patron of the arts. Rather he is a rich merchant who, by virtue of his economic standing, has the literary avant-garde at his beck and call. Merten's party is a bourgeois capitalistic perversion of the salon just as much of the tea party conversation is a corruption of the salon conversation. The actors here are no longer representing themselves; they are playing a role. Most of the conversations at Merten's no longer fit the paradigm of Romantic conversation. Instead they are closer to our commonplace understanding of the term, namely that mode of discourse common to urbane society, circumscribed by certain expectations, in which form rather than content is of the essence, in which the speaker feels compelled to demonstrate his or her own erudition. The impetus for these conversations arises less from the desire to communicate than from the need to excel. Informed by the principle of one-upmanship, the conversation loses its dialogic structure and becomes self-perpetuating.

While Merten's tea party does not recreate the Romantic salon, traces of Romantic interaction are perceptible, notably in Günderrode's interaction with her friends. When Clemens Brentano asks Günderrode for forgiveness after their altercation, Kleist notes that the

matter seems to have been settled. Kleist has never before been among people who trespass so greatly on each other's territory and yet do not become enemies as a result. A glimmer of hope that certain dreams of his young manhood, of which he now feels ashamed, might conceivably come true after all: trust might not be an absurdity, love not a phantasm.

(*NP* 75).

In her Günderrode essay Wolf described the intersubjectivity of the Romantics as follows:

Productive relations – she [Günderrode] knows them, she engages in them consciously. "Communication is a necessity for me." The new values of these young people, which they cannot realize in the rigidified or quickly rigidifying institutions, are formulated, discussed, and tried out in circles of friends with similar ideas. That is what I want to call anticipation, adumbration, the attempt to break through isolation and to move in new productive forms of life, forms of life arising out of the spirit of a group.

(GE 333-4)

Helen Fehervary's argument that the salon serves as a model for Christa Wolf's writing,[69] while overstated, offers an interesting perspective on her work. It is certainly true that Wolf's transposition of the epistolary (her sources) to the dramatic mode (verbal enactment) closely approximates the salon. However, the main point of convergence between Wolf's writing and the Romantic salon is the dialogic nature common to both. Dialogism, as defined by Bakhtin, "represents an epistemological mode which is neither authoritative nor absolute."[70] The dialogic informs all of Wolf's writing since "An Afternoon in June" and embraces the author–reader relationship as well as the relationship of the author–narrator to her subject matter, that is, to her characters.

The dialogic also informs one of the central documents of Romantic literary theory, Friedrich Schlegel's *Gespräch über die Poesie* (*Dialogue on Poetry*, 1800).[71] In this essay Schlegel claims that poetry (that is, the spirit of poetry, *Poesie*, as opposed to poetic production, *Dichtung*) unites all who love it; that all human beings carry their own poetry as a means of subjective transformation of objective reality within themselves; that the world of poetry is inexhaustible; that there is conscious poetry in the form of works of art and unconscious poetry in nature and human experience, but that the earth is the one great poem which it is our human task to celebrate. Poetry is thus necessarily democratic, and the function of the poet is vatic. He is a prophet not of divine mysteries inaccessible except to the elect, but of the liberating gospel that we are all creators and therefore all godlike. The poet teaches us our own poetry.

Gespräch is structured polyphonically because Schlegel rejects out of hand the notion that there can be one correct view of poetry; that is, that there can be a single valid aesthetic. In his nonsystematic presentation, a number of voices are allowed to speak about poetry, and there is no overarching corrective perspective. The inclusion of disparate, often contradictory points of view allows him to show the intermediate steps in the development of an argument and to capture the process of thinking; it illustrates his pluralistic, nonauthoritarian stance. Reason is monolithic, says Schlegel, the same for all humans, but poetry exists in a different form in each human being. Implicit in his *Gespräch* is the idea that poetry is the refuge of the imagination from the tyranny of reason.

The inclusive, egalitarian Romantic politics of art clearly appealed to Wolf. Its claim that art can be a force for increasing human freedom makes it consonant with the goals of Marxism. Thus, given the Romantic view that formal experimentation is a means of teaching freedom, there is no inherent conflict between , socialism and formal experimentation in literature.

No Place on Earth calls to mind a salon only to disappoint that expectation, but in their dialogue the poets Günderrode and Kleist do carry on a counterpoint of significance to the small talk around them. The untimeliness of their views is still untimely; their perspectives are enlightening for our society as well. Kleist's reflections on the encroachment of the intellect to the detriment of the imagination obviously have relevance for a contemporary audience as well. It is precisely at this point that art can be the most useful to us, by revitalizing the humanly necessary sphere of the imagination.

Christa Wolf not only concurs with Schlegel's view of the function and importance of poetry; she follows his *Gespräch* still further in calling *No Place on Earth* an "erwünschte Legende" (wished-for legend). She creates the legend of two artists meeting, talking, and touching, leaving their words behind for us. This is a literary myth and as such evokes Schlegel's call for a new mythology to express the (new) Romantic view of nature and the human creative role in the world. In the section "Rede über die Mythologie" ("Talk on Mythology") he explains the need to incorporate new knowledge into symbolic art, to make it more than mere rational knowledge. He also asks for an eclectic revival of old mythologies, pieces of which can function as epistemes in the new mythology. In *No Place on Earth* Wolf has criticized contemporary society using Romantic characters, themes, and formal devices in the service of the Romantic view of art's function. In her next work, *Cassandra*, she deconstructs a significant myth and constructs it anew, in order to give aesthetic form to her insights about the self-destructive nature of Western civilization.

6

CASSANDRA: MYTH, MATRIARCHY, AND THE CANON

Re-vision – the act of looking back, of seeing with fresh eyes, of entering an old text from a new critical direction – is for us more than a chapter in cultural history: it is an act of survival. Until we can understand the assumptions in which we are drenched we cannot know ourselves. And this drive to self-knowledge, for woman, is more than a search for identity: it is part of her refusal of the self-destructiveness of male-dominated society. A radical critique of literature, feminist in its impulse, would take the work first of all as a clue to how we live, how we have been living, how we have been led to imagine ourselves, how our language has trapped as well as liberated us; and how we can begin to see – and therefore live – afresh . . . We need to know the writing of the past, and to know it differently than we have ever known it; not to pass on a tradition but to break its hold over us.[1]

Adrienne Rich

In her Cassandra project of 1983, Christa Wolf undertakes the radical feminist critique of literature and society described by Adrienne Rich, in a re-vision of the myth of Cassandra. Her narrative and her critique of the Western literary tradition in "Conditions of a Narrative," the four essays that accompany the literary text,[2] are important contributions to a female aesthetic of resistance. Impelled by a drive for self-knowledge, they constitute "part of her refusal of the self-destructiveness of male-dominated society."

Human self-destructiveness is a recurrent theme in Wolf's work. In her search for the possible causes of this pervasive phenomenon, she has focused increasingly on hierarchal structures and patriarchal values. She has repeatedly implicated male inability to love, the perversion of reason, and atrophy of imagination as causes of (self-) alienation. In her Cassandra project, Wolf broadens her analysis by exploring how the patriarchy's systematic exclusion of women has helped shape our present catastrophic world political situation.

Christa Wolf's work of the eighties has been stamped by the fear of nuclear catastrophe. In 1980 she received West Germany's Georg Büchner Prize for Literature. In her acceptance speech, she again paid tribute to the writer she so highly esteems as she reaffirmed her commitment to *littérature engagée*. The Büchner Prize Acceptance Speech[3] reiterates issues familiar since *Patterns of Childhood* and *No Place on Earth* and points forward to concerns specifically addressed in *Cassandra*. In it Wolf expands on her analysis of Büchner in "The Reader and the Writer" (1969), where she characterized him as a writer whose subjective presence in his work served as a model for her own authorship. In the speech delivered twelve years later, she views him primarily as a social critic. Her interpretation of Büchner as a spiritual cousin of the Romantics, as an untimely phenomenon, as a precursor of us moderns is an obvious carry-over from her work on Kleist and Günderrode and allowed her to express her current concerns.

In 1980 Christa Wolf's overriding concern was the survival of Europe. With the resurgence of the Cold War in the seventies, Wolf found herself grappling with the same issues she had had her Moscow delegation debate in *Moscow Novella*. She feared that humankind's momentous decision – permanent peace or self-annihilation – was dangerously close to being made. Written from the perspective of a Central European confronted with the imminent stationing of Cruise and Pershing ii missiles in Western Europe and the presence of SS–20s in the Warsaw Pact nations, watching the superpowers use Europe as a pawn on their battle-field, her Büchner Prize Speech reasserts the redemptive potential of literature.

Wolf's mandate that "today literature must be peace research" (BP 10) must be viewed in the context of a broad-based European reaction to the precarious political situation. Peace conferences in East Berlin, The Hague, Cologne, and West Berlin in the early eighties were widely attended by writers from both East and West. These conferences, reflective of wide-scale peace movements in the FRG and GDR, broke down traditional political barriers and united participants in a condemnation of the militarism of both sides. The first Berlin meeting of writers for the advancement of peace was held in East Berlin on 13–14 December 1981[4] and the second was held in West Berlin on 22–3 April 1983.[5] The transcripts reveal that most of the participants framed their protests in the discourse of politics instead of exploring the potential of literary language for furthering the goals of peace. As Alexander Stephan has pointed out, only the small group of women writers who had been invited to participate in the peace conferences called for a qualitatively new language. They criticized their (male) colleagues for appropriating the very militaristic jargon that they themselves repudiated in politicians. They pointed to the specific task of the writer: since language is their artistic medium, writers may well be able to "correct the concepts" currently being (mis)used. Rejecting the prevailing pragmatism and progress-oriented thinking of male-dominated society, these women expressed their commitment to formulating and creating a more humane way of being in the world.[6]

In "A Letter," written in December 1981, Christa Wolf, contemplating whether Europe could be saved, gave voice to precisely these concerns. According to her:

A civilization which is capable of planning its own demise and which, through incredible sacrifices, creates the means to do so, seems sick to me. Rockets and bombs are after all not by-products of this culture; they are the consistent manifestation of thousands of years of expansionist behavior; they are the inevitable embodiments of the syndrome of industrial societies, which with their more! faster! more accurately! more efficiently! have subordinated all other values, many of which were measured by more human norms ... Anything that cannot be measured, weighed, counted, verified, might as well not exist. I am plagued by the thought that our culture, which could only attain what it calls 'progress' through force, through domestic repression, through the annihilation and exploitation of foreign cultures, which has narrowed its sense of reality by pursuing its material interests, which has become instrumental and efficient – that such a culture necessarily has to reach the point it has now reached.[7]

Inextricably connected with Wolf's denunciation of instrumental rationality in our current situation is her criticism of patriarchal society's exclusion of women: "For three thousand years, wherever 'reality,' things of real importance, were drafted, planned, and produced, women have not counted and do not count. Half the population of a culture have *by their very nature* no part in those phenomena through which that culture recognizes itself." And, she adds, almost as an afterthought, "it occurs to me that they therefore have no part in the experiments in thought and production that concern its destruction."[8]

The Büchner Prize Speech, Wolf's most overtly political statement to that time, was written somewhat earlier than "Ein Brief," but its explicitly pacifist focus links it directly to the women writers' contribution to the peace conferences (in which she participated) and to *Cassandra*. Reflecting on the fact that a mere fifty years separate Goethe's humanistic enjoinder "Let man be noble" from Büchner's despairing assessment that "a mistake was made when we were created,"[9] Wolf credits Büchner with an untimely modern sensibility. She notes: "We are not the first. Courage, backbone, hope, immediacy – much that is necessary for speaking is broken on the fracture points between epochs. Fear leaps into the vacant spaces. The literary vanguard nearly always anticipates the fear that later overcomes many" (BP 5).

Wolf also credits Büchner with the awareness that "progress, just then being cranked up in the grand style, had the makings of a new myth" and that "the passion the new era found in itself was rooted in the passion for destruction" (BP 6), insights his contemporaries had no interest in hearing. Precisely the passionate belief in progress, based on a corruption of the enlightenment concept of reason, has in her view brought us to the brink of the abyss. "Sober to the marrow," she maintains, "we stand aghast before the dreams made real by instrumental thinking that still calls itself reason, although it has long since lost its enlightened impulse toward emancipation, toward maturity, and has entered the Industrial Age as barefaced utilitarian mania" (BP 4). In analyzing the "precursor" Büchner, she attributes to him an anachronistic sensibility for the spiritual vicissitudes attending the rise of industrialization, materialism, and commercialism, the recognition that the "sign of the approaching age was the paradox" (BP 5), and "the desire to accomplish the impossible: to render the blind spot of this culture visible" (BP 6–7). Thus she credits her predecessor with addressing what to her is an essential function of literature: to examine society's self-destructive blind spot. In Büchner's works she sees prefigured that self-destructiveness and reduction of livable alternatives that she had begun to record in *Christa T.*, *Patterns of Childhood*, and *No Place on Earth* and that she explores to the full in her indictment of the Western social and cultural tradition in *Cassandra*.

Interweaving quotations from Büchner's works throughout her text, Wolf criticizes the exclusion to which women have traditionally been subjected as she speaks of her cautious faith in the civilizing power of literature. Written when Wolf was already working on her Cassandra project, the Büchner Prize Speech contains a brilliant passage intended to illuminate the changing, yet fundamentally unchanged, position of women throughout history. Women's lot as depicted in *Cassandra* – exclusion, invisibility, objectification – is traced in all of Büchner's heroines. Variations on a theme, the treatment they suffer at the hands of the male figures testifies for Wolf to their interchangeability. The fate of Rosetta, a figure in Büchner's drama *Leonce and Lena*, becomes for Wolf the symbol of women *per se*: "Invisible to herself and Leonce, mute, deprived of reality, Rosetta is fated to dwell in a repudiated, soundless, forfeited space, wholly incomprehensible to the world, to which she too belongs. She is definable by what she is not" (BP 7).

Wolf traces her interpretation of literary representations of the eternal feminine by way of Büchner and Georg Hauptmann to Ibsen:

Rosetta lets herself be deprived of her rights. Robbed of her voice. Of sadness. Joy. Love. Work. Art. She lets herself be raped. Prostituted. Locked up. Driven crazy. Lets herself, as Rose,[10] be oppressed, exploited: "doubly," it's called. Lets herself be forced to bear children. Lets herself be forced to abort children. Lets her sex be analyzed away. Entangles herself in the net of impotence. Becomes the nag. The slut. The vamp. The cricket on the hearth. Leaves, as Nora, the doll's house.   (BP 7)

She does not restrict her catalogue of victims to literary projections of the male imagination[11] but extends it to include such diverse figures as Rosa Luxemburg, Marlene Dietrich, and the wartime and post-war everywoman worker, thus illustrating how fluid the boundaries are for her between art and life. Common to all these variations on the theme of womanhood is that

Rosetta under her many names lets herself be destroyed rather than admitting to herself what is happening to her: that when Leonce the thinker says "subject," he never means her, the real woman. That for him she has become an object ... Here she pauses. Does not strive for the ultimate insight. Prefers to deny herself. Suppresses her talent. Supports, under her many names, some familiar to you, the genius of the contemplative, poetic, artistic male.[12]   (BP 7)

As in "Ein Brief," in the Büchner Prize Speech Wolf's feminist critique meshes with her appraisal of the immediate European political situation. Forfeiting her East German identity, she speaks to her West German audience[13] as a German woman writer. She notes that in the event of a "'nuclear confrontation,' the two countries on both sides of the Elbe River would be among the first to be obliterated" and speculates on the existence of maps that have already "plotted the phases of this obliteration" (BP 10–11). Noting that "with the help of specialized language, scientists have shielded their discoveries from their own feelings; pseudological linguistic constructions support the politicians' obsession that the salvation of humanity lies in the possibility of exterminating it several times over," Wolf maintains that "today, literature must be peace research" (BP 10). She calls upon literature to confront that "map of death with its own map." It is her hope that

all the localities and landscapes, human relations that literature described so accurately, justly and in bias, painfully, critically, devotedly, fearfully and happily, ironically, rebelliously, and lovingly, should be erased from that map of death and be considered rescued ... Perhaps a General Staff may really find it harder to target a city that was described intimately and accurately than to target one that no one knows. One that nobody was moved to describe as one's hometown, as the place of one's humiliation or first love. (BP 11)

Through its ability to infuse objective reality with subjective experience and response, Wolf hopes that literature will at long last "be taken at its word and applied to the preservation of human affairs" (BP 11).

Christa Wolf interjects a seemingly parenthetical remark about Cassandra into her deliberations on annihilation in the Büchner Prize Speech: she imagines that Cassandra "must have loved Troy more than herself when she dared to prophesy to her compatriots the downfall of their city" (BP 11). As her Cassandra project makes clear, this figure is in fact germane to her recent considerations on literature and politics. Christa Wolf's first literary work to appear after the Büchner Prize Speech, *Cassandra* (1983) is clearly intended as a contribution to peace research. The tension between patriotism and self-love implied in her evocation of Cassandra in the acceptance speech underlies the structure of Wolf's narrative. An essential subtext of this work is the question of whether and how the fall of Troy could have been avoided and by extension whether Europe can be saved.

Wolf's *Cassandra* is not simply the story of an ancient civilization's extinction. Instead, in the four essays that accompany the narrative, "Conditions of a Narrative," she gives explicit contemporary relevance to questions raised in her literary text. Originally delivered as a series of "Lectures on Poetics" at the University of Frankfurt in May 1982, the Cassandra complex represents Wolf's tightest interweaving of literature and biography to date. Indeed, Wolf effectively erases the generic boundaries between fiction and essay (literature and biography) by appending the narrative *Cassandra* as the fifth lecture on poetics.

The multilayered, multitemporal essays, an amalgam of travelogue, work diary, and letter, contain Christa Wolf's unsystematic reflections about her fictional character, about the inception, development, and ramifications of her story, about war, peace, the status of women, about the conditions for women's writing. In addition to depicting the genesis of her Cassandra project, Wolf reflects on current world political events, condemns the bellicosity of both NATO and Warsaw Pact nations, and draws explicit parallels between Cassandra's Troy and our world. The closed-ended story, on the other hand, consists almost exclusively of Cassandra's memories and reflections as, immediately before her Greek captors slay her, she reconstructs her personal history (hence the history of her people) and, in creating herself, recreates her city in imagination.

Apart from a small frame, whose opening prong serves to evoke the figure of Cassandra and whose closing prong, in its shift to the present tense, indicates that Cassandra has succeeded in (re)creating herself,[14] the narrative consists of Cassandra's interior monologue.

Unlike *Patterns of Childhood* with its overlay of fictional narration and essayistic commentary, *Cassandra* makes it the reader's responsibility, as it was in *No Place on Earth*, to establish connections between the self-reflective essays and narrative, to determine the contemporaneity in Wolf's most temporally distant work to date. In many respects Wolf's most stinging indictment of contemporary society, *Cassandra* offers striking analogies between prehistoric times and our current situation, between Cassandra's doomed Troy and Wolf's Europe, inextricably caught up in the deadly arms race between East and West, teetering on the brink of destruction. Two common factors in Wolf's equation of prehistoric Troy and our contemporary culture are the prevalence of a delusional war mentality and the exclusion and objectification of women – both attributable to patriarchal values.[15]

Christa Wolf clearly articulates her indignation, her fears, and her call to reason: she advocates unilateral disarmament as a last-ditch attempt to put an end to the war madness, knowing that her call will probably be misconstrued, that she speaks with the voice of Cassandra. Wolf is not a pacifist in the traditional sense. That is, she does not absolutely reject the use of force. She can justify the use of weapons for self-defense in specific historical contexts: in the case of those European countries invaded by Hitler in the thirties; in Vietnam's self-defense against American oppression; in wars of liberation and self-defense in South America today.

Her pacifism arises from a recognition of the specific historical situation of postwar Europe. As she says: "I am a European woman. Europe cannot be defended against an atomic war. Either it will survive in one piece or be destroyed in one piece. The existence of nuclear weapons has reduced to absurdity all conceivable strategies for defending our little continent" (CON 229). Her reasonable analysis stands in sharp contrast to the "delusional thinking" currently prevalent among military and political leaders. Wolf defines "delusional thinking" as follows:

What do I actually mean when I say "delusion"? I mean the absurdity of the claim that the excessive atomic armament of both sides creates a "balance of terror" that reduces the danger of war; that in the long run it even offers a minimum of security. I mean the grotesque calculation based on strategies that were devastating when applied to conventional weaponry, but which are senseless and irrational in relation to atomic weapons. Hence the cynical saying: He who strikes first will die second.

(CON 229)

In a bold line of attack, Wolf derives our current dead-ended situation from that of Troy: she sees it as the logical conclusion of an inevitable process of self-estrangement initiated by the victory of the patriarchal Achaian princes. She locates the beginning of alienation in a much earlier historical period than is generally accepted, above all in Marxist thought. In her interpretation, alienation is no longer the result of industrialization; it can no longer be circumscribed as alienation of labor. Instead its roots are to be found in the cradle of Occidental civilization. According to her, alienation came about when a patriarchal culture displaced a matriarchal one, introduced hierarchical thinking, banned women from the public sphere; when societal structures became rigid and human beings for political or other reasons were treated as means to an end. In this analysis, Western civilization from the outset has carried within itself the seeds of its own destruction.

Wolf arrives at this radical perspective through a change in what she terms her "view-scope." In the "Letter to A," the fourth Frankfurt lecture on poetics,[16] she testifies to the far-reaching implications of this new perspective:

Ever since I took up the name Cassandra and began to carry it around like a sort of credential and watchword; ever since I entered these realms where it now leads me, everything I encounter seems to be related to it. Things that in the past were separate have merged without my realizing it. A little light is falling into previously dark, unconscious rooms. Underneath them or previous to them (places and times flow together), further rooms can be sensed in the dim light. The time of which we are aware is only a paper-thin, bright strip on a vast bulk that is mostly shrouded in darkness. With the widening of my visual angle and the readjustment to my depth of focus, my viewing lens (through which I perceive our time, all of us, you, myself) has undergone a decisive change. It is comparable to that decisive change that occurred more than thirty years ago, when I first became acquainted with Marxist theory and attitudes; a liberating and illuminating experience which altered my thinking, my view, what I felt about and demanded of myself. When I try to realize what is happening, what *has* happened, I find that (to bring it down to the lowest common denominator) there has been an expansion of what for me is "real." Moreover, the nature, the inner structure, the movement of this reality has also changed and continues to change almost daily.[17]   (CON 277–8)

Seen through Wolf's new view-scope, all Greek literature and poetics undergoes a reinterpretation. According to this re-vision, both arose from that patriarchal reevaluation of values characterized in the religious realm by the displacement of the cult(s) of the goddesses, the coming into prominence of Zeus in the heavens, and the increasing dominance of the cult of Apollo. Wolf believes, however, that the concept of Zeus was not possible until a monarchy with a male line of inheritance arose. This amalgamation of patriarchy, property, and hierarchy, coupled with the simultaneous displacement, exclusion, and objectification of women is, according to her, an essential characteristic of the origins of the Greek epic. Occidental literature, which begins with the Homeric hero stories, is for Wolf a literature of the victors, "a heroization of bloody crimes."[18] Wolf has no interest in the Homeric epic, based on conquest and violence. She applies gender-based aesthetic criteria to Homer and rejects the *Iliad* as boring. Conceived around the rage of Achilles, dealing with battle and slaughter, focused on male experience, the epic can evoke no response in Wolf as a woman. *Cassandra*, written against the male tradition, offers a female interpretation of the Cassandra myth. As such, it represents Wolf's confrontation with the patriarchal mythological and poetic canon.

In the Cassandra essays, Wolf consciously reflects on the gender specificity of writing. She thus makes explicit what she has from the outset, but ever more consciously, been working to achieve: her self-understanding as a woman writer. In the third Frankfurt lecture on poetics, Wolf reflects on the prerequisites for women's writing:

To what extent is there really such a thing as "women's writing"? To the extent that women, for historical and biological reasons, experience a different reality than men. Experience a different reality than men and express it. To the extent that women belong not to the rulers but to the ruled, and have done so for centuries. To the extent that they are the objects of objects, second-degree objects, frequently the objects of men who are themselves objects, and so, in terms of their social position, unqualified members of the subculture. To the extent that they stop wearing themselves out trying to integrate themselves into the prevailing delusional systems. To the extent that, writing and living, they aim at autonomy. In this case they encounter the men who aim at autonomy. Autonomous people, nations, and systems can promote each other's welfare; they do not have to fight each other like those whose inner insecurity and immaturity continually demand the demarcation of limits and postures of intimidation. (CON 259)

Wolf's deliberations on women's writing are consistent with her views on the function of literature as formulated in her early essay, "The Reader and the Writer." In that essay, she had maintained that in our modern, troubled world, "the only way left is the narrow path of reason, of growing up, of a maturing of the human consciousness, the deliberate step out of prehistory into history. The decision to grow up remains to be taken."[19] In "Conditions of a Narrative" Wolf again expresses her belief that the basis for caring human community is the full development of its individual subjects, defined here as "autonomy" of the individual. In "The Reader and the Writer," Wolf stated that "epic prose" "can push the frontiers of our knowledge about ourselves farther forward. It can keep awake in us the memory of the future that we must not abandon on pain of destruction. It helps mankind [*sic*] to become conscious subjects. It is revolutionary and realistic; it entices and encourages people to achieve the impossible."[20] Since literature helps humankind become conscious subjects, it can only be created by conscious subjects, that is, by autonomous individuals. Given her debt to Idealist philosophy, it is hardly surprising that Christa Wolf frames her reflections on women's writing in terms of autonomy and conscious subjectivity.

In "Conditions of a Narrative" Wolf rejects the reality depicted in the Homeridae because it fails to correspond to the experienced reality of women. But she also rejects Homer for other aesthetic reasons: the *Iliad*, with its concentration on what is most important for the male imagination, represents a simplification and reduction of the material and ultimately excludes what is most important for her. Often precisely what a male writer considers unimportant is the most essential thing for her as a woman writer. Through her

Cassandra figure Wolf seeks to inscribe what has traditionally been excluded from accounts of the Trojan War: the experienced reality of women.

Wolf's study of the literary, mythological, and historical sources of the Cassandra tradition convinced her that Cassandra represents "one of the first women figures handed down to us whose fate prefigures what was to be the fate of women for three thousand years: to be turned into an object" (CON 227). Yet she also assigns to her advantages peculiar to women: because they are not part of the ruling system, women's underprivileged status as outsiders grants them a greater ability to perceive false consciousness and misconstructions, that is, delusional societal structures. Wolf's Cassandra is not a prophet in the traditional sense. Her clairvoyance is not a divinely granted "ability" to see the future. Consistently referred to as a "seeress," Cassandra "sees" the future because she has the courage to confront the actual state of affairs. She must, however, first secure this courage by freeing herself from "the prevailing delusional system" – by becoming an autonomous subject.

Carrying over her feminist critique of Greek literature to poetic theory, Wolf objects to the absence of women in Greek theater. She sees further evidence that the development of patriarchy displaced women in the fact that women's roles in tragedy were played by men. Aristotle's *Poetics* is a product of this new social order. Aristotle calls upon the mimetically creative artist to represent agents, who must of necessity be either good or bad; Wolf emphatically rejects this antinomic thinking, just as she rejects the one-sidedness of male rationality and false objectivity as detrimental to integration and totality: to life. Reaffirming a holistic (literary) subjectivity, Wolf asserts her belief

that everything is fundamentally related; and that the strictly one-track-minded approach – the extraction of a single "skein" for purposes of narration and study – damages the entire fabric, including the "skein." Yet to put it in simplified terms, this one-track-minded route is the one that has been followed by Western thought: the route of segregation, of the renunciation of the manifoldness of phenomena, in favor of dualism and monism, in favor of closed systems and pictures of the world; of the renunciation of subjectivity in favor of a sealed "objectivity." (CON 287)

Christa Wolf introduced her Frankfurt lectures on poetics by maintaining that she had no poetics. The lectures were meant to clarify the reasons for her rejection of the traditional concept of a poetics, which according to the *Classical Antiquity Lexicon* is "a theory of the art of poetry, which at an advanced stage – Aristotle, Horace – takes on a systematic form and whose norms have been accorded 'wide validity' in numerous countries since the period of humanism" (CON 141). In "Conditions of a Narrative," Wolf makes us privy to her highly intuitive, associative way of working, determined in large measure by the unconscious and by fortuitous factors. The first two lectures make us aware of her increasing fascination – to the point of obsession – with the figure of Cassandra. We note how the figure changes and evolves as Wolf becomes ever more immersed in her subject matter. We thus must recognize that for Christa Wolf, "Cassandra" is not literary content to be mastered by being compressed into a suitable form but living material, not an object but a subject. Wolf's respect for her character's autonomy, her conscious attempt to present Cassandra as operating according to her own inner laws, prompted her to rewrite her story, originally begun in third-person narration, in the form of an interior monologue. According to Wolf, she wanted to reserve judgment, wanted the neutrality of the first-person singular for her Cassandra.[21] It is remarkable that Wolf, who explores the theme of the difficulty of saying "I" in her more autobiographical works, should choose a consistent first-person narrative voice for her temporally most distant figure.

Her rejection of a mediated third-person narrative in favor of the spontaneity and directness of the first person is consistent with the goals she has set for herself as a writer. The narrative documents the coming-into-being of female subjectivity. Such an undertaking by definition excludes the possibility of a poetics since the normative component of a poetics, according to Christa Wolf, cannot prevent "the living experience of countless perceiving subjects from being killed and buried in art objects ... ('works')" (CON 142). Wolf strives for precisely the opposite. Recognizing that literature based on poetics objectifies and that poetics kills and buries, Wolf resists these dangers by rejecting poetics and by empathizing with her literary figure. Identifying with Cassandra ("So, is pain the point at which I assimilate her, a particular kind of pain, the pain of becoming a knowing subject?" CON 230), Wolf opposes the subjectivity of the first person to literature's process of objectification.

Nonetheless, she recognizes that the closed structure of *Cassandra* also makes it a work, an art object, and is aware of the inherent contradiction in her Cassandra project. Sigrid Weigel has discussed this paradox in the context of Christa Wolf's rejection of the male literary tradition.[22] In Weigel's view, the multitemporal, open-ended, self-reflexive "Conditions of a Narrative" is consistent with Wolf's rejection of heroic literature. As Wolf herself noted, the lectures on poetics constitute a "fabric." "Many of its motifs are not followed up, many of its threads are tangled. There are wefts which stand out like foreign bodies, repetitions, material that has not been worked out to its conclusion" (CON 142). In the first four lectures no single skein has been extracted for purposes of narration and study. The fifth "lecture," the narrative, on the other hand follows one single strand: it tells the story of Cassandra's development into a conscious subject. Weigel quotes Wolf's analysis of the genesis of the heroic epic.

The choral song of the priestesses, completely embedded in the unfolding seasons among a largely undifferentiated group of human beings, is a hymn; there is no narration. Only the advent of property, hierarchy, and patriarchy extracts a blood-red thread from the fabric of human life, which the three ancient crones, the Moirae, had in hand; and this thread is amplified at the expense of the web as a whole, at the expense of its uniformity. The blood-red thread is the narrative of the struggle and victory of the heroes, or their doom. The plot is born. The epic, born of the struggles for patriarchy, becomes *by its structure* an instrument by which to elaborate and fortify the patriarchy. The hero is made to serve as a model, and still does so down to the present day. The chorus of female speakers has vanished, swallowed up by the earth. The woman can now become the object of masculine narrative, in the role of heroine. Helen, for example, who, rigidified into an idol, lives on in the myths.   (CON 296–7)

Weigel then argues that the story (plot) of Cassandra emulates the male tradition Wolf repudiates, in that it too is exemplary. Unlike Wolf's earlier characters who are shown in the process of coming-to-themselves, Cassandra realizes this goal: by attaining autonomy she becomes a heroine.[23] Weigel raises an interesting point. Despite the fact that by calling *Cassandra* the fifth lecture, Wolf has made it clear that "Conditions of a Narrative" and the narrative itself constitute an integral whole, there is a formal discrepancy between the first four lectures and the narrative *Cassandra*. Yet as Weigel herself notes, "Conditions of a Narrative" relativizes and partially counterbalances *Cassandra*'s "maturity" and narrative closure.[24] However, she fails to draw the conclusion from this observation. Just as the Bettine and Günderrode essays opened up the closed narrative structure of *No Place on Earth*, "Conditions of a Narrative" expands the (closed) parameters of *Cassandra*, calling upon the reader to draw connections between essays and narrative.

Thus the act of reading explodes the closed structure of the *Cassandra* narrative.

Moreover, while Weigel is correct in underscoring the modellike nature of *Cassandra*, she fails to consider this aspect adequately in her analysis. Since "Conditions of a Narrative" relativizes Cassandra's maturity, and the reader is meant to integrate the essays into the story, to draw conclusions about the status of women in our own society, Cassandra's exemplary subjectivity should be read as encouraging female resistance to the patriarchal socialization. Its function is thus diametrically opposed to male heroic literature, which elaborates and fortifies the patriarchy. Wolf's outrage at the objectification of women found expression in her portrayal of female autonomy in *Cassandra*. The almost cultish popularity this work has attained attests to the need it fills for women all over the world. By presenting the possibility of attaining autonomy, the exemplary narrative *Cassandra* meets Wolf's utopian definition of literature: it keeps "awake in us the memory of the future . . . It is revolutionary and realistic; it entices and encourages people to achieve the impossible."[25]

The story of Cassandra has a rich tradition from antiquity to the present.[26] While Wolf specifically mentions Aeschylus and Homer in "Conditions of a Narrative," it is obvious that she is also thoroughly familiar with the late antique and medieval Troy story. The anti-Homeric tradition, particularly the pseudochronicles of Dictys of Crete and Dares the Phrygian, obviously influenced her conception of Achilles.[27] Wolf's Cassandra begins to come into being by confronting Aeschylus's creation. Wolf rejects as distorted by a male perspective the figure she encounters in the *Oresteia*. By virtue of a sympathetic understanding similar to the eidetic intuition between Kleist and Günderrode in *No Place on Earth*, Wolf believes she knows the essential Cassandra. In the lectures on poetics Wolf describes her spontaneous reaction to Aeschylus's figure:

Cassandra. I saw her at once. She, the captive, took me captive; herself made an object by others, she took possession of me. Later I would ask when, where, and by whom the pacts were joined that made this magic. It worked at once. I believed every word she said; so there was still such a thing as unqualified trust. Three thousand years – melted away.

(CON 144–5)

As a result, Wolf cannot concur when the Greek dramatist presents Cassandra's sympathy with Agamemnon's fate. Moreover, the repulsion Aeschylus depicts between Clytemnestra and Cassandra appears to Wolf to rest on the poet's patriarchal prejudice.

That is how the male poet chooses to see these women: vindictive, jealous, petty toward each other – as women can be when they are driven out of public life, chased back to home and hearth. This is exactly what happened in the decades which Aeschylus sums up in his great drama. (CON 179)

Thus Christa Wolf suggests that friendship between women constitutes a threat to the patriarchy and that the myth of female animosity has been propagated by men out of self-interest.

Wolf's re-vision of the Cassandra story can be understood as an attempt to correct this distorted male image. For her the relationship between Cassandra and Clytemnestra is based on an unexpressed understanding, a sisterliness[28] comparable to Wolf's own relationship to her protagonist. Unlike Aeschylus, Wolf does not present Clytemnestra as the unfaithful wife and assassin, but rather as someone who is unwillingly drawn into events and compelled to carry out her act of revenge.[29] In so doing, she rehabilitates this female figure.

In addition to rehabilitating Clytemnestra, Wolf goes further than her anti-Homeric sources in revising the male figures as part of her correction of the literary canon. Her criterion for evaluating the Greeks is totally different from Homer's. The decisive factor is not the boldness of bellicose acts but rather self-knowledge and the capacity for interpersonal relationships – and in this regard the male figures fail miserably. Thus Cassandra rejects the "hero" Agamemnon as a "weakling who lacks self-esteem," as an "imbecile," as a "nonentity." Using Agamemnon as a yardstick,[30] she generalizes that "all men are self-centered children" (*C* 9), an assessment based on her experiences among both the Greeks and the Trojans. Christa Wolf thus elaborates on reservations about the Greek king already expressed in the *Iliad* and developed more fully in Euripides' *Iphigenia at Aulis* and *Hecuba*. With the exception of Aeneas[31] and his father Anchises, in whom she finds autonomous human beings, she is continually confronted with narcissistic men. For Christa Wolf's Cassandra, men remain infantile, closed off to themselves, incapable of self-knowledge and autonomy, hence also closed off to others, emotionally immature, and incapable of love.

This male inability to love is presented most strikingly in the figure of Achilles. Wolf goes back to the tradition in which Achilles, after killing Penthesilea in battle, falls in love with and rapes her corpse.[32] Achilles' desecration of the corpse is the most compelling evidence for Wolf's belief in the connection between aggression and the inability to love.[33] Through Achilles' necrophilia, Wolf also establishes a link between the inability to love and inability to live. Achilles cannot love a living woman who is his equal, only a dead or, as in the case of Cassandra's sister Polyxena, a subservient one.[34] In Wolf's view, for human beings incapable of loving, sexuality can only be expressed through violence. The Achilles–Penthesilea subplot, a variation on the theme of irresolvable conflict, of unviable alternatives, familiar to us from *No Place on Earth*, carries Cassandra's dilemma to its logical extreme. Penthesilea, who embodies for Wolf the "doomed line of the matriarchy" (CON 263), refuses to submit to male domination. Incapable of subservience, she strives for equality by assuming an untraditional female role as a warrior. Yet in adapting to a male norm, caught in an either-or situation, Penthesilea is caught between the unlivable alternatives of killing or dying. She finds only death.

Since Christa Wolf is writing after Homer, she cannot fulfill Cassandra's fervent wish to extirpate the name of Achilles from humankind's memory.[35] She can, however, question the Homeric image of Achilles. In *Cassandra* the famous son of Peleus as well as his entire entourage of heroes undergoes a fundamental revision. The *Iliad* deals with the rage, the *menis* of Achilles; Wolf, following the anti-Homeric tradition, reinterprets his heroic acts as atrocities: "Achilles, the brute,"[36] Cassandra consistently calls him. In affixing this derogatory epithet to Achilles, Wolf appears to grant Cassandra's wish that between the brute and posterity an abyss of contempt might appear (*C* 79).

Like Agamemnon, Achilles is depicted as a weakling without self-esteem. Undermining traditional heroic models of the brave warrior, Wolf portrays Achilles (and Odysseus) as cowards: both initially attempted to get out of battle.[37] Forced to fight against his will, Achilles appears on the battlefield as the élite Greek warrior, to be protected at all costs including the sacrifice of all his comrades. Violating all rules of conduct for competition between high-born men, he is concerned only with winning – with winning at all costs. He thus represents the new utilitarian mentality that views people as means to an end.

Seen through the eyes of Cassandra, the nonvictor, he is a barbarian: consumed by sadomasochistic, homoerotic lust he slaughters and decapitates her unarmed brother, Troilus, who had sought refuge in the temple of Apollo. The desecration of the holy site underscores the brutal perversity of Achilles' act, proving that nothing is sacred to him. For Christa Wolf, Achilles is the epitome of the new morality of the patriarchy, a morality propagated by the violent Achaian princes who, bent on plunder, destroyed the order of peace in the eastern Mediterranean (CON 247).

Cassandra, witness to this historical transition, wants to testify. Her desire to bear witness, even if there is no longer a single human being who calls for her testimony, points to an essential aspect of her character, her unconditionality. Tormented by the thought of dying without leaving a trace, Cassandra, prisoner outside the fortress of Mycenae, considers begging Clytemnestra for a reprieve. In her imagined conversation with the Greek queen, Cassandra implores:

Send me a scribe, or better yet a young slave woman with a keen memory and a powerful voice. Ordain that she may repeat to her daughter what she hears from me. That the daughter in turn may pass it on to her daughter, and so on. So that alongside the river of heroic songs this tiny rivulet, too, may reach those faraway, perhaps happier, people who will live in times to come. (*C* 81)

Cassandra thus differentiates between the heroic (written) songs of the male tradition and a female oral tradition and recognizes that the latter, that of the subculture, is more suitable for recording her story. But she realizes that Clytemnestra, having entered the power structure, cannot grant her wish even if she should care to. She can no longer act as a private individual, but must fulfill her public role. By deciding not to ask, Cassandra relinquishes the hope for a written or oral account of her story.

When Christa Wolf tells Cassandra's previously unwritten story, she moves the previously peripheral figure into the foreground. Her tale consists not of heroic deeds of war, but rather of everyday history; her focus is not the extraordinary heroic feat but rather the subjective, the commonplace, the interpersonal. The story that Cassandra relates is told not from the perspective of the victors but rather of the losers, second-degree losers (objects of objects).[38] It is the story of the fall of Troy as filtered through female consciousness.

Wolf's Cassandra is not heroic in Homer's sense. Wolf calls her "utopian," meaning that Cassandra achieves that autonomy which for her is a prerequisite for women's writing. Giving in to her spontaneous reaction while reading the *Oresteia* that Cassandra is the only figure who knows herself, Wolf presents Cassandra's quest for self-knowledge as a difficult process of liberation from all family and social ties. In depicting her struggle for autonomy, *Cassandra* becomes yet another manifestation of Wolf's theme of coming-to-oneself.

Wolf's explicit purpose in creating *Cassandra* was to "retrace the path out of the myth, into its (supposed) social and historical coordinates" (CON 256). For this reason she sets her story at that historical seam marking the transition from a matriarchal to a patriarchal society. For Wolf, Cassandra is the "daughter of a royal house in which patrilinear succession seems secure; but in which the queen, Hecuba – who many scholars believe comes from the matriarchal culture of the Locrains – has not yet sunk into insignificance on that account" (CON 293).

Presumably Wolf conceived of Troy as "a model for a kind of utopia" (CON 224) because the social and historical coordinates which she invented for her Cassandra, the historical overlaps resulting from the "seam" she (re)constructs, enabled her to depict a dimension of depth, a multitude of realities not possible in a purely patriarchal society. In Wolf's Troy, remnants of matriarchal modes of thought still exist and offer an alternative to the prevailing social structures. In "Conditions of a Narrative," Wolf tells us that she wanted to know who Cassandra was before anyone wrote about her (CON 273), that is, before she was distorted into a *Frauenbild*, a male image of women, by the male literary tradition.[39]

The questions Wolf poses in order to realize her figure reflect her concern with the interpersonal. Her psychologically and sociologically based characterization incorporates questions concerning the character of individual family members and family relationships: "What kind of a man was Priam, Cassandra's father? And how did her mother, Hecuba, so superabundantly blessed with sons, treat her few daughters?" as well as questions concerning the way of life of a sociologically privileged member of her society who is nonetheless subservient by virtue of her gender: "What kind of life did this king's daughter lead in Troy, her father's city?" (CON 153). The story that presented itself to Wolf:

Cassandra, the eldest and best-loved daughter of King Priam of Troy, a vivacious person interested in society and politics, does not want to be confined to the house, to get married like her mother Hecuba, like her sisters. She wants to learn a profession. For a woman of rank, the only possible profession is that of priestess, seeress, which was practiced only by women in remote antiquity, in the days when the chief deity was a woman, Ge, Gaea, the earth goddess. (CON 238)

Although as always with Wolf, the personal is in the foreground, here it is inextricably connected with the political. In this story the dialectic between the individual and society manifests itself in the tension between Cassandra's birth and her office. Cassandra's self-reflection is prompted by the knowledge of her imminent death. At the hour of her death, however, Cassandra possesses the new view-scope that Christa Wolf describes in her lectures on poetics. Hence her insights are also characterized by a widened visual angle and a readjusted depth of focus. Although Wolf felt bound by her sources to retain the fatal conclusion to her story,[40] she deviates from the tradition in not presenting Cassandra simply as Agamemnon's war booty. Instead, Cassandra appears on Greek soil of her own volition, having refused to flee with her lover Aeneas, who she knows will survive. Her acceptance of necessity is based on the recognition that survival in these times means subservience and submission to violence: "It was obvious: The new masters would dictate their law to all the survivors. The earth was not large enough to escape them" (*C* 138). For Cassandra, so long oppressed, her hard-won autonomy takes precedence. She recognizes that Aeneas has no choice: in order to preserve Trojan culture, he must rescue a few hundred people from death. In founding Rome, he will perpetuate patriarchal culture. He will be a hero. Cassandra refuses to share this future, the hero's fate imposed upon him. She knows she is incapable of loving a hero and refuses to witness his transformation into an idol. She freely chooses to be a loser.[41] Thus Wolf's Cassandra chooses death[42] in order not to jeopardize her autonomy and because she refuses to watch the objectification of her lover, his loss of autonomy. The existential freedom Cassandra attains, her emancipation from family, state, and religion, comes only at the cost of death. Her life is another example of unlivable alternatives.

The narrating consciousness of *Cassandra* is infidel: although a priestess of Apollo, she no longer believes in the power of religion. Yet as becomes apparent from her story, this was not always the case. Wolf assigns to her character the question that was paramount in her conception of Cassandra. Before the gates of Mycenae Cassandra probes why she had so desperately wanted the gift of prophecy. Her self-searching reveals that ultimately those characteristics used to describe her – the "inclination to conform with those in power" and a "craving for knowledge" (*C* 62–3) – were at work in this instance as well.

Only after she had been initiated as priestess did she realize that

her craving for knowledge was diametrically opposed to her inclination to conform with those in power. While her office is a means
to self-actualization, she is ultimately confronted with the choice
between her birth, that is, her family and her privileged status, and
herself. Only by eschewing privilege can Cassandra attain clairvoyance in Wolf's sense – a clear vision of the present. The more
she liberates herself from the false values resulting from the rise of a
war mentality, the more she can carry out her office as seeress.

At first, however, she merely plays a role, for she too is caught up
in the delusions. She comes to realize that priesthood cannot grant
her the independence she seeks because priestly duties are inextricably bound up with the existing social structures. Thus, the royal
house places real-political demands on the priests: the so-called
"oracles made to order" (*C* 89). Not self-actualization but rather
self-alienation is initially Cassandra's fate. Only when she realizes
that the war, which has dehumanized the men, also threatens her
with spiritual ruin does she resist.

The reason the Greeks win in Wolf's view is not merely because
of their new utilitarian morality, not merely because of their
military superiority, which arises out of their win-at-all-costs mentality, but because the morality of the Trojans is compromised by
this new militaristic victor mentality. In Christa Wolf's rewriting of
the history of the Trojan War, the Greeks are victorious only
because the Trojans have already accepted their new morality.
Troy is defeated by both the internal and the external enemy.

Eumelos, who embodies the new order, symbolizes the infiltra-
tion of the new morality in Troy. Slowly but irresistibly, he
insinuates himself into a position of power. Starting with the court,
his sphere of influence gradually spreads until it ultimately encompasses the entire city. His main tactic – polarization – testifies to
that antinomic thought which for Wolf has led to our current world
political situation. Eumelos's initial antagonism toward the Greeks
polarizes Greeks and Trojans. Soon he also polarizes the Trojans:
whoever criticizes the actions of the royal house is viewed as an
enemy.

The new morality increasingly violates tradition. This new view is
expressed by Priam when he notes that war invalidates all rules in
effect during peacetime. It is predominantly women who suffer at
the hands of the new morality, an indication that the new epoch is a
strictly patriarchal one. Exclusion and objectification are portrayed
as fundamental experiences of women under patriarchy. First of
all, Hecuba, presented as Priam's equal in every respect, is

excluded from the council. The flimsy excuse: what is being discussed is not for women's ears. Later Briseis, daughter of the renegade prophet Calchas, sent to the Greeks after the death of her lover, is declared a traitor for reasons of political expediency. Most debasing, however, is the treatment the royal daughters must endure: Polyxena is sold to Achilles[43] and later used as bait; Cassandra is married off, for military-political reasons, to a man she does not love. It becomes the norm in Troy to barter with women.

Priam's spiritual degeneration is the most striking example of the casualties wrought by the war and the rise of the new morality. Increasingly caught up in the spell of the war, he allies himself with Eumelos, excludes Hecuba, whom he had always respected, and treats Cassandra, who had been his favorite daughter, as an object. In his attempt to coerce the once dutiful, now disobedient daughter, he declares her insane, locks her up, and forces her into an unwanted marriage. The forced marriage of Cassandra constitutes a violation not only of the daughter but of women *per se* and provides an excellent example of how the personal becomes the political. On the one hand it brings about an inner division among Trojan women: they are forced to hate Troy, whose victory they desire. On the other hand this ambivalence leads to female solidarity – to sisterliness – and contributes to the creation of an alternative subculture.

Three enterprises that Cassandra identifies as points in the development toward war chronicle the rise of the new morality: the so-called first, second, and third ships represent distinct levels of moral decay. They crystallize phases in the development of an image of the enemy and point to the creation of a myth in the commonplace modern sense of false consciousness. It is part of Wolf's deconstruction of the mythological canon, her tracing of myth back to its supposed social and historical coordinates, to show how historical events are manipulated into myth.

The prevailing lack of clarity (even on Cassandra's part) regarding the highly secret Trojan missions to Greece is striking. The actual purpose of the first enterprise, called "the ship to Delphi," is never revealed. Speculations abound, however. Anchises, Aeneas's father, maintains that the maneuver was an attempt to appease the powerful Greek princes who wanted access to the Hellespont.[44] Cassandra's brother Hector, on the other hand, claims that Lampos was sent as ambassador of the royal house to ask the Delphic Oracle about the security of the city of

Troy. In Delphi he had met the priest of Apollo, Panthous. Out of passion for Lampos, Panthous had followed him to Troy.

Which, if either, version is true, is immaterial. What is important is what is proclaimed as truth to the people: namely that Panthous had been brought back to Troy as Lampos's booty. According to Anchises, the Trojans had been forced to negotiate with the more powerful Greeks about their hereditary rights of access to the Hellespont. "The Greeks did not agree on terms, Lampos brought rich offerings to Delphi which we could barely afford . . . And our palace scribes, who as you must know are a breed unto themselves, have belatedly rechristened this the FIRST SHIP, bragging about an enterprise that halfway miscarried" (*C* 32).

The distortion of reality regarding the first ship was due to an antagonistic juxtaposition of Greeks and Trojans, and the Trojans sought to interpret the events to their own advantage. This delusionary tactic is intensified in the case of the second ship. The alleged motive for this undertaking is to retrieve Priam's sister, who, according to the king, has been "taken by force" and was being held captive by the Spartan Telamon. Hecuba unsuccessfully criticizes Priam's (mis)use of language. "'Now, now, "held,"'" mocked Hecuba, "'"taken by force."'" Hesione could hardly be considered a humble prisoner. According to reports Telamon had after all made her his wife, made her his queen. Hecuba's protests fall on deaf ears: "That wasn't the point . . . "'A king who does not try to win back his sister when she is abducted loses face'" (*C* 35).

Later, a second ship is sent to Greece out of a false sense of honor – for Priam is motivated neither by a sense of affection for his sister, nor by his sense of personal conviction but rather by socio-political coercion – with disastrous results. The prophet Calchas, who had accompanied Anchises on the journey, does not return. Clearly this enterprise is an unambiguous failure: Telamon laughed at the Trojans' demand and Calchas, fearing that he would be held accountable for the favorable prophecies he had made before leaving Troy, defected to the Greeks. Those in power fail to realize that the royal house, by forcing him to make favorable prophecies, is in part responsible for Calchas's desertion. Instead, they polarize still further by allowing the people to believe that the prophet is being kept hostage by the Greeks.

Reports of the third ship develop the characteristics of those of the earlier expeditions; they intensify lying and deception to an extreme. Led by Paris, the prodigal son, long believed dead, the third ship no longer purports to be for Hesione's sake. It is clearly launched to satisfy Paris's ambition. Referring to Aphrodite's alleged promise that he would be given the world's most beautiful woman, Paris, on the eve of Menelaus's departure from the palace in Troy, announces: "'It is I, Paris, who will fetch the king's sister back from the enemy. But if they refuse to give her to me, I'll find another woman more beautiful than she. Younger. Nobler. Richer. That's what I have been promised, if you all want to know!'" (*C* 58–9). Paris thus reveals his violent intentions: he had already dreamed of possessing Menelaus's wife, Helen, the most beautiful woman in Greece.

Reverting to the tradition in which Paris abducts Helen only to lose her to the king of Egypt, Wolf reveals the cause of the Trojan War to be a phantom. The gullible populace is, however, led to believe that the provocative abduction, undeniably a challenge to war, is a heroic act. Cassandra bears witness to the efficacy of the courtly propaganda machine and the collusion between the secular and the religious:

I was witness to the scurrying back and forth between the palace and the temple priests, to the sessions of the council that went on day and night; I saw how a news report was manufactured, hard, forged, polished like a spear. At the behest of our dear goddess Aphrodite, the Trojan hero Paris had abducted Helen, the most beautiful woman in Greece, from the boastful Greeks, and so had erased the humiliation once inflicted on our mighty King Priam by the theft of his sister. (*C* 64)

Aphrodite, Helen, Hesione – variations on a theme. Women are constantly being used as a pretense and means to an end in this warring state. When Paris returns to Troy months later he consciously intends to deceive. He is accompanied by a heavily veiled woman presumed to be Helen, but whom no one actually sees face to face. The shrouded woman is, however, merely the objective correlative of the prevailing linguistic obscurantism. The circle of deception has broadened while the circle of initiates has shrunk. Years later no one any longer asks to see the woman who does not exist. Everyone is too occupied with the war allegedly being fought on her account.

In her attempt to locate origins of war, Cassandra says:

You can tell when a war starts, but when does the prewar start? If there are rules about that, we should pass them on. Hand them down inscribed in clay, in stone. What would they say? Among other things they would say: Do not let your own people deceive you. (*C* 66)

Recognizing that the escalation manifested itself linguistically she notes how her own people manipulated the word "enemy." It was already part of the "mental armament" deemed necessary for defense before a single Greek had stepped aboard a single Trojan ship. This mental armament consisted of a "defamation of the enemy." Yet upon closer scrutiny it reveals itself to be a projection of Trojan aggression and hostility. By creating this image of the Greeks, the Trojans unleash a self-fulfilling prophecy.

The portentous effects of designating the Greeks "enemies" becomes apparent during Menelaus's visit. The old word "guest-friend" no longer exists – it has been replaced by "provocateur." The Greek is greeted by suspicion, and a new word, "security net," which is cast around the future enemy, usurps the old term "guest-friend." Thus Christa Wolf, by examining the ways in which language influences social behavior, in examining the corruption of concepts, responds to the call for a correction of concepts made by the women writers at the Berlin peace conferences.

Linguistic haste in designating the enemy is coupled with an unwillingness to call things by their proper name, a tendency toward self-deception. After Paris has lost Helen to the Egyptian king, Cassandra asks her father to call a halt to the course of events, warning him that a war waged for the sake of a phantom cannot be won. Priam defends himself by saying: "'Why not? ... All you have to do is make sure the army does not lose faith in the phantom ... And why should there even be a war? You always use these big words. What I think is, we'll be attacked, and what I think is, we'll defend ourselves'" (*C* 69–70). Priam's statement is the most striking evidence that the new pragmatism is morally bankrupt. When war perforce does come, it is forbidden to speak of war. The official term is "surprise attack." That is the blindness linked with power: it begins as deception of others and boomerangs, as self-deception, as blindness, back to those in power.

On the other hand, Cassandra, from the outset intent upon calling a spade a spade, works against the devaluation of language. Prophetic not because she possesses divine insight but because she can see clearly, she is punished because she names the deeds. Hence not the crimes themselves but their naming is punishable. By severing herself from her family, she comes to recognize that self-imposed blindness which is linked with power. Initially her tendency to agree with those in power and her compulsion to conform make her guilty of this blindness as well. Deluded into believing it was a powerful ship, she had as a child cheered on the ship to Delphi. Upon the return of the second ship, she refuses to believe that Calchas had deserted of his own volition. Cassandra chooses to have her servant Marpessa punished for bearing this news rather than listen to her inner voice, which knows that Marpessa is speaking the truth. Long after everyone else has ceased to believe in the existence of Helen, an incredibly naive Cassandra still believes in her. Reflecting on her own powers of self-delusion, she notes: "Every fiber in me shut itself off, refused to recognize that there was no beautiful Helen in Troy" (*C* 67).

Her blindness arises out of the misapprehension of her own situation. By orienting herself to those in power, by identifying herself with the oppressors, she works against her own interests as a woman. In her childhood, when Hecuba still had political stature, her desire to integrate herself into the system was understandable. But her position changes qualitatively as Troy becomes increasingly patriarchal and hierarchical. For a time Cassandra endures the self-estrangement brought on by the events in Troy and the suppression of her inner voice. Ultimately, however, it becomes intolerable. In a crisis, Cassandra must decide whether actually to succumb to the madness into which she had fled[45] in order to put an "end to the torture of pretense" and to lose herself, or to listen to her inner voice, open her inner eye and to come to herself. Paraphrasing Günderrode's situation, Christa Wolf has Cassandra articulate the dilemma of unlivable alternatives:

> To be forced to give birth to what will destroy you: the terror beyond terror. I could not stop producing madness . . . Two adversaries had chosen the dead landscape of my soul as their battlefield and were engaged in a life-and-death struggle. Only madness stood between me and the intolerable pain which these two would otherwise have inflicted on me, I thought.
> (*C* 60)

Finally, with the guidance of Arisbe, Priam's former concubine who becomes her matriarchal mentor, Cassandra decides to pursue her authentic inclinations.

The voice of protest emerges slowly. It comes by way of silence. When Eumelos designates the ill-suited Hector as first hero, Cassandra resists. Seeking out her mother, Cassandra finds Anchises with her. Hecuba knows that her favorite son is caught between two unviable alternatives: he can refuse to fulfill the heroic role and suffer the derision of the city or he can succumb to the image foisted upon him, be the first to enter battle, and fall. When her mother curses the war, all three remain silent. "I learned that protest begins with this silence in which more than one takes part"

(*C* 91), says Cassandra. Silence offers the possibility of listening to one's inner voice; communal silence represents a refusal to conform with those in power: it is the beginning of resistance.

When her father abuses her sister, however, Cassandra expresses her protest in sisterly solidarity. When she learns that Polyxena is to be used as a decoy to lure Achilles into the temple to be murdered, that is, when the actions of the Trojans become indistinguishable from those of the Greeks, Cassandra refuses to endorse the royal family's plans. At the same time she recognizes that from their vantage point the duty to kill Troy's deadliest foe might well have devoured the question of rights:

Rapidly, with uncanny rapidity I considered the possibility that they might be right. What does that mean, "right"? Considered the possibility that the question of rights – Polyxena's right, my right – did not even arise because a duty, the duty to kill our worst enemy, ate up the right. And Polyxena? She was headed for ruin, no doubt about it. She was already a hopeless case.

(*C* 127)

In Wolf's most emphatic assertion of individualism, she has Cassandra, in an autonomous act of noncompliance, reject the demands of the community (duty). Through her silence Cassandra has listened to her own voice. In saying "no" for the first time she speaks in her own voice. It is the voice of dissent. Her rejection of the absolute abstract principle of duty in favor of a context-oriented responsibility and caring for her sister reflect Carol Gilligan's findings on gender-based difference in moral decision making even more clearly than *Christa T.* did.[46] In essence Cassandra rejects the male moral code based on duty and justice as unviable.

Christa Wolf's meshing of a female ethic with dissidence in *Cassandra* is a logical conclusion of her reflections on the status of women in contemporary society. The utilitarianism of male-dominated societal structures based on a perversion of reason to instrumental rationality represents for her a dangerous one-sidedness, an exclusion of essential human qualities. The same reductionism, at work in the patriarchy's exclusion of women, is, in her view, detrimental to both sexes, has fostered delusional thinking, and has brought us to the brink of self-annihilation. Addressing the current situation in the GDR, Wolf argues that while socialism has granted women the basis for equality, their legal advantages have been overshadowed by the tenacity and pervasiveness of patriarchal attitudes and values. She interprets the increasing numbers of women who reject their (theoretically possible) integration into the existing hierarchical structures as a sign of hope.

Their desire to explore sexual differences productively, based on "a self-esteem arising not out of a will for power, domination and subjugation but rather on an ability to cooperate,"[47] can prove liberating for both sexes. Wolf does not assert that "women by nature are more immune than men to political delusionary thinking. Only that a specific particular historical period has given them conditions which enable them to express a claim to life for men as well,"[48] that is, a claim to live as full human beings.

Thus when Cassandra, realizing that the war that has corrupted her countrymen threatens her as well, resists, she expresses the claim to life of which Wolf speaks. Her refusal is her spiritual defense and her first public step toward self-actualization. By breaking her pattern of conforming with those in power, it allows her the freedom to pursue her thirst for knowledge. Her punishment – imprisonment in the grave of heroes – represents Cassandra's final break with her origins. Released after Achilles' death, she finds refuge in the community of women residing in caves in the hills outside the city.

This culture of the marginalized has grown up far removed from the prevailing culture. True, the female cave community is an outgrowth of the oppression of women. Excluded from Trojan society, the women congregate in the surrounding mountainside. Only because the men are preoccupied with the war, which has long since been lost, can the female community exist. Nonetheless, for Cassandra, for whom the citadel of Troy has become the symbol of her own imprisonment, the cave community with its closeness to nature represents emancipation. It becomes her chosen home after she renounces her origins. The key to Christa Wolf's alternative to patriarchal society is *Cybele*. The Frankfurt lectures on poetics illuminate this word: Cybele is the Anatolian form of the old Cretan goddess of birth, Eileithyia (CON 245–6). Wolf conceives the primitive life in the caves as a remnant of a matriarchal civilization. Whereas the war stands under the sign of Apollo (the battles invariably occur under the scorching sunny sky), the matriarchal community is under the sign of life.

The most striking feature of this community is the absence of a hierarchy. Wolf consistently uses the term "community" (*Gemeinschaft*), familiar from Ferdinand Toennies' *Community and Society*, to distinguish it from the hierarchical "society" (*Gesellschaft*) of the court.[49] In the caves, where Cassandra is first brought by the slave Marpessa, there are no advantages arising from birth or office. Here the royal princess is neither mistress nor priestess.

Indeed, the privileged Cassandra is initially an outsider among these outsiders and must earn acceptance. It takes a while before Arisbe includes her in the communal "we."

The cave community is characterized above all by interaction between women of all social levels. In contrast to the closed, élitist society of the court, which excludes more and more people, no one is rejected from this open community. Outcasts and outsiders of Trojan society (such as Greeks and Amazons) are all welcomed here. The laws of this community testify to those "characteristics of sisterliness: sympathy, self-respect, trust and friendliness" that Christa Wolf had described in "Berührung" (Touching).[50]

The concept of "touching," inextricably connected to the ability to love, plays an important role in *Cassandra*. Sara Lennox, who regards Christa Wolf's work as "the most radical feminist critique of any woman writing in German today," considers "touching" the key to what Wolf considers a specifically female stance. Conceived as a female epistemological alternative to positivistic objectivity, "touching" "regards its object with sympathy and under-standing."[51]

A spontaneous "touch-fest" develops out of the illiterate Trojan women's desire to leave behind a trace of themselves for poster-ity.[52] With it, a utopian spirit arises in their community. As in "Berührung," here again touching is seen as a means to self-understanding as well as mutual understanding and knowledge. That this understanding must occur through the senses is consonant with Wolf's call in her letter on Bettine for an integration of the rational and the sensible.[53] In *Cassandra* Wolf achieves a union between the sensual and the rational in part by means of the erotic. The erotic had already played a role in *No Place on Earth*, where, however, it had remained a subtext. In *Cassandra* the erotic is of unprecedented importance for Wolf. It has been noted that in Wolf's previous work the search for identity did not include sexual identity;[54] this is not the case in *Cassandra*. Nor does the liberation of the erotic restrict itself to heterosexual relationships. By includ-ing love between women Wolf grants to her Cassandra free development of her sexuality.[55] By exploring her full erotic potential, Cassandra becomes a sexual subject and capable of love in its broadest sense. Wolf's Cassandra loves men, women, and knowledge.

Although an intimate relationship exists between the women, the condition for acceptance into this community is not gender but humanity (*Menschlichkeit*), a concept which Christa Wolf has defined in the Kantian tradition: "never, under any circumstances to make another human being a means for one's own ends."[56] Anchises' completely integrated role in the cave community is consonant with Wolf's rejection of a separatist feminism. His significance for the cave community cannot be minimized. Together with Arisbe this nature-bound person is seen as exemplary. Indeed the cave community, which consists predominantly of women, appears as a mirror image of an earlier Troy, the Troy in which Hecuba still played an important role within patrilinear society. Since antinomic thinking does not exist among them, these people (*Menschen*) are able to cultivate that which is no longer possible in patriarchal Troy: life. A mutually supportive existence devoted to communal work enables them to develop their potential freely. In an exchange of learning and teaching, they share their special talents with the others. In the brief period before the patriarchy brings about the fall of Troy, a period described as a "gap in time" (*C* 124), these people are permitted to live out their utopia, in which no one is objectified and where everyone is regarded as an independent and mature subject. Cassandra, speaking of their life in the caves, says of Anchises: "He was fulfilling a dream of his and was teaching us younger ones how to dream with both feet on the ground" (*C* 135). Her words, essentially a paraphrase of Bloch's notion of "dreaming with our eyes open," link the cave community with his principle of hope.[57] In creating this concrete utopia, Wolf's literature of hope serves as a constant reminder that our memory of a future, indeed our future itself, is in mortal danger.

In the midst of death and destruction Cassandra comes to herself. Her path leads by way of the unconscious to madness and to life. Increasingly self-awareness, that is, awareness of herself as a female subject, replaces false consciousness. Her dreams, presented as acts of liberation, chart the course of her personal integration. As the expression of the unconscious and the preconscious, they document not only her restlessness, increasing alienation and crisis, but also a psychic breakthrough and healing process. The dream state provides Cassandra with the key to overcoming her self-alienation. Appointed judge, Cassandra in a dream must determine which of the heavenly bodies, the sun or the moon, can shine more brightly. Although she senses that something is wrong with this contest, Cassandra decides in favor of Phoebus Apollo. The fact that the lady of the moon, Selene, thereupon sinks to the horizon is an indication that Cassandra has betrayed her own gender. Arisbe's didactic interpretation of the dream: "'the most important thing about your dream ... was that faced with a completely perverted question, you nevertheless tried to find an answer'" (*C* 87), leads Cassandra to recognize that it is not in the moon's nature to shine more brightly and that such questions are perverse.

By recognizing the fundamental difference of the moon goddess and rejecting criteria oriented toward the male sun god, Apollo, Cassandra reevaluates and revalues her own gender. The awareness she attains through her dream is an important step in her search for herself. This is not merely a cerebral knowledge, as becomes obvious from her description of the relief she felt: "One coil in the rope that bound me, the outermost coil, snapped, dropped away; many others remained. It was a time to draw breath, to stretch stiff joints; a blossoming of the flesh" (*C* 88). Cassandra's experience calls to mind the Leonardo da Vinci statement Christa Wolf cites in the lectures on poetics: "'know-ledge which has not passed through the senses can produce none but destructive truth'" (CON 268). Cassandra's sensuous know-ledge leads to an increased solidarity with women. While her relationship to some women remains ambivalent (for example her fascination with yet aversion to Penthesilea), on the whole Cas-sandra's liberation from the male values of Troy brings about a greater identification with the more humane values cultivated by the women. By increasingly surrendering herself to the cave community, by relinquishing male-oriented criteria, Cassandra overcomes her split. Her last dream, with its harmonious inter-play of the most disparate elements, testifies to her spiritual recovery:

I saw colors, red and black, life and death. They interpenetrated, they did not fight each other as I would have expected even in a dream. They changed form continually, they continually produced new patterns which could be unbelievably beautiful. They were like waters, like a sea. In the middle of the sea I saw a bright island which I was approaching rapidly in my dream – for I was flying; yes, I was flying! What was there on the island? What kind of creature? A human being? An animal? It glowed the way only Aeneas glows at night. What joy. Then headlong fall, breeze, darkness, awakening. (*C* 124)

This dream of integrated life, reminiscent of the narrator's dream at the conclusion of *Patterns of Childhood*, is a sign that Cassandra has found the third possibility between dying and killing – life, which for Christa Wolf can only be attained through the self-awareness of a mature individual. Thereafter Cassandra never again, not even in the grave of heroes, reverts to madness.

Whereas Cassandra's dreams offer insight into her soul and document her recovery, her madness must be seen as a process of spiritual death and rebirth. Initially all Cassandra's serious attacks of madness are escape maneuvers. As such, they fulfill a similar function in Wolf's story as loss of consciousness does in Kleist's writing: they offer a way out of a painful, unendurable reality. Cassandra, upon learning that Marpessa had told the truth about Calchas's desertion, is forced to admit that she had always known it. Unable to cope with the knowledge that she had allowed Marpessa to be punished for speaking the truth, she is overcome with remorse and retreats into madness. This mechanism fails, however, on the eve of the third ship when she "sees" the fall of Troy. In contrast to her other attacks of insanity in which in some sense she had remained in control, this is a genuine, life-threatening crisis. Not until she heeds Arisbe's advice to open her inner eye is Cassandra able to find her way out of madness. In her presentation of Arisbe's and Anchises' exemplary didactic function, Wolf again inverts the paradigm of the *Bildungsroman*. Instead of social integration, Cassandra is educated to segregation, to autonomous thinking. Thus *Cassandra* can be regarded as a negative *Bildungsroman*.

In her process of desocialization, madness, the "lack of rapport with ordinary reason" (BP 4), plays an important role. Cassandra's insanity must be seen not as the weakness of the individual, but rather as the defense mechanism of a sensitive psyche confronted with a pathological time. "Verkehrt," meaning "perverse,"[58] is the term Wolf uses both in the Büchner Prize Speech and in *Cassandra* to describe the world situation that has arisen out of the propagation of patriarchal values.

Cassandra's courage to be autonomous is born out of the apparent weakness of madness, under the pressure of the pain of living in a perverse world. With it is born the possibility of touching society's blind spot, that is, of violating social taboos. From the perspective of her society, Cassandra's insights remain unrealized. She does not find any listeners, she speaks into the void. The victors, who send her to her death, have the final word. Like Christa T. and Karoline von Günderrode, Cassandra is unable to find a viable alternative. And yet, her story offers a glimmer of hope. For Cassandra's pain is not totally in vain; it does enable her to attain psychic integration, to overcome self-destructiveness.

Although the historical situation denies her the possibility for life, she goes to her death more alive than ever before.

Cassandra achieves the task of literature which Christa Wolf has set for herself. By writing down Cassandra's supposed story, Wolf raises it to the rank of women's literature. More than that, she attributes to Cassandra the fiction of being the first female author. If, as Helen Fehervary has noted, "the historical 'I' of female authorship lies in what has been concealed by the literary canon, in the silent tradition of oral history, letters, diaries, autobiography and fiction that has never been written down, let alone published,"[59] then in *Cassandra*, Christa Wolf succeeds in inventing one of these female "I"s. By writing down Cassandra's story, told into the void, by creating the third component necessary for female authorship, the active listener, a real public,[60] Wolf once again points to the utopian potential of literature. The silenced tradition of female authorship has broken through. Cassandra becomes the first woman writer.

7

IN LIEU OF A CONCLUSION.[1]
STÖRFALL: THE DESTRUCTION
OF UTOPIA?

The events of 26 April 1986 have left an indelible impression on all of us old enough to understand their import. At 1.25 a.m. local time, in Chernobyl, a small Ukranian city some 130 kilometers north of Kiev, reactor four in the nuclear power plant exploded, starting the graphite fire that could have culminated in the nuclear nightmare of core meltdown. Alerted by Swedish scientists' reports of alarmingly high levels of radiation, a terrified world watched the unthinkable happen.

The fact that the Soviets waited nearly three days before reporting the world's worst nuclear accident fanned the fires of outrage in Western and Eastern Europe, which were still burning high from the missile showdown between the superpowers in Autumn 1983. Chernobyl rapidly became one of the most volatile issues in recent European history.

Christa Wolf's reactions to the Chernobyl disaster are documented in *Störfall* (Breakdown, 1987),[2] her latest work, written between June and September 1986. In effect an unplanned sequel to *Cassandra*, *Störfall* continues that work's criticism of one-sided rationality, the growing role of technocracy in modern life, male domination of nature, and the exclusion of women.

In *Störfall*, Christa Wolf does not distance herself temporally from the events that so profoundly affected her, as she did in *No Place on Earth* and *Cassandra*. Nor does she displace them into obviously fictional constructs and respond to contemporary issues indirectly through analogy, as she had done in those works. In a sense *Störfall* has more in common with "Conditions of a Narrative" than with the narrative *Cassandra*, in that it presents the author's intellectual and emotional insights directly. Without mentioning Chernobyl by name,[3] the narrator/author elucidates the enormous impact it had on her life. But *Störfall* is so obviously about Chernobyl that not mentioning it becomes a *tour de force*: it is left to the reader constantly to fill in the gap in the text with the missing name. Like the radioactivity in the atmosphere all around us, Chernobyl becomes omnipresent in the reader's consciousness.

The work's subtitle, *Nachrichten eines Tages* (News of a Day), recalls the third Frankfurt lecture on poetics, "A Work Diary about the Stuff Life and Dreams are Made of," as it does Wolf's diaristic story, "Tuesday, 27 September." Through the technique of free association, the text makes us privy to the narrator/author's thoughts and emotions as it records her responses to the news of a single day. Although the precise date remains unspecified, the reader, on the basis of the narrated news reports, can readily identify it as several days after news of the Chernobyl explosion became known, that is, early May 1986.[4]

Western critics may well chastize Wolf for not criticizing the Soviet delay in reporting the accident. *Störfall* may also be faulted for manifesting the same intellectual (anti-Western) dishonesty which Hans Mayer found in *Patterns of Childhood*. Yet one could argue that by not identifying Chernobyl or laying blame directly, Christa Wolf gives this event its proper global resonance. The (mis)use of nuclear power, as the recent resumption of underground nuclear testing by the United States makes clear, is hardly peculiar to the East. Chernobyl has rendered national and political boundaries meaningless.

But ultimately *Störfall* is more than a work of antinuclear protest. Its criticism runs deeper: it raises existential questions concerning human aggression, moral responsibility, and fundamental human needs. Here, as in her Cassandra project, Christa Wolf no longer speaks primarily as an East German, but rather as a woman writer. Probing both her own and our age's self-destructive blind spot, she examines the fallacies and delusional thinking of the dominant male culture and sees connections rather than distinctions between the East and the West.

Störfall makes far less extensive use of intertextuality than other works by Wolf, notably *No Place on Earth*. It does, however, contain a prime example of self-quotation in the narrator's repeated reference to Chernobyl as "the news" ("die Nachricht"). This circumlocution refers back to another event of great historical import that Wolf had described similarly. In chapter twenty-three of *Divided Heaven* she drew a parallel between GDR and Soviet scientific and technological endeavors by having the work brigade's outing to test their railroad car coincide with the 1961 Soviet launching of the first man into space. The narrator builds suspense by repeatedly referring to "the news" before finally revealing this news to be the manned space flight. By using the identical word to describe the disparate phenomena of the space flight of Juri Gagarin and Chernobyl, Christa Wolf points to the underlying connection between them: both the space program and the "peaceful" use of nuclear power are anchored in a blind faith in technology. Juri Gagarin's flight and Chernobyl are opposite sides of the same coin. At the same time, by using the same word and the same technique of indirect reference, Wolf makes us aware of how fundamentally her own assessment of technology has changed. Whereas her early work had enthusiastically embraced scientific progress and technology and the Soviet mastery of space, Wolf's latest work inextricably links science and technology with male (self-) destructiveness, aggression, and inability to love.

Wolf's scepticism regarding technology is scarcely new. It had begun to manifest itself as early as *Christa T.*: there the space program greeted euphorically in *Divided Heaven* is underplayed and depicted as essentially disappointing.[5] But Wolf's criticism of technology was still relatively unfocused in *Christa T.* Not until "Self-Experiment" did it mesh with a criticism of instrumental rationality and with a feminist critique of patriarchal values. This dual critical perspective characterizes *No Place on Earth*, Wolf's essays on the Romantics, and her Cassandra project, and leads directly to *Störfall*.

Störfall accomplishes more successfully what Wolf had attempted in the Cassandra complex in appending the narrative as the fifth lecture on poetics: it effaces the distinctions between essayistic and narrative prose. It can (and doubtless will) as readily be called an essay as a fictional narrative. Perhaps more than any of her other works, *Störfall* so interweaves literature and biography as to render traditional genre classifications meaningless. It evinces the intense subjective engagement we have come to expect from Christa Wolf's essays. It also has much in common with Wolf's autobiographical stories, "Tuesday, 27 September," "An Afternoon in June," and "Change of Perspective," and ultimately of course with her autobiographical *magnum opus*, *Patterns of Childhood*.

After experimenting with more closed forms of narration in *No Place on Earth* and *Cassandra*, Christa Wolf has returned to the open-ended, process-oriented mode of writing that is most uniquely her own and that first earned her critical acclaim. Clearly autobiographical, *Störfall* recalls *Patterns of Childhood* by referring back to individuals (the narrator's mother, her maternal grandparents, and her Aunt Lisbeth) and events (the dislocation of her brother's arm and Nelly's typhus) from the earlier work.[6] It shares with the earlier work an intimate, self-exploratory, self-reflexive nature and a desire to use literature to work through traumatic experiences. It differs, however, from Wolf's auto-biographical novel in that the narrator/author writes consistently in the first person: Christa Wolf has, it seems, finally overcome the difficulty of saying "I." Unlike *No Place on Earth*, in which Wolf uses the historical figures of Kleist and Günderrode as mouthpieces for her own ideas and feelings, or the *Cassandra* narrative, in which she uses the mythological figure of Cassandra in the same way, Wolf is able to speak in her own voice in *Störfall*.

Moreover, this voice is no longer split, as it was in *Patterns of Childhood*. True, Wolf is acutely aware of the schizophrenia she considers characteristic of our age. "How remarkable," the narrator notes, "that in Greek 'a-tom' means the same as 'individual' in Latin: indivisible. Those who invented these words knew neither atomic fission nor schizophrenia. Whatever is the source of the modern compulsion to divide into ever smaller parts, to split off whole parts of a personality from that ancient person thought to be indivisible?"[7] Yet if she still suffers from this modern malaise, it is obviously no longer as debilitating as it once was. It is as though Wolf had benefited vicariously from her fictional Cassandra's journey to selfhood, as though her character's process of self-integration were also therapeutic for her.

Like *Christa T.* and *Patterns of Childhood*, *Störfall* is preceded by a disclaimer cautioning readers against identifying the book's characters with living persons and maintaining that all figures are invented by the author, Christa Wolf. Yet more clearly than in any of her other works, the free "invention" of *Störfall* is based on authentic authorial experiences and hence fulfills Christa Wolf's self-imposed mandate of "subjective authenticity."

From the outset, the text makes it clear that Chernobyl consti-tutes an historical and personal watershed for the narrator/author: "Once again, so it seemed to me, the age had created a before and an after for itself. I could describe my life as a series of such incisions, as a series of darkenings through ever denser shadows. Or on the contrary, as an increasing accommodation to harsher lighting, sharper insights, greater sobriety" (*S* 43).

Yet this event is not an absolute hiatus. Instead, it is the culmination of a preexisting condition. Like Cassandra, who was able to interpret signs of pre-war only in retrospect, after war had broken out, the narrator of *Störfall* recognizes after the nuclear disaster that there had been warning signals all along: "That was one of those days on which I recalled all the signs that we had been given to see without understanding them" (*S* 94). She recalls, for instance, the first demonstrations against the construction of a nuclear power plant in the city of Whyl, West Germany and recognizes that the young protestors' warnings about the dangers of atomic power fell for the most part on deaf ears. They did not carry the stamp of authority of the "experts," experts who after Chernobyl are forced to confess how little they really know about nuclear power. Stunned, the narrator marvels at the "unconscious certainty with which everything works together: most people's desire for a comfortable life, their tendency to believe the speakers behind the elevated podiums and the men in their white smocks. Everybody's mania to conform and their fear of contradicting seem to correspond to the thirst for power and the arrogance, the greed, the unscrupulous curiosity and self-infatuation of the few. What was it in the end that made this equation impossible to solve?" (*S* 23). Reiterating her antiauthoritarian view (she has repeatedly held the Germans' exaggerated love of authority in part responsible for the rise of Nazism), Christa Wolf implicates us all in Chernobyl and calls upon us to resist.

It is characteristic of the writer Wolf's attention to language that she defines the "before" and "after" created by Chernobyl in terms of its far-reaching linguistic implications for the narrator. The danger of worldwide nuclear contamination renders such traditional nature metaphors as "the glowing heavens" (*S* 28) inviable. It also inhibits the creation of new metaphors, such as "the green explodes" (*S* 8) to describe the verdant spring day on which "the news" comes. Furthermore, it compromises formerly benign words such as "cloud." Reflecting that in her grandmother's day "cloud" denoted a natural phenomenon pure and simple, the narrator attributes its current contamination to our own ineptitude: "The fact that we call it a 'cloud' is after all only a sign of our own inability to keep pace linguistically with the advances of science" (*S* 34).

Although a misnomer, the atomic "cloud" has colonized the connotative resonance of the original word. Recalling lines from Bertolt Brecht's love poem, "Memory of Marie A.," in which the poet uses the metaphor of a white cloud to describe his ephemeral love: "but that cloud bloomed only for minutes and as I looked up it was already disappearing in the wind," the narrator reflects:

I hope. I hope it's only for minutes, was all I could think, even though this was a song from the time when clouds were "white" and composed of poetry and pure condensed steam. But, I thought, now we could anxiously wait to see which poet would be the first to dare to praise a white cloud again. An invisible cloud of a completely different substance had taken it upon itself to attract our emotions – totally different emotions. And, I thought again with dark glee at the misfortunes of others, it has pushed the white cloud of poetry into the archive.   (*S* 62)

Wolf's observations about the difficulty of writing nature poetry after Chernobyl recall Adorno's dictum that it is barbaric to write poems after Auschwitz.[8] By inviting a parallel between the Holocaust and the nuclear holocaust, she makes clear just how profound a caesura that accident is for the narrator. After Chernobyl nothing can ever be the same for her.

Just as it has contaminated "cloud," Chernobyl estranges well-known literary quotations by imbuing verbs such as "radiate" and "glow" with a new, sinister meaning. The opening lines of Goethe's famous love poem "Maifest" (Rites of Spring): "How magnificently nature radiates for me" (*S* 44) and the jubilant evocation: "Oh Heaven, glowing azure" (*S* 15) take on a dark implication. In the wake of Chernobyl, increasingly alarming news reports about the medical and agricultural implications of the disaster transform milk, lettuce, and venison into storehouses of radioactivity: ordinary means of sustenance have become transmuted into means of death.

The global crisis triggers a crisis of language in the narrator that manifests itself first as a revulsion toward words (*Wortekel*) in general, then as a revulsion at her own words, and finally as self-revulsion. Chernobyl calls into question the validity of the entire enterprise of writing: "What," she ponders, "can any, even the most successful formulation mean. So much has already been spoken and written" (*S* 108). News of Chernobyl not only calls into question literary discourse, it also forces the narrator to acquire the scientific discourse of the atomic age. Whereas Wolf had previously resisted appropriating the militaristic jargon of the superpowers, indeed had appealed to writers to oppose the language of literature to the language of war and destruction, she now finds herself compelled to learn the vocabulary of nuclear holocaust. Words like "contaminate," "rads," "iodine 131," and "half-life" enter her speech almost against her will.

Chernobyl, in short, threatens to destroy everything for which the narrator has been working for years.

And I informed that authority which early on began to regard me attentively from a very distant future – a look, nothing more – that I would henceforth no longer feel bound to anything. Free to do and above all to leave undone whatever I desired. That very distant future goal, toward which until then all lines had moved, had been exploded away. Along with the fissionable material in a reactor encasement, it was in the process of burning out. An unusual case – . (*S* 9)

I interpret the "very distant future goal" to be Marx's vision of social community, a goal to which Christa Wolf had remained committed and which had sustained her in the face of great adversity. If this goal has now been exploded away, what support remains to her? Chernobyl has, it appears, definitively called into question Wolf's utopian ideal. Specifically addressing the concept of utopia, the narrator/author declares that those scientists dedicated to the peaceful uses of the atom had a utopian goal: enough energy for all, forever. She speculates whether the failure of those scientists means that

the utopias of our time necessarily breed monsters? Were we monsters, when, for the sake of a utopia – justice, equality and humanity for all – that we didn't want to postpone, we fought those whose interests were not (are not) served by this utopia and, with our own doubts, fought those who dared to doubt that the ends justify the means? That science, the new God, would deliver us all the answers we would solicit from him. (*S* 37)

In *Christa T.* Wolf had already criticized herself and other dedicated socialists of the *Aufbau* period for an immoral disregard of those with dissenting perspectives. There she had also questioned the GDR's emphasis on the revolution in science and technology. In the context of Chernobyl, these reservations take on a new meaning. In retrospect, the narrator's unease in *Christa T.* can be interpreted as one of the signs not properly understood to which the narrator of *Störfall* refers.

Given the enormous emotional impact Chernobyl had upon her, given Christa Wolf's decision to write about it in the first person, and given her fear of writing "naturalistically,"[9] that is, myopically, how does she avoid the pitfalls of excessive affect in *Störfall*? As in all her fictional works, Wolf gains distance from the immediacy of her personal experiences by transforming them imaginatively, by stylizing herself into a fictional character. Like *Patterns of Childhood*, the locus of narration in *Störfall* is not based on an identity between the experiencing and narrating consciousness of the narrator/author. Although the point of intersection between the two is temporally much closer than in her earlier work, here too the narrator is removed from herself, observing herself from a distance. The author, writing her story several months after the fact, has the benefit of hindsight as she seeks to reconstruct that day in early May 1986. Shifting between present and past tenses, the narrative reproduces both states of consciousness. Thus the author's writing consciousness often uses the past tense to comment on or augment the events of that day and/or the narrator's reactions to them (often related in the present tense). This alternation between present and past, the text's interweaving of self-reflexivity and (recreated) spontaneity, prevents affect from dominating.

In addition, Wolf's opening passage, with its stylized and idiosyncratic use of tenses, its play with narrative perspective, effectively estranges readers. The narrative begins: "One day, about which I cannot write in the present tense, the cherry trees will have blossomed. I will have avoided thinking 'exploded'; the cherry trees have exploded, as only a year before, although even then no longer totally unwittingly, I could not only think but say" (*S* 9).

With respect to her experiencing consciousness, the narrator's writing consciousness is in the future. Yet this writing consciousness is unable to reconstruct the present tense of her experiencing consciousness's perception of that day. Instead, looking back at that experiencing consciousness, Wolf projects it forward into the future by using the future perfect to create a new time structure in which experiencing and narrating consciousnesses converge. Wolf's use of this complicated narrative structure enables her to approximate linguistically the significance this day has for her. Its implications are so far-reaching that she is incapable of conceiving of it without immediately thinking of its ramifications for the future. Chernobyl's radioactive future has a far longer half-life than the future toward which she was working.

But *Störfall* does not focus solely on Chernobyl. Instead the narrative intertwines the global castastrophe with the narrator/author's family crisis. News about and reflections on Chernobyl are interspersed with news about and reflections on her brother, who during the time narrated is undergoing brain surgery for removal of a malignant tumor. This dual focus lends greater resonance to the book's subtitle: *News of a Day*. It also intensifies the impact of the Chernobyl accident by pairing it with a personal "breakdown."

Addressing her brother throughout the text, the narrator/author creates the aura of conversation so characteristic of Wolf's mature work. *Störfall* sustains this conversational mode even more consistently than *Christa T.* had done.[10] In *Christa T.* Wolf had used the simple past, which is the usual narrative tense. In *Störfall*, she uses the nonliterary, that is, conversational, present perfect tense to describe past events. Her renunciation of the epic preterite[11] in *Störfall* is the grammatical manifestation of her process-oriented, antiauthoritarian narrative stance. As the linguist Harald Weinrich has shown, German speakers use the present perfect tense when discussing past events that have relevance for them in the present and when they seek to impart the emotional residue of these events. In other words, it is the tense used when a person is still working through past events.[12] It is therefore singularly appropriate to Wolf's current undertaking.

Written to and for the narrator's brother, *Störfall* records for him details of the momentous events he is missing. It also documents the narrator's very unextraordinary everyday activities: domestic chores, such as cooking, cleaning, and gardening; a visit to the neighbors; telephone conversations with a woman friend, her daughters, and her sisiter-in-law; a bicycle ride; and a trip to the grocery store. And these familiar undertakings, by virtue of their ordinariness, serve as a bulwark against those extraordinary and terrifying events over which she has no control. Nowhere in Christa Wolf's work are the personal and the political more tightly interwoven than in *Störfall*.

The dialogic structure allows Wolf to create an intensely personal historical document. By projecting a fictional dialogue partner who for the most part remains silent yet allows her to associate freely, the text also simulates Freud's patient–analyst relationship and thus enables her, through her self-styled "talking cure," to work through emotions that both Chernobyl and her brother's cancer unleash.

Thus Wolf's dialogism has a therapeutic function for the narrator. In another sense the therapy encompasses her brother as well, to whom the narrator directs concentrated psychic energy to help him withstand the rigors of the six-hour operation and ensure his recovery. In effect, the narrator wills her brother back to good health.

It is no accident that the narrator consistently refers to her brother as "brother-heart" ("Bruderherz"). It is as though by means of this epithet she were trying to counteract the imbalance of an overly developed, hence dis-eased brain. Wolf's emphasis on psychic healing in *Störfall* is consonant with her holistic world view and her repeated admonishments that we must overcome our debilitating mind/body dichotomy if we are to survive. This sympathetic healing rests on the narrator's empathy with her brother, an identification similar to Günderrode's with Kleist and Wolf's with her fictional character Cassandra.

Before her brother is anesthetized, the narrator assures him:

Everything will go well. That is the message that I transmit to you as a concentrated ray of energy. Can you perceive it? Everything will go well. Now I let your head appear before my inner eye, search for the most vulnerable spot which my thought can penetrate to reach your brain, which they will lay bare soon. Everything will go well. (*S* 10)

Later she transmits the thought that he can trust the experienced and skilled hands of his surgeon (*S* 16). About two hours into the operation, she is overcome by the feeling that something is wrong. Sensing that her brother is losing his will to live, the narrator reminds him of the joys of life, assures him that he can recover fully, and reenacting the childhood role of the older sister entrusted with the care of her younger sibling familiar to us from *Patterns of Childhood*, demands that he not let himself go. "But you've got to hold tight. Don't let go, brother! Hold tight! That's it. I'll pull a bit now, can see you already, nearer and nearer, clearer and clearer. Now very near. There. Now we've done it. Please don't do that again. It's against our pact" (*S* 20).

Just as the narrator can sense a particularly crucial moment in the operation, she also intuits when her brother is out of danger. Thus at precisely 1.25 p.m. she suddenly and inexplicably begins to sing Schiller's "Ode to Joy" – only to learn later that this was precisely the moment her brother regained consciousness.

In both *Patterns of Childhood* and *Störfall*, the narrator's brother is presented as the rational, sober, unemotional antipode of his sister, as a scientist fascinated by computers and technology. It cannot be coincidence that he undergoes brain surgery on precisely the day when our blind faith in technology ought to have been irrevocably shattered, on which the limitations, if not the ultimate dead end of modern technology was brought home with a vengeance. Wolf's juxtaposition of public and private events leads us to infer that the overly developed brain of *homo technicus* is diseased and that our runaway technology is like a cancer that takes over our bodies, incessantly, abnormally reproducing itself.

Such an interpretation is reinforced by the narrator's reflections on the "star warriors," that is, the scientists committed to implementing the Reagan administration's Star Wars defense initiative.

219

In linking Chernobyl to these American scientists at the Livermore laboratories, Wolf effectively undercuts attempts to differentiate between peaceful and militaristic uses of nuclear power. Describing their fascination with abstract research, with the pursuit of an idea, Wolf characterizes these star warriors as extraordinarily intelligent, precocious young American scientists who, "driven ... by the hyperactivity of certain centers of their brain, have sold their souls not to the devil ... but to their fascination with a technical problem" (*S* 70), and allow themselves to be incarcerated in their research laboratories. There, deprived of all human relationships, these young men live in utter isolation, "without women, without children, without friends, without any pleasures besides their work, subjected to the most rigorous rules of security and secrecy" (*S* 70).[13]

Again sounding the theme of *kennen*, knowing another human being (and concomitantly being known), Wolf's narrator maintains that these star warriors

know neither father nor mother. Neither brother nor sister. Neither wife nor child (there are no women there, brother-heart! Is this oppressive fact the reason for young people's love of computers? Or the result of this love?) What they do know, these boy geniuses, with their highly trained brains, with the restless left hemisphere of their brains working feverishly day and night, what they know is their machine. Their beloved computer. To which they are bound, chained, just as any slave to his galley ... The only goal they know: to construct an atom-powered x-ray laser, the foundation of that fantasy of a totally secure America achieved by displacing future nuclear battles into space.   (*S* 70–1)

Since *kennen* is an intersubjective act, the isolation of these scientists, their incapacity to know another subject, their inability to love, is a manifestation of the perversion of social relations in our time. Their ability to know and care only for inanimate objects (their computers) is an expression of their (and our) alienation. Without the ability to love, either ourselves or one another, we are, as Christa Wolf has often reminded us, in mortal danger of self-annihilation. Thus the narrator quickly recognizes that it is "not the phantom of 'security,' no: it is the attraction of death, the realizability of nothingness, that has driven some of America's finest brains together here" (*S* 72).

Fascinated by the scientist Peter Hagelstein, the star warrior profiled in a journal article she is reading, the narrator follows his career. For her this nuclear-age Faust embodies those traits that have distinguished Wolf's recent male figures such as Kleist and

Achilles, in whom desire and aggression, Eros and Thanatos converge. "At what crossroad," the narrator ponders, "did human evolution possibly go astray, that we have coupled satisfaction of desire with a drive for destruction?" (*S* 73).

Hagelstein-Faust differs from the Goethean model in that he is driven not by a thirst for knowledge, but by ambition: the desire to win the Nobel prize by inventing an x-ray laser for peaceful purposes. At Livermore his goal is subverted and Hagelstein, who abhors bombs, is persuaded, against his own better judgment, to work on his invention for military rather than for pure research purposes. Thus, instead of working for humankind as Goethe's Faust had done, Hagelstein works toward its destruction. This perversion of a humanistic goal is attributable to the negative dialectics of the Enlightenment. Originally liberating, the concept of reason as thirst for knowledge in the service of the community is perverted to instrumental rationality (Hagelstein is motivated by pragmatism and personal ambition). The narrator is also intrigued by Hagelstein's lover, Josephine Stein, the Gretchen figure who in the modern version is no longer a passive victim, destroyed by Faust, but rather a moral agent who seeks to redeem him. When Hagelstein, in violation of his conscience, produces a blueprint which will help implement devices for the creation of an x-ray laser for Star Wars, Stein protests and ultimately leaves him. Instead of Goethe's bourgeois tragedy, we have a contemporary *Lysistrata*. This reinterpretation is in keeping with Christa Wolf's belief that women, because they are marginalized and excluded from existing patriarchal structures, can better withstand the pressures to conform and often become a force of resistance and a catalyst for peace.

Five months later, news that Peter Hagelstein has left the Livermore atomic research center mitigates the narrator's pessimism. Upon hearing the news, she rejoices: "One of them has done it. Nothing is final. I must think anew about the fate and decisions of the modern Faust" (*S* 102).

The tension between hope and despair, so characteristic of Wolf's work since *No Place on Earth*, is the structuring principle of *Störfall*. It is embodied in two quotations that precede the text. The first, by Carl Sagan, the American astronomer, astrophysicist, popular scientist, and outspoken critic of nuclear weapons, stresses humankind's potential for destruction. Linking aggression and progress, it reads: "The connection between murder and invention has been with us ever since. Both derive from agriculture and civilization." Taken from his book *The Dragons of Eden. Specu-*

lations on the Evolution of Human Intelligence, the passage cited by Wolf summarizes Sagan's line of argument and warrants fuller quotation. In his chapter "Eden as a Metaphor," Sagan maintains that the biblical account of humankind after the exile from Eden corresponds in good part to the archeological and historical evidence. According to Sagan,

civilization develops not from Abel, but from Cain the murderer. The very word "civilization" derives from the Latin word for city . . . The first city, according to Genesis, was constructed by Cain, the inventor of agriculture – a technology that requires a fixed abode. And it is his descendants, the sons of Lamech, who invent both "artifices in brass and iron" and musical instruments. Metallurgy and music – technology and art – are in the line from Cain . . . The connection between murder and invention has been with us ever since. Both derive from agriculture and civilization.[14]

The second quotation, from the animal behaviorist Konrad Lorenz, best known in the scientific community as the father of ethology, reads like an expression of Bloch's principle of hope. At once an encouragement and a challenge, it makes us aware of our potential and our task: "The long-sought missing link between animals and the really humane being is ourselves" (*S* 7).

In his book *On Aggression*,[15] Lorenz argues for the existence of an innate aggressive drive in human beings. Based on his studies of animals with highly developed intraspecific aggression, such as the greylag goose, which also form bonds of individual friendship, that is, manifest highly developed social behavior, Lorenz concludes that "intra-specific aggression can certainly exist without its counterpart, love, but conversely there is no love without aggression."[16] Noting the striking similarities in complex norms of behavior between the greylag and man (for example, strife for ranking order, falling in love, jealousy, grieving), Lorenz maintains that in both the greylag and man each of these instincts has a special, virtually identical value for the survival of the species.[17]

The final three chapters of Lorenz's book are, by his own admission, the most speculative. Here he applies data gleaned from the science of comparative ethology to humans in the hope of curbing man's aggressive drives. It should be noted that this aspect of Lorenz's work is highly controversial. Indeed, there are many scientists and social scientists who dispute the existence of an innate aggressive drive in humans.[18] The issue here, however, is not the validity of Lorenz's arguments. What is of interest is that Christa Wolf should choose a passage from this final portion, specifically from the chapter entitled "On the Virtue of Humility."

In this chapter, Lorenz asserts that man's pride and his androcentricity are handicaps to self-knowledge. Praising the virtues of humility, he calls on humankind to know itself. He indicts German Idealist philosophy for its dualistic world view, for dividing humankind into a natural, material and a moral, spiritual being. As a confirmed Darwinian, he believes that human beings are moral not by virtue of some divine inner will but because they are more highly evolved beings. "The functions of reason and moral responsibility . . . first come into the world with man and . . . provided he does not blindly and arrogantly deny the existence of his animal inheritance, give him the power to control it."[19] Self-knowledge, according to Lorenz, is essential if we are not to remain powerless "against the pathological disintegration of our social structure, and if, armed with atomic weapons, we cannot control our aggressive behavior any more sensibly than any animal species."[20] Arguing for the unique position of man, Lorenz maintains:

We are the highest achievement reached so far by the great constructors of evolution. We are their "latest" but certainly not their last word . . . To regard man, the most ephemeral and rapidly evolving of all species, as the final and unsurpassable achievement of creation, especially at his present-day particularly dangerous and disagreeable stage of development, is certainly the most arrogant and dangerous of all untenable doctrines. If I thought of man as the final image of God, I should not know what to think of God. But when I consider that our ancestors, at a time fairly recent in relation to the earth's history, were perfectly ordinary apes, closely related to chimpanzees, I see a glimmer of hope. It does not require considerable optimism to assume that from us human beings something better and higher may evolve. Far from seeing in man the irrevocable and unsurpassable image of God, I assert – more modestly and, I believe, in greater awe of the Creation and its infinite possibilities – that the long-sought missing link between animals and the really humane being is ourselves![21]

It is obvious why Wolf would be interested in Lorenz's teachings. He not only offers us a materialist explanation for human morality but also, like Wolf, stresses the link between self-knowledge and moral responsibility. By placing the Lorenz quotation last, Wolf calls upon us to counteract the seemingly inevitable link between progress and destruction that, according to Sagan, has characterized human civilization thus far. It challenges us to engage our imagination (invention) toward positive ends: to make the world a proper home for truly humane beings instead of using it for inhuman ends (killing).

For the narrator, Peter Hagelstein thus becomes the emblem of the conflict she herself is experiencing and to which she gives expression in the text's double motto. As a star warrior at Livermore, Hagelstein seems to validate Sagan's perceptions about the interrelationship between human creativity and destructiveness. His decision to leave breaks an established pattern of behavior and encourages both the narrator and the reader to hope that we, as the link between the animal and the truly humane being, can realize our potential. By relinquishing his ambitious drive for success, Hagelstein is free to use his considerable intellect for productive ends.

It is typical of Christa Wolf's indebtedness to Bloch's philosophy that she ends her realistic, if despondent, appraisal of the current situation on a more optimistic note. However traumatic Chernobyl is, it is paradoxically also liberating. Like Cassandra, telling her story before the gates of Mycenae in the face of imminent death, the narrator/author (as she herself repeatedly tells us) no longer feels bound to anything. Like Cassandra, hers is an existential freedom born of despair. Precisely the urgency of the situation has enabled Christa Wolf to overcome those remaining forms of self-censorship against which she has so tenaciously struggled. It enables her definitively to reject the male generic modes of expression that had to some degree still bound her and to speak in her own (female) voice. *Störfall*'s conversational mode breaks with the male literary tradition; it simulates an oral transmission, which has traditionally been women's province. Even more emphatically than *Christa T.*, it overcomes the opposition between speech and writing, thereby again deconstructing the system of dichotomous oppositions that informs patriarchal discourse and perception. In presenting the narrator's sympathetic healing of her brother, the text carries Wolf's specifically female holistic epistemological stance of "touching" to its logical conclusion. It serves as an example of the bonding Lorenz and Wolf considered necessary for the survival of the species.

It is significant that the narrator's reflections on writing do not end pessimistically, but with a reaffirmation of literature's potential. As the narrator is going to bed, she picks up a book she has been meaning to read for a long time. Her enthusiastic assessment of *The Heart of Darkness* as a work of subjective authenticity and of Joseph Conrad as an author who probed the blind spot of his culture stand in sharp contrast to her earlier statements. Conrad's artistic genius has obviously rekindled her faith in the power of literature to touch the innermost core of the reader and to effect change. However severely Chernobyl may have endangered her belief in the realizability of Marx's social vision, it has not totally destroyed her faith in the utopian dimension of literature.

Störfall ends with the narrator's recollection of a dream out of which she awoke with a scream. A comparison of this dream with the one that concludes *Patterns of Childhood* demonstrates just how precarious Wolf's position has become. Whereas the earlier hopeful dream, with its fluid transitions, enabled the narrator to overcome limitations experienced in the waking state, the terrifying dream in *Störfall* graphically records her fears. "In my dream a gigantically close, disgustingly decomposed moon had sunk very quickly behind the horizon. A large photo of my dead mother was fastened to the jet-black sky. I screamed" (*S* 119). Unlike *Patterns of Childhood*, the dream in *Störfall* does not offer the narrator the possibility of a reprieve. There appears to be no recourse for her (or for us) out of this world of our own making. The pairing of the images of the decomposed moon,[22] symbolic of our own planet that we are destroying, and the narrator's dead mother establish the connection between man's domination of nature and his domination of women. It is, after all, not the narrator's mother, but a photo of her, that is, her reified image, symbolic of male objectification of women, that appears fastened to the sky. The dream also reinforces the narrator's deliberations on language in a post-Chernobyl age. For so long a repository of metaphors, images, ideals, and aspirations, the moon is no longer innocent. Technology, by sending a man to the moon, has intruded on cosmic space. It has also invaded our private corporeal and imaginative spheres. True, technology cures the narrator's brother. But its benign side is inseparable from its destructive side; the same technology has greatly increased our risk of cancer. Technology has taken us over body and soul.

Störfall does not conclude with the narrator's dream, but with her remark to her brother: "How hard it would be, brother, to bid farewell to this earth" (*S* 116). Viewed in conjunction with the narrated dream, this statement must be read as a warning. The use of the conditional (in German, "würde es sein"), instead of the indicative, mitigates the pessimism of the dream. Had Wolf said "How hard it *will* be to leave this earth," there would be no room for hope. As it stands, the conclusion contains a prophetic vision of what will come into being if we continue on our self-destructive course. It is a warning that we cannot afford to ignore. Perhaps there is still time.

NOTES

1 Introduction: setting the context

1 This recent assessment (1983) was related by Christa Wolf's husband, Gerhard Wolf, during a lecture and discussion on GDR poetry at Ohio State University (3 June 1983).

2 The Socialist Unity Party was created in the GDR in 1946 when the Communist Party (KPD) merged with the Socialist Party (SPD). The SED nominated Wolf to the list of candidates for the Central Committee in 1963. In 1967 she was removed from the list by the Party leadership for coming into conflict with them over cultural political issues.

3 Wolf's Marxism continues to be guided by anthropological concerns; her focus remains on the individual and on the possibility of developing all aspects of one's personality. While we know very little about her excursions into Marxist thought, we *do* know that the first Marxist work she read was Engels's essay "Ludwig Feuerbach and the End of Classical German Philosophy." Christa Wolf, "Zu einem Datum," in *Lesen und Schreiben* (Darmstadt/Neuwied: Luchterhand, 1972), p. 52. Judging from her concern with human self-actualization, one can conclude that the early Marx of the *Economic and Philosophic Manuscripts of 1844* and the Marx/Engels of *Theses on Feuerbach* and *The German Ideology* had the greatest impact on her.

4 Frank Trommler, "Kulturpolitik der Nachkriegszeit," in *Kulturpolitisches Wörterbuch: Bundesrepublik Deutschland/Deutsche Demokratische Republik im Vergleich*, ed. Wolfgang R. Langenbucher *et al.* (Stuttgart: J. B. Metzler, 1983), p. 409.

5 This law was based on the pedagogical reform of the Weimar Republic and drawn up by exiles of the Nazi regime. Trommler, p. 412.

6 From the inscription on the Soviet war memorial in East Berlin, erected 1949.

7 Biographical information on Christa Wolf is scarce. The following data are gleaned from Alexander Stephan, *Christa Wolf* (Munich: C. H. Beck, 1976), pp. 7–22, 161–2, and Jack Zipes, "Christa Wolf: Moralist as Marxist," Introduction to *Divided Heaven*, trans. Joan Becker (New York: Adler's Foreign Books, 1974), pp. xi–xxx.

8 Wolf, "Zu einem Datum," p. 52.

9 Not only had the university attracted eminent Third Reich émigrés who had chosen to return to East rather than West Germany, but the founding of the GDR Literary Institute (1955; renamed the Johannes R. Becher Institute in 1959) aimed at developing the literary talents of writers culled from the working and peasant classes, ensured that Leipzig would become an important literary center as well.

10 For many years critics assumed Wolf had read Bloch's works and/or attended his lectures during her years in Leipzig because of echoes of Blochian utopian thought in her writing. Recently, however, Wolf has denied that she was familiar with Bloch's work until well after completing *Christa T.* See editor's note in *Christa Wolf Materialienbuch*, ed. Klaus Sauer, 2nd, revised edn (Darmstadt/Neuwied: Luchterhand, 1983), p. 115. In a letter to me dated 13 January 1986, Wolf reiterated that she had not read Bloch until very late in her career. The similarities between Wolf's work and Bloch's philosophy of hope, his emphasis on subjectivity and on the everyday, and his call for humankind to assume the ethical posture of "the upright stance" (*der aufrechte Gang*) are so striking that one must speculate that the main tenets of Bloch's utopian thinking had become common intellectual currency. Wolf was perhaps exposed to them indirectly, either through Hans Mayer, who while Christa Wolf was studying in Leipzig was engaged in an intense debate with Bloch, or at some later period. See Andreas Huyssen, "Auf den Spuren Ernst Blochs: Nachdenken über Christa Wolf," in *Christa Wolf Materialienbuch*, pp. 99–115, for a discussion of parallels between Bloch's philosophy and especially *The Quest for Christa T.*, and Klaus K. Berghahn's recent article, "Die real existierende Utopie im Sozialismus. Zu Christa Wolfs Romanen," in Berghahn and Hans Ulrich Seeba, eds., *Literarische Utopien von Morus bis zur Gegenwart* (Königstein: Athenäum, 1983), pp. 275–97, for a broader analysis of Bloch's significance. Far from overstating the importance of Bloch's thought for her *œuvre*, Wolf scholarship has not yet explored its full significance.

11 David Bathrick, "Geschichtsbewusstsein als Selbstbewusstsein. Die Literatur der DDR," in *DDR-Literatur*, ed. Klaus von See, vol. 21, *Neues Handbuch der Literaturwissenschaft* (Wiesbaden: Akademische Verlagsgesellschaft, 1979), p. 274. Bathrick quite rightly points out a fallacy informing this aesthetic, namely the tacit assumption that everyone knew what "real life" was and that the writer would be guided by this knowledge.

12 For a discussion of the reevaluation of Romanticism in the GDR, see Patricia Herminghouse, "Die Wiederentdeckung der Romantik: Zur Funktion der Dichterfiguren in der neueren DDR-Literatur," in Jos Hoogeveen and Gerd Labroisse, eds., *DDR-Roman und Literaturgesellschaft*, pp. 217–48 (Amsterdam: Rodopi, 1981); Herminghouse, "The Rediscovery of Romanticism," in *Studies in GDR Culture and Society*, vol. 2, ed. Margy Gerber *et al.* (Washington, DC: University Press of America, 1982), pp. 1–17.

13 See Peter Uwe Hohendahl, "Ästhetik und Sozialismus: Zur neueren Literaturtheorie der DDR," in *Literatur und Literaturtheorie in der DDR*, ed. Hohendahl and Patricia Herminghouse (Frankfurt/Main: Suhrkamp, 1976), pp. 103–14; 123–38 for a discussion of the reception, criticism, and influence of Western literary theory.

14 Her dissertation, "The Problems of Realism in the Work of Hans Fallada," treats a novelist who was a progressive social critic of the Weimar Republic. The study shows that she was familiar with current theories of literary realism. In her work as editor, she rigorously applied Party line norms. In essays and discussions Wolf has recalled restrictive aspects of her study of German literature. She believes that her literary studies retarded her emergence as a creative writer.

15 Helen Fehervary and Sara Lennox, Introduction to Christa Wolf, "Self-Experiment: Appendix to a Report," trans. Jeanette Clausen, *New German Critique* 13 (Winter 1978): 112. I am indebted to Fehervary and Lennox for my reading of this story.

16 Christa Wolf, "Self-Experiment: Appendix to a Report," trans. Jeanette Clausen, *New German Critique* 13 (Winter 1978): 113–31, here 122. "Anders," the protagonist's new name, means "different, other."

17 This holistic appropriation of reality by the female subject would also account for the significant role played by illness in Wolf's work. In *Moscow Novella, Divided Heaven, Christa T., Patterns of Childhood* and *No Place on Earth* her protagonists respond to external events by becoming ill. In *Cassandra* the response is madness. In each case the etiology of illness and madness is a situation that is emotionally intolerable to the woman. In a talk delivered at a conference of medical doctors in October 1984, Christa Wolf argued that particularly for women, illness is often psychosomatic, arising from a feeling of not being loved. She urged doctors not merely to treat physical symptoms, but to explore the psychological roots of these illnesses. Published as "Christa Wolf. Krankheit und Liebesentzug. Fragen an die psychosomatische Medizin" in *Neue deutsche Literatur* 34/10 (October 1986): 84–102.

18 Fehervary/Lennox, Introduction to "Self-Experiment," p. 111.

19 *Guten Morgen, du Schöne* (Berlin, GDR: Buchverlag Der Morgen, 1978). West German edition Luchterhand, 1978.

20 Also published in Christa Wolf, *Fortgesetzter Versuch: Aufsätze, Gespräche, Essays* (Leipzig: Reclam, 1982), pp. 312–22.

21 Christa Wolf, *Fortgesetzter Versuch*, p. 312. My translation.

22 Sara Lennox, "Trends in Literary Theory: The Female Aesthetic and German Women's Writing," *German Quarterly* (Winter 1981): 71.

23 "Der Schatten eines Traumes" (Shadow of a Dream, 1978), written as an introduction to an anthology of the work of Karoline von Günderrode by the same name; "Nun ja! Das nächste Leben geht aber heute schon an" (Yes indeed! But the next life starts today!, 1979), written as an afterword to the recently reissued biography of Günderrode by Bettina von Arnim (both essays appear in *Fortgesetzter Versuch*); and

an essay on Heinrich von Kleist's *Penthesilea* (1982) written as an afterword for a new edition of the play (Berlin, GDR: Buchverlag Der Morgen, 1983), pp. 157–66. Also published in a volume of fiction and essays on Romanticism by Christa Wolf and Gerhard Wolf, *Ins Ungebundene gehet eine Sehnsucht: Gesprächsraum Romantik* (Berlin/ Weimar: Aufbau, 1985), pp. 195–210.

24 Since *Divided Heaven* Wolf's works have appeared both in the GDR and in the Federal Republic of Germany (FRG) and have been translated into English within a relatively short period of time. Since *No Place on Earth* Wolf has been published simultaneously in the GDR and the FRG.

Publication history of Wolf's major works:

Divided Heaven: GDR (Mitteldeutscher Verlag: 1963)
               FRG (Rowohlt: 1968)
               USA (Adler's Foreign Books: 1965)
Christa T.: GDR (Mitteldeutscher Verlag: 1968)
               FRG (Luchterhand: 1969)
               USA (Farrar, Straus & Giroux: 1972)
Patterns of Childhood: GDR (Aufbau: 1976)
               FRG (Luchterhand: 1977)
               USA (Farrar, Straus & Giroux: 1984)
               (originally published as *A Model Childhood*, 1980)
No Place on Earth: GDR (Aufbau: 1979)
               FRG (Luchterhand: 1979)
               USA (Farrar, Straus & Giroux: 1982)
Cassandra: GDR (Aufbau: 1983)
               FRG (Luchterhand: 1983)
               USA (Farrar, Straus & Giroux: 1984)
Störfall: GDR (Aufbau: 1987)
               FRG (Luchterhand: 1987)

In a recent interview about *No Place on Earth* (1982), Christa Wolf admitted that she was no longer readily able to distinguish between letters from East and West German readers. Describing an experiment she sometimes does, namely reading her mail without checking the return address, Wolf said she frequently could not tell if a letter was from the Federal Republic or from the GDR. According to her, "apparently there's a similar need that the texts respond to. Often, by the way, they are similar people – I meet them at public readings. There's a similar human type that's neither East nor West German, GDR or FRG. Rather, it's a type, usually a young person, with very specific expectations that aren't 'divided.'" Christa Wolf, "Culture is What You Experience – An Interview with Christa Wolf," trans. Jeanette Clausen, *New German Critique* 27 (Fall 1982): 98.

25 Wolfgang Emmerich, *Kleine Literaturgeschichte der DDR* (Darmstadt/ Neuwied: Luchterhand, 1981), pp. 20–1; 29–32.

26 The freedom of expression of GDR writers at any given moment is dependent upon the political climate. The *cause scandaleuse* expatriation of the vociferously critical but committed socialist poet and songwriter Wolf Biermann is the most recent testimony to the GDR's unwillingness to countenance internal criticism.

27 Publication of the book was delayed a year. According to Wolf, *Christa T.* had been completed for a year when she started to write "The Reader and the Writer," published in 1968, the same year as *Christa T.*; see "Die Dimension des Autors" in Christa Wolf, *Fortgesetzter Versuch: Aufsätze, Gespräche, Essays* (Leipzig: Reclam, 1982), p. 78. Moreover, there is speculation that a large part of the original GDR edition was sold to the West (see Heinrich Mohr, "Produktive Sehnsucht. Struktur, Thematik und politische Relevanz von Christa Wolfs *Nachdenken über Christa T.*," in *Basis: Jahrbuch für deutsche Gegenwartsliteratur*, vol. 2, ed. Reinhold Grimm and Jost Hermand (Frankfurt/Main: Athenäum, 1971), 217, footnote 20. There are also vast discrepancies in reports regarding the actual number of copies printed in the first edition of *Christa T.* (estimates range from 500 to 15,000 copies). This first edition sold out almost immediately. A second edition was not printed until 1972. See Dieter Sevin, *Christa Wolf: Der geteilte Himmel; Nachdenken über Christa T.: Interpretation* (Munich: R. Oldenbourg, 1982), p. 62, footnote 54.

28 This is true, for example, of the anti-Nazi novels *Das siebte Kreuz* (*The Seventh Cross*, 1939/42) by Anna Seghers and *Nackt unter Wölfen* (Naked Among Wolves, 1958) by Bruno Apitz. It is, however, also increasingly true that more controversial works, including those of Christa Wolf, are enjoying the greatest popularity.

29 GDR writers have a larger readership relative to population, hence a more significant public voice. For a discussion of the book and publishing industry in the GDR, see Emmerich, pp. 21–6.

30 The reprisals against Biermann's supporters following his expatriation seriously called this assumption into question and precipitated a crisis in Christa Wolf, which found its expression in *No Place on Earth*.

31 Robert Minder, quoted by Emmerich, p. 19. The following overview of the GDR as *Literaturgesellschaft* is indebted to Emmerich, pp. 19–33.

32 As Emmerich has pointed out, Becher's statements reflect not only the perspective of classical critical Marxist thinkers such as Rosa Luxemburg but also the utopian legacy of Enlightenment Idealist thought (Emmerich, p. 20). This dual legacy plays an important role in Christa Wolf's work.

33 See Horst Redeker, *Abbildung und Aktion: Versuch über die Dialektik des Realismus* (Halle/Saale: Mitteldeutscher Verlag, 1966).

34 Hans Georg Hölsken, "Zwei Romane: Christa Wolf 'Der geteilte Himmel' und Hermann Kant 'Die Aula,'" *Deutschunterricht* 5/21 (1969): 64.

35 It remains an open question whether the literary praxis of Socialist Realism corresponds to the theory arising out of Bitterfeld.

36 Unpublished public discussion with Christa Wolf at Ohio State University, 2 June 1983.

37 Christa Wolf, "Die Dimension des Autors," discussion with Hans Kaufmann, *Fortgesetzter Versuch*, p. 83.

38 Heinrich Mohr, "Die zeitgemässe Autorin – Christa Wolf in der DDR," in *Erinnerte Zukunft – 11 Studien zum Werk Christa Wolfs*, ed. Wolfgang Mauser (Würzburg: Königshausen & Neumann, 1986), p. 47.

2 Beginnings: experimentation with Socialist Realist paradigms. *Moscow Novella* and *Divided Heaven*

1 In her essay "Über Sinn und Unsinn von Naivität" (On the Sense and Nonsense of Naiveté, 1973), Christa Wolf proves to be her own most severe critic. Published in *Fortgesetzter Versuch: Aufsätze, Gespräche, Essays* (Leipzig: Reclam, 1982), pp. 49–58. All quotations will refer to this edition and will be in my translation.

2 The essay "Zu einem Datum" documents the transformative power Wolf attributed to socialism. *Lesen und Schreiben* (Darmstadt/ Neuwied: Luchterhand, 1972), pp. 47–53. In the essayistic component of her work on Cassandra, "Conditions of a Narrative", Wolf's description of her shift to a feminist perspective, or "view scope," as she calls it, is measured against the earlier shift to a Marxist view scope, leaving little doubt as to the significance of this experience. *Cassandra: A Novel and Four Essays*, trans. Jan van Heurck (New York: Farrar, Straus & Giroux, 1984), p. 278.

3 Jack Zipes, "Christa Wolf: Moralist as Marxist," Introduction to *Divided Heaven*, trans. Joan Becker (New York: Adler's Foreign Books, 1981), p. xvi.

4 Originally written for Gerhard Schneider, ed., *Eröffnungen: Schriftsteller über ihr Erstlingswerk* (Berlin/Weimar: Aufbau, 1974), p. 13–48. It is remarkable that Wolf refused to disclose the genesis and development of *Moscow Novella* when she does precisely that in "Conditions of a Narrative" with regard to *Cassandra*. Clearly her sense of privacy will only allow her to reveal information of her own volition, not when it is elicited by others.

5 "Über Sinn und Unsinn von Naivität," in *Fortgesetzter Versuch*, p. 54. My translation. All subsequent quotations from this text will be in my translation.

6 *Ibid.*, p. 52.

7 *Ibid.*, pp. 54–5.

8 *Ibid.*, p. 53.

9 Christa Wolf, *Moskauer Novelle* (Halle: Mitteldeutscher Verlag, 1961), p. 11. My translation. All subsequent quotations will refer to this edition, in my translation, and be cited as *MN* in the text.

10 Helen Fehervary, "Christa Wolf's Prose: A Landscape of Masks," *New German Critique* 27 (Fall 1982): 67.

11 See, for example, Gerda Schulz, "Ein überraschender Erstling," *Neue deutsche Literatur* 7 (1961): 130. Schulz's generally positive review takes exception to the descriptions of the Moscow milieu, deeming them too lengthy and detailed for the circumscribed genre of the novella.

12 Thus mankind's potential for self-annihilation, which is the impetus for Wolf's most recent works, *Cassandra* and *Störfall*, has been an important concern of hers since the beginning of her writing career.

13 Zipes, "Christa Wolf: Moralist as Marxist," p. v.

14 Willkie K. Cirker, "The Socialist Education of Rita Seidel: The Dialectics of Humanism and Authoritarianism in Christa Wolf's *Der geteilte Himmel*," *University of Dayton Review* 13/2 (Winter 1978): 105–11.

15 "She no longer shrank from admitting to herself that the place and the time she had collapsed had been no accident. She had seen the two heavy green coaches rolling toward her, inexorably, quietly, certainly. They're coming right at me, she had thought, and she knew quite well that she was bringing it upon herself." *Divided Heaven*, trans. Joan Becker (New York: Adler's Foreign Books, 1981), p. 202. Unless otherwise indicated, all further quotations will refer to this edition and will be cited as *DH* in the text.

16 "Dienstag, der 27. September," in Christa Wolf, *Gesammelte Erzählungen* (Darmstadt/Neuwied: Luchterhand, 1982), pp. 20–33, here pp. 32–3, my translation. In the story the names of the narrator's children, Tinka and Annette, are identical with Wolf's, and the initial G. of her husband obviously stands for Gerhard Wolf, to whom Christa Wolf dedicated *Der geteilte Himmel*, using the initial G. The dedication is not included in the English translation. Together with "Juninachmittag" (*Gesammelte Erzählungen*, pp. 35–53), "An Afternoon in June," trans. Eva Wulff, *Cross-Section*, ed. Wieland Herzfelde and Günther Cwojdrak (Leipzig: Edition Leipzig, 1970), pp. 256–72 (Anthology of the PEN Centre German Democratic Republic), and "Blickwechsel" (*Gesammelte Erzählungen*, pp. 5–19), "Change of Perspective," trans. A. Leslie Willson (*Dimension* [Special Issue 1973]: 180–201), also in Elisabeth Rütschi Herrmann and Edna Huttenmaier Spitz, eds., *German Women Writers of the Twentieth Century* (Oxford, New York: Pergamon, 1978), pp. 94–100, "Dienstag, der 27. September" belongs to Wolf's most autobiographical short stories. Indeed, the spontaneity of the journal entry form blurs the distinction between fiction and life to an unprecedented degree.

17 We must bear in mind that at this time the FRG not only refused to recognize the GDR, it actively sought to isolate the Ulbricht government. The Hallstein Doctrine threatened any country that established diplomatic relations with the GDR with severance of diplomatic ties with the Federal Republic. Dieter Sevin, *Christa Wolf, Der geteilte Himmel; Nachdenken über Christa T.: Interpretation* (Munich:

R. Oldenbourg, 1982), pp. 25–6. See Sevin, pp. 24–6, for a concise overview of this political and economic situation of the GDR in the early sixties.

18 Christa Wolf, *Der geteilte Himmel* (Halle/Saale: Mitteldeutscher Verlag, 1967), p. 260. My translation. Joan Becker's translation does not capture the bitterness and frustration of Rita's statement.

19 Christa Wolf, "Kann man eigentlich über alles schreiben?" (Can one really write about everything?), *Neue deutsche Literatur* 6 (1958): 13–14.

20 Martin Reso, *'Der geteilte Himmel' und seine Kritiker. Dokumentation* (Halle: Mitteldeutscher Verlag, 1965).

21 This objection certainly has validity from a GDR standpoint, and Western critics have concurred with this evaluation. Alexander Stephan, for example, has pointed out that Manfred's dilemma is in many ways more compelling than Rita's. In his opinion it is Manfred, not Rita, who enacts the conflict between the individual and society. Alexander Stephan, *Christa Wolf. Autorenbuch* (Munich: Beck, 1979), pp. 44–5. Furthermore, more similarities exist between Manfred and Christa Wolf than between the author and her heroine, a not insignificant fact for a writer whose aesthetic point of departure is experiential.

22 See Reso's concluding essay in *'Der geteilte Himmel' und seine Kritiker*, pp. 256–98.

23 Walter Ulbricht, *Über die Entwicklung einer volksverbundenen sozialistischen Nationalkultur* (Berlin: Dietz Verlag, 1964), p. 21.

24 Stephan, *Christa Wolf*, p. 49.

25 In *Wilhelm Meister* this telos is the *Turmgesellschaft* (Society of the Tower), a group that oversees and guides Wilhelm's development toward the principles of usefulness, productivity, and specialization. Recent scholarship has pointed to the oppressiveness if not inhumanity of the secret Society of the Tower. See Karl Schlechta, *Goethes Wilhelm Meister* (Frankfurt/Main: Suhrkamp, 1977); Heinz Schlaffer, "Exoterik und Esoterik in Goethes Romanen," *Goethe Jahrbuch* 95 (1978): 212–26; Hannelore Schlaffer, *Wilhelm Meister. Das Ende der Kunst und die Wiederkehr des Mythos* (Stuttgart: Metzler, 1980).

26 For a discussion of the *Bildungsroman* in the GDR, see Frank Trommler, "Von Stalin zu Hölderlin: Über den Entwicklungsroman in der DDR," in *Basis: Jahrbuch für deutsche Gegenwartsliteratur*, vol. 2, ed. Reinhold Grimm and Jost Hermand (Frankfurt/Main: Athenäum, 1971), pp. 141–90. Trommler points out that in *Das Erlebnis und die Dichtung* (Leipzig/Berlin, 1905), Wilhelm Dilthey anchored his definition of the *Bildungsroman* firmly in the sociohistorical situation of the German burghers of the nineteenth century. He therefore suggests using the more general term *Entwicklungsroman* (novel of development) when dealing with this phenomenon in twentieth-century socialist society. However, given the important role of Enlightenment and

classical humanist thought for the GDR in general and Christa Wolf in particular, I have chosen to retain this term (keeping in mind Trommler's considerations) as a point of departure against which to measure experimentations and deviations from the norm.

27 Hans Vaget, "Goethe the Novelist," in *Goethe's Narrative Fiction: The Irvine Goethe Symposium*, ed. William J. Lillyman (Berlin/New York: Walter de Gruyter, 1983), p. 15.

28 In speaking about *Patterns of Childhood*, Wolf rejects the antifascist tradition created by the GDR, maintaining that while leading public offices were held by resistance fighters, the "masses of course were the same as in the Federal Republic." Discussion with Christa Wolf at Ohio State University (24 May 1983). Published as "Dokumentation: Christa Wolf; Eine Diskussion über *Kindheitsmuster*," *German Quarterly* 51/1 (Winter 1984): 91. My translation. Thus as early as 1963 Wolf avoided creating figures that did not conform to what she herself had experienced.

29 Christa Wolf, "Eine Rede" (A Speech), in *Lesen und Schreiben*, p. 22. My translation.

30 Cirker, "The Socialist Education of Rita Seidel," p. 108.

31 Myra Love, "Das Spiel mit offenen Möglichkeiten: Subjectivity and the Thematization of Writing in the Works of Christa Wolf" (Ph.D dissertation, University of California/Berkeley, 1983), p. 107.

32 Cirker, p. 108.

33 *Ibid.*, p. 110.

34 Christa Wolf, "Kann man eigentlich über alles schreiben?" p. 13. My translation.

35 Alexander Stephan sees this juxtaposition as examples of "the two basic possibilities of life between which, according to Christa Wolf, every modern human being today must choose." Stephan, *Christa Wolf*, p. 35. My translation.

36 Wolf has spoken of this process with regard to herself. "Erfahrungsmuster" (Patterns of Experience), in *Fortgesetzter Versuch*, p. 105.

37 In *Patterns of Childhood*, Wolf in the figures of the narrator and her daughter Lenka again raises the issue of the possibility of communicating experience from one generation to another.

38 "Über Sinn und Unsinn von Naivität," in *Fortgesetzter Versuch*, p. 56. My translation.

39 Rita, in assessing the reasons for Manfred's flight, concludes that "he had simply given up the struggle and if he had given up loving or hating he could live anywhere. He had not gone away out of protest, but had just given up. This going to the West was not a new experiment, but the end of all experiments . . . It did not matter any more what he did" (*DH* 189).

40 Stephan, *Christa Wolf*, p. 45.

41 *Forum* 18 (1963). Quoted by Reso, ed., *Der geteilte Himmel und seine Kritiker*, p. 256. My translation.

42 Silke Beinssen-Hesse, "Zum Realismus in Christa Wolfs *Der geteilte Himmel*," in *Wolf: Darstellung, Deutung, Diskussion*, ed. Manfred Jurgensen (Bern/Munich: Francke, 1984), p. 44.

43 "Nicht mehr aus verzweifelter Liebe, sondern aus Verzweiflung darüber, daß Liebe vergänglich ist wie alles und jedes." Christa Wolf, *Der geteilte Himmel*, p. 275. My translation.

44 Interview with Karl Corino on Hessian radio on 27 November 1974 in the series "Transit: Culture in the GDR." Quoted by Stephan in *Christa Wolf*, p. 35. My translation.

45 Wolf's essay on Karoline von Günderode, "Der Schatten eines Traumes" (The Shadow of a Dream), was written as an introduction to a recent reissue of Günderrode's work which she edited. Her essay on Bettina von Arnim, "Nun ja! Das nächste Leben geht aber heute an" (Yes, indeed! But the future starts today!) was written as an afterword to the re-release of Bettina's biography of her friend Karoline, *Die Günderode*.

46 Stephan, *Christa Wolf*, pp. 36–7.

47 Jack Zipes points out the irony of the fact that Wolf's portrayal of a male-dominated sphere of production was probably not intended as a conscious critique. "Christa Wolf: Moralist as Marxist," p. xxxv.

48 After the party at the professor's, in effect a role reversal takes place in Rita and Manfred's relationship. It is now she who seeks to protect him. Increasingly it appears that she is the one in control, not he.

49 Although never explicitly stated, the Wall is the danger alluded to in the frame, which registers the reactions of the GDR populace to the "silent voices of imminent dangers, all fatal in that period" and speaks of a resumption of daily work following the "shadow" that had fallen over the city but had retreated again (*DH* 1).

50 *Der geteilte Himmel*, p. 274. My translation.

51 Wolfgang Joho, ed., "Notwendiges Streitgespräch; Bemerkungen zu einem internationalen Kolloquium," *Neue deutsche Literatur* 3 (1965): 103.

52 Love, "Das Spiel mit offenen Möglichkeiten," p. 112.

3 Christa T.: the quest for self-actualization

1 For a representative sample of critical responses, see *Wirkungsgeschichte von Christa Wolfs 'Nachdenken über Christa T.,'* ed. Manfred Behn (Königstein: Athenäum Verlag, 1978).

2 No official information regarding actual numbers of the first edition is available. According to Heinrich Mohr, the Mitteldeutsche publishing house failed to respond to his inquiry regarding publication details. An unofficial source, the critic Roland Wiegenstein, provided the following information: a version of *Christa T.* existed as early as 1965. Five thousand copies of the revised version were printed in 1968. Of these, 800 copies were delivered in 1969. After the critical rejection of the

book, the remaining 4,200 copies were sold to Luchterhand in West Germany. Since many of the original 800 copies were sent to critics, Party functionaries, and library officials, the number of copies actually sold in bookstores in the GDR was quite small. Heinrich Mohr, "Produktive Sehnsucht: Struktur, Thematik und politische Relevanz von Christa Wolfs *Nachdenken über Christa T.*," in *Basis: Jahrbuch für deutsche Gegenwartsliteratur*, vol. 2, ed. Reinhold Grimm and Jost Hermand (Frankfurt/Main: Athenäum, 1971), 216–17, footnote 20.

3 After the initial primarily negative response (reviews appeared in *Sinn und Form* and *Neue deutsche Literatur* in 1969), public debate about *Christa T.* largely ceased. Apart from passing remarks in longer essays and entries in literary histories, no further mention was made of Wolf's work. There is still no full-length GDR study of *Christa T.* Alexander Stephan, *Christa Wolf: Forschungs-Berichte zur DDR-Literatur* 1, ed. Gerd Labroisse (Amsterdam: Rodopi, 1980), p. 38.

4 "Christa T. stirbt an Leukemie, aber ihre wirkliche Krankheit ist die DDR." Marcel Reich-Ranicki, "Christa Wolfs unruhige Elegie," *Die Zeit*, 25 May 1969. My translation.

5 The text's inherently revolutionary impetus might help to explain why the book was extolled in East-bloc countries and why it has found such resonance in the West, especially among women. Adam Krzemiński in the Warsaw weekly *Polityka* for example praised *Christa T.* as the event of 1969, and an anonymous review in the well-known Moscow paper *Literaturnaja gazeta* lauded *Christa T.* as a moral model. Adam Krzemiński, "Rytm pokoleniowy" (Rhythm of generations) in *Polityka*, 17 May 1969 and Anonymous, "Istorijia Kristy T." (The Story of Christa T.) in *Literaturnaja gazeta*, 14 May 1969: 15. Quoted by Alexander Stephan, *Christa Wolf* (Munich: Beck, 1979), p. 91.

6 Campaigns against modernism were standard fare of GDR cultural politics in the fifties. This interdiction against modernist literary experimentation was reiterated by the central committee of the SED in 1965. See Gerhard Probst's interpretation of *Christa T.* based on Hans Robert Jauss's concept of alterity (*University of Dayton Review* 13/2 [1978]: 25–35) and Dieter Sevin's application of Wolfgang Iser's reader-response theories in Sevin, *Christa Wolf: Der geteilte Himmel; Nachdenken über Christa T.: Interpretation* (Munich: R. Oldenbourg, 1982), pp. 72–6.

7 A summary of the colloquium proceedings as well as selected contributions by individual authors, among them Christa Wolf, was published under the title Necessary Dispute. Wolfgang Joho, ed., "Notwendiges Streitgespräch: Bemerkungen zu einem internationalen Kolloquium," *Neue deutsche Literatur* 13/3 (1965): 88–112; Wolf's contribution, 97–104.

8 *Ibid.*, p. 98. My translation. All subsequent quotations from the proceedings are in my translation.

9 *Ibid.*, p. 99.

10 *Ibid.*

11 *Ibid.*, pp. 101–2.

12 *Ibid.*, p. 103.

13 *Ibid.*

14 If it is true, as Heinrich Mohr has suggested (see note 2), that a version of *Christa T.* existed in 1965, then this work and "An Afternoon in June" are actually parallel works, not sequential ones.

15 "Juninachmittag," in Christa Wolf, *Gesammelte Erzählungen* (Darmstadt/Neuwied: Luchterhand, 1982), p. 34. My translation. English translation, "An Afternoon in June," trans. Eva Wulff, in *Cross-Section*, ed. Wieland Herzfelde and Günther Cwojdrak (Leipzig: Edition Leipzig, 1970), pp. 256–72.

16 The family situation, ages of the first-person narrator's children and the proximity of the garden to Berlin all point to a convergence between narrator and author.

17 This appellation is not limited to the opening passage, but is repeated six times throughout the text.

18 Christa Wolf, "Die zumutbare Wahrheit," in *Fortgesetzter Versuch* (Leipzig: Reclam, 1982), p. 269.

19 *Ibid.*, p. 272.

20 *Ibid.*, p. 277.

21 *Ibid.*, pp. 280–1.

22 Since "Juninachmittag" constitutes a turning point in Christa Wolf's work in its new emphasis on the reader's involvement it is significant that the narrator is herself engaged in the act of reading in the story.

Although her name is never mentioned in the text, Helen Fehervary argued that the narrator was reading a story by Ingeborg Bachmann. Fehervary, "Christa Wolf's Prose: A Landscape of Masks," *New German Critique* 27 (Fall 1982): 86. References to Italy (where Bachmann lived until her death) and to the writer's style that correspond to Wolf's discussion of Bachmann in her essay "Die zumutbare Wahrheit" (The Acceptable Truth) led Fehervary to infer that she was the author of the story being discussed. This was incorrect. The narrator/author was actually reading Marie Luise Kaschnitz's "Lange Schatten" (Long Shadows). See revised reprint of Fehervary's essay in *Responses to Christa Wolf: Critical Essays*, ed. Marilyn Sibley Fries (Detroit: Wayne State University Press, forthcoming).

23 Fehervary, "Christa Wolf's Prose," p. 86.

24 Sevin, *Christa Wolf*, implies as much on p. 62.

25 Published as "Die Dimension des Autors," in Christa Wolf, *Fortgesetzter Versuch*, p. 77–104. Here p. 78.

26 Published as "Unruhe und Betroffenheit," in *Fortgesetzter Versuch*, pp. 59–76.

27 Published in Christa Wolf, *The Reader and the Writer: Essays, Sketches, Memories*, trans. Joan Becker (New York: International

Publishers, 1977), pp. 76–80. All further references to this collection will be cited as *RW* in the text.

28 In her interview with Hans Kaufmann, Christa Wolf points to this overlap between her literary and essayistic work: "To this extent my successive (or interpenetrating) fictional and essayistic utterances are not essentially distinct from each other." *Fortgesetzter Versuch*, p. 78. My translation.

29 In *Patterns of Childhood* Wolf compounds the issue by appending the subtitle "novel" to the West German edition: *Kindheitsmuster: Roman* (Darmstadt/Neuwied: Luchterhand, 1979), a designation missing in the original East German edition.

30 "The Reader and the Writer," in Christa Wolf, *The Reader and The Writer*, p. 198.

31 Interview with Hans Kaufmann, in "Die Dimension des Autors," *Fortgesetzter Versuch*, p. 83.

32 This is articulated for instance by Wolfgang Kayser in his essay, "Wer erzählt den Roman?" (Who narrates the novel?), in *Zur Poetik des Romans*, ed. Volker Klotz (Darmstadt: Wissenschaftliche Buchgesellschaft, 1969), pp. 197–216. He maintains (pp. 206–7) that "the narrator in all forms of narration is never the known or as yet unknown author, but rather a role that the author invents and assumes, that the narrator is a fictive person into which the author has transformed himself." My translation.

33 In German, the passage reads: "Christa T. ist eine literarische Figur. Authentisch sind manche Zitate aus Tagebüchern, Skizzen and Briefen." Christa Wolf, *Nachdenken über Christa T.* (Darmstadt/Neuwied: Luchterhand, 1969), p. 6.

34 Interview with Karl Corino on Hessian radio on 27 November 1974 in the series "Transit: Culture in the GDR." Quoted by Alexander Stephan, *Christa Wolf*, p. 79. My translation.

35 In "The Reader and the Writer," Wolf ironically rejects the reflection theory of literature: "Let us leave mirrors to do their job: to mirror. They cannot do anything else. Literature and reality do not stand face to face like a mirror and what it reflects. They merge in the author's mind" (*RW* 206).

36 "Die Dimension des Autors," in *Fortgesetzter Versuch*, p. 83. My translation.

37 *Ibid.* My translation.

38 Unpublished group discussion with Christa Wolf at Ohio State University, 2 June 1983.

39 Interview with Hans Kaufmann, "Die Dimension des Autors," in *Forgesetzter Versuch*, p. 78.

40 Clearly all Wolf's work after *Christa T.* has had this therapeutic effect for her.

41 In "The Reader and the Writer," Wolf also connects the exigencies of Dostoyevsky's situation while writing *Crime and Punishment* with his

portrayal of Raskolnikov, pointing out that, in order not to kill his own creditors in reality, Dostoyevsky may well have had to let Raskolnikov kill his landlady. Thus, "Dostoyevsky, as if possessed, plays out with shadow figures and can to some extent overcome what has brought him to the brink of destruction or self-destruction in the real world" (*RW* 203–6, here 206).

42 "Unruhe und Betroffenheit," in *Fortgesetzter Versuch*, p. 65. My translation.

43 *Ibid.*, p. 64. My translation.

44 *Ibid.*, p. 63.

45 "Die Dimension des Autors," in *Fortgesetzter Versuch*, p. 81.

46 This is Hans Mayer's reading. He sees Christa T.'s death as paradigmatic. Christa T. dies so that her author can continue to live and write in the GDR. Mayer, "Christa Wolf: *Nachdenken über Christa T.*," *Neue Rundschau* 81/1 (1970): 180–6.

47 In her interview with Joachim Walther, Wolf admits to a burning interest in questions concerning the morality of her generation. Examining the achievements, failures, and aspirations of the generation around 1930, Wolf is particularly interested in her age group's self-perception, maturation, and conscience. "Unruhe und Betroffenheit," *Fortgesetzter Versuch*, p. 72. In her discussion with Hans Kaufmann she elucidates the unique position of her generation:

> What our generation has experienced, no other generation will encounter: to grow up, be educated and formed by one society and to have the possibility for radical social criticism and self-criticism in another – our – society. To be able to think, understand and act and in doing so to be placed in new, certainly not easy, contradictions and conflicts. To help, in fact, create these contradictions and to help work toward overcoming them and yet to not be able to deny patterns of behavior that determined our childhood and youth.

"Die Dimension des Autors," in *Fortgesetzter Versuch*, p. 93. My translation.

48 See Christa Thomassen, *Der lange Weg zu uns selbst. Christa Wolfs Roman 'Nachdenken über Christa T.' als Erfahrungs- und Handlungsmuster* (Kronberg: Skriptor, 1977), pp. 20–33 for a detailed analysis of the question of author–narrator identification.

49 Christa Wolf, *The Quest for Christa T.*, trans. Christopher Middleton (New York: Farrar, Straus & Giroux, 1970), p. 5. All further quotations will refer to this edition and will be cited as *CT* with page references in the text.

50 While Stalinism is never explicitly mentioned in the text, the emphasis Wolf places on this period indicates her concern with this phenomenon. In *Patterns of Childhood* Wolf explicitly addresses Stalinism and her self-censorship on the subject.

51 Sevin, *Christa Wolf*, p. 68.

52 Wolf, *Nachdenken über Christa T.*, p. 7.
53 Myra Love, "Christa Wolf and Feminism: Breaking the Patriarchal Connection," *New German Critique* 16 (Winter 1979): 35.
54 "Unruhe und Betroffenheit," in *Fortgesetzter Versuch*, pp. 74–5. My translation.
55 Wolf's frame of reference in the "The Reader and the Writer" is explicitly scientific. In a long section she discusses the relationship between Heisenbergian physics and literature with regard to language (*RW* 199–201). See Alexander Stephan, "Die wissenschaftlich-technologische Revolution in der Literatur der DDR," *Deutschunterricht* (BRD) 2 (1978): 18–34 for a discussion of the scientific technological revolution in GDR literature.
56 The concept of touching (*berühren*), which will play an important role in *No Place on Earth* and *Cassandra*, where it will be portrayed mainly as the intuitive silent understanding of another person, is here still connected with language; it is the *voice* of another person that touches the reader.
57 In her emphasis on the educative function of literature in facilitating humanity's coming-of-age, Wolf recalls earlier trends of thought compatible with the goals of epic prose: the German Enlightenment and the German *Klassik*. Immanuel Kant's famous essay "What is Enlightenment?," in which he defines Enlightenment as "the emergence of man from his self-imposed minority," parallels Christa Wolf's views. Immanuel Kant, "An Answer to the Question: What is Enlightenment?," trans. Patricia Crampton, in *Enlightenment in Germany*, ed. Paul Raabe and Wilhelm Schmidt-Biggemann (Bonn: Hohwacht Verlag, 1979), p. 9. Both hold humanity culpable for our lack of maturity and look to reason as the vehicle of maturation.

Similarly, Wolf's hope of effecting social change through a change in individual consciousness with the help of epic prose also calls to mind Friedrich Schiller's *On the Aesthetic Education of Man in a Series of Letters* (1795). In *The Aesthetic Education* Schiller attributes to art the role of healing the wounds of civilization. By overcoming the split between the human being and nature, between intellect and senses, art helps us overcome our alienation; it makes us whole again and reconciles us with ourselves and with the world. The closing image of Schiller's treatise, that of a society of aesthetically educated individuals emanating out in concentric circles from a nucleus, is compatible with Wolf's view of the personal and social transformational power of prose. Friedrich Schiller, *On the Aesthetic Education of Man in a Series of Letters*, trans. Elizabeth M. Wilkinson and L. A. Willoughby (Oxford: Clarendon Press, 1967), esp. The Twenty-Seventh Letter, pp. 204–19.
58 In essays and commentary, Wolf has stressed the importance of the visual for her in the act of literary creation. In "The Reader and the Writer," she speaks of "seeing" the world in a new way. She elucidates

this phenomenon by describing her experience in Moscow in which past and present events left their imprint on her in terms of *seeing* everything differently (*RW* 177; 179). Similarly, Wolf's discussion of her new feminist "view scope" in "Conditions of A Narrative" is framed in visual terms. Christa Wolf, *Cassandra, A Novel and Four Essays*, trans. Jan van Heurck (New York: Farrar, Straus & Giroux, 1984), esp. 277–8. In an unpublished discussion held at Ohio State University (2 June 1983), Wolf extended this metaphor to the reader as well. Before she can begin writing, she maintained, she must be able to "see" her potential reader. Invariably this means visualizing the reader's eyes.

59 In her interview with Hans Kaufmann, Christa Wolf attributed to her study of German her inhibited spontaneity and creativity and a retardation in her development as a writer. "Die Dimension des Autors," in *Fortgesetzter Versuch*, p. 80.

60 This passage is strikingly similar to Wolf's description of plot-oriented, mechanistic writing. See the "Celestial Mechanics" section in "The Reader and the Writer" (*RW* 193–7).

61 Throughout the text italics are used to indicate verbatim quotations from Christa T.

62 The use of modal verb *müssen*, in German, "to have to do something," clearly implies that Christa T. does not watch this spectacle of her own volition. *Nachdenken über Christa T.*, p. 25.

63 In Mann's novella the bourgeois-manqué artist caught between two worlds is at once contemptuous of and longs for entry into the world of the bourgeoisie. In describing Tonio Kröger's reactions to the failure of his relationship with Hans Hansen and Ingeborg Holm, the narrator says: "His heart beat richly: longing was awake in it, and a gentle envy; a faint contempt, and no little innocent bliss." Thomas Mann, "Tonio Kröger," in *Death in Venice and Seven Other Stories*, trans. H. T. Lowe-Porter (New York: Vintage, 1954), p. 85. Wolf continues her quotation of "Tonio Kröger" in her portrayal of the love triangle in which Christa T. is involved by having her ironically allude to Kostia's other lover as the blond Inge. There is a plethora of literary allusions in *Christa T.* See Fritz Raddatz, "Mein Name sei Tonio K.," *Spiegel* 23 (2 June 1969): 153–4 for a discussion of literary influence in *Christa T.*

64 "Es ist die Erfüllung aller der Möglichkeiten, wie sie dem Menschen gegeben sind," in *Auf andere Art so grosse Hoffnung. Tagebuch 1950, Eintragungen 1951* (Berlin [DDR]/Weimar: Aufbau, 1969), p. 224. My translation.

65 See Heinrich Mohr, "Produktive Sehnsucht."

66 Ernst Bloch, *Tübinger Einleitung in die Philosophie* 1 (Frankfurt/Main: Suhrkamp, 1963), p. 11. *A Philosophy of the Future*, trans. John Cummings (New York: Herder and Herder, 1970), p. 1.

67 Bloch, *A Philosophy of the Future*, p. 12.

68 *Ibid.*, p. 36.

69 Ernst Bloch, *Das Prinzip Hoffnung* 1 (Frankfurt/Main: Suhrkamp,

1959), p. 16. *The Principle of Hope* I, trans. Neville Plaice, Stephen Plaice, and Paul Knight (Oxford: Blackwell, 1986), p. 7.

70 *Ibid.*, p. 14.

71 Ehrhard Bahr, "The Literature of Hope: Ernst Bloch's Philosophy and its Impact on the Literature of the German Democratic Republic," in *Fiction and Drama in East and Southeast Europe: Evolution and Experiment in the Postwar Period*, ed. Henrik Birnbaum and Thomas Eckman (Ohio: Slovica Publications, 1980), pp. 11–26, here p. 13. See Bahr for a concise overview of Bloch's philosophy.

72 See Heinrich Mohr, "Die zeitgemässe Autorin – Christa Wolf in der DDR," in Wolfram Mauser, ed., *Erinnerte Zukunft: 11 Studien zum Werk Christa Wolfs* (Würzburg: Könighausen & Neumann, 1985), pp. 17–52 for a discussion of Christa Wolf as a writer representative of her time.

73 Wolf refers to Novalis's *Heinrich von Ofterdingen* through her introduction of the Klingsor figure, who in the original is instrumental in helping Heinrich find the blue flower. In *Christa T.* the exotic Indian she calls Klingsor first appears to Christa T. in a dream and fulfills her most fervent wish: he calls her a poet.

74 This motif is picked up by Thomas Mann in "Tonio Kröger." In his juxtaposition of artist and burgher, the leitmotif of the blue cornflower in the father's buttonhole is a symbol of his longing for the exotic.

75 The English translation fails to specify that it is the early part of the summer, rendering *Frühsommer* simply as "summer" (*CT* 70).

76 Johann Wolfgang von Goethe, "Das Göttliche," *Goethes Werke*, Hamburger Ausgabe, vol. I (Hamburg: Christian Wegner Verlag, 1966), pp. 147–9; here 149. My translation.

77 "Zu einem Datum," in *Lesen und Schreiben* (Darmstadt/Neuwied: Luchterhand, 1972), pp. 47–53.

78 Their correspondence, which spanned the years 1965–9, was published in *Was zählt ist die Wahrheit. Briefe von Schriftstellern der DDR* (Halle: Mitteldeutscher Verlag, 1975), pp. 9–33.

79 The narrator tells us: "It's a striking fact that it needn't have been she, Christa T., sitting in front of him. In this scene she's interchangeable with countless other people her age. Many, but not all. The time was approaching when she'd become different, but we didn't realize this. Until we stood in it up to our necks" (*CT* 107).

80 The difference between the technique employed by Wolf in Christa T.'s "conversation" with the principal (*CT* 103–7) and interior monologue is that care is always taken to identify the speaker.

81 This sentiment is presumably a direct quotation from Christa T.'s manuscript of the Toad Story. The italicized quotation reads: "*It seems to me that when I started I somewhat underestimated my profession and the psychological make-up of my students . . .*" (*CT* 108).

82 In the essay "Berührung," Wolf uses Kant's categories to credit Maxie Wander with precisely such humanity. "If humaneness means never,

under any circumstances, making someone else the means for one's own ends, then Maxie Wander was humane." "Berührung," in *Fortgesetzter Versuch*, p. 313. My translation.

83 Carol Gilligan, *In A Different Voice* (Cambridge, Mass.: Harvard University Press, 1983), p. 164.

84 Gilligan, lecture given at the *Beyond The Second Sex* conference, University of Pennsylvania, 7 April 1984.

85 Perhaps Christa T.'s androgynous nature allows her to embody a vision of maturity similar to the one articulated by Gilligan. Krischan, as she is known to everyone, could be either a male or a female name.

86 See Werner Krogmann, "Moralischer Realismus – ein Versuch über Christa Wolf," in Gerd Labroisse, ed., *Zur Literatur und Literaturwissenschaft der DDR* (1978): 233–61, Amsterdamer Beiträge zur neueren Germanistik, 7; Myra Love, "Das Spiel mit offenen Möglichkeiten: Subjectivity and the Thematization of Writing in the Works of Christa Wolf" (Ph.D Dissertation, University of California, Berkeley, 1983), pp. 83–145; and Heinrich Mohr, "Produktive Sehnsucht."

87 This attitude she again shares with Friedrich Schiller. See Schiller, "The Stage as a Moral Institution," in *Aesthetical and Philosophical Essays*, vol. 2, ed. Nathan Haskell Dole (London/Berlin/New York: Robertson, Ashford and Bentley, 1902), pp. 53–61.

88 Wolf refers to Bobrowski's question in her interviews with both Joachim Walther and Hans Kaufmann.

89 "Die Dimension des Autors," in *Fortgesetzter Versuch*, pp. 103–4.

90 *Ibid.*, p. 103.

91 *Ibid.*, p. 104.

92 Hans Kaufmann, in a Postscript to his Discussion with Christa Wolf, published separately, "Zu Christa Wolfs poetischem Prinzip: Nachbemerkung zum Gespräch," *Weimarer Beiträge* 6 (1974): 113–25.

93 Myra Love, "Das Spiel mit offenen Möglichkeiten," p. 131.

94 *Ibid.*

95 See Bernd W. Seiler, "Nachdenken über Theodor S.: 'Innerlichkeit' bei Storm und Christa Wolf," *Schriften der Theodor-Storm-Gesellschaft* 27 (1978): 10.

96 In a discussion at Ohio State University on 2 June 1983, Christa Wolf addressed the issue of the pseudo-objectivity of scientific inquiry and lamented the fact that the humanities and social sciences as well as the sciences perpetuate the same questions instead of coming up with questions that are meaningful to those who pose them. Discussion published as "Ein Gespräch über *Kassandra*," *German Quarterly* (Winter 1984): 105–15; here 114–15.

97 *Fortgesetzter Versuch*, p. 82. My translation.

98 Sevin, *Christa Wolf*, pp. 105–7.

99 A broadening of the concept of realism to include a "subjective" dimension to augment the "objectivity" of the reflection theory was the object of debate among literary historians and theoreticians in the

GDR in the late fifties and early sixties (Horst Redeker, Walter Besenbruch, Erhard Jahn). However, the parameters of this subjectivity were circumscribed by class while individualistic subjectivity was denounced as "subjectivistic." For a discussion of the change in the concept of realism, see Peter Uwe Hohendahl, "Ästhetik and Sozialismus: Zur neueren Literaturtheorie der DDR," in *Literatur und Literaturtheorie in der DDR*, ed. Hohendahl and Patricia Herminghouse (Frankfurt/Main: Suhrkamp, 1976), pp. 138–56.

100 Jeanette Clausen, "The Difficulty of Saying 'I' as Theme and Narrative Technique in the Works of Christa Wolf." in Marianne Burkhard, ed., *Gestaltet und Gestaltend: Frauen in der deutschen Literatur* (1980): 319–331 Amsterdamer Beiträge zur neueren Germanistik, 10, here 319. See Manfred Jäger, "Die Grenzen des Sagbaren: Sprachzweifel im Werk von Christa Wolf," in *Christa Wolf: Materialienbuch*, pp. 130–45, for a general discussion of Christa Wolf's attitude toward language.

101 *Ibid.*

102 Mary Daly, *Gyn/Ecology. The Metaethics of Radical Feminism* (Boston: Beacon, 1968), p. 18. Quoted by Clausen, p. 319.

103 In *New German Critique* 16 (Winter 1979): 31–53.

104 I am indebted to Sara Lennox, "Trends in Literary Theory: The Female Aesthetic and German Women's Writing," *German Quarterly* (1981): 63–75 for an excellent, concise overview of the French feminist appropriation of deconstructionist theory.

105 Love, "Christa Wolf and Feminism," p. 34.

106 *Ibid.*, p. 33.

107 *Ibid.*

108 *Ibid.*, p. 34.

109 See Elizabeth Abel, "(E)merging Identities: The Dynamics of Female Friendship in Contemporary Fiction by Women," and the response by Judith Kegan Gardiner, "The (Us)es of (I)dentity: A Response to Abel on '(E)merging Identities,' " as well as Abel's response to Gardiner, in *Signs: Journal of Women in Culture and Society* 16 (1981): 413–35, esp. 421–3; pp. 436–42; and pp. 422–44 respectively for an example of the debate among feminist scholars on the importance of sociopolitical specificity in feminist analysis of literature. Abel, using Nancy Chodorow's research on mother–daughter relationships, applies object relations theory to examine the dynamics of several fictional women's friendships, including that of Christa T. and the narrator in Wolf's *Christa T.* Gardiner takes issue with Abel for her failure to establish a sociological context for the works considered.

110 In his most recent article, "Frieden, Frauen und Kassandra," in *Wolf: Darstellung, Deutung, Diskussion*, ed. Manfred Jurgensen (Bern/Munich: Francke, 1984), pp. 149–60, Stephan does consider the role of gender in the creation of the text of *Cassandra*. However, his reading of the text as a call for women to work actively for peace does not do justice to the complexity of Wolf's enterprise.

111 Alexander Stephan, "Christa Wolf," in *Neue Literatur der Frauen: Deutschsprachige Autorinnen der Gegenwart*, ed. Heinz Puknus (Munich: Beck, 1980), pp. 149–58, here 150, 153. My translation. For an excellent refutation of Stephan's argument, see Katharina von Hammerstein "Warum nicht Christian T.? Christa Wolf zur Frauenfrage, untersucht an einem frühen Beispiel: *Nachdenken über Christa T.*," *New German Review*, 3 (1987): 17–29.

112 Karin McPherson, "Christa Wolf in Edinburgh. An Interview," *GDR Monitor* 1 (Summer 1979): 1–12; here 11.

113 Wolf has expressed concern about men's more restricted receptivity to her work. Unpublished discussion with Christa Wolf at Ohio State University (2 June 1983).

114 *Fortgesetzter Versuch*, p. 312.

4 *Patterns of Childhood*: the confrontation with the self

1 See Patricia Herminghouse, "Vergangenheit als Problem der Gegenwart: Zur Darstellung des Faschismus in der neueren DDR-Literatur," in *Literatur der DDR in den 70er Jahren*, ed. Peter Uwe Hohendahl and Patricia Herminghouse (Frankfurt/Main: Suhrkamp, 1983), pp. 259–94, for an excellent discussion of this literature.

2 See Christa Wolf "Erfahrungsmuster" (Patterns of Experience), in *Fortgesetzter Versuch: Aufsätze, Gespräche, Essays* (Leipzig: Reclam, 1982), pp. 105–36, and "Dokumentation: Christa Wolf, Eine Diskussion über *Kindheitsmuster*," *German Quarterly* 57/1(Winter 1984): 91–5.

3 Wolf, "Erfahrungsmuster," pp. 107–8; 112.

4 Christa Wolf, *Patterns of Childhood*, originally published as *A Model Childhood*, trans. Ursule Molinaro and Hedwig Rappolt (New York: Farrar, Straus & Giroux, 1980). Paperback edition (1984) entitled *Patterns of Childhood*. Unless otherwise indicated, all quotations will refer to the paperback edition and be cited as *PoC* in the text.

5 I have chosen to render the word *unheimlich* as "uncanny" rather than "strange," as the English translators have done.

6 Christa Wolf, *Kindheitsmuster* (Darmstadt/Neuwied: Luchterhand, 1979), p. 9. My translation.

7 Wolf, "Erfahrungsmuster," p. 112.

8 It is true that Wolf's process-oriented mode of writing makes closure difficult and that her endings are sometimes abrupt, as if the author had arbitrarily decided to stop the flow of her narrative at a certain point. This is true to a greater degree of *Patterns of Childhood* than of *Christa T.* and may have prompted part of the negative critical response.

9 Among these are the death of the farmer Wilhelm Grund, shot by strafing planes in full view of his son; the encounter with the just-released concentration camp inmates from Oranienburg; the Polish foreign worker's resistance to the German landowner, Herr Volk; the eleventh-hour desertion by the Poles of the German caravan to return

to their homes in the East; and the narrator's success at preventing her wristwatch from being confiscated by American GIs.

10 "What? said the SS officer, tired of living? You want to fall into the hands of those Asiatic hordes? The Russians slice the breasts off all of the women!" Christa Wolf, "Change of Perspective," trans. A. Leslie Willson, in *German Women Writers of the Twentieth Century*, ed. Elizabeth Rütschi Herrmann and Edna Huttenmaier Spitz (New York: Pergamon, 1978), pp. 94–100, here p. 94. All further quotations will refer to this edition and be cited as CP.

11 Sandra Frieden, "In eigener Sache: Christa Wolfs *Kindheitsmuster*," *German Quarterly* 54 (1981): 476–7.

12 *Ibid.*, p. 477.

13 Christa Wolf, "Diary, Aid to Work and Memory," in *The Reader and the Writer: Essays, Sketches, Memories*, trans. Joan Becker (New York: International Publishers, 1977), pp. 63–76.

14 Sandra Frieden, *Autobiography: Self Into Form* (Frankfurt/Main: Lang, 1983), p. 13.

15 The discussion with Christa Wolf at Ohio State University was published as "Dokumentation: Christa Wolf, Ein Gespräch über *Kassandra*," *German Quarterly* 57/1 (Winter 1984):105–15; here 114–15. My translation.

16 Wolfgang Iser, *The Implied Reader* (Baltimore: Johns Hopkins, 1974), p. xii.

17 Frieden, "In eigener Sache," p. 483.

18 *Ibid.*, p. 485.

19 Neil Jackson and Barbara Saunders point out that Wolf's opening paraphrase of Faulkner: "What is past is not dead; it is not even past" (*PoC* 3) had been incorporated by Joho into his preface and that her disclaimer has similarities with Joho's afterword, where he maintained that his readers would not find the characters in his novel anywhere, even though they all exist. Jackson and Saunders argue that these similarities, possibly conscious allusions, ultimately serve to draw attention to the enormous differences between the two works. In their view, Joho's portrayal represents precisely the official Party line toward the Nazi past that Wolf is challenging in *Patterns of Childhood*. "Christa Wolf's *Kindheitsmuster*: An East German Experiment in Political Autobiography," *German Life and Letters* 33/4 (1980):320.

Patricia Herminghouse's recent essay illuminates the broader context of the Faulkner quotation. She points out that in addition to Joho and Wolf, the West German writer Alfred Andersch also used it as a motto for his novel *Winterspelt* (1974). Moreover, it serves as the conclusion of another work of GDR literature: Erich Loest's story "Pistole mit sechzehn" (A Pistol at Age Sixteen, 1977). In her view the common currency of Faulkner's quotation in both Germanies can be attributed to the European success of the dramatic adaptation of Faulkner's novel *Requiem for a Nun*, from which the quotation is taken. This in turn may be attributable to the fact that Faulkner's story of guilt and responsibility could be regarded as paradigmatic for the situation of the Germanies after the war. "Vergangenheit als Problem der Gegenwart," pp. 260–1.

20 An exception among GDR critics is Sigrid Bock, who does address the issue of narrative structure and political content. Sigrid Bock, "Christa Wolf: 'Kindheitsmuster,'" *Weimarer Beiträge* 23/9 (1977): 102–30. Yet Bock also falls prey to GDR ideology when she criticizes aspects of the reflective contemporary level of narration for failing adequately to differentiate between pre-1945 and post-1945 conditions and when she stresses the petty bourgeois milieu of the Jordan family.

21 Annemarie Auer, "Gegenerinnerung," *Sinn und Form* 4 (1977): 847–78. Auer's comments elicited a good deal of reader response in *Sinn und Form*, most of which took issue with her affective, accusatory style.

22 Hans Mayer, "Der Mut zur Unaufrichtigkeit," *Der Spiegel*, 11 April 1977, pp. 185–90.

23 Fritz Raddatz, "Wo habt ihr bloss alle gelebt," *Die Zeit*, 4 March 1977.

24 Marcel Reich-Ranicki, "Christa Wolfs trauriger Zettelkasten," *Frankfurter Allgemeine Zeitung*, 19 March 1977.

25 Norbert Schachtsiek-Freitag, "Vom Versagen der Kritik: Die Aufnahme von 'Kindheitsmuster' in beiden deutschen Staaten," in *Christa Wolf Materialienbuch*, ed. Klaus Sauer (Darmstadt/Neuwied: Luchterhand, 1979), pp. 117–30.

26 See Jackson and Saunders and Frieden for an interpretation of *Patterns of Childhood* as political autobiography and Susan Wendt-Hildebrandt, "*Kindheitsmuster*: Christa Wolfs 'Probestück,'" *Seminar* 17/2 (May 1981): 164–76 for a discussion of the book in the context of Wolf's previous fictional and theoretical work.

27 Jackson and Saunders, "Christa Wolf's *Kindheitsmuster*," p. 324.

28 *Ibid.*, p. 325.

29 The German word *Probestück*, derived from the verb *proben*, to rehearse, points to the experimental, nondefinitive nature of Wolf's narrative.

30 Wolf, *Kindheitsmuster*, p. 39. My translation. The English translation is misleading here.

31 Wolf, "Erfahrungsmuster," p. 117.

32 Even after such a long time, Wolf's resistance to writing down her personal history is apparent and is transmitted to the reader both directly, through the narrator's editorial comments, and indirectly. Significantly, the reader also has difficulty becoming involved in the narrative. My experience with *Patterns of Childhood*, that it took a concentrated effort and numerous starts before I could actually become engrossed in the work, is one shared by most people I know.

33 Wolf, "Erfahrungsmuster," p. 109.

34 *Ibid.*, pp. 123–4.

35 *Ibid.*, p. 105.
36 *Ibid.*, pp. 119–20.
37 *Ibid.*, p. 127.
38 Sigmund Freud, "Construction in Analysis," in *Standard Edition of the Complete Psychological Works of Sigmund Freud*, vol. 23, trans. and ed. James Strachey (London: Hogarth Press, 1923), p. 259.
39 Wolf, "Erfahrungsmuster," p. 106.
40 *Ibid.*
41 *Ibid.*, pp. 108–9.
42 Originally published in German as *Die Unfähigkeit zu trauern: Grundlagen kollektiven Verhaltens* (Munich: Piper, 1967). English translation by Beverly R. Placzek (New York: Grove Press, 1975). Unless otherwise indicated, all citations will refer to the English edition.
43 Mitscherlich and Mitscherlich, *The Inability to Mourn*, p. 26.
44 *Ibid.*, p. 28.
45 *Ibid.*, p. 14.
46 *Ibid.*, pp. xvi–xvii.
47 Judith Ryan regards the narrator's discussion with her brother concerning the existence and ramifications of black holes as the crux of *Patterns of Childhood*, dramatizing Christa Wolf's opposition to the official Party line about the Nazi past. Ryan, *The Uncompleted Past: Postwar German Novels and the Third Reich* (Detroit: Wayne State University Press, 1983), pp. 144–6.
48 Mitscherlich and Mitscherlich, *The Inability to Mourn*, p. 24.
49 Sigmund Freud, "Mourning and Melancholia," in *Standard Edition*, vol. 14, p. 246. Quoted by the Mitscherlichs, p. 26.
50 *Ibid.*, p. 24.
51 Ryan, *The Uncompleted Past*, p. 15.
52 Mitscherlich and Mitscherlich, *The Inability to Mourn*, pp. 64–5.
53 *Ibid.*, p. 14.
54 Personal comment to me at Ohio State University, 2 June 1984.
55 Although several critics have alluded to the mourning work (see Charles Linsmayer, "Die wiedergefundene Fähigkeit zu trauern," *Neue Rundschau* 88/3 (1977): 472–8, and Margarethe Mitscherlich, "Die Frage der Selbstdarstellung: Überlegungen zu den Autobiographien von Helene Deutsch, Margaret Mead und Christa Wolf," *Neue Rundschau* 2/3 (1980: 291–316, only Klemens Renolder, *Utopie und Geschichtsbewusstsein: Versuche zur Poetik Christa Wolfs*, Stuttgarter Arbeiten zur Germanistik 92 (Stuttgart: Akademischer Verlag, 1981), pp. 124–34, and Patricia Herminghouse, "Die Vergangenheit als Problem der Gegenwart," pp. 269–76, elucidate this aspect of *Patterns of Childhood*.
56 Wolf, "Erfahrungsmuster," p. 115.
57 The English edition omitted the essentially content-oriented chapter headings of the original.

58 Wolf, *Kindheitsmuster*, p. 346. My translation.
59 Ryan, *The Uncompleted Past*, p. 146. Ryan points to the shock value of the narrator's omission of the Scholls' execution and the Warsaw ghetto uprising in her description of Nelly's confirmation.
60 "Dokumentation: Christa Wolf; Eine Diskussion über *Kindheitsmuster*," *German Quarterly* 57 (Winter 1984): 91–5, here 92. My translation.
61 Alice Miller, *The Drama of the Gifted Child*, trans. Ruth Ward (New York: Basic Books, 1981), p. 4.
62 Margarethe Mitscherlich, "Die Frage der Selbstdarstellung," p. 311. Mitscherlich reads *Patterns of Childhood* as a reflection of the life-long mourning process that constitutes the process of maturation. She views Christa Wolf's confrontation with her past in the context of work to be done during midlife. Characteristic of this period, according to Mitscherlich, is not only Wolf's mourning for her mother's death, but also a heightened awareness of the possibility of her own death. While Mitscherlich's analysis is on the whole illuminating, I find her explanation of Wolf's impetus for writing the book: to mourn for her mother, overstated and oversimplified, an example of overpsychologizing reductionism.
63 *Ibid.*, p. 313. My translation.
64 *Ibid.*, p. 311.
65 Originally published as *Das Drama des begabten Kindes* (Frankfurt/Main: Suhrkamp, 1979); original English title, *Prisoners of Childhood*, trans. Ruth Ward (New York: Basic Books, 1981), and *Am Anfang war Erziehung* (Frankfurt/Main: Suhrkamp, 1980); English edition trans. Hildegarde and Hunter Hannum (New York: Farrar, Straus & Giroux, 1983). All citations will refer to the English editions.
66 Miller, *The Drama of the Gifted Child*, p. ix.
67 *Ibid.*, p. 9.
68 *Ibid.*, p. 12.
69 *Ibid.*, p. 15.
70 *Ibid.*, p. 12.
71 The technique of quotation is one that Wolf employs extensively in *No Place on Earth*.
72 Wolf continues her playing with the Christa T./Christa Wolf/narrator identity in *Patterns of Childhood* by varying the motif of the child frozen in the snow and presenting it as an experience of the narrator in *Patterns of Childhood* on her flight west.
73 See for example Hans Mayer, "Der Mut zur Unaufrichtigkeit," *Der Spiegel*, 11 April 1977, pp. 185–90.
74 Ryan, *The Uncompleted Past*, p. 151.
75 *Ibid.*
76 Wolf, "Erfahrungsmuster," p. 106.
77 Ryan, *The Uncompleted Past*, p. 148.

5 *No Place on Earth*: revision of the Romantic heritage

1 Sonja Hilzinger, *Christa Wolf* (Stuttgart: Metzler, 1986), p. 106.
2 Christa Wolf, "The Reader and the Writer," in *The Reader and the Writer: Essays, Sketches, Memories*, trans. Joan Becker (New York: International Publishers, 1977), p. 206. All future citations will refer to this edition and be cited as RW in the text.
3 See, for example, Günter Kunert, "Zweige vom selben Stamm," in *Christa Wolf Materialienbuch*, ed. Klaus Sauer, 2nd, revised edn (Darmstadt/Neuwied: Luchterhand, 1983), pp. 15–20.
4 "Culture Is What You Experience – An Interview with Christa Wolf," trans. Jeanette Clausen, *New German Critique* 27 (Fall 1982): 89–90. Interview originally published in *alternative* 144/45 (April/June 1982): 117–27.
5 Wolf emphasized this dimension of her narrative following a reading on 8 May 1979 in Münster, West Germany. Recounted by Renate Knoll, "Das 'innerste Innere.' Christa Wolf und die Tradition des 18. Jahrhunderts. Ein phänomenologische Skizze," *Text und Kontext* 7/11 (1979): 161, footnote 13.
6 Ute Thoss Brandes notes that Kleist's statement that "one's fatherland always looks better the farther one gets away from it" (*No Place on Earth* 66) contains a Biermann quotation. Brandes, "Das Zitat als Beleg. Christa Wolf. *Kein Ort. Nirgends*," in Brandes, *Zitat und Montage in der neueren DDR-Prosa* (Frankfurt/Main: Lang, 1984), p. 61. As Patricia Herminghouse has shown, Christa Wolf tailors historical data to make a political point about a contemporary issue in the GDR. Herminghouse, "Die Wiederentdeckung der Romantik: Zur Funktion der Dichterfiguren in der neueren DDR-Literatur," in Jos Hoogeveen and Gerd Labroisse eds., *DDR-Roman und Literaturgesellschaft*, pp. 217–48, here p. 247 (Amsterdam: Rodopi, 1981), Amsterdamer Beiträge zur neuren Germanistik 10/11. (English version published as "The Rediscovery of Romanticism: Revisions and Reevaluations," in *Studies in GDR Culture and Society* 2, ed. Margy Gerber *et al.* (Washington, DC: University Press of America, 1982), pp. 1–17.) In the Bettine essay, Wolf recalls the situation of the professors in Göttingen (including the Grimm brothers), who signed a petition requesting the Prussian king to uphold the constitution. Wolf has dated the signing of this petition the 18th of November [*sic!* P.H.], the date on which GDR intellectuals signed the petition protesting Biermann's expulsion.
7 *Kein Ort. Nirgends* (Berlin/Weimar: Aufbau Verlag, 1979; BRD edition Darmstadt/Neuwied: Luchterhand, 1979); English edition *No Place on Earth*, trans. Jan van Heurck (New York: Farrar, Straus & Giroux, 1982). While the English translation is, for the most part, excellent, the title is somewhat misleading. "No Place on Earth" implies a somewhere not on earth. A better choice would have been "No Place. Nowhere." Unless otherwise indicated, all quotations will be from the English edition and will be cited as *NP* in the text.

8 *Kein Ort. Nirgends*, p. 6. My translation. Heurck's translation, "legend that suits us" (4), does not capture the longing connoted by the original.

9 Anna Seghers's fantastical story of 1972, "Reisebegegnung," in which she has the writers E. T. A. Hoffmann, Franz Kafka, and Nikolai Gogol meet in Prague and discuss writing, may have served as an inspiration for Wolf's meeting between Kleist and Günderrode. In Anna Seghers, *Sonderbare Begegnungen* (Berlin/Weimar: Aufbau, 1973), pp. 109–48.

10 Thus in one sense *No Place on Earth* has a point of departure similar to that of *The Quest for Christa T.* Just as the narrator of *Christa T.* had invented situations for Christa T. based on her knowledge of her friend, so Christa Wolf has invented the meeting between Kleist and Günderrode based on her knowledge of their characters and situation.

11 For a detailed analysis of the use of quotation and citation in *No Place on Earth*, see Brandes, "Das Zitat als Beleg," pp. 61–100. An English translation of Brandes' chapter on *No Place on Earth* will appear in Marilyn Sibley Fries, *Christa Wolf: Some Critical Perspectives* (Detroit: Wayne State University Press, forthcoming.)

12 Wolf extends this principle to other historical characters such as Clemens Brentano and Carl Savigny as well.

13 See Sandra Frieden, " 'Falls es strafbar ist, die Grenzen zu verwischen': Autobiographie, Biographie und Christa Wolf," in *Vom Anderen und vom Selbst*, ed. Reinhold Grimm and Jost Hermand (Königstein: Athenäum, 1982), pp. 153–66, for a discussion of *No Place on Earth* as biography (pp. 161–5).

14 For a discussion of GDR reception of Romanticism, see Claus Träger, "Ursprünge und Stellung der Romantik," *Weimarer Beiträge* 21/2 (1975): 37–73; Träger, "Historische Dialektik der Romantik und Romantikforschung," *Weimarer Beiträge* 24/4 (1978): 47–73; Hans-Dietrich Dahnke, "Zur Stellung und Leistung der deutschen romantischen Literatur," *Weimarer Beiträge* 24/4 (1978): 5–20; Herminghouse, "Die Wiederentdeckung der Romantik"; and Monika Totten, "Zur Aktualität der Romantik in der DDR: Christa Wolf und ihre Vorläufer(innen)," *Zeitschrift für deutsche Philologie* 101/2 (1982): 244–62.

15 Georg Lukács, "Die Tragödie Heinrich von Kleists," in *Deutsche Realisten des 19. Jahrhunderts* (Berlin: Aufbau, 1951), pp. 19–48, and "Ein Briefwechsel zwischen Anna Seghers und Georg Lukács," in Lukács, *Essays über Realismus* (Berlin: Aufbau, 1948), pp. 171–215. English version, "A Correspondence with Anna Seghers," in *Essays on Realism*, trans. David Fernbach, ed. Rodney Livingstone (London: Lawrence and Wishart, 1980), pp. 167–97.

16 Johann Wolfgang von Goethe, "Klassisch ist das Gesunde, romantisch das Kranke," Maxim 863, *Schriften zur Kunst, Schriften zur Literatur, Maximen und Reflexionen, Goethes Werke. Hamburger Ausgabe in 14 Bänden*, vol. 12 (Hamburg: Christian Wegner Verlag, 1953), p. 487. My translation.

17 Lukács, "A Correspondence with Anna Seghers," p. 168.

18 See Christa Wolf's essays on Anna Seghers, "Glauben an Irdisches" and "Begegnungen mit Anna Seghers," in *Fortgesetzter Versuch* (Leipzig: Reclam, 1982), pp. 212–37; 238–49.

19 Comment by Christa Wolf in a seminar at Ohio State University, June 1983. See also Wolf, "Culture Is What You Experience," p. 91, and "Christa Wolf in Edinburgh: An Interview," *GDR Monitor* 1 (Summer 1979): 10.

20 As part of this rehabilitation Christa Wolf, together with her husband Gerhard Wolf, recently published a collection of essays and narratives on Romanticism. *Ins Ungebundene gehet eine Sehnsucht: Gesprächsraum Romantik* (Berlin/Weimar: Aufbau, 1985) contains *No Place on Earth* and Christa Wolf's essays on Bettine von Arnim, Karoline von Günderrode, and Kleist's *Penthesilea* as well as Gerhard Wolf's essays and narrative on Friedrich Hölderlin, a contemporary of Kleist's and Günderrode's who went insane, and his essays on Bettine and Achim von Arnim and Heinrich Heine.

21 Karoline von Günderrode, *Der Schatten eines Traumes: Gedichte, Briefe, Zeugnisse von Zeitgenossen*, ed. Christa Wolf (Berlin, GDR: Buchverlag Der Morgen, 1979); licensed West German edition (Darmstadt/Neuwied: Luchterhand, 1979).

22 Jeanette Clausen's translation: Wolf, "Culture Is What You Experience," p. 92, footnote 4.

23 Bettine's work *Die Günderode*, written in 1839 in the form of the epistolary novel popular at the time, is based on correspondence between the two women dating from 1805 to 1806. Bettine's work is characteristically Romantic in its innovative use of authentic material and her mingling of fact and fiction. In its conflation of the biographical and the poetic, art and life, it also reflects Christa Wolf's own aesthetic of "subjective authenticity." Bettina von Arnim, *Die Günderode* (Frankfurt/Main: Insel, 1982). For a discussion of this work and *The Quest for Christa T.* as examples of auto/biographical fiction see my article, "The 'Failure' of Biography, the Triumph of Women's Writing," forthcoming in *Revealing Lives: Gender in Autobiography* (Philadelphia: University of Pennsylvania Press). Regarding the discrepancies in the orthography of the names: the original spelling of the family name Günderrode contained two *r*'s. However, for a long time the name was spelled with only one *r*. Anna Seghers also followed this convention. Since the 1960s, the trend has been to go back to the original spelling. Christa Wolf insists on the proper orthography. The historical Bettina von Arnim wrote her name with an *a*; in her epistolary novel, however, she signed her letters Bettine. Wolf goes back to the spelling used in *Die Günderode* and consistently refers to her in both the essay about Bettine: "Nun ja! Das nächste Leben geht aber heute an" and about Günderrode in "Der Schatten eines Traumes" and in *No Place on Earth* as Bettine, presumably to establish a correspondence between *her* Bettine and the Bettine of the *Günderode*

book. I shall adhere to Christa Wolf's orthography. Both essays were reprinted in *Fortgesetzter Versuch* (Leipzig: Reclam, 1982), "Der Schatten," pp. 325–76; "Nun ja!," pp. 377–409. All quotations will be taken from this edition and will be cited as the Günderrode and Bettine essays (GE and BE) respectively.

24 Letter to Karoline von Barkhaus, 26 July 1799, in Wolf, *Der Schatten eines Traumes*, p. 136.
25 Brandes was able to locate over ninety authentic quotations in Wolf's text. *Zitat und Montage*, p. 64.
26 Wolf, *Der Schatten eines Traumes*, p. 193.
27 The poem "Die Einzige," from Günderrode's *Melete*, a collection of lyric and dramatic verses and letters, was addressed to her lover Friedrich Creuzer. Cast in the voice of a male lyrical ego, it serves as a poignant reminder of how Günderrode denied her sex in order to write.
28 I use the term here as coined by Dorrit Cohn, "Narrated Monologue: Definition of a Fictional Style," *Comparative Literature* 18 (1966): 97–112.
29 The reader is thus granted a privileged status which none of the characters possesses. At no time, not even in their most personal exchanges, is any one character given access to the entire emotional spectrum of another. The fact that readers are granted this intimacy allows us to approximate the perspective of the creative authorial consciousness.
30 The original German: "Vorgänger ihr, Blut im Schuh" with its image of "blood in the shoe" evokes the story of *Aschenputtel* (Cinderella). It conjures up the image of those who, like Cinderella's step-sisters, attempt by self-mutilation to fit a slipper made for someone else. The fairy tale, as recorded by the Grimm brothers, reads as follows: "Rucke di guck, rucke di guck. Blut ist im Schuck. Der Schuck ist zu klein, – die rechte Braut sitzt doch daheim." The Brothers Grimm, *Kinder- und Hausmärchen* (Stuttgart: Reclam, 1980), p. 143.
31 Sigrun D. Leonhard, "Strategie der Annäherung; Zur Erzähltechnik in Christa Wolfs *Kein Ort. Nirgends*," *The Germanic Review* 60/3 (Summer 1985):100.
32 Bettina von Arnim, *Die Günderode*, p. 13. My translation.
33 *Ibid.*, pp. 12–13.
34 The original quotation, from Günderrode's letter to Clemens Brentano (1803?), reads "But for this reason I fancy that (when I read what I wrote a while ago), I am seeing myself in the coffin, and my two selves stare at each other in wonderment." *Der Schatten eines Traumes*, p. 184. By deleting the parenthetical phrase, Wolf has intensified Günderrode's sense of alienation: the passage no longer refers specifically to her work, but to an existential condition.
35 See Ernst Bloch, *Erbschaft dieser Zeit*, in Bloch, *Gesamtausgabe*, vol. 4 (Frankfurt/Main: Suhrkamp, 1962), pp. 45–204.

36 Über Gleichzeitigkeit, Provinz und Propaganda: Ein Gespräch mit Rainer Traub und Harold Wieser," in *Gespräche mit Ernst Bloch*, ed. Rainer Traub and Harold Wieser (Frankfurt/Main: Suhrkamp, 1975), p. 196.

37 I am indebted to Angelika Bammer, whose unpublished paper on the possible implications of Ernst Bloch's philosophy for feminist scholarship, delivered at the Women in German Conference in Portland, Oregon in October 1986, helped clarify my thoughts and encouraged me to pursue the concept of *Ungleichzeitigkeit* in connection with *No Place on Earth*.

38 Bloch, "Über Gleichzeitigkeit, Provinz und Propaganda," in *Gespräche mit Ernst Bloch*, p. 199.

39 Wolf, "Culture Is What You Experience," p. 96.

40 *Ibid.*, p. 93.

41 This last vision anticipates her death. Two years later, in 1806, Günderrode, while again visiting Merten, will commit suicide by stabbing herself. Her body will be found by the Rhine River.

42 Wolf takes the original quotation from Kleist's letter of 10 October 1801 to his fiancée, Wilhelmine von Zenge, and radicalizes its content by appending it to a fictive passage in which Kleist questions whether the state actually sees to the needs of the common person. See Heinrich von Kleist, *Sämtliche Werke und Briefe in sieben Bänden*, ed. Helmut Sembder (Munich: Carl Hanser Verlag), vol. 6, p. 217.

43 When Kleist does succeed in killing himself, he does so with another person, whereas Günderrode dies alone.

44 Kleist's dream differs from Günderrode's in two significant ways: first, he is an active agent while she is the passive victim; and second his dream is focused on himself, whereas Günderrode's involves other people. Again, these differences can be attributed both to gender-specific acculturation processes and to individual psychological make-up.

45 Christa Wolf, "Kleist's 'Penthesilea,'" in Christa Wolf and Gerhard Wolf, *Ins Ungebundene gehet eine Sehnsucht*, p. 204. My translation.

46 *Ibid.*

47 Wolf explicitly rejects unrequited love as the reason for Günderrode's suicide, maintaining that her unhappy affair was a symptom of a more pervasive malaise rather than the cause of her death (GE 330).

48 This passage, another example of Wolf's ambiguous narrative perspective, could arguably also be read as Günderrode's narrated monologue. As such it would be an example of Günderrode's prescience.

49 Once again the Günderrode essay furnishes important background information as a complement to the literary work, making explicit what is implicit in the narrative. Here we learn that the identity of Günderrode, who had published her poems under the pseudonym Tian, had become known to a reviewer, who had subsequently published a censorious review in *Der Freimüthige* (GE 347).

50 Brentano had enclosed this poem to Günderrode in a letter dated 1 May 1804. See *Der Schatten eines Traumes*, pp. 185–8.

51 See *Der Schatten eines Traumes*, pp. 148–75.

52 See Brandes, *Zitat und Montage*, pp. 75–6.

53 Günderrode's recognition that clairvoyance can arise out of intense pain or concentration, which in turn can bring about the illumination of one's inner landscape (*NP* 106) foreshadows the main themes of *Cassandra*.

54 Christa Wolf ironically dubs the Günderrode–Creuzer affair a "*bürgerliche[s] Trauerspiel*," a middle-class tragedy (GE 359). An important dramatic genre in Germany since the Enlightenment, this form of tragedy is often melodramatic and sentimental.

55 One copy of the manuscript consisting in part of printed pages and in part of manuscript pages survived. In 1896 several excerpts were printed; in 1906 *Melete* appeared for the first time in an unabridged form; in 1920 it was published as part of the collected works of Günderrode (GE 373).

56 Günter Kunert, "Zweige vom selben Stamm," in *Christa Wolf Materialienbuch*, ed. Klaus Sauer (Darmstadt/Neuwied: Luchterhand, 1979), p. 17.

57 Wolf, "Culture Is What You Experience," p. 100.

58 It is remarkable that Wolf, in presenting their sexual ambiguity, portrays Günderrode's androgynous nature positively, whereas Kleist's is seen as something incomplete.

59 Schiller's juxtaposition of naive and sentimental poetry was later taken up by the Schlegels, who reformulated his dichotomy as the opposition of Classical and Romantic literature.

60 The play relates the life of the Duke of Normandy, whose goal of capturing Byzantium for the Norman empire is thwarted by the plague that decimates his army. Made complacent by a prophecy that he would die in Jerusalem, Guiscard tends the plague victims himself. Too late he discovers that a city called Jerusalem once lay on Corus, where he finds himself.

61 See Christa Wolf's discussion of the relationship between psychosomatic illness and the withdrawal of love, "Christa Wolf. Krankheit und Liebesentzug. Fragen an die psychosomatische Medizin," *Neue deutsche Literatur* 34/10 (October 1986): 84–102.

62 For a discussion of *No Place on Earth* as an example of Bloch's concrete utopia, see Klaus L. Berghahn, "Die real existierende Utopie im Sozialismus: Zu Christa Wolfs Romanen," in *Literarische Utopien von Morus bis zur Gegenwart*, ed. Berghahn and Hans Ulrich Seeber (Königstein: Athenäum, 1983), pp. 275–97; here 286–93.

63 As in *Moscow Novella, Divided Heaven, Christa T.*, and *Patterns of Childhood*, in *No Place on Earth* illness, whether physical or psychic, is the response of the characters to an untenable social situation. Günderrode's severe headaches and her sensitivity to light and Kleist's attacks

of weakness and mental breakdown are responses to a time that does not permit integration of the emotional and the rational components of human life.

64 Both in Christa Wolf, *Gesammelte Erzählungen* (Darmstadt/Neuwied: Luchterhand, 1974, 1980); "Unter den Linden," pp. 54–96; "Kater," pp. 97–123.

65 Friedrich Schiller, *On the Aesthetic Education of Man in a Series of Letters*, fifteenth letter, trans. Elizabeth M. Wilkinson and L. A. Willoughby (Oxford: Clarendon Press, 1967), p. 107.

66 Hannah Arendt, *Rahel Varnhagen: The Life of a Jewish Woman*, trans. Richard and Clara Winston (New York: Harcourt Brace Jovanovich, 1974), p. 38. Quoted by Helen Fehervary, "Christa Wolf's Prose: A Landscape of Masks," *New German Critique* 27 (Fall 1982):78–9.

67 Fehervary, "Christa Wolf's Prose," p. 79.

68 *Ibid.*

69 *Ibid.*

70 Anne Christine Herrmann, "Toward a Female Dialogic: Virginia Woolf and Christa Wolf," Ph.D dissertation, Yale University, 1983, p. 16. See M. M. Bakhtin, *The Dialogic Imagination: Four Essays*, ed. Michael Holquist, trans. Caryl Emerson and Michael Holquist (Austin: University of Austin Press, 1981).

71 Friedrich Schlegel, *Dialogue on Poetry*, in *Dialogue on Poetry and Literary Aphorisms*, trans. and intro. Ernst Behler and Roman Struc (University Park/London: Pennsylvania State University Press, 1968), pp. 53–117.

6 *Cassandra*: myth, matriarchy, and the canon

1 Adrienne Rich, "When We Dead Awaken: Writing as Re-Vision," *College English* 34/1 (October 1972): 18–19.

2 The essays, originally delivered as a series of lectures on poetics at the University of Frankfurt, and the narrative were published as one volume in the GDR (Berlin: Aufbau, 1983). The West German edition (Darmstadt/Neuwied: Luchterhand, 1983) published the essays and the narrative separately. For obvious commercial reasons, the story appeared in an expensive hardcover and the lectures in an inexpensive paperback edition. Happily, the English translation by Jan van Heurck, *Cassandra: A Novel and Four Essays* (New York: Farrar, Straus & Giroux, 1984), based on the West German edition, has rejoined the lectures with the story in one volume. However, the narrative appears first, followed by the lectures on poetics. Since Wolf intended *Cassandra* as the fifth lecture and since the literal meaning of *Voraussetzungen einer Erzählung* is "prerequisites of a narrative," this sequence seems ill-advised. All quotations from *Cassandra* and "Conditions of a Narrative" will refer to the English version and will be cited as *C* and CON in the text.

3 "Von Büchner sprechen (Darmstädter Rede)" in Christa Wolf *Fortgesetzter Versuch: Aufsätze, Gespräche, Essays* (Leipzig: Reclam, 1982), pp. 149–60. Translated into English as "Shall I Garnish a Metaphor with an Almond Blossom?" by Henry J. Schmidt in *New German Critique* 23 (Spring/Summer 1981): 3–11. Unless otherwise indicated, citations will refer to the Schmidt translation and be cited as BP in the text.

4 See *Berliner Begegnung zur Friedensförderung. Protokolle des Schriftstellertreffens am 13/14 Dezember 1981* (Darmstadt/Neuwied: Luchterhand, 1983).

5 See *Zweite Berliner Begegnung. "Den Frieden erklären." Protokolle des zweiten Schriftstellertreffens am 22/23 April 1983* (Darmstadt/Neuwied: Luchterhand, 1983).

6 Alexander Stephan, "Frieden, Frauen und Cassandra," in Manfred Jurgensen, ed., *Wolf. Darstellung, Deutung, Diskussion* (Bern: Francke, 1984), pp. 149–73; here p. 151.

7 Christa Wolf, "Ein Brief," in Ingrid Krüger, ed., *Mut zur Angst. Schriftsteller für den Frieden* (Darmstadt/Neuwied: Luchterhand, 1982), pp. 152–9; here 154–5; 157. "Ein Brief" is Wolf's response to a letter from a young West German medical student who shares her fears and asks her advice.

8 *Ibid.*, p. 155.

9 "Von Büchner sprechen," in *Fortgesetzter Versuch*, p. 151. My translation.

10 An allusion to Rose Bernd, the heroine of Gerhard Hauptmann's naturalistic bourgeois tragedy of the same name.

11 See Silvia Bovenschen, *Die imaginierte Weiblichkeit: Exemplarische Untersuchungen zur kulturgeschichtlichen und literarischen Präsentationsformen des Weiblichen* (Frankfurt/Main: Suhrkamp, 1980) for a critical discussion of images of women created by men. Wolf lists Bovenschen's work in the bibliography to *Voraussetzungen einer Erzählung* and she was most likely familiar with it when she wrote the Büchner Prize Speech.

12 To this list, as Wolf's previous work makes clear, we must add Karoline von Günderrode and Ulrike von Kleist.

13 The speech was held in Darmstadt, Büchner's birthplace.

14 The narrative starts: "It was here. This is where she stood. These stone lions looked at her; now they no longer have heads" (*C* 3). It concludes with: "Here is the place. These stone lions looked at her. They seem to move in the shifting light" (*C* 138).

15 While her criticism certainly is not directed solely against the East bloc, the GDR clearly indicated its sensitivity to her feminist–pacifist message by excising overt criticism of Warsaw Pact countries or the mere contemplation of unilateral disarmament. Wolf's criticism was unwelcome on two counts: just as a woman's movement is deemed superfluous in the GDR, a peace movement is considered redundant, since the SED by definition regards itself as the party of peace. See the

virulent polemic by Wilhelm Girnus, "Wer baute das siebentorige Theben?," *Sinn und Form* 2 (1983): 439–47, in which he attacks Wolf's feminist analysis, faulting her for failing to differentiate the status of women in East and West and accusing her of assuming a bourgeois-capitalist stance. Girnus's article precipitated a great deal of debate. See Christa Wolf's response, "Christa Wolf: Zur Information," *Sinn und Form* 4 (1983): 863–6, and overwhelmingly supportive letters from readers, *Sinn und Form*, 5 (1983): 1087–105.

16 The fourth lecture is entitled: "A Letter, about Unequivocal and Ambiguous Meaning, Definitiveness and Indefiniteness: about Ancient Conditions and New View-Scopes; about Objectivity" (CON 272).

17 The almost magical integrative power of her new view-scope is probably attributable to Wolf's experiences while researching Minoan civilization. Her descriptions of the reconstructed frescos in the Palace of Knossos (see CON 192–4) contain a similar interpenetration of various layers of reality. Pursuing traces of Minoan civilization both on Crete and in archeological books, Wolf again and again encountered a prepatriarchal society, the cults of the goddesses.

18 Discussion with Christa Wolf at Ohio State University. Published as "Dokumentation: Christa Wolf – Ein Gespräch über *Kassandra*," *German Quarterly* (Winter 1984): 105–15; here 106.

19 Christa Wolf, "The Reader and the Writer," in *The Reader and the Writer: Essays, Sketches, Memories* (New York: International Publishers, 1977), p. 212.

20 *Ibid.*

21 Wolf, "Ein Gespräch über *Kassandra*," p. 108.

22 Sigrid Weigel, "Vom Sehen zur Seherin. Christa Wolfs Umdeutung des Mythos und die Spur der Bachmann-Rezeption in ihrer Literatur," in *Text + Kritik* 46, 3rd, expanded edn, Heinz Ludwig Arnold, ed. (Munich: Text + Kritik, 1985), pp. 67–92, esp. 69–80.

23 *Ibid.*, p. 69.

24 *Ibid.*, p. 78.

25 Wolf, "The Reader and the Writer," p. 212.

26 Homer, Aeschylus, Euripides, Dictys, Dares, Boccaccio, and Shakespeare are among those who have treated the story of Cassandra. The male tradition has propagated the image of Cassandra as Apollo's servant, who is later punished by the god for rejecting him sexually. According to this commonly accepted view, Cassandra is granted the gift of prophecy, but no one believes her. For a discussion of the myth of Cassandra in antiquity and early Christian writing, see Karl Ledergerber, *Kassandra. Das Bild der Prophetin in der antiken und insbesondere in der älteren abendländischen Dichtung* (Buochs: Das Aufgebot, 1940). More recently, women writers have broken with this tradition. In an essay of 1852, Florence Nightengale evokes the name Cassandra to lament women's inferior social status in the nineteenth century (Nightengale, *Cassandra* [Old Westbury: The Feminist Press, 1979]); in

The Autobiography of Cassandra. Princess & Prophetess of Troy (USA: Archer Editions Press, 1979), Ursule Molinaro incorporates neglected aspects of the Cassandra tradition to present a more positive image of women. I am grateful to Tamara Evans for making me aware of the Molinaro text.

27 Although believed to have been written during the first century after the common era, Dictys's and Dares' prose narratives claim to be eye-witness accounts of the Trojan war. That is, they claim to antedate Homer. Dictys's account, written from the perspective of the Greeks, and Dares', from that of the Trojans, frequently contradict Homer and undermine the heroism of his figures. See *The Trojan War: The Chronicles of Dictys of Crete and Dares the Phrygian*, trans., intro., notes by R. M. Frazer, Jr. (Bloomington: Indiana University Press, 1966).

28 Wolf has her Cassandra say: "She [Clytemnestra] indicated to me with a shrug of her shoulders that what was happening had nothing to do with me personally. In different times nothing would have prevented us from calling each other sister. That is what I read in my adversary's face" (*C* 41). And when Clytemnestra realizes that Cassandra is wearing the mate to her necklace (Agamemnon had given it to her because she reminded him of his daughter Iphigenia), Cassandra says: "We reached up to touch our necklaces with an identical gesture, looked at each other, agreed as only women agree" (*C* 104).

29 By making Clytemnestra's downfall dependent on her action, Wolf underscores the relationship between power and blindness. Through her act of revenge Clytemnestra is drawn into the established structures. Yet Cassandra credits her with "knowing that she, too, will be stricken with the blindness that comes with power. She, too, will fail to see the signs. Her house, too, will fall" (*C* 42).

30 On the trip to Greece, the boat gets into a storm and is in danger of sinking. Agamemnon accuses Cassandra of inciting Poseidon against him. He had, he maintained, after all "sacrificed three of his best horses to the god before the crossing." When Cassandra asks him what he had offered Athena, Agamemnon pales. The king's inability to concern himself with anything non-male elicits Cassandra's reproach of narcissism (*C* 9).

31 The figure of Aeneas is consciously anachronistic. In "Conditions of a Narrative" Wolf maintains: "Quick as a flash Aeneas sprang up before my inner eye, and Cassandra had known him. Merely known him? What was there about him that might have touched her more deeply? Consideration, coupled with strength? So, I was transferring a contemporary ideal to a mythological figure who cannot possibly have been that kind of a person? Of course. What else?" (CON 184). The relationship between Cassandra and Aeneas is Christa Wolf's invention.

32 This tradition, which also informed the conception of Kleist's *Penthesi-*

lea, goes back to Quintus of Smyrna's *Posthomerica* (fourth century CE) in which Achilles falls in love with Penthesilea when, after killing her on the battlefield, he removes her helmet and discovers how beautiful she is. For a discussion of Achilles as lover, see Katherine King, "Achilles Amator," *Viator. Medieval and Renaissance Studies* 16 (1985): 21–64.

33 Wolf defines this ability to love both literally and figuratively. Thus, the bully Agamemnon is portrayed as sexually impotent. Yet to cover up his inadequacies and to retain his standing with his men, he insists upon imprisoning a slave girl in his tent.

34 The romantic relationship between Achilles and Polyxena is part of the late antique and medieval tradition of the Trojan War. It can be found in Benoit de Sainte-Maure's *Le Roman de Troie* (*c.* 1160 CE), a work based on the chronicles of Dictys and Dares. In contrast to her sources, however, Christa Wolf is more concerned with Polyxena than with Achilles, more precisely with the relationship between Polyxena and Cassandra. See Frazer, *The Trojan War*, pp. 3–4. For a detailed discussion of the development of the Achilles–Polyxena tradition, see Katherine King, "Achilles Amator," pp. 31–64.

35 Cassandra maintains that if she were able to do this, she would not have lived in vain (*C* 9; 79).

36 In German, the epithet is even stronger: Achilles is called "das Vieh," which connotes bestiality.

37 According to the seer Calchas, Odysseus literally dragged Achilles out of a homosexual love nest into battle (*C* 82–3).

38 Since Christa Wolf consciously deviates from the Greek sources, it is not surprising that her study of the Cassandra figure leads her precisely to those aspects that are not dealt with in the main traditions. She is particularly interested in those controversial sources that tell of Cassandra's abuse at the hands of both friend and foe: her rape by the Achaian Ajax-the-Lesser and the undesired marriage forced upon her by her father.

39 Inge Stephan defines *Frauenbild* as follows: "a form of male wish and ideology production in literary texts ... in which memories of women's real lives and mythical structures are incorporated." Stephan, "Bilder, und immer wieder Bilder," in Stephan and Sigrid Weigel, eds., *Die verborgene Frau* (Berlin: Argument, 1983), pp. 26–7. My translation.

40 Unpublished discussion with Christa Wolf at Ohio State University, 3 June 1983.

41 According to Christa Wolf, she was shocked by the insight she gained regarding the status of women while working with the Greek epic, namely how early they were forced into the loser's position, out of which they have not emerged in over three thousand years. "Gespräch über *Kassandra*," p. 106.

42 By freely choosing death, Cassandra exhibits Schiller's concept of dignity (*Erhabenheit*) and again reveals Christa Wolf's debt to the German Idealist tradition.

43 Polyxena's implication in Achilles' death refers back to the versions of Dares and Dictys, which deviate from the standard account in which he dies in battle, struck by Paris's arrow.

44 Wolf interprets the historical events of the Trojan War differently from her sources. Whereas the gods determine the course and outcome of the events in the Homeric epic, Wolf precludes divine intervention. The cause of the war is for her purely economic: it arises out of the Greeks' need to gain access to the Trojan-controlled Dardanelles and hence to the Bosporus. Her economic interpretation of the Trojan War is in part indebted to the Marxist classicist George Thompson, whom she lists in her bibliography.

45 Wolf's description of Büchner's Lenz, who "goes insane by losing his rapport with ordinary reason" (BP 4) is applicable to her Cassandra as well.

46 Carol Gilligan, *In A Different Voice* (Cambridge, Mass.: Harvard University Press, 1983). In a personal conversation with Christa Wolf (19 June 1983) it became clear that she was not familiar with Gilligan's work when she wrote *Cassandra*. The similarities between the literary presentation and the psychological study are therefore all the more remarkable.

47 "Berührung," in *Fortgesetzer Versuch*, p. 321.

48 *Ibid.*, p. 322.

49 Ferdinand Toennies, *Community and Society* (New York: Harper and Row, 1966).

50 "Berührung," p. 312.

51 Sara Lennox, "Trends in Literary Theory: The Female Aesthetic and German Women's Writing," *German Quarterly* (Winter 1981): 61–75; here 71. See also Lennox, "Christa Wolf and the Women Romantics," in Margy Gerber *et al.*, eds., *Studies in GDR Culture and Society 2: Proceedings of the Seventh International Symposium on the GDR* (Washington, DC: University Press of America, 1982), pp. 31–43.

52 The desire to record experience for succeeding generations is an important recurring theme in *Cassandra*.

53 "Nun ja! Das nächste Leben geht aber heute an," in *Fortgesetzter Versuch*, pp. 404–5.

54 Dagmar Ploetz, "Vom Vorteil eine Frau zu Sein: Frauenbild und Menschenentwurf in Christa Wolfs Prosa," in Klaus Sauer, ed., *Christa Wolf Materialienbuch* (Darmstadt/Neuwied: Luchterhand, 1979), p. 104.

55 Wolf's presentation of female and male homosexuality differs markedly. Whereas the love between women is presented positively in *Cassandra*, male homosexuality, as linked to the figure of Achilles, is seen as destructive and aggressive. The implications of Wolf's presentation need to be explored. A possible explanation for this discrepancy can be found in the furtive nature of Achilles' desire, his unwillingness to admit to his inclination. Hence, male homosexuality could be seen as

another variation on Wolf's theme of the fear of self-knowledge, which she had described as "the mortal sin of our time" in *Patterns of Childhood*.

56 "Berührung," p. 313.

57 Ernst Bloch, *The Principle of Hope*, trans. Neville Plaice, Stephen Plaice, and Paul Knight (Oxford: Basil Blackwell, 1986), vol. 1, p. 77.

58 Henry Schmidt's rendering of "verkehrt" as "awry" in the English translation of the Büchner Prize Speech does not adequately capture Wolf's sense of the word. Jan van Heurck's choice of "perverse" approximates the contextual meaning much more closely.

59 Helen Fehervary, "The Gender of Authorship: Heiner Müller and Christa Wolf," in *Studies in Twentieth Century Literature* 5/1 (Fall 1980), pp. 41–58; here p. 47.

60 Helen Fehervary, "Autorschaft, Geschlechtsbewusstsein und Öffentlichkeit," in *Entwürfe von Frauen in der Literatur des 20. Jahrhunderts*, Literatur im historischen Prozess, Neue Folge, 5, ed. Irmela von der Lühe (Berlin: Argument Verlag, 1982), pp. 151–2. According to Fehervary, the "female author . . . does *not have* a narrative voice in the traditional sense. She must create a third component in order to realize both the narrating and narrated I. This person is the active listener, a real public sphere, which history has banned from the literary process, by means of which the female narrative voice was silenced" (p. 151). My translation.

7 In lieu of a conclusion. *Störfall*: the destruction of utopia?

1 My original concluding remarks were preempted by the appearance of *Störfall* in April 1987. This new publication enhanced my discomfort at trying to make definitive statements about a living author. I had sensed all along that, particularly in the case of Christa Wolf, any attempt at closure would violate her art. I had, however, been properly taught that "good" critical writing required a beginning, a middle, and an end. It is with a sense of relief that I now reject that dictum. This book will not have a conclusion in the traditional sense. Instead, I will analyze *Störfall* in relation to Wolf's other works.

2 It is difficult to find an adequate English equivalent for Wolf's title. In its technical context, *Störfall* denotes a disturbance or breakdown. In the postatomic age it has entered common scientific discourse, where it is used to refer to a technical disturbance or breakdown in a nuclear power system. A sensationalistic rendering might be "Code Red." In a more general, nontechnical sense, *Störfall* could be translated as "a cause for concern." I have chosen to render the title as "Breakdown" because this term captures both the technical and the subjective, emotional aspects of the original. It comes closest to duplicating the play on words suggested by Wolf's title. Within the text, however, I will refer to Wolf's work by its original title, and will abbreviate it to *S*.

3 The narrator does mention Kiev (*S* 33), which, as the closest metropolis, was in the news a great deal in those days.

4 News about the explosion began to emerge on 28 April. In the following days news reports dealt with the evacuation of the city of Chernobyl, conflicting reports regarding the number of casualties directly related to the explosion and fire, and speculations as to the anticipated number of long-range Chernobyl-related deaths. A battery of experts gave widely divergent testimony on what constituted "safe" and "dangerous" levels of exposure to radioactivity. Europeans were warned against eating produce, especially leafy vegetables. The hazards of drinking milk and sitting on the ground were discussed. All these details are mentioned in *Störfall*. Since the narrator states that the reactor had exploded the previous week (*S* 48), we are able to fix the date in question as sometime during the first week of May. In addition, she mentions that she had been in Kiev only once, also in May. Reports concerning the large turnout of Soviet citizens for the May Day celebration in Kiev were widely publicized and may well have triggered the narrator's memory of her visit there.

5 The mastery of space was part of the ethos of the *Aufbau* period, with its glorification of "reason ... science, the scientific age" (*CT* 143). After waiting in vain to catch a glimpse of Sputnik, the narrator remarks laconically, "we tipped the last of the wine into the apple tree. The new star hadn't appeared. We were cold and went back into the room, where the moonlight was coming in" (*CT* 144).

6 Not only does the text reintroduce several family figures from her autobiographical work, *Patterns of Childhood*, it also refers to Wolf's two daughters and their children and alludes to her husband, Gerhard.

7 Christa Wolf, *Störfall. Nachrichten eines Tages*, (Darmstadt/Neuwied: Luchterhand, 1987), pp. 35–6. My translation. All future quotations will be from this edition in my translation.

8 Theodor Adorno, "Kulturkritik und Gesellschaft," in *Prismen* (Frankfurt/Main: Suhrkamp, 1955), p. 31. English version, "Cultural Criticism and Society," in *Prisms*, trans. Samuel Weber and Shierry Weber (London: Spearman, 1967), p. 34.

9 See "'Culture Is What You Experience' – An Interview with Christa Wolf," trans. Jeanette Clausen, *New German Critique* 27 (Fall 1982):82 for her discussion of this fear in relation to Biermann's expatriation.

10 In this respect, *Störfall* again resembles "Conditions of a Narrative," specifically the epistolary essay, "A Letter, about Unequivocal and Ambiguous Meaning, Definiteness and Indefiniteness; about Ancient Conditions and New View-Scopes; about Objectivity" in which Wolf throughout addresses A., to whom the essay-letter is directed.

11 See Käte Hamburger, *Die Logik der Dichtung*, 2nd, revised edn (Stuttgart: Klett, 1968). English version, *The Logic of Literature*, trans. Marilyn J. Rose (Bloomington: Indiana University Press, 1973), pp. 64–81.

12 Harald Weinrich, *Tempus*, 2nd, revised edn (Stuttgart: Kohlhammer, 1971), pp. 36, 39.

13 Wolf's excessively negative view of the Livermore laboratories is obviously based on her uncritical acceptance of official Party doctrine. The GDR equates Livermore with Starwars and systematically condemns the activities of the scientrists working there. Wolf perpetuates this one-sided view in *Störfall*.

14 Carl Sagan, *The Dragons of Eden. Speculations on the Evolution of Human Intelligence* (New York: Random House, 1977), p. 94.

15 Konrad Lorenz, *Das sogenannte Böse. Zur Naturgeschichte der Aggression* (Vienna: Dr. G. Borotha-Schoeler Verlag, 1963). English version, *On Aggression*, trans. Marjorie Kerr Wilson (New York: Harcourt, Brace & World, 1966). All references will be to the English version.

16 Lorenz, *On Aggression*, p. 217.

17 *Ibid.*, p. 218.

18 See, for example, Ashley Montague, ed., *Man and Aggression*, 2nd edn (New York: Oxford University Press, 1973), a series of essays written against the popular writings of Lorenz and Robert Ardrey.

19 Lorenz, *On Aggression*, p. 225.

20 *Ibid.*, p. 223.

21 *Ibid.*, pp. 228–9.

22 The narrator's dream calls to mind the grandmother's (anti)fairy tale in Büchner's *Woyzeck*, in which a child visits the moon and discovers that it is a piece of rotten wood. Georg Büchner, *Woyzeck*, trans. Henry J. Schmidt (New York: Avon, 1969), pp. 50–1.

SELECT BIBLIOGRAPHY

Christa Wolf's works in German

"Kann man eigentlich über alles schreiben?" *Neue deutsche Literatur* 6 (1958): 3–16.

Moskauer Novelle. Halle: Mitteldeutscher Verlag, 1961.

Der geteilte Himmel. Erzählung. Halle: Mitteldeutscher Verlag, 1963.

"Notwendiges Streitgespräch: Bemerkungen zu einem internationalen Kolloquium." *Neue deutsche Literatur* 13/3 (1965): 88–112. Wolf's contribution, 97–104.

Nachdenken über Christa T. Halle: Mitteldeutscher Verlag, 1968; Darmstadt/Neuwied: Luchterhand, 1969.

Lesen und Schreiben. Aufsätze und Betrachtungen. Darmstadt/Neuwied: Luchterhand, 1972. 2nd, revised edition, 1980.

(with Gerhard Wolf) *Till Eulenspiegel*. Erzählung für den Film. Darmstadt/Neuwied: Luchterhand, 1973.

Unter den Linden. Drei unwahrscheinliche Geschichten. Darmstadt/Neuwied: Luchterhand, 1974.

"Gerti Tetzner–Christa Wolf." Correspondence. In *Was zählt ist die Wahrheit. Briefe von Schriftstellern der DDR*. Halle: Mitteldeutscher Verlag, 1975, pp. 9–33. Reprinted in Klaus Sauer, ed., *Christa Wolf Materialienbuch*, pp. 39–56. Darmstadt/Neuwied: Luchterhand, 1983.

Kindheitsmuster. Darmstadt/Neuwied: Luchterhand, 1977.

"Der Schatten eines Traumes." Introduction to Karoline von Günderrode. *Der Schatten eines Traumes. Gedichte, Briefe, Zeugnisse von Zeitgenossen*. Edited by Christa Wolf. Darmstadt/Neuwied: Luchterhand, 1978. Reprinted in *Fortgeseter Versuch*, 1982.

" 'Ich bin schon für eine gewisse Masslosigkeit' – Christa Wolf im Gespräch." In Klaus Sauer, ed., *Christa Wolf Materialienbuch*, pp. 53–63. Darmstadt/Neuwied: Luchterhand, 1979.

Kein Ort. Nirgends. Darmstadt/Neuwied: Luchterhand, 1979.

"Nun ja! Das nächste Leben geht aber heute an." (Ein Brief über die Bettine.) Afterword to Bettina von Arnim, *Die Günderode*. Frankfurt/Main: Insel, 1982. Reprinted in *Fortgesetzter Versuch*, 1982.

Fortgesetzter Versuch. Aufsätze, Gespräche, Essays. Leipzig: Reclam, 1982.

Select bibliography

"Ein Brief." In *Mut zur Angst: Schriftsteller für den Frieden.* Ed. Ingrid Krüger. Darmstadt/Neuwied: Luchterhand, 1982, pp. 152–9.

Gesammelte Erzählungen. Darmstadt/Neuwied: Luchterhand, 1982.

"Kultur ist was gelebt wird," *alternative* (April/June 1982): 118–27.

Kassandra. Erzählung. Darmstadt/Neuwied: Luchterhand, 1983.

Voraussetzungen einer Erzählung: Kassandra. Frankfurter Poetik-Vorlesungen. Darmstadt/Neuwied: Luchterhand, 1983.

"Dokumentation: Christa Wolf; Eine Diskussion über *Kindheitsmuster.*" *German Quarterly* 57/1 (Winter 1984): 91–5.

"Dokumentation: Christa Wolf; Ein Gespräch mit Christa und Gerhard Wolf." *German Quarterly* 57/1 (Winter 1984): 95–105.

"Dokumentation: Christa Wolf; Ein Gespräch über *Kassandra.*" *German Quarterly* 57/1 (Winter 1984): 105–15.

"Kleists 'Penthesilea.'" Afterword in Heinrich von Kleist. *Penthesilea,* pp. 157–66. Berlin/GDR: Buchverlag Der Morgen. Reprinted in Christa Wolf and Gerhard Wolf. *Ins Ungebundene gehet eine Sehnsucht,* pp. 195–210. Berlin/Weimar: Aufbau, 1985. Also in Heinz Ludwig Arnold, ed. *Text + Kritik 46: Christa Wolf,* pp. 1–11. 3rd edition Munich: Text + Kritik, 1985.

"Christa Wolf. Krankheit und Liebesentzug. Fragen an die psychosomatische Medizin." *Neue Deutsche Literatur* 34/10 (October 1986): 84–102.

Die Dimension des Autors. Essays und Aufsätze, Reden und Gespräche 1959–1985. Darmstadt/Neuwied: Luchterhand, 1987.

Störfall. Nachrichten eines Tages. Darmstadt/Neuwied: Luchterhand, 1987.

Christa Wolf's works in English

Divided Heaven. Trans. Joan Becker. Berlin/GDR: Seven Seas Books, 1965. Third Printing, New York: Adler's Foreign Books, 1981.

"An Afternoon in June." Trans. Eva Wulff. In Wieland Herzfelde and Günther Cwojdrak, eds., *Cross-Section,* pp. 256–72. Leipzig: Edition Leipzig, 1970. Anthology of the PEN Centre German Democratic Republic.

The Quest for Christa T. Trans. Christopher Middleton. New York: Farrar, Straus & Giroux, 1972.

"Change of Perspective." Trans. A. Leslie Willson. *Dimension* (Special Issue 1973): 180–201. Also published in Elizabeth Rütschi Herrmann and Edna Huttenmaier Spitz, eds., *German Women Writers of the Twentieth Century,* pp. 94–100. New York: Pergamon, 1978.

The Reader and the Writer: Essays, Sketches, Memories. Trans. Joan Becker. Berlin/GDR: Seven Seas Books, 1977; New York: International Publishers, 1977.

"Self-Experiment: Appendix to a Report." Trans. Jeanette Clausen. *New German Critique* 13 (Winter 1978): 109–31.

A Model Childhood. Trans. Ursule Molinaro and Hedwig Rappolt. New

Select bibliography

York: Farrar, Straus & Giroux, 1980. Paperback edition, *Patterns of Childhood*, 1984.

"'Shall I Garnish a Metaphor with an Almond Blossom?': Büchner Prize Acceptance Speech." Trans. Henry J. Schmidt. *New German Critique* 23 (Spring/Summer 1981): 3–11.

"Culture is What You Experience–An Interview with Christa Wolf." Trans. Jeanette Clausen. *New German Critique* 27 (Fall 1982): 89–100.

No Place on Earth. Trans. Jan van Heurck. New York: Farrar, Straus & Giroux, 1982.

Cassandra. A Novel and Four Essays. Trans. Jan van Heurck. New York: Farrar, Straus & Giroux, 1984.

Secondary works in German

A   BOOKS ON CHRISTA WOLF

Arnold, Heinz Ludwig, ed., *Text + Kritik 46: Christa Wolf*. Munich: Text + Kritik, 1975, ²1979, ³1985.

Behn, Manfred, ed., *Wirkungsgeschichte von Christa Wolfs 'Nachdenken über Christa T.'* Königstein: Athenäum, 1978.

Greif, Hans-Jürgen. *Christa Wolf: 'Wie sind wir so geworden wie wir heute sind?'* Bern: Lang, 1978.

Hilzinger, Sonja. *Christa Wolf*. Stuttgart: Metzler, 1986.

Kassandra: Über Christa Wolf. Frankfurt/Main: Haag und Herchen, 1982. 2nd, revised edition, 1984.

Jurgensen, Manfred, ed., *Wolf: Darstellung, Deutung, Diskussion*. Bern/Munich: Francke, 1984.

Mauser, Wolfram, ed., *Erinnerte Zukunft: 11 Studien zum Werk Christa Wolfs*. Würzburg: Königshausen und Neumann, 1985.

Renolder, Klemens. *Utopie und Geschichtsbewusstsein. Versuche zur Poetik Christa Wolfs*. (Stuttgarter Arbeiten zur Germanistik 92.) Stuttgart: Akademischer Verlag Hans-Dieter Heinz, 1981.

Reso, Martin. *'Der geteilte Himmel' und seine Kritiker. Dokumentation*. Halle: Mitteldeutscher Verlag, 1965.

Salisch, Marion von. *Zwischen Selbstaufgabe und Selbstverwirklichung. Zum Problem der Persönlichkeitsstruktur im Werk Christa Wolfs*. Stuttgart: Klett, 1975.

Sauer, Klaus, ed. *Christa Wolf Materialienbuch*. Darmstadt/Neuwied: Luchterhand, 1979. 2nd, revised and expanded edition 1983; ³1985.

Sevin, Dieter. *Christa Wolf, 'Der geteilte Himmel'; 'Nachdenken über Christa T.': Interpretationen*. Munich: R. Oldenbourg, 1982.

Stephan, Alexander. *Christa Wolf*. München: Beck, 1976. 2nd, expanded edition 1979; ³1987.

Christa Wolf: Forschungs-Berichte zur DDR-Literatur 1, ed. Gerd Labroisse. Amsterdam: Rodopi, 1980.

Select bibliography

Thomassen, Christa. *Der lange Weg zu uns selbst. Christa Wolfs Roman 'Nachdenken über Christa T.' als Erfahrungs- und Handlungsmuster.* Kronberg: Scriptor, 1977.

Zahlmann, Christel. *Christa Wolfs Reise "ins Tertiär": Eine literatur- psychologische Studie zu "Kindheitsmuster."* Würzburg: Königs- hausen & Neumann, 1986.

B ARTICLES AND REVIEWS

Adams, Marion. "Christa Wolf: Marxismus und Patriarchat." In Manfred Jurgensen, ed., *Frauenliteratur: Autorinnen – Perspektiven – Kon- zepte*, pp. 123–37. Bern/Frankfurt/Main: Lang, 1983.

"Christa Wolf und die Vergangenheit." In Manfred Jurgensen, ed., *Wolf: Darstellung, Deutung, Diskussion*, pp. 77–88. Bern/Munich: Francke, 1984.

Auer, Annemarie. "Gegenerinnerung." *Sinn und Form* (1977): 847–78. (On *Kindheitsmuster*)

Beinssen-Hesse, Silke. "Zum Realismus in Christa Wolfs *Der geteilte Himmel.*" In Manfred Jurgensen, ed., *Wolf: Darstellung, Deutung, Diskussion*, pp. 23–50. Bern/Munich: Francke, 1984.

Berghahn, Klaus L. "Die real existierende Utopie im Sozialismus. Zu Christa Wolfs Romanen." In Klaus Berghahn and Hans Ulrich Seeba, eds., *Literarische Utopien von Morus bis zur Gegenwart*, pp. 275–97. Königstein: Athenäum, 1983.

Bock, Sigrid. "Christa Wolf: *Kein Ort. Nirgends.*" *Weimarer Beiträge* 26/5 (1980): 145–57.

"Kindheitsmuster." *Weimarer Beiträge* 23 (1977): 102–30.

"'Kassandra' von Christa Wolf." *Weimarer Beiträge* 30/8 (1984): 1353–81.

Böll, Heinrich. "Wo habt ihr bloss gelebt?" In Klaus Sauer, ed., *Christa Wolf Materialienbuch*, pp. 7–14. Darmstadt/Neuwied: Luchterhand, 1979.

Bradley, Brigitte L. "Christa Wolfs Erzählung 'Unter den Linden': Unerwünschtes und erwünschtes 'Glück.'" *German Quarterly* (Spring 1984): 231–49.

Brandes, Ute Thoss. "Das Zitat als Beleg: Christa Wolf, *Kein Ort. Nirgends.*" In Ute Thoss Brandes. *Zitat und Montage in der neueren DDR-Prosa*, pp. 61–100. Frankfurt/Main: Lang, 1984.

Cramer, Sibylle. "Eine unendliche Geschichte des Widerstandes." In Klaus Sauer, ed., *Christa Wolf Materialienbuch*, 2nd, revised edition, pp. 121–42. Darmstadt/Neuwied: Luchterhand, 1983.

Dahlke, Günther. "'Geteilter Himmel' und geteilte Kritik. Über die Dialektik von Glück und Unglück und einige andere Fragen." *Sinn und Form* (1964): 307–17.

De Bruyn, Günter. "'Sie, Kleist, nehmen das Leben gefährlich ernst.'" In Klaus Sauer, ed., *Christa Wolf Materialienbuch*, pp. 21–3. Darmstadt/Neuwied: Luchterhand, 1979. (On *Kein Ort. Nirgends*)

Select bibliography

Eifler, Margaret. "Christa Wolf: Materialistische Blickpunkte ihrer Romantikdarstellung." In Manfred Jurgensen, ed., *Wolf: Darstellung, Deutung, Diskussion*, pp. 89–106. Bern/Munich: Francke, 1984.

Emmerich, Wolfgang. "Identität und Geschlechtertausch. Notizen zur Selbstdarstellung der Frau in der neueren DDR-Literatur." *Basis: Jahrbuch für deutsche Gegenwartsliteratur* 8 ed. Jost Hermand and Reinhold Grimm (Frankfurt: Suhrkamp, 1978): 127–54.

"Der Kampf um die Erinnerung." In Klaus Sauer, ed., *Christa Wolf Materialienbuch*, pp. 111–16. Darmstadt/Neuwied: Luchterhand, 1979.

Engler, Jürgen. "Im Spannungsfeld von Gedanke und Tat. Christa Wolf: *Kein Ort. Nirgends.*" *Neue deutsche Literatur* 27/7 (1979): 128–33.

Fehervary, Helen. "Autorschaft, Geschlechtsbewusstsein und Öffentlichkeit: Versuch über Heiner Müllers 'Die Hamletmaschine' und Christa Wolfs 'Kein Ort. Nirgends.'" In Irmela von der Lühe, ed., *Entwürfe von Frauen in der Literatur des 20. Jahrhunderts*, pp. 132–53. Literatur im historischen Prozess, Neue Folge 5. Berlin: Argument Verlag, 1982.

Frieden, Sandra. "'Falls es strafbar ist, die Grenzen zu verwischen': Autobiographie, Biographie und Christa Wolf." In Reinhold Grimm and Jost Hermand, eds., *Vom Anderen und vom Selbst*, pp. 153–66. Königstein: Athenäum, 1982.

Girnus, Wilhelm. "Wer baute das siebentorige Theben?" *Sinn und Form* (1983): 439–47. (On *Kassandra*)

Greiner, Bernhard. "'Mit der Erzählung geh ich in den Tod': Kontinuität und Wandel des Erzählens im Schaffen von Christa Wolf." In Wolfram Mauser, ed., *Erinnerte Zukunft. 11 Studien zum Werk Christa Wolfs*, pp. 107–40. Würzburg: Königshausen und Neumann, 1985.

Gutjahr, Ortrud. "'Erinnerte Zukunft.' Gedächtnisrekonstruktion und Subjektkonstitution im Werk Christa Wolfs." In Wolfram Mauser, ed., *Erinnerte Zukunft. 11 Studien zum Werk Christa Wolfs*, pp. 53–80. Würzburg: Königshausen und Neumann, 1985.

Hammerstein, Katharina von. "Warum nicht Christian T.? Christa Wolf zur Frauenfrage, untersucht an einem frühen Beispiel: *Nachdenken über Christa T.*," *New German Review*, 3 (1987): 17–29.

Hilzinger, Sonja. "Weibliches Schreiben als eine Ästhetik des Widerstands. Über Christa Wolfs 'Kassandra'-Projekt." *Neue Rundschau* 96/1 (1985): 85–101.

Hinck, Walter. "Die vielen Botschaften der Christa Wolf. Ihre Erzählung 'Kassandra' und der Text ihrer Frankfurter-Poetik-Vorlesungen." *Frankfurter Allgemeine Zeitung*, 23 April 1983.

Huyssen, Andreas. "Auf den Spuren Ernst Blochs. Nachdenken über Christa Wolf." *Basis: Jahrbuch für deutsche Gegenwartsliteratur* 5 (1975): 100–16. Reprinted in Manfred Behn, ed., *Wirkungsgeschichte von Christa Wolfs 'Nachdenken über Christa T.'*, pp. 147–55. König-

269

Select bibliography

stein: Athenäum, 1978. Also reprinted in Klaus Sauer, ed., *Christa Wolf Materialienbuch*, pp. 81–7. Darmstadt/Neuwied: Luchterhand, 1979. English version to appear in Marilyn Sibley Fries, ed., *Responses to Christa Wolf: Critical Essays*. Detroit: Wayne State University Press, forthcoming.

Jäger, Manfred. "Auf dem langen Weg zur Wahrheit: Fragen, Antworten und neue Fragen in den Erzählungen, Aufsätzen und Reden Christa Wolfs." In Manfred Jäger, ed., *Sozialliteraten; Funktion und Selbstverständnis der Schriftsteller in der DDR*, pp. 11–101. Düsseldorf: Bertelsmann, 1973.

"Die Grenzen des Sagbaren." In Klaus Sauer, ed., *Christa Wolf Materialienbuch*, pp. 130–45. Darmstadt/Neuwied: Luchterhand, 1979.

Jurgensen, Manfred. "Christa Wolf: *Moskauer Novelle*." In Manfred Jurgensen, ed., *Wolf: Darstellung, Deutung, Diskussion*, pp. 11–22. Bern/Munich: Francke, 1984.

Krogmann, Werner. "Moralischer Realismus – ein Versuch über Christa Wolf." In Gerd Labroisse, ed., *Zur Literatur und Literaturwissenschaft der DDR*, pp. 233–61. Amsterdam: Rodopi, 1978. Amsterdamer Beiträge zur neueren Germanistik 7.

Kunert, Günter. "Zweige vom selben Stamm." In Klaus Sauer, ed., *Christa Wolf Materialienbuch*, pp. 15–20. Darmstadt/Neuwied: Luchterhand, 1979.

Lennox, Sara. " 'Der Versuch, man selbst zu sein': Christa Wolf und der Feminismus." In Wolfgang Paulsen, ed., *Die Frau als Heldin und Autorin: Neue kritische Ansätze zur deutschen Literatur*, pp. 217–22. Bern: Francke, 1979. Amherster Kolloquium zur deutschen Literatur 10.

Leonhard, Sigrun. "Strategie der Annäherung: Zur Erzähltechnik in Christa Wolfs 'Kein Ort. Nirgends.'" *The Germanic Review* 60/3 (Summer 1985): 99–106.

Linn, Marie-Luise. "Doppelte Kindheit – Zur Interpretation von Christa Wolfs 'Kindheitsmuster.'" *Deutschunterricht* 2 (1978): 52–66.

Linsmayer, Charles. "Die wiedergefundene Fähigkeit zu trauern." *Neue Rundschau* (1977): 472–8. (On *Kindheitsmuster*)

Marx, Jutta. "Die Perspektive des Verlierers – ein utopischer Entwurf." In Wolfram Mauser, ed., *Erinnerte Zukunft. 11 Studien zum Werk Christa Wolfs*, pp. 161–80. Würzburg: Königshausen und Neumann, 1985.

Mauser, Helmtrud. "Zwischen Träumen und Wurfspeeren. *Kassandra* und die Suche nach einem neuen Selbstbild." In Wolfram Mauser, ed., *Erinnerte Zukunft. 11 Studien zum Werk Christa Wolfs*, pp. 291–315. Würzburg: Königshausen und Neumann, 1985.

Mauser, Wolfram. " 'Gezeichnet zeichnend.' Tod und Verwandlung im Werk Christa Wolfs." In Wolfram Mauser, ed., *Erinnerte Zukunft. 11 Studien zum Werk Christa Wolfs*, pp. 181–206. Würzburg: Königshausen und Neumann, 1985.

Select bibliography

"Subjektivität – Chance oder Verirrung? Christa Wolfs 'Nachdenken über Christa T.' " *Sprachkunst* 12 (1981): 171–85.

Mayer, Hans. "Christa Wolf: *Nachdenken über Christa T.*" *Neue Rundschau* 81/1 (1970): 180–6.

"Der Mut zur Unaufrichtigkeit." *Der Spiegel*, 11 April 1977, pp. 185–90. (On *Kindheitsmuster*)

Mohr, Heinrich. "Produktive Sehnsucht: Struktur, Thematik und politische Relevanz von Christa Wolfs *Nachdenken über Christa T.*" *Basis: Jahrbuch für deutsche Gegenwartsliteratur* 2 (1971): 191–233.

"Die zeitgemässe Autorin – Christa Wolf in der DDR." In Wolfram Mauser, ed., *Erinnerte Zukunft. 11 Studien zum Werk Christa Wolfs*, pp. 17–52. Würzburg: Königshausen und Neumann, 1985.

Neumann, Gerhard. "Christa Wolf: *Kassandra*. Die Archäologie der weiblichen Stimme." In Wolfram Mauser, ed., *Erinnerte Zukunft. 11 Studien zum Werk Christa Wolfs*, pp. 233–64. Würzburg: Königshausen und Neumann, 1985.

Nieraad, Jürgen. "Pronominalstrukturen in realistischer Prosa: zu Erzählebene und Figurenkontur bei Christa Wolf." *Poetica* 10/4 (1978): 485–506.

"Subjektivität als Thema und Methode realistischer Schreibweise: Zur gegenwärtigen DDR-Literaturdiskussion am Beispiel Christa Wolf." *Literaturwissenschaftliches Jahrbuch im Auftrag der Görres-Gesellschaft* 19 (1978): 289–316.

Ploetz, Dagmar. "Vom Vorteil, eine Frau zu sein. Frauenbild und Menschenentwurf in Christa Wolfs Prosa." In Klaus Sauer, ed., *Christa Wolf Materialienbuch*, pp. 97–110. Darmstadt/Neuwied: Luchterhand, 1979.

Reich-Ranicki, Marcel. "Christa Wolfs unruhige Elegie." *Die Zeit* 25, May 1969. (On *Christa T.*)

"Christa Wolfs trauriger Zettelkasten." *Frankfurter Allgemeine Zeitung*, 19 March 1977. (On *Kindheitsmuster*)

Renner, Rolf Günter. "Mythische Psychologie und psychologischer Mythos. Zu Christa Wolfs *Kassandra*." In Wolfram Mauser, ed., *Erinnerte Zukunft. 11 Studien zum Werk Christa Wolfs*, pp. 265–90. Würzburg: Königshausen und Neumann, 1985.

Roebling, Irmgard. " 'Hier spricht keiner meine Sprache, der nicht mit mir stirbt.' Zum Ort der Sprachreflexion in Christa Wolfs *Kassandra*." In Wolfram Mauser, ed., *Erinnerte Zukunft. 11 Studien zum Werk Christa Wolfs*, pp. 207–32. Würzburg: Königshausen und Neumann, 1985.

Sander, Volkmar. "Erinnerung an die Zukunft: Christa Wolfs *Nachdenken über Christa T.*" In Ralph Ley et al., eds., *Perspectives and Personalities: Studies in Modern German Literature Honoring Claude Hill*, pp. 320–9. Heidelberg: Carl Winter Verlag, 1979.

Sauer, Klaus. "Der lange Weg zu sich selbst. Christa Wolfs Frühwerk." In Klaus Sauer, ed., *Christa Wolf Materialienbuch*, pp. 64–80. Darmstadt/Neuwied: Luchterhand, 1979.

Select bibliography

Schachtsiek-Freitag, Norbert. "Vom Versagen der Kritik." In Klaus Sauer, ed., *Christa Wolf Materialienbuch*, pp. 117–29. Darmstadt/Neuwied: Luchterhand, 1979.

Schlenstedt, Dieter. "Motive und Symbole in Christa Wolfs Erzählung 'Der geteilte Himmel.'" *Weimarer Beiträge* 1/1 (1964): 77–104.

Stephan, Alexander. "Christa Wolf." In Heinz Puknus, ed., *Neue Literatur der Frauen: Deutschsprachige Autorinnen der Gegenwart*, pp. 149–58. München: Beck, 1980.

"Christa Wolf: Unter den Linden." *Neue deutsche Hefte* 1 (1975): 144–7.

"Frieden, Frauen und Kassandra." In Manfred Jurgensen, ed., *Wolf: Darstellung, Deutung, Diskussion*, pp. 149–60. Bern/Munich: Francke, 1984.

Stephens, Anthony. "Vom Nutzen der zeitgenössischen Metafiktion: Christa Wolfs *Kindheitsmuster*." In Rolf Kloepfer and Gisela Janetzke-Dillner, eds., *Erzählung und Erzählforschung im 20. Jahrhundert*, pp. 359–79. Stuttgart: Kohlhammer, 1981.

"'Die Verführung der Worte' von *Kindheitsmuster* zu *Kassandra*." In Manfred Jurgensen, ed. *Wolf: Darstellung, Deutung, Diskussion*, pp. 127–48. Bern/Munich: Francke, 1984.

Tanner, Anne. "Wendepunkt: Christa Wolfs *Juninachmittag*." In Manfred Jurgensen, ed., *Wolf: Darstellung, Deutung, Diskussion*, pp. 51–76. Bern/Munich: Francke, 1984.

Tunner, Erika. "Auf der Suche nach Kassandra." In Manfred Jurgensen, ed., *Wolf: Darstellung, Deutung, Diskussion*, pp. 107–26. Bern/Munich: Francke, 1984.

Walther, Joachim. "Persönlich werden." In Klaus Sauer, ed., *Christa Wolf Materialienbuch*, 2nd, revised edition, pp. 24–9. Darmstadt/Neuwied: Luchterhand, 1983.

Weber, Heinz-Dieter. "'Phantastische Genauigkeit.' Der historische Sinn der Schreibart Christa Wolfs." In Wolfram Mauser, ed., *Erinnerte Zukunft. 11 Studien zum Werk Christa Wolfs*, pp. 81–106. Würzburg: Königshausen und Neumann, 1985.

Zahlmann, Christel. "*Kindheitsmuster*: Schreiben an der Grenze des Bewusstseins." In Wolfram Mauser, ed., *Erinnerte Zukunft. 11 Studien zum Werk Christa Wolfs*, pp. 141–60. Würzburg: Königshausen und Neumann, 1985.

C GENERAL

Books

Emmerich, Wolfgang. *Kleine Literaturgeschichte der DDR*. Darmstadt/Neuwied: Luchterhand, 1981.

Select bibliography

Articles

Dahnke, Hans-Dietrich. "Zur Stellung und Leistung der deutschen romantischen Literatur." *Weimarer Beiträge* 24/4 (1978): 5–19.

Herminghouse, Patricia. "Vergangenheit als Problem der Gegenwart: Zur Darstellung des Faschismus in der neueren DDR-Literatur." In Peter Uwe Hohendahl and Patricia Herminghouse, eds., *Literatur der DDR in den 70er Jahren*, pp. 259–94. Frankfurt/Main: Suhrkamp, 1983.

"Die Wiederentdeckung der Romantik: Zur Funktion der Dichterfiguren in der neueren DDR-Literatur." In Jos Hoogeveen and Gerd Labroisse, eds., *DDR-Roman und Literaturgesellschaft*, pp. 217–48. Amsterdam: Rodopi, 1981. Amsterdamer Beiträge zur neueren Germanistik 11/12.

"Wunschbild, Vorbild oder Porträt? Zur Darstellung der Frau im Roman der DDR." In Peter Uwe Hohendahl and Patricia Herminghouse, eds., *Literatur und Literaturtheorie in der DDR*, pp. 281–334. Frankfurt/Main: Suhrkamp, 1976.

Hohendahl, Peter Uwe. "Ästhetik und Sozialismus: Zur neueren Literaturtheorie der DDR." In Peter Uwe Hohendahl and Patricia Herminghouse, eds., *Literatur und Literaturtheorie in der DDR*, pp. 100–62. Frankfurt/Main: Suhrkamp, 1976.

Stephan, Alexander. "Die wissenschaftlich-technische Revolution in der Literatur der DDR." *Deutschunterricht* (BRD) 2 (1978): 18–34.

Totten, Monika. "Zur Aktualität der Romantik in der DDR: Christa Wolf und ihre Vorläufer(innen)." *Zeitschrift für deutsche Philologie* 101/2 (1982): 244–62.

Träger, Claus. "Ursprünge und Stellung der Romantik." *Weimarer Beiträge* 21/2 (1975): 37–73.

Trommler, Frank. "DDR-Erzählung und Bitterfelder Weg." *Basis: Jahrbuch für deutsche Gegenwartsliteratur* 3, eds., Jost Hermand and Reinhold Grimm, (Frankfurt: Athenäum, 1972): 61–97.

"Von Stalin zu Hölderlin: Über den Entwicklungsroman in der DDR." *Basis: Jahrbuch für deutsche Gegenwartsliteratur* 2, eds. Jost Hermand and Reinhold Grimm, (Frankfurt: Athenäum, 1971): 141–90.

Werner, Hans-Georg. "Zum Traditionsbezug der Erzählungen in Christa Wolfs 'Unter den Linden.'" *Weimarer Beiträge* 4 (1976): 36–64. Reprinted in Günter Hartung *et al.*, eds., *Erworbene Tradition. Studien zu Werken der sozialistischen deutschen Literatur*, pp. 256–98. Berlin/DDR: Aufbau, 1977.

Secondary works in English

A   FULL-LENGTH STUDIES

Fries, Marilyn Sibley, ed., *Responses to Christa Wolf: Critical Essays*. Detroit: Wayne State University Press, forthcoming.

Select bibliography

Herrmann, Anne Christine. "Toward a Female Dialogic: Virginia Woolf and Christa Wolf." Ph.D Dissertation, Yale University, 1983.

Love, Myra. "Das Spiel mit offenen Möglichkeiten: Subjectivity and the Thematization of Writing in the Works of Christa Wolf." Ph.D Dissertation, University of California at Berkeley, 1983.

B ARTICLES AND REVIEWS

Abel, Elizabeth. "(E)Merging Identities: The Dynamics of Female Friendship in Contemporary Fiction by Women." *Signs: Journal of Women in Culture and Society* 6/3 (Spring 1981): 413–35.

Caute, David. "Divided Hearts at the Wall." *The Nation* 13, 2 (1967): 215–16. (On *Divided Heaven*)

Cicora, Mary. "Language, Identity, and the Woman in *Nachdenken über Christa T.*: A Post-Structuralist Approach." *The Germanic Review* 57/1 (Winter 1982): 16–22.

Cirker, Willkie K., "The Socialist Education of Rita Seidel: The Dialectics of Humanism and Authoritarianism in Christa Wolf's *Der geteilte Himmel.*" *University of Dayton Review* 13/2 (Winter 1978): 105–11.

Clausen, Jeanette. "The Difficulty of Saying 'I' as Theme and Narrative Technique in the Works of Christa Wolf." In Marianne Burkhard, ed., *Gestaltet und gestaltend. Frauen in der deutschen Literatur*, pp. 319–33. Amsterdam: Rodopi, 1980. Amsterdamer Beiträge zur neueren Germanistik 10.

Crick, Joyce, "Dichtung und Wahrheit: Aspects of Christa Wolf's *Kindheitsmuster.*" *London German Studies* 2, pp. 168–83. University of London, Institute of Germanic Studies, 1983.

Fehervary, Helen. "Christa Wolf's Prose: A Landscape of Masks." *New German Critique* 27 (Fall 1982): 57–87.

"The Gender of Authorship: Heiner Müller and Christa Wolf." *Studies in Twentieth Century Literature* 5/1 (Fall 1980): 41–58.

Fehervary, Helen and Sara Lennox. Introduction to Christa Wolf's "Self-Experiment: Appendix to a Report." Trans. Jeanette Clausen. *New German Critique* 13 (Winter 1978): 109–12.

French, Marilyn. "Henrich von Kleist Could Not Last." (Review of *No Place on Earth.*) *New York Times Book Review*, 10 October 1982.

"Trojan Woman." (Review of *Cassandra.*) *Women's Review of Books* 2/3 (December 1984).

Frieden, Sandra. "Christa Wolf's *Kindheitsmuster.*" In Sandra Frieden, *Autobiography: Self into Form. German-Language Autobiographical Writings of the 1970s*, pp. 154–77. Frankfurt/Main: Lang, 1983.

"'In eigener Sache': Christa Wolf's *Kindheitsmuster.*" *German Quarterly* 54 (1981): 473–87.

Fries, Marilyn Sibley. "Christa Wolf's Use of Image and Vision in the Narrative Structuring of Experience." In Margy Gerber *et al.*, eds.,

Studies in GDR Culture and Society 2, pp. 59–74. Washington, DC: University Press of America, 1982.

Gardiner, Judith Kegan. "The (US)es of (I)dentity: A Response to Abel on '(E)merging Identities.'" *Signs: Journal of Women in Culture and Society* 6/3 (Spring 1981): 436–42.

Jackson, Neil and Barbara Saunders. "Christa Wolf's *Kindheitsmuster*: An East German Experiment in Political Autobiography." *German Life and Letters* 33/4 (1980): 319–29.

Kane, B. M. "In Search of the Past: Christa Wolf's *Kindheitsmuster*." *Modern Languages* 59/1 (March 1978): 19–23.

Koerner, W. Charlotte. "*Divided Heaven* – by Christa Wolf? A Sacrifice of Message and Meaning in Translation." *German Quarterly* (Spring 1984): 213–30.

Kuhn, Anna K. "Telling the Myth of Cassandra in Feminist Terms." *Philadelphia Inquirer*, 19 August 1984. (On *Cassandra*)

Lamse, Mary Jane. "*Kindheitsmuster* in Context: The Achievement of Christa Wolf." *University of Dayton Review* 15/1 (Spring 1981): 49–55.

Lefkowitz, Mary. "Can't Fool Her." *New York Times*, 9 September 1984. (On *Cassandra*)

Lehmann-Haupt, Christopher. "*Cassandra: A Novel and Four Essays*. (Review) *New York Times*, 31 July 1984.

Lennox, Sara. "Christa Wolf and the Women Romantics." In Margy Gerber *et al.*, eds., *Studies in GDR Culture and Society* 2, pp. 31–44. Washington, DC: University Press of America, 1982.

Love, Myra. "Christa Wolf and Feminism: Breaking the Patriarchal Connection." *New German Critique* 16 (Winter 1979): 31–53.

McPherson, Karin. "Christa Wolf in Edinburgh. An Interview." *GDR Monitor* 1 (Summer 1979): 1–12.

"In Search of the New Prose: Christa Wolf's Reflections on Writing and the Writer in the 1960s and 1970s." *New German Studies* 9/1 (Spring 1981): 1–13.

Parkes, K. S. "An All-German Dilemma: Some Notes on the Presentation of the Theme of the Individual and Society in Martin Walser's *Halbzeit and Christa Wolf's Nachdenden über Christa T.*" *German Life and Letters* 28 (1974–5): 58–64.

Pawel, Ernst. "The Quest for Christa T." *New York Times Book Review*, 31 January 1971, pp. 7, 33.

"Prophecies and Heresies. *Cassandra: A Novel and Four Essays*." (Review) *The Nation*, 22 September 1984.

Pickle, Linda S. "'Unreserved Subjectivity' as a Force for Social Change: Christa Wolf and Maxie Wander's *Guten Morgen, du Schöne*." In Margy Gerber *et al.*, eds., *Studies in GDR Culture and Society* 2, pp. 217–30. Washington, DC: University Press of America, 1982.

Probst, Gerhard F. "Thematization of Alterity in Christa Wolf's 'Nachdenken über Christa T.'" *University of Dayton Review* 13/2 (1978): 25–35.

Select bibliography

Ryan, Judith. "The Discontinuous Self: Christa Wolf's *A Model Childhood*." In Judith Ryan, *The Uncompleted Past: Postwar German Novels and the Third Reich*, pp. 141–54. Detroit: Wayne State University Press, 1983.

Sevin, Dieter. "The Plea for Artistic Freedom in Christa Wolf's 'Lesen und Schreiben' and *Nachdenken über Christa T.*: Essay and Fiction as Mutually Supportive Genre Forms." In Margy Gerber *et al.*, eds., *Studies in GDR Culture and Society* 2, pp. 45–58. Washington, DC: University Press of America, 1982.

Spender, Stephen. "The Mortal Sin of Our Time" (on Christa Wolf's *A Model Childhood*). *New York Times Book Review*, 12 October 1982.

Stephan, Alexander. "The Emancipation of Man: Christa Wolf as a Woman Writer." *GDR Monitor* 2 (1979/1980): 23–30.

Review of Christa Wolf, *Kindheitsmuster*. Darmstadt/Neuwied: Luchterhand, 1977. In *New German Critique* 11 (1977): 178–82.

Wendt-Hildebrandt, Susan. "*Kindheitsmuster*: Christa Wolf's 'Probestück.'" *Seminar* 17/2 (May 1981): 164–76.

Willett, John. "The Quest for East Germany." *New York Review of Books*, 2 September 1971, pp. 21–3. (Review article of *The Quest for Christa T.*)

Zipes, Jack. "Christa Wolf: Moralist as Marxist." Introduction to *Divided Heaven*. Trans. Joan Becker. New York: Adler's Foreign Books, 1974, pp. v–xxxvii.

C GENERAL

Herminghouse, Patricia. "The Rediscovery of Romanticism: Revisions and Reevaluations." In Margy Gerber *et al.*, eds., *Studies in GDR Culture and Society* 2, pp. 1–17. Washington, DC: University Press of America, 1982.

Lennox, Sara. "Trends in Literary Theory: The Female Aesthetic and German Women's Writing." *German Quarterly* (1981): 63–75.

Stern, Dagmar Cäcilia. "From the Mouths of GDR Babes." *Publications of the Arkansas Philological Association* 6/2: 86–96.

INDEX

Note: Titles refer to works by Christa Wolf unless otherwise stated.

Index

Index

Index

Index